CLAIRE CROMPTON
& SUE WHITING

The Knitting & Crochet Bible

The Complete Handbook for Creative Knitting and Crochet

CLAIRE CROMPTON & SUE WHITING

The Knitting & Crochet Bible

The Complete Handbook for Creative Knitting and Crochet

David and Charles

www.mycraftivity.com

About the authors

Claire Crompton is a talented needlewoman with over 15 years experience. Her degree in Knitwear Design took her to the knitting industry and she has worked as a pattern designer for major wool manufacturers such as Sirdar, Courtaulds and Hayfield, as well as for the needlework company DMC. She is the author of *Cross Stitch Card Collection*, also published by David & Charles.

Sue Whiting is an accomplished crochet and knitwear designer. She graduated from the London College of Fashion and has been involved in the needlecrafts and fashion industry for more than 30 years. She has written several books on needlecraft subjects, and works regularly for many of the major yarn manufacturers.

A DAVID & CHARLES BOOK

F&W Media International, LTD is a subsidiary of F+W Media Inc.,
10151 Carver Road, Suite #200,
Blue Ash, OH 45242, USA

First published in the UK and US as *The Knitter's Bible*, 2004, 2006, and *The Crochet Bible*, 2008
Reprinted in 2010 (twice), 2011, 2012

A catalogue record for this book is available from the British Library.

ISBN-13: 978-0-7153-3280-1 paperback
ISBN-10: 0-7153-3280-5 paperback

Printed in China by RR Donnelley
for David & Charles
Brunel House, Newton Abbot, Devon

David & Charles publish high quality books on a wide range of subjects.
For more great book ideas visit: **www.stitchcraftcreate.co.uk**

contents

Introduction

This section will take you through the
basic techniques that you need to begin
knitting, such as casting on, and knit and
purl stitches. It encourages you to try new
techniques including cables and fair isle
knitting. There is a wide range of
projects for you and your home,
ranging from simple ones to
more challenging designs
as your confidence
and skills grow.

to knitting

How to use this section

This section has been divided into colour coded sub-sections to help you find the information you need quickly and easily. Each new technique is explained with clear diagrams, photographs and step-by-step instructions.

Getting Started is colour coded purple and teaches you the basic techniques you need to begin knitting straight away. It offers invaluable information about yarns and choosing the correct needles for your work. At the end of the Getting Started section is a page of useful hints and tips to improve your knitting and a list of the abbreviations that are used throughout this book, each clearly explained.

Creative Options pages are coded blue, and introduce more techniques to expand your range of knitted fabrics, such as lace knitting, cables and colour knitting. Circular knitting is also explained.

Exploring Choices is colour coded green and features many exciting techniques to encourage you to experiment and discover the wide variety of fabrics that can be knitted. Beads, embroidery and looped knitting decorate the surface whilst mitred squares and entrelac illustrate the creative use of shapes. The Exploring Choices section also includes information on working from knitting patterns, how to alter patterns to fit and how to adapt patterns with new stitches.

Throughout these three sub-sections, there are Knit Perfect boxes, which focus on the important points of each technique and give tips to improve your knitting.

The Stitch Library pages are coded turquoise and include a wide range of over 100 stitches that you can use in the projects or for your own designs.

All the techniques are illustrated by projects, beginning with a simple garter stitch scarf that can be knitted with three basic techniques. Other projects include a cable throw, and bootees, sweater and blanket for baby.

The smaller items like gift bags and scented sachets are quick and easy to knit and will encourage you to try new techniques.

Measurements are given in imperial with metric conversions in brackets. Use either imperial or metric when working, do not combine them since in many cases they are not a direct conversion.

Two ways of holding the needles and knitting are explained: the English method and Continental method. To avoid confusion, throughout this book the diagrams show the English method of holding the needles. Knitters who prefer the Continental method can easily use the diagrams since the position of the needles and the working yarn around the needles are the same for both methods.

Whether you are a complete novice wanting to start knitting, or an experienced knitter searching for fresh ideas and inspirations, this is the essential handbook that will always be at your side.

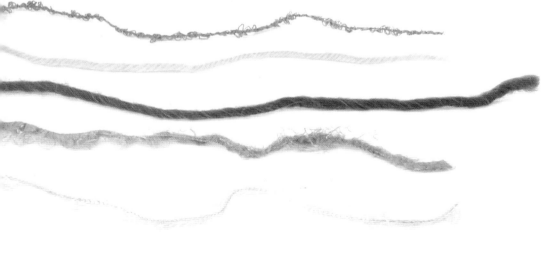

Getting Started

This section contains all the techniques you need to start knitting, beginning with how to hold the needles and yarn, how to cast on and work the knit stitch, and how to bind (cast) off. These basic techniques will then allow you to complete your first project. Learn how to purl, the other basic stitch, and combine it with the knit stitch to produce stockinette (stocking) stitch and ribs. More projects follow, using the techniques just learnt. There is useful information on choosing and using different yarns, and an explanation of the different needles and equipment you will need to begin knitting confidently.

INTRODUCING YARNS

Fibres

Yarns are spun from natural or synthetic fibres. Natural fibres include wool, silk, linen, cotton, cashmere and alpaca. Synthetic fibres include polyester, acrylic, viscose, rayon and nylon. Yarn can also be a mixture of each, for example, wool and acrylic, or wool and cotton.

The following list describes the most common fibres used in knitting yarns:

NATURAL FIBRES

Alpaca hair from the alpaca (llama)
Angora hair from the angora rabbit
Cashmere hair from the cashmere goat
Cotton plant fibre, from the boll of the cotton plant
Lambswool sheep's first shearing, usually the softest
Linen plant fibre, from the stem of the flax plant
Merino wool from the fleece of the merino sheep
Mohair from the angora goat, the softer and finer kid mohair is from the kid goat
Shetland wool traditionally from Shetland sheep
Silk continuous filament secreted by the silkworm larva
Wool from the fleece of a sheep

SYNTHETIC FIBRES

Acetate, rayon and viscose chemical treatment of cellulose fibres from wood pulp
Acrylic, polyester and nylon made from petro-chemicals, nylon is the strongest textile fibre, elastane is an elastic fibre

PLY OR THICKNESS

A ply is a single twisted strand and, as a general rule, the more plies that are twisted together, the thicker the yarn but, confusingly, the plies from different manufacturers can be different thicknesses themselves. A tightly spun ply will be thinner than a loosely spun one. In order of thickness they are:

1 ply which is used for gossamer lace knitting like traditional Shetland shawls
Baby and fingering (UK 2ply or 3ply)
Sport (UK 4ply)
Worsted (UK DK – double knitting) the most widely used weight which is suitable for most garments without being too bulky for indoor wear.
Fisherman or medium weight (UK aran)
Bulky (UK chunky)
Super bulky (UK super chunky)
and **Big** yarns are even thicker

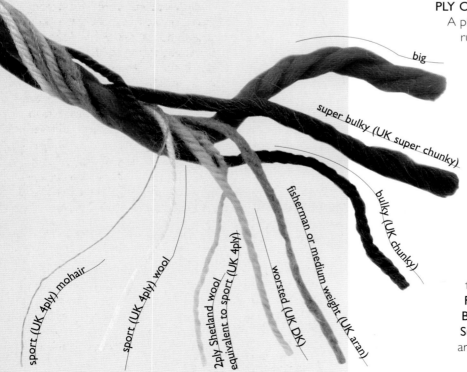

big

super bulky (UK super chunky)

bulky (UK chunky)

fisherman or medium weight (UK aran)

worsted (UK DK)

2ply Shetland wool/ equivalent to sport (UK 4ply)

sport (UK 4ply) wool

sport (UK 4ply) mohair

Texture

Most yarns are plain — simply plies twisted together but there are other yarns called novelty or specialist yarns.

Chenille has a core of strong plies spun together to trap the short velvet pile threads.

Boucle has two plies spun together at different speeds so one bunches up around the other creating a towelling look when knitted up.

Slub yarns alternate between thick and thin creating a very textured fabric.

Ribbon yarns are exactly what they sound like; knitted up they form a loose fabric with plenty of drape.

Mohair or angora yarns have been brushed to raise the hairs of the fibre and make a soft fluffy fabric.

Fun fur yarns with short or long piles knit up for an extra furry garment.

Fleece yarns knit up to make a soft all-over pile.

Special features

Due their different characteristics, some yarns are more suitable for certain uses than others. A child's garment that needs frequent washing should be knitted in a hardwearing, machine-washable yarn rather than one that has to be hand washed. Fun fur yarns make cosier cushions than rough natural wool and linen yarns drape better than crisp cotton.

Wool is the best yarn to use. It is strong, durable, elastic, takes dye well and feels soft against the skin. A garment knitted in wool will hold its shape, have excellent insulation properties and the surface will not pill like some synthetics. As there are different breeds of sheep so there are different types of wool; lambswool is soft, merino and wensleydale have long fibres and a lustrous sheen when knitted, and shetland wool is available in a wide range of colours for traditional fair isle knitting. Natural, undyed yarn, usually straight from the wool producers, comes in range of colours from cream through to soft browns and charcoals, and has a real rustic look and feel. Wool

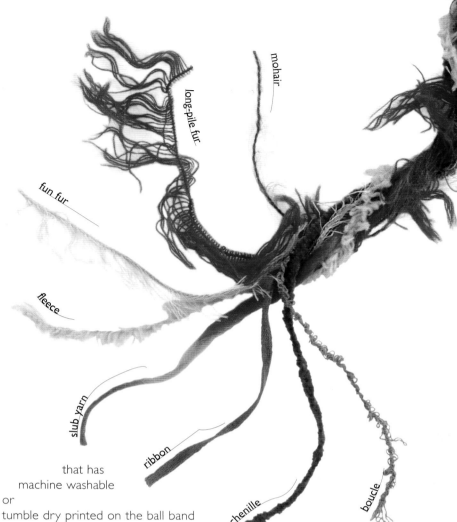

that has machine washable or tumble dry printed on the ball band has been treated to not shrink or full in the washing machine and drier.

Cotton is a heavy yarn, so the weight of a finished garment can cause it to drop and the garment will get longer. It also lacks elasticity and so ribs become baggy, though this is restored after washing. Cotton blended with a synthetic fibre will have more stability. However, cotton is a great yarn to use for crisp stitch textures and looks beautiful in lace knitting. Mercerized cotton has been treated to add lustre and take brighter dyes; it is stronger than untreated cotton and harder wearing.

Silk is a luxury fibre that is beautiful to knit with and creates soft, fluid garments to wear against the skin. If loosely spun, it will not be hard wearing, so use it for special garments only.

Cashmere is an expensive yarn but its soft, light and luxurious qualities make it a good investment. Knit it into classic garments that never go out of fashion.

Synthetic yarns are hard wearing, and can be pulled in and out of the washing machine without suffering shrinkage or fulling, making them ideal for children's clothes. But some knitters find them uncomfortable to knit with, as stitches tend to cling to the needles. The surface pills easily, and submit them to a steam iron and they lose all elasticity and life.

Blended yarns of natural and synthetic fibres combine the natural yarn's qualities with the hardwearing and stable features of the synthetic.

When you are learning to knit, start as you mean to go on — choose a 100 per cent wool yarn; it is easy to work with, can be unravelled and reused, and whatever you knit will look gorgeous.

CHOOSING YARNS

When selecting yarn for a particular garment or accessory, bear in mind the way in which it will be used once finished, and the overall effect you want to achieve through the colour and texture.

Yarns for baby

Yarns specifically for babies are treated to be softer, and made to withstand frequent machine washing and tumble drying. Suitable yarns are baby and fingering (2ply) in 100 per cent wool for white lacy heirloom shawls, sport (4ply) nylon/acrylic mix in traditional blue and pink, fashion worsted (DK) nylon/acrylic mix with a pearlized thread or 100 per cent wool in soft colours for cosy sweaters and bootees.

Crisp cool yarns

Pure 100 per cent cotton, cotton mixes and natural fibres such as linen and silk are perfect for summer but can look good all year round. Hardwearing, they also give a classic look to soft furnishings, knitted into throws and cushions. Worsted (DK) denim yarn fades and ages like jeans, tweed yarns with a touch of silk make relaxed holiday wear, and spaced-dyed yarns give a blended look. Worsted (DK) cotton comes in bright colours for crisp ribbed sweaters, worsted (DK) linen mixed with viscose has drape, sport (4ply) mercerized cottons have a sheen, and a cotton ribbon yarn is ideal for slinky summer evening wear.

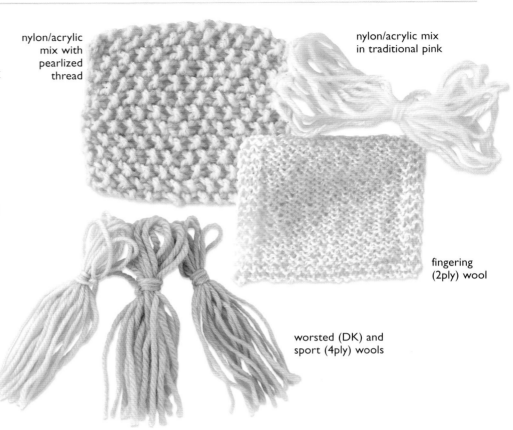

nylon/acrylic mix with pearlized thread

nylon/acrylic mix in traditional pink

fingering (2ply) wool

worsted (DK) and sport (4ply) wools

cotton denim yarns

worsted (DK) cotton

cotton ribbon yarn

tweed and space dyed cotton mix yarns

sport (4ply) mercerized cotton

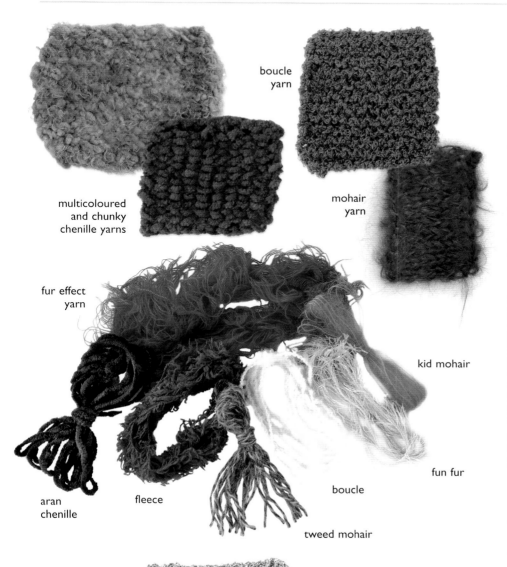

boucle yarn

multicoloured and chunky chenille yarns

mohair yarn

fur effect yarn

kid mohair

fun fur

boucle

aran chenille

fleece

tweed mohair

Yarns with texture

Knit them in simple stockinette (stocking) stitch and let the yarn make the difference. Use soft, velvety chunky chenille for opulence and a multi-coloured version for fun. Mohair makes huggable sweaters in medium (aran) weight mohair/wool mix, sport (4ply) kid mohair creates a delicate fabric and a sophisticated tweed is ideal for city wear. Boucle yarns are great for summer tops. For a fun look, knit a top in funky fur yarns in variegated or bold colours while fleece yarns are great for outdoor wear.

✓ Knit Perfect

Dye lots of the same colour may differ slightly in shade, so always buy enough yarn of the same dye lot to complete your project. The dye lot number is printed on the ball band next to the shade number.

Yarns with sparkle

A lurex and viscose mix is perfect for evening wear and adds an unexpected accent to fair isle knits. Metallic embroidery threads add small glints of sparkle when combined with a plain yarn.

sport (4ply) fashion lurex yarns

metallic embroidery threads

13

choosing yarns

Natural fibre yarns

The best knitting yarns are made from natural fibres. Tweeds for a cosy country look, thick yarns for warmth in the great outdoors and stylish yarns for urban wear. Try using small amounts of tapestry wools for their great range of colours in fair isle or for embroidery. Shown here are truly rustic fisherman (aran), bulky (chunky) and worsted (DK) weight yarns in tweeds and soft greens, a soft sport (4ply) 100 per cent alpaca yarn, traditional shetland wool sweater yarn and tapestry wools equivalent to worsted (DK) weight.

bulky (chunky) tweed wool

aran weight rustic natural wool

sport (4ply) tweed wool

2ply shetland wool

luxury alpaca

bulky (chunky) wool/ alpaca mix

worsted (DK) tweed wool

two skeins tapestry wool

aran weight tweed wool

worsted (DK) soft merino wool

bulky (chunky) tweed wool

worsted (DK) tweed yarn

Every one of these adorable bags was knitted in basic stockinette (stocking) stitch (see pages 20–25) and measures 4in (10cm) square, but the varying choices of yarn and needle size have resulted in very different effects. See page 154 for the full pattern and details of trimmings.

Heart and bird knitted in stockinette (stocking) stitch using a chunky fleece effect yarn on size 9 (5.5mm/UK5) needles.

Rosebud knitted in stockinette (stocking) stitch using a silk and kid mohair yarn used double on size 5 (3.75mm/ UK9) needles.

Gold ribbon star knitted in stockinette (stocking) stitch using a cotton ribbon yarn on size 8 (5mm/UK6) needles.

aran weight chenille

100% pure silk
hand dyed yarn

super bulky
slub yarn

sport
(4ply)
thread

skeins of
sport (4ply)
weight
hand-dyed
embroidery
threads

thick slub
wool yarn

aran weight cotton
ribbon yarn

Hand painted, hand made yarns

For a really exclusive garment, how about an individual yarn, hand painted in multi-colours or a big bold slub yarn for texture and colour? Add an extravagant touch by using small amounts of embroidery thread, the mixed colours guarantee no two are alike. Multi-coloured chenille and ribbon yarn come in sophisticated colours like these berry shades and for pure luxury try a sport (4ply) 100 per cent silk yarn in soft azure shades. Slub yarns make unusual fun sweaters and embroidery silks can be added for a little touch of magic.

Denim heart bag knitted in stockinette (stocking) stitch using a cotton yarn on size 7 (4.5mm/UK7) needles.

Hologram daisy bag knitted in stockinette (stocking) stitch using a lurex yarn on size 3 (3.25mm/UK10) needles.

Fluffy pink ribbon bag knitted in stockinette (stocking) stitch using a funky fur yarn on size 6 (4mm/UK8) needles.

Snowflake bag knitted in stockinette (stocking) stitch using a boucle yarn on size 6 (4mm/ UK8) needles.

NEEDLES AND EQUIPMENT

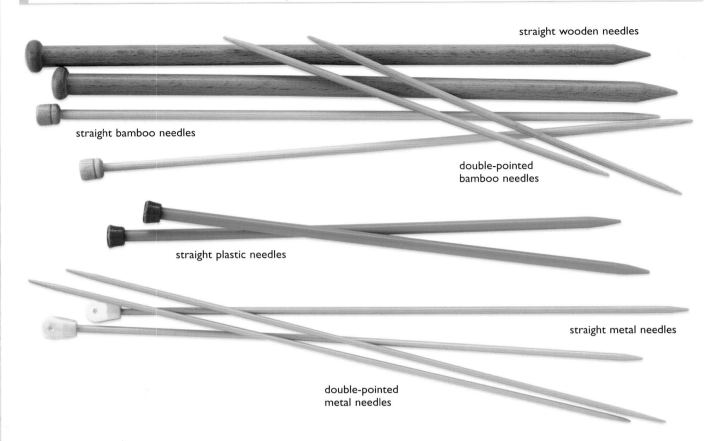

straight wooden needles

straight bamboo needles

double-pointed
bamboo needles

straight plastic needles

straight metal needles

double-pointed
metal needles

There are three types of needles, in a range of sizes, lengths and made from different materials.

Straight needles are used in pairs and have a point at one end with a fixed knob at the other. Stitches are worked using the pointed end; they cannot be removed from the other end. They are used for flat knitting, working across a row of stitches moving them from one needle to the other, turning the work and working back again, and continuing back and forth.

Double-pointed needles are used in sets of four or five and have a point at each end. Stitches can be worked with one end and can also be removed from the other end. This means you don't have to turn your work at the end of each row. In fact you can continue knitting in a spiral and produce a seamless continuous tube. This is called circular knitting.

Circular needles consist of a pair of needles joined by a flexible nylon wire. They have a point at each end and, like double-pointed needles, you can work from both ends and so knit in rounds to produce a seamless tube.

Plastic, metal or wood, including bamboo are used to make needles. Each has its own characteristics and can help or hinder your knitting experience. Metal can be cold and inflexible to work with, but it is more slippery than other materials and can help you knit faster. Wood, bamboo or plastic on the other hand are warmer and more flexible, and are smooth rather than slippery. They grip the stitches a bit more which is quite useful when you're beginning to knit and don't want stitches sliding off your needles. Wood and bamboo warm up in the hands and are light to use. Try different materials and find the one you are most comfortable with.

The tip of the needle is also something to consider. Some needles have a blunt tip and some have a sharp tip. A blunt tip is harder to insert into stitches but is better to use with a loosely spun or thick yarn. A sharp tip can split the stitches but is useful when working pattern stitches or knitting with a tight gauge (tension).

The size of a needle is determined by its diameter and there are three sizing systems. In the US, needles have the American size and metric equivalent. In Britain, they have the metric size with the old UK size. The table shows you how these sizes compare; however some needles have no exact equivalent.

Three standard lengths are available, 10in (25cm), 12in (30cm) and 14in (35cm). Use longer needles for projects with a large number of stitches and shorter needles for fewer stitches. The stitches should fit snugly along the length of the needle, not crammed together where they can easily fall off the end. Long needles can be awkward to knit with; you need a lot of elbowroom to work comfortably. Many knitters find it easier to use a circular needle instead, working as for flat knitting, and turning the work at the end of every row.

Needle sizes

US	METRIC	UK	US	METRIC	UK
0	2mm	14	10	6mm	4
1	2.25mm	13	10½	6.5mm	3
	2.5mm			7mm	2
2	2.75mm	12		7.5mm	1
	3mm	11	11	8mm	0
3	3.25mm	10	13	9mm	00
4	3.5mm		15	10mm	000
5	3.75mm	9	17	12.75mm	
6	4mm	8	19	15mm	
7	4.5mm	7	35	19mm	
8	5mm	6		20mm	
9	5.5mm	5			

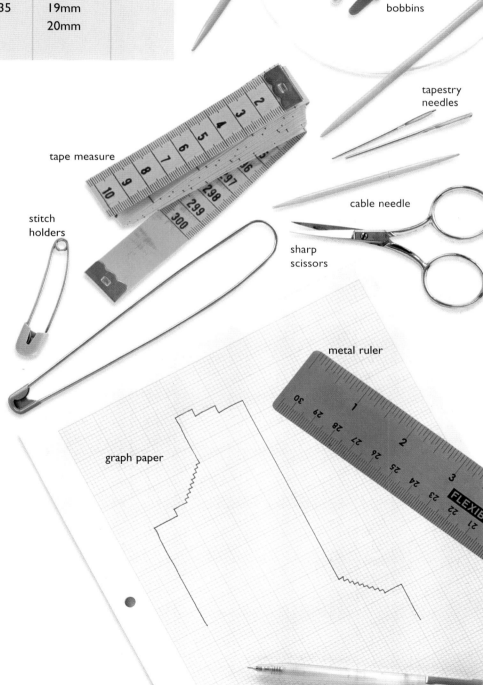

circular needles

bobbins

tapestry needles

cable needle

tape measure

stitch holders

sharp scissors

metal ruler

graph paper

Additional items beside needles and yarn will be needed as you progress with your knitting. These include:

- A needle gauge to check the size of a needle; circular needles and double-pointed needles tend not to be marked.
- A pair of small sharp scissors to cut the yarn; never be tempted to break the yarn, you will stretch the fibres.
- A non-stretch fibreglass tape measure for checking your garment measurements and a ruler for measuring your gauge (tension) square.
- Cable needles are used for manipulating stitches whilst working cables. They are short needles, pointed at both ends, and some have a kink in the middle.
- Stitch holders to hold stitches not being worked; you can use a safety pin for a small number of stitches.
- A tapestry needle with a large eye and a blunt end for sewing pieces together and sewing in ends.
- Bobbins for winding off lengths of coloured yarns for intarsia or fair isle knitting.
- A pad of graph paper is useful for charting garment shaping or stitches, giving a clearer picture than written instructions.
- A row counter that slides on to the needle to keep track of the row being knitted.

HOLDING THE NEEDLES

Not every knitter holds their needles and yarn in the same way. The yarn can be held in either the right or left hand, the needles can be held from above or below. Try each of the methods described here and work in a way that is most comfortable for you. They are all bound to feel awkward and slow at first.

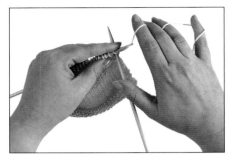

English method
(yarn in the right hand)

Left hand: hold the needle with the stitches in your left hand with your thumb lying along the needle, your index finger resting on top near the tip and the remaining fingers curled under the needle to support it. The thumb and the index finger control the stitches and the tip of the needle.

Right hand: pass the yarn over the index finger, under the middle and over the third finger. The yarn lies between the nail and the first joint and the index finger 'throws' the yarn around the right-hand needle when knitting. The yarn should be able to move freely and is tensioned between the middle and third finger. You can wrap the yarn around the little finger if you feel it is too loose and it keeps falling off your fingers. Hold the empty needle in your right hand with your thumb lying along the needle, your index finger near the tip and the remaining fingers curled under the needle to support it (see right hand in Continental method).

Some knitters prefer to hold the end of the right-hand needle under their right arm, anchoring it firmly. Whilst knitting this needle remains still and the right hand is above the needle and moves the yarn around it.

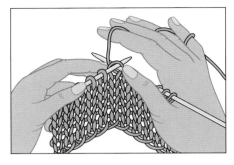

Alternative hold

Left hand: hold the needle in the same way as shown left.

Right hand: hold the yarn in the fingers the same way as shown left. Hold the needle like a pen, on top of the hand between thumb and index finger. The end of the needle will be above your right arm, in the crook of the elbow. As the fabric grows longer, the thumb will hold the needle behind the knitting.

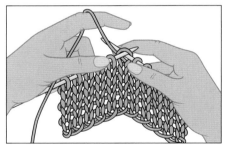

Continental method
(yarn in the left hand)

Left hand: wrap the yarn around your little finger, under the middle two fingers and then over the index finger between the nail and the first joint. The yarn is held taut between the index finger and the needle. Hold the needle with your thumb lying along the needle, your index finger near the tip and remaining fingers curled under the needle to support it. The thumb and index finger control the stitches, yarn and needle tip.

Right hand: hold the empty needle in your right hand with your thumb lying along the needle, index finger resting on top near the tip and remaining fingers curled under the needle to support it. The thumb and index finger control the stitches and the needle tip, which hooks the yarn and draws the loop through.

✓ Knit Perfect

If you learn both the English and Continental ways of knitting, you will be able to hold a different colour yarn in each hand which will make fair isle knitting (see page 39) easier and quicker. As you start to knit you will soon find a way of holding the yarn and needles that is right for you. Whether you hold the yarn differently, have it wrapped around more or less fingers to control the tension or hold the needles from above or below, as long as the yarn flows freely through your fingers and the tension on it is consistent, stick to the most comfortable method.

CASTING ON

To begin knitting, you need to work a foundation row of stitches called casting on. There are several ways to cast on depending on the type of edge that you want (see also page 26). The cast on edge should be firm; too loose and it will look untidy and flare out, too tight and it will break and the stitches unravel. If your casting on is always too tight, use a size larger needle. If it is always too loose, use a size smaller needle. Remember to change back to the correct size needle to begin knitting.

✓ Knit Perfect

The slip knot counts as the first cast on stitch. It is made some distance from the end of the yarn and placed on the needle. Pull the ends of the yarn to tighten it. You now have two ends of yarn coming from the slip knot; the ball end attached to the ball and a shorter free end.

For the thumb method of casting on, you will need approximately 1in (2.5cm) for every stitch you want to cast on. When you have cast on, you should have at least a 6in (15cm) length to sew in.

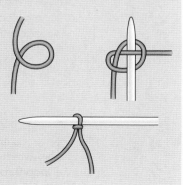

Thumb method

This is the simplest way of casting on and you will need only one needle.

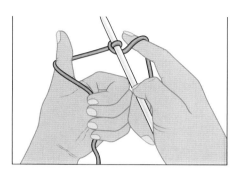

1 Make a slip knot some distance from the end of the yarn (see Knit Perfect) and place it on the needle. Hold the needle in your right hand. Pass the ball end of the yarn over the index finger, under the middle and then over the third finger. Holding the free end of yarn in your left hand, wrap it around your left thumb from front to back.

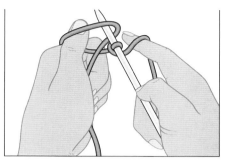

2 Insert the needle through the thumb loop from front to back.

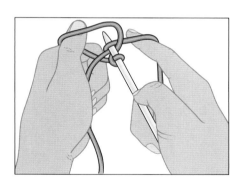

3 Wrap the ball end over the needle.

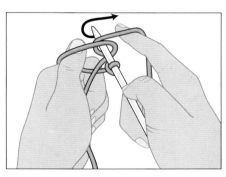

4 Pull a new loop through the thumb loop by passing the thumb loop over the end of the needle. Remove your thumb and tighten the new loop on the needle by pulling the free end. Continue in this way until you have cast on the required number of stitches.

INTRODUCING KNIT STITCH

In knitting there are only two stitches to learn - knit stitch (k) and purl stitch (p). They are the foundation of all knitted fabrics. Once you have mastered these two simple stitches, by combining them in different ways, you will soon be knitting ribs, textures, cables and many more exciting fabrics.

English method *(yarn in the right hand)*

In knit stitch the yarn is held at the back of the work (the side facing away from you) and is made up of four steps.

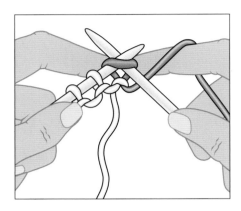

1 Hold the needle with the cast on stitches in your left hand, and insert the right-hand needle into the front of the stitch from left to right.

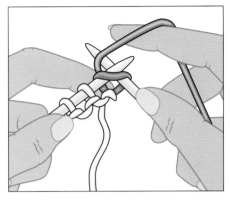

2 Pass the yarn under and around the right-hand needle.

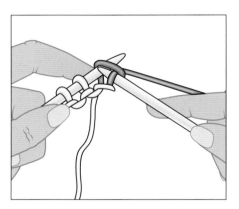

3 Pull the new loop on the right-hand needle through the stitch on the left-hand needle.

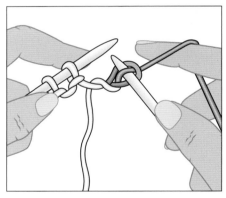

4 Slip the stitch off the left-hand needle. One knit stitch is completed.

To continue...
Repeat these four steps for each stitch on the left-hand needle. All the stitches on the left-hand needle will be transferred to the right-hand needle where the new row is formed. At the end of the row, swap the needle with the stitches into your left hand and the empty needle into your right hand, and work the next row in the same way.

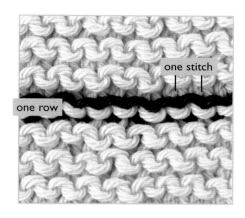

one row
one stitch

the result:

GARTER STITCH

knit every row

When you knit each row the fabric you make is called garter stitch (g st) and has rows of raised ridges on the front and back of the fabric. It looks the same on the back and the front so it is reversible. Garter stitch lies flat, is quite a thick fabric and does not curl at the edges. These qualities make it ideal for borders and collars, as well as for scarves and the main fabric of a garment.

Continental method *(yarn in the left hand)*

In this method the right-hand needle moves to catch the yarn; the yarn is held at the back of the work (the side facing away from you) and is released by the index finger of the left hand. This knit stitch is made up of four steps.

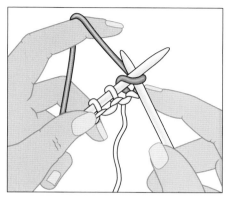

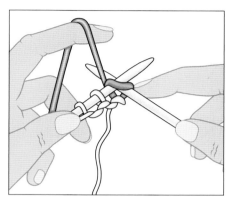

1 Hold the needle with the cast on stitches in your left hand and the yarn over your left index finger. Insert the right-hand needle into the front of the stitch from left to right.

2 Move the right-hand needle down and across the back of the yarn.

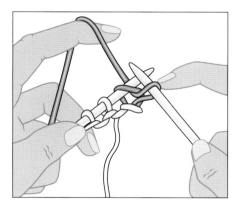

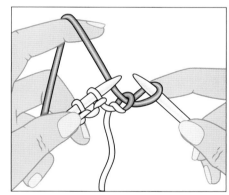

3 Pull the new loop on the right-hand needle through the stitch on the left-hand needle, using the right index finger to hold the new loop if needed.

4 Slip the stitch off the left-hand needle. One knit stitch is completed.

To continue...
Repeat these four steps for each stitch on the left-hand needle. All the stitches on the left-hand needle will be transferred to the right-hand needle where the new row is formed. At the end of the row, swap the needle with the stitches into your left hand and the empty needle into your right hand, and work the next row in the same way.

BINDING (CASTING) OFF

Bind (cast) off stitches when you have finished using them. This links stitches together to stop them unravelling and is the simplest method of binding (casting) off. See page 27 for advanced binding (casting) off.

✓ Knit Perfect

Like a cast on edge, it is important that a bind (cast) off edge is elastic. This means that it should not be so tight that it pulls the knitted fabric in. This is important when binding (casting) off a neckband, if it is too tight it will not stretch over your head and the edge may break, unravelling the stitches.

If you bind (cast) off too tightly, use a needle one or two sizes larger than that used for the knitted fabric. Always spend time undoing the edge and binding (casting) off again if it isn't right.

Bind (cast) off knitwise

This is the easiest method to bind (cast) off on a knit row.

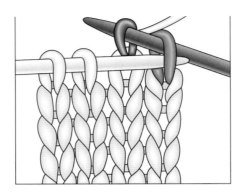

1 Knit two stitches, insert the tip of the left-hand needle into the front of the first stitch on the right-hand needle.

2 Lift this stitch over the second stitch and off the needle.

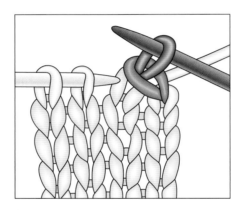

3 One stitch is left on the right-hand needle.

4 Knit the next stitch and lift the second stitch over this and off the needle. Continue in this way until one stitch remains on the right-hand needle.

To finish...
Cut the yarn (leaving a length long enough to sew in), thread the end through the last stitch and slip it off the needle. Pull the yarn end to tighten the stitch.

Bind (cast) off purlwise

To bind (cast) off on a purl row, simply purl the stitches instead of knitting them.

◀ KNIT SOMETHING NOW!

With what you have learnt so far – cast on, knit and bind (cast) off – you can easily complete this scarf, worked in one colour or in a simple striped pattern.

Plain scarf knitted in garter stitch in a bulky (chunky) wool yarn on size 11 (8mm/UK0) needles.
Striped scarf knitted in a fisherman (aran) merino wool yarn on size 7 (4.5mm/UK7) needles. Finished size for each scarf is 6in (15cm) wide by 62in (158cm) long. See page 131 for patterns.

INTRODUCING PURL STITCH

You may find purl stitch a little harder to learn than knit stitch. But really it is just the reverse of a knit stitch. If you purled every row, you would produce garter stitch (the same as if you knitted every row). It is not often that you will work every row in purl stitch; it is easier and faster to knit every row if you want garter stitch.

English method (*yarn in the right hand*)

In purl stitch the yarn is held at the front of the work (the side facing you) and is made up of four steps.

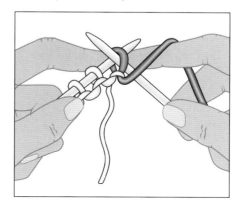

1 Hold the needle with the cast on stitches in your left hand, and insert the right-hand needle into the front of the stitch from right to left.

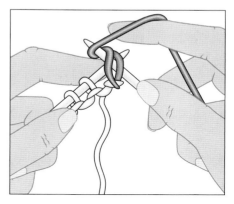

2 Pass the yarn over and around the right-hand needle.

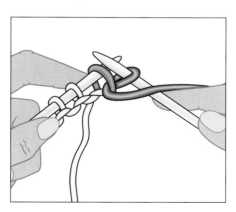

3 Pull the new loop on the right-hand needle through the stitch on the left-hand needle.

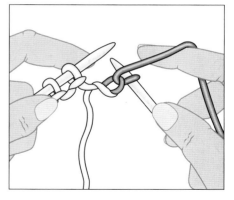

4 Slip the stitch off the left-hand needle. One stitch is completed.

To continue...

Repeat these four steps for each stitch on the left-hand needle. All the stitches on the left-hand needle will be transferred to the right-hand needle where the new purl row is formed. At the end of the row, swap the needle with the stitches into your left hand and the empty needle into your right hand, and work the next row in the same way.

As with knit stitch there are two ways of holding the needles and yarn to work purl stitch. The left-hand index finger controls the yarn which is hooked through on to the right-hand needle.

Continental method *(yarn in the left hand)*

In purl stitch the yarn is held at the front of the work (the side facing you) and is made up of four steps.

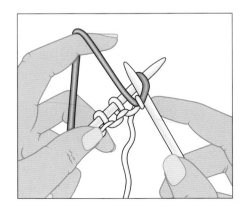

1 Hold the needle with the cast on stitches in your left hand, and insert the right-hand needle into the front of the stitch from right to left, keeping the yarn at the front of the work.

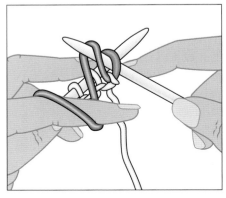

2 Move the right-hand needle from right to left behind the yarn and then from left to right in front of the yarn. Pull your left index finger down in front of the work to keep the yarn taut.

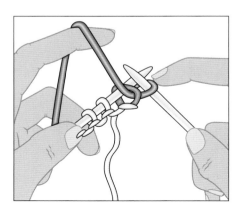

3 Pull the new loop on the right-hand needle through the stitch on the left-hand needle, using the right index finger to hold the new loop if needed.

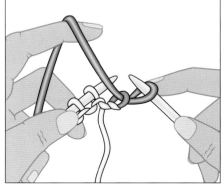

4 Slip the stitch off the left-hand needle. Return the left index finger to its position above the needle. One stitch is completed.

To continue...
Repeat these four steps for each stitch on the left-hand needle. All the stitches on the left-hand needle will be transferred to the right-hand needle where the new purl row is formed. At the end of the row, swap the needle with the stitches into your left hand and the empty needle into your right hand, and work the next row in the same way.

COMBINING KNIT AND PURL

If you work one row of knit stitches followed by one row of purl stitches, and repeat these two rows, you will produce stockinette (stocking) stitch (st st), the most widely used fabric in knitting. Work a row of knit stitches. At the end of the row, swap the needle with the stitches into your left hand and the empty needle into your right hand, and then work the next row in purl stitch.

In knitting instructions, stockinette (stocking) stitch is written as follows:
Row 1 (RS) Knit.
Row 2 Purl.
or the instructions may be:
Work in st st (1 row k, 1 row p), beg with a k row...

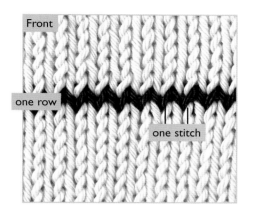

Front — one row — one stitch

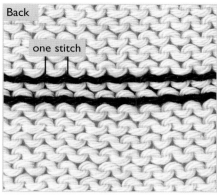

Back — one stitch

the result:

STOCKINETTE STITCH
(stocking stitch)

knit one row, purl one row

The front or right side (RS) of stockinette (stocking) stitch is smooth or flat, and the back or wrong side (WS) has rows of raised ridges and is rough. If you lay a piece of stockinette (stocking) stitch down you will see that the side edges curl towards the back of the fabric whilst the cast on and bind (cast) off edges curl towards the front of the fabric. This is why a garment in stockinette (stocking) stitch usually has a rib or garter stitch edging.

If the back of the fabric is used as the right side it is called reverse stockinette (stocking) stitch (rev st st). This is commonly used as the background for cables and embossed knitting.

✓ Knit Perfect

In stockinette (stocking) stitch, to identify which row to work next, look at the fabric on the left-hand needle as though you were ready to start. If the smooth (knit) side is facing you, work a knit row. If the rough (purl) side is facing you, purl the next row. To count rows in stockinette (stocking) stitch either count the V's on the knit side or the top loops of the ridges on the purl side.

Knit and purl stitches can also be combined to make a wide range of textured fabrics; (see Stitch library page 91–102).

◀ KNIT SOMETHING NOW!

Once you have mastered the two basic stitches, and know how to combine them to make stockinette (stocking) stitch, you can make this handy little bag.

Striped bag knitted in stockinette (stocking) stitch using a sport (4ply) weight mercerized cotton yarn on size 3 (3.25mm/UK10) needles. Finished size is 6½ × 7in (17 × 18cm). See page 133 for pattern.

ADVANCED CASTING ON

Using the correct method of casting on and off is important, whether it is at the start of a piece of knitting, adding or removing stitches part way through or finishing off.

Knitting on

This simple method of casting on needs two needles. Begin by making a slip knot about 6in (15cm) from the end of the yarn and slip it on to a needle held in your left hand. This method produces a loose cast on edge, ideal for lace fabrics where a hard edge is not necessary.

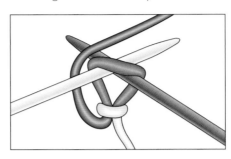

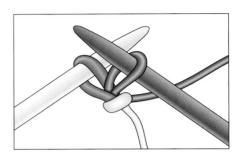

1 Insert the right-hand needle into the slip knot as though to knit it and wrap the yarn around the tip.

2 Pull a new loop through but do not slip the stitch off the left-hand needle.

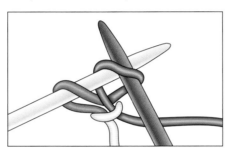

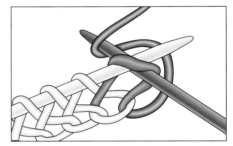

3 Place the loop on to the left-hand needle as shown by inserting the left-hand needle into the front of the loop from right to left as shown.

4 Insert the right-hand needle (as though to knit) into the stitch just made and wrap the yarn around the tip. Pull a new loop through and place it on to the left-hand needle.
  Repeat step 4 until you have cast on the required number of stitches.

Cable cast on

Work the same as knitting on but instead of going into a stitch the needle goes between stitches. It should be worked quite loosely so the needle slips between stitches easily. This produces a rope-like edge used when working buttonholes where stitches are cast off on one row and cast on again on the next row (see page 71).

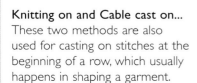

Knitting on and Cable cast on...
These two methods are also used for casting on stitches at the beginning of a row, which usually happens in shaping a garment.

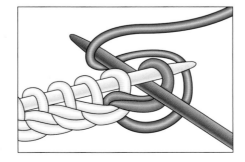

Cast on two stitches using the knitting on method. Insert the right-hand needle between the first and second stitches and wrap the yarn round the tip. When the new loop is pulled through between the stitches, place it on to the left-hand needle as for knitting on step 3.

ADVANCED BINDING (CASTING) OFF

Picot bind (cast) off

This is a pretty, decorative finish used when the bind (cast) off edge is part of the design, for example across the top of a pocket or around a collar.

1 Using the simple bind (cast) off method cast off two stitches (see page 22).

2 Slip the stitch on the right-hand needle back to the left-hand needle and, using the cable cast on method, cast on two stitches (see left).

3 Bind (cast) off four stitches. These are the two stitches just cast on and the next two stitches of the bind (cast) off edge.

To continue...
Repeat steps 2 and 3 until only one stitch remains on the right-hand needle. Cut the yarn, pull it through the last stitch and draw up tightly.
   The picots can be spaced wider apart by binding (casting) off five or more stitches.

Seam bind (cast) off

This is used to join two edges with the same number of stitches. It is often used for shoulder seams where the stitches have been left on stitch holders. You need three needles for this method.

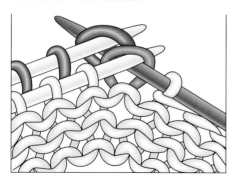

1 Slip each set of stitches on to a needle, place together with right sides facing and hold in the left hand.

2 Insert the third (right-hand) needle through both sets of stitches and draw a loop through, knitting the stitches together. Repeat for the next set of two stitches.
   Using the simple bind (cast) off method (see page 22), bind (cast) off stitches on the right-hand needle.

To finish...
With right sides together the bind (cast) off seam will be inside the garment; with wrong sides facing it will be a decorative seam on the outside as shown above.

Bind (cast) off in pattern

You should always bind (cast) off in the same stitch that you are using for the main fabric. On a knit row, you knit all the stitches when you bind (cast) off and on a purl row you purl all the stitches when you bind (cast) off. To cast off in rib, you must knit the knit stitches and purl the purl stitches of the rib. If you are working a pattern of cable stitches or lace, you would bind (cast) off in pattern; again knit the knit stitches and purl the purl stitches.

KNIT SOMETHING NOW!

Use the techniques you have already learned together with more advanced methods which you will learn further on to make this simple sweater.

The flower top is knitted in worsted (DK) weight wool and cotton yarn on size 3 (3.25mm/UK10) and size 6 (4mm/UK8) needles. See page 132 for pattern.

INCREASING STITCHES

To shape knitting, stitches are increased or decreased. Increases are used to make a piece of knitting wider by adding more stitches, either on the ends of rows or within the knitting. Some increases are worked to be invisible whilst others are meant to be seen and are known as decorative increases. You can increase one stitch at a time or two or more.

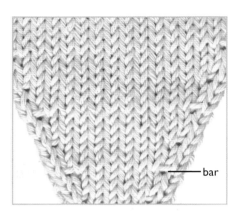

bar

Increasing one stitch (inc 1)

The easiest way to increase one stitch is to work into the front and back of the same stitch. This produces a small bar across the second (increase) stitch and is very visible. This makes counting the increases easier.

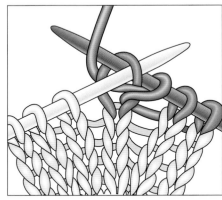

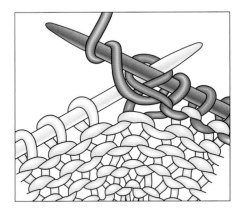

On a knit row knit into the front of the stitch as usual, do not slip the stitch off the left-hand needle but knit into it again through the back of the loop. Then slip the original stitch off the left-hand needle.

On a purl row purl into the front of the stitch as usual, do not slip the stitch off the left-hand needle but purl into it again through the back of the loop. Then slip the original stitch off the left-hand needle.

the result:

FULL FASHIONING

To make a neater edge when working increases at the beginning and end of rows, work the increase stitches a few stitches from the end. This leaves a continuous stitch up the edge of the fabric that makes sewing up easier. Because the made stitch lies to the left of the original stitch, at the beginning of a knit row you knit one stitch, then make the increase, but at the end of a knit row you work the increase into the third stitch from the end. The increase stitch lies between the second and third stitches at each end (see page 28–29 for more information on full fashioning).

On a purl row you work in exactly the same way; the bar will be in the correct position two stitches from either end.

KNIT SOMETHING NOW! ▶

This simple beret comes in three sizes, small, medium and large and is knitted in stockinette (stocking) stitch with a k1, p1 rib border.

Plain beret knitted in a worsted (DK) tweed wool yarn.
Two colour striped beret knitted in two colours of a worsted (DK) wool yarn on size 3 (3.25mm/UK10) and size 6 (4mm/UK8) needles. Finished head circumference measures 18 [20:22]in (45.5 [51:56]cm). See page 139 for pattern.

Make 1 (M1)

This is another way to increase one stitch and is often used when increasing stitches after a rib. The new stitch is made between two existing stitches using the horizontal thread that lies between the stitches – called the running thread. This is an invisible increase and is harder to see when counting.

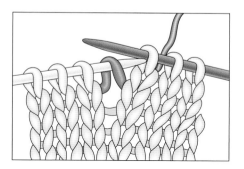 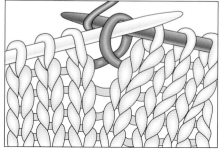 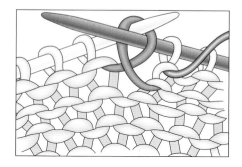

To twist the made stitch to the left
1 Knit to the point where the increase is to be made. Insert the tip of the left-hand needle under the running thread from front to back.

2 Knit this loop through the back to twist it. By twisting it you prevent a hole appearing where the made stitch is.

3 If you are working M1 on a purl row, you purl the loop through the back.

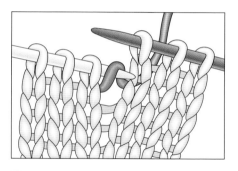 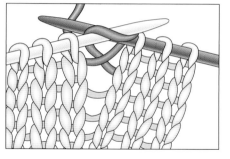 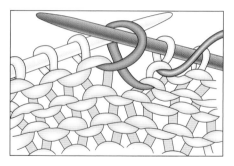

To twist the made stitch to the right
1 Knit to the point where the increase is to be made. Insert the tip of the left-hand needle under the running thread from back to front.

2 Knit this loop through the front to twist it.

3 If you are working M1 on a purl row, you purl the loop through the front.

the result:

INVISIBLE INCREASES

Being able to twist M1 to the right or left is useful when using this increase to shape a sleeve; the increases will be in pairs.
On a knit row, you knit two stitches, then work a M1 twisted to the right, knit to the last two stitches, then work a M1 twisted to the left. On a purl row, purl two stitches and work a M1 twisted to the left, then purl to the last two stitches and work a M1 twisted to the right.

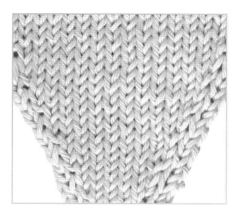

Increasing more than one stitch

To increase two stitches simply knit into the front, back and then the front again of the same stitch. When knitting bobbles (see page 44), you will sometimes make five, six or seven stitches out of one stitch in this way. For example, to make seven stitches the instructions would read (k into front and back of same st) 3 times, then k into front again.

DECREASING STITCHES

Decreasing is used at the ends of rows or within the knitted fabric to reduce the number of stitches being worked on. This means that you can shape your knitted fabric by making it narrower.

▼ KNIT SOMETHING NOW!

The baby's bootees are worked in stockinette (stocking) stitch and shaped by using increases and decreases creatively.

Baby bootees knitted in a worsted (DK) merino yarn on size 6 (4mm/UK8) needles. See page 149 for pattern.

Decreasing one stitch

The simplest way to decrease one stitch is to knit or purl two stitches together (k2tog or p2tog). Both of these methods produce the same result on the front (knit side) of the work; the decrease slopes to the right.

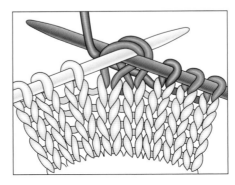 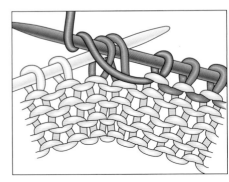

K2tog on a k row Knit to where the decrease is to be, insert the right-hand needle (as though to knit) through the next two stitches and knit them together as one stitch.

P2tog on a p row Purl to where the decrease is to be, insert the right-hand needle (as though to purl) through the next two stitches and purl them together as one stitch.

Decorative decreasing one stitch purlwise

Sometimes decreases are decorative, especially in lace knitting where they form part of the pattern. Then you have to be aware of whether the decrease slants right or left. Each decrease has an opposite and the two of them are called a pair. There is one way to work the decrease that is the pair to p2tog which slopes to the left when seen on the front (knit side) of the work. See page 34 for ways to slip stitches.

Slip one, slip one, purl two together through backs of loops (ssp or p2tog tbl)

1 Slip two stitches knitwise, one at a time, from the left-hand needle to the right-hand needle (they will be twisted), pass these two stitches back to the left-hand needle in this twisted way.

2 Purl these two stitches together through the back loops.

Decorative decreasing one stitch knitwise

There are two ways to work the decrease that is the pair to k2tog. They both produce the same result and slope to the left. See page 34 for ways to slip stitches.

Slip one, slip one, knit two together (ssk or p2tog tbl)

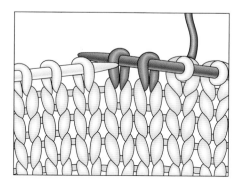 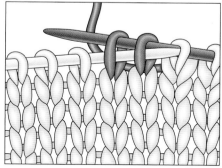

1 Slip two stitches knitwise one at a time from left-hand needle to right-hand needle.

2 Insert the left-hand needle from left to right through the fronts of these two stitches and knit together as one stitch.

Slip one, knit one, pass slipped stitch over (skpo)

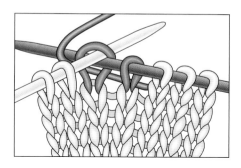 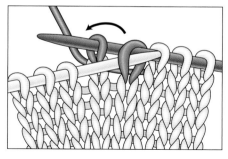

1 Insert the right-hand needle knitwise into the next stitch and slip it on to the right-hand needle without knitting it. Knit the next stitch.

2 With the tip of the left-hand needle, lift the slipped stitch over the knitted stitch and off the needle. This is like binding (casting) off one stitch.

Central decreasing

Slip two stitches knitwise, knit one, pass the two slipped stitches over (sl2tog-k1-psso)

Double decreases can also be worked where the two decreased stitches are arranged around a central stitch. Sk2po (see right) is a central decrease. To make a feature of the double decrease with its unbroken chain stitch running up the centre, work the central decrease as follows.

Insert the right-hand needle into the next two stitches as if to knit them together, slip them off together on to the right-hand needle without knitting them. Knit the next stitch. With the tip of the left-hand needle, lift the two slipped stitches together over the knitted stitch and off the needle.

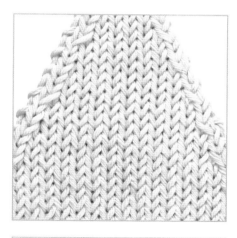

the result:

FULL FASHIONED DECREASES

You can use decreases in full fashioning in the same way as increases.

Slope to the right
knit row – k2tog
purl row – p2tog

Slope to the left
knit row – ssk or skpo
purl row – ssp

Decreasing two stitches at once

The two simplest ways are to knit three stitches together (k3tog) or purl three stitches together (p3tog). These are worked the same as k2tog and p2tog, but worked over three stitches instead of two.

The pair to k3tog is slip one, knit two together, pass slipped stitch over (sk2po), which is worked in the same manner as skpo but k2tog instead of k1.

Alternatively, the pair can be worked like ssk but slip three stitches knitwise instead of two.

The pair to p3tog is worked like ssp but over three stitches instead of two.

RIBS

Ribs are the result of alternating columns of knit and purl stitches. The knit columns stand out at the front and the purl columns sink to the back. When you lay a piece of ribbing flat, you will only see the knit columns as they pull together and cover the purl columns. This means that ribbing is very elastic; you can pull it out horizontally and it will spring back. When used at the waist, neck and wrists of garments, the ribs will expand when you put it on and then spring back to fit snugly.

The number of stitches in a rib fabric can be even, for example knit 1, purl 1 (k1, p1), knit 2, purl 2 (k2, p2), knit 3, purl 3 (k3, p3) or it can be uneven, for example knit 2, purl 3 (k2, p3), knit 2, purl 4 (k2, p4). Work a few samples of rib in different combinations to see the elastic effect of ribbing.

✓ Knit Perfect

Ribs are usually worked on needles two sizes smaller than those used for stockinette (stocking) stitch, because the action of moving the yarn backwards and forwards between the knit and purl stitches can loosen the work. Try and keep a regular tension when working a rib pattern.

KNIT SOMETHING NOW! ▶

This snug winter scarf uses six different ribs. It will grow quickly and give you lots of practise in ribbing

Ribbed scarf is knitted in a bulky (chunky) yarn using size 10½(6.5mm/UK3) needles. Finished size is 6in (15cm) wide by 64in (162cm) long. See page 137 for pattern.

Single rib (k1, p1)

Cast on an odd number of stitches.

1 With the yarn at the back of the work, knit the first stitch.

2 Bring the yarn to the front of the work between the needles and purl the next stitch.

3 Take the yarn to the back of the work, and knit the next stitch.

Single rib – k1, p1

Double rib – k2, p2

To continue...

Repeat steps 2 and 3 to the end of the row. On the return row knit the knit stitches and purl the purl stitches.

Double rib (k2, p2) is worked the same, but cast on a multiple of four stitches plus two stitches and knit or purl two stitches each time.

the result:

SINGLE AND DOUBLE RIB
k1, p1, or k2, p2

When using ribs for garments, it is usual to start and finish each row with the same stitch so the rib looks balanced when the garment is sewn up. So for a knit 1, purl 1 rib you would cast on an odd number of stitches, and for a knit 2, purl 2 rib you would need to cast on a multiple of four stitches plus two stitches.

GAUGE (Tension)

At the beginning of any knitting pattern, the designer will state the gauge (tension) that you need to achieve and this is used to calculate the finished dimensions of the garment. It is a very important part of knitting and is the number of stitches and rows to 1in (2.5cm). If you do not get the correct gauge (tension) the garment will not be the correct size. More stitches to 1in (2.5cm) and the garment will be smaller; fewer stitches to 1in (2.5cm) and the garment will be bigger. A tight fitting sweater may end up big and baggy.

In knitting patterns, the gauge (tension) is given over 4in (10cm). For example, 22 stitches and 28 rows to 4in (10cm) measured over stockinette (stocking) stitch on size 6 (4mm/UK8) needles. You must work a square of fabric measuring at least 6in (15cm), using the stated yarn, needle size and stitch. You can then measure the fabric in the middle of the square, avoiding the edge stitches which will be distorted.

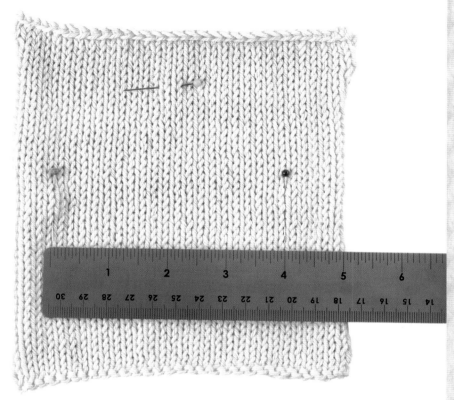

 Knit Perfect

Many knitters do not check their gauge (tension) because they think it is boring and a waste of time and yarn. They assume that they have the same gauge (tension) as the designer, but this is not necessarily the case.

Everyone holds the yarn at a different tension when they knit, this makes the stitches tighter or looser than someone else knitting exactly the same yarn on the same size needles.

Knitting a gauge (tension) square

To knit a gauge (tension) square for stockinette (stocking) stitch cast on the number of stitches stated for 4in (10cm) plus 10 extra stitches.

1 Work in stockinette (stocking) stitch for at least 6in (15cm) and then bind (cast) off loosely.

2 Steam or block the square in the way that you will use for your finished project (see page 68). The knitting pattern will tell you whether to block the pieces or not.

3 Lay the square on a flat surface without stretching it. Place a ruler horizontally on the square and place a pin four stitches in from the edge and place another at 4in (10cm) from the first pin.

4 Do the same for the rows by placing the ruler vertically, keeping away from the cast on and bind (cast) off edges, which may pull the fabric in.

5 Count the number of stitches and rows between the pins and this will be your gauge (tension):
Too many stitches means that your stitches are too small; you need to use a size larger needle to make the stitches bigger and so get fewer to 4in (10cm).
Too few stitches means your stitches are too big; you need to use a size smaller needle to make the stitches smaller and therefore get more to 4in (10cm).

6 Work more gauge (tension) squares until you achieve the gauge (tension) stated in the pattern.

If the gauge (tension) is quoted over a stitch pattern like a lace stitch, cast on enough stitches to work complete repeats. For aran patterns, cast on enough stitches to work all the different cables.

Checking your gauge (tension) will save you time spent unravelling your work and starting again, and it means the difference between a perfect garment and a disaster!

KNIT PERFECT

Here is some useful information and handy tips to improve the appearance of your knitting.

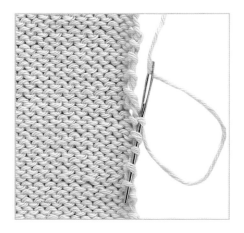

Knit Perfect

✓ Hairy yarns are sometimes difficult to unravel, the hairs become tangled into several stitches. Use a pair of sharp scissors to carefully cut the tangled hairs. Be careful not to cut the yarn completely. If the yarn is too damaged to re-use, cut it off and rejoin new yarn at the beginning of the row.

✓ If you snag a stitch in your knitted piece, a loop of yarn is pulled out drawing up several stitches tightly. Using a tapestry needle, ease the extra yarn back through the distorted stitches, one by one, starting with the stitch closest to the snag and yarn loop.

Joining a new ball

When you run out of yarn and need to start a new ball in the same colour or need to change to another colour, always start a new ball of yarn at the beginning of a row, at a seam edge where the ends can be woven in without showing on the front.

Simply drop the old yarn, wrap the new yarn around the needle and work a few stitches. Tie the two ends securely together at the beginning of the row so neither one will work its way free and unravel your stitches. When you've finished the piece, undo the knot and weave one end up the edge for a couple of inches, and then double back over a few stitches to secure the end.

Make sure you haven't pulled it too tightly and distorted the edge. Weave the other end down the edge using the same method. Use this method when knitting stripes and changing colours at the beginning of a row.

If you are coming to the end of a ball, to see if you have enough yarn to work one more row, lay the knitting flat and measure the yarn four times across the width. This will be sufficient to work one row of stockinette (stocking) stitch; textured and cabled fabric will need more yarn. When in doubt, join in a new ball of yarn to avoid running out of yarn halfway through and having to unravel stitches.

Slip stitches

Slipping stitches from one needle to another is part of many of the techniques already described and it is important to slip them correctly.

To slip a stitch, you pass it from one needle to the other without working into it. In the instructions you will usually be told how to slip the stitch, knitwise (kwise) or purlwise (pwise). To slip knitwise (sl1 kwise), insert the right-hand needle as if to knit and pull the stitch off the left-hand needle. This will twist the stitch as if you have worked it. To slip purlwise (sl1 pwise), insert the

right-hand needle as if to purl and pull the needle off the left-hand needle. The stitch will not be twisted.

Slipping either knitwise or purlwise makes a difference to the appearance of your work. In decreasing you always slip the stitch knitwise on a knit row and purlwise on a purl row, otherwise, when it is pulled over the other stitches in the decrease, it will appear to be twisted. When instructed to slip a stitch at the beginning of a row, to form a neat edge, slip knitwise on knit rows and purlwise on purl rows.

Stopping knitting

When you wish to stop knitting always finish the complete row. Finishing in the middle of a row will stretch the stitches and they may slide off the needle. If you need to put your knitting aside for several weeks or even months and do not have time to finish the piece beforehand mark on the pattern or

make a note of where you have got to. If you are working in a regular pattern like stockinette (stocking) stitch, when re-starting again it is worth unravelling a couple of rows and re-knitting them as stitches left over time on the needles can get stretched and leave an unsightly ridge where you stopped.

ABBREVIATIONS

Abbreviations are used to shorten techniques and words to make written knitting instructions easier to read and a manageable length. There are some standard abbreviations but others can vary. Always read the abbreviations on your pattern's knitting instructions carefully. The following are the most common abbreviations used throughout this book.

alt	alternate
approx	approximately
beg	begin/beginning
CC	contrast colour
cm	centimetre(s)
CN	cable needle
cont	continue
dec(s)	decrease(s)/decreasing
DK	double knitting
dpn	double-pointed needle
foll	following
g	gram
g st	garter stitch (k every row)
in(s)	inch(es)
inc(s)	increase(s)/increasing
k	knit
k2tog	knit 2 stitches together (1 stitch decreased)
k3tog	knit 3 stitches together (2 stitches decreased)
kwise	knitwise
LH	left hand
LT	left twist
m	metre(s)
mm	millimetre(s)
M1	make one (increase 1 stitch)
M1L	make one twisted to the left (increase 1 stitch)
M1R	make one twisted to the right (increase 1 stitch)
M1p	make one purlwise (increase 1 stitch)
MB	make a bobble
MC	main colour
oz	ounces
p	purl
patt(s)	pattern(s)
patt rep(s)	pattern repeat(s)
PB	place bead
PM	place marker
p2tog	purl 2 stitches together (1 stitch decreased)
p3tog	purl 3 stitches together (2 stitches decreased)
psso	pass slipped stitch over
p2sso	pass 2 slipped stitches over
pwise	purlwise

rem	remain/ing
rep(s)	repeat(s)
rev st st	reverse stockinette stitch (1 row p, 1 row k) (UK: reverse stocking stitch)
RH	right hand
rnd(s)	round(s)
RS	right side
RT	right twist
skpo	slip 1 stitch, knit 1 stitch, pass slipped stitch over (1 stitch decreased)
sk2po	slip 1 stitch, knit 2 stitches together, pass slipped stitch over (2 stitches decreased)
sl2tog-k1-psso	slip 2 stitches together, knit 1 stitch, pass 2 slipped stitches over (2 stitches decreased)
ssk	slip 2 stitches one at a time, knit 2 slipped stitches together (1 stitch decreased)
ssp	slip 2 stitches one at a time, purl 2 slipped stitches together through the back of the loops (1 stitch decreased)

sl	slip
sl st	slip stitch
sl 1	slip 1 stitch
sl 1k	slip 1 stitch knitwise
sl 1p	slip 1 stitch purlwise
st(s)	stitch(es)
st st	stockinette stitch (1 row k, 1 row p) (UK: stocking stitch)
tbl	through back of loop
tog	together
WS	wrong side
wyib	with yarn in back
wyif	with yarn in front
ybk	yarn to the back
yd(s)	yard(s)
yfwd	yarn forward
yo	yarn over
yrn	yarn round needle
yon	yarn over needle
*	repeat directions following
*	as many times as indicated or until end of row
[ ]	instructions in square brackets refer to larger sizes
( )	repeat instructions in round brackets the number of times indicated

Throughout the book US terms are given with UK terms in brackets. These are the most commonly used:

Instructions	US	UK
	bind off	cast off
	gauge	tension
	stockinette stitch	stocking stitch
	reverse stockinette stitch	reverse stocking stitch
	work even	work straight/work without shaping

Yarns	US	UK
	fingering/baby yarn	2ply/3ply
	sport weight	4ply
	worsted	DK
	fisherman/medium weight	aran
	bulky	chunky

Creative Options

In this section, you will build upon the techniques that you have learnt so far. You will see new ways of working stitches, such as lace knitting, using yarn overs and decreases decoratively. The sections on cables, twisted stitches and embossed knitting introduce manipulating stitches, twisting them and carrying them across the fabric, to add a three dimensional aspect to your knitting. Colour knitting is covered by the sections on two techniques; intarsia and fair isle knitting. There is a section on circular knitting and how to use four or more needles, or circular needles. Short rows are useful for shaping and can produce wonderful structural effects.

KNIT SOMETHING NOW! ▶

Knit a trio of lace sachets to hold pot pourri or lavender and practise three lace stitch patterns.

The **lace bags** are knitted in a sport (4ply) mercerized cotton yarn on size 2 (3mm/UK11) needles. See page 145 for the patterns.

LACE KNITTING

The general term used to cover eyelets, faggoting and lace is lace knitting. These form categories on their own, but many stitch patterns overlap between two or even three of them.

Eyelets are single holes worked in rows or in groups on a background of stockinette (stocking) stitch; for example, a drawstring can be threaded through a row of eyelets with three or four stitches between them.

Knitted faggoting is the same term as that used in embroidery and describes a line of horizontal or vertical holes, next to each other and separated by a few strands of thread. It is often used as an open insertion around a hem or cuff. All-over faggoting forms a net or mesh.

Lace is the most open variation where the holes and decreases are arranged to form patterns. A lace stitch pattern can be repeated as an all-over fabric or worked as an insertion on stockinette (stocking) stitch. The stitch and row repeat can vary from simple patterns of less than ten stitches and two rows up to complex patterns of 20 or 30 stitches and as many rows.

The holes in lace knitting are made by working a yarn over. This makes (increases) a stitch so it has to be accompanied by a decrease. The way you work a yarn over depends on the stitches either side of it. In patterns, where yarn over (yo) is given, you decide which yarn over method to use. Some patterns will tell you which one to use.

Working a yarn over

Between two knit stitches
(k1, yo, k1) or (k1, yfwd, k1)

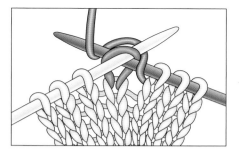

Bring the yarn forward (yfwd or yf) between the two needles. Knit the next stitch, taking the yarn over the right needle.

Between two purl stitches
(p1, yo, p1) or (p1, yrn, p1)

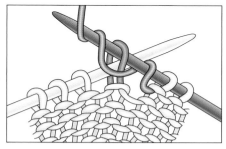

Take the yarn back over the right-hand needle and forward between the needles to bring yarn round needle (yrn). Purl the next stitch.

Between knit and purl stitches
(k1, yo, p1) or (k1, yfrn, p1)

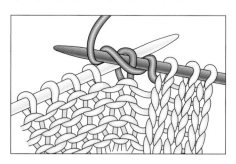

Bring the yarn forward between the two needles, take it back over the right-hand needle and forward again between the two needles – yarn forward and round needle (yfrn). Purl the next stitch.

Between purl and knit stitches
(p1, yo, k1) or (p1, yon, k1)

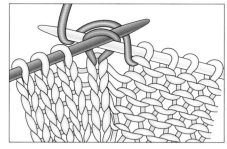

Take the yarn back over the right-hand needle – yarn over needle (yon). Knit the next stitch.

✓ Knit Perfect

When working a lace pattern you may find it helpful to place a marker (make several slip knot loops of a contrasting colour yarn) between each repeat, where the asterisks are, and slip them on every row. Then you can keep track of each small repeat instead of having to work back through a long row of stitches if you make a mistake.

lace knitting

At the edge of work

Sometimes you have to work a yarn over at the edge of the work, before the first stitch.

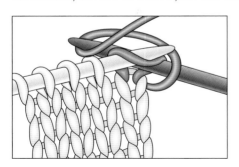

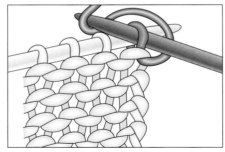

Before a knit stitch bring the yarn forward as if to purl, knit the first stitch bringing the yarn over the right needle as you do so.

Before a purl stitch take the yarn back as though to knit, purl the first stitch, bringing the yarn over the needle as you do so.

Multiple yarn overs
(yo twice)

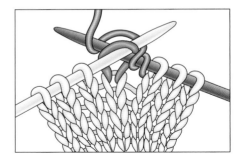

These are used to make bigger holes. Wrap the yarn around the needle twice. On the return row, you must knit then purl into the double yarn over.

✓ ## Knit Perfect

Decreases in lace stitches play a decorative part and the lace stitch pattern will tell you which decrease to work (see page 76).

the result:

SIMPLE LACE PATTERN
To see the lace pattern at its best the knitting needs to be stretched slightly to open it out and then blocked. Lace patterns look particularly good knitted in a smooth cotton yarn.

Working a lace stitch pattern

A simple lace pattern is written as follows:

Row 1 K1, * yfwd, k1, sk2po, k1, yfwd, k1; rep from * to end.
Row 2 P to end.
Row 3 K1, * k1, yfwd, sk2po, yfwd, k2; rep from * to end.
Row 4 P to end.

This pattern is worked over a multiple of six stitches plus one and over four rows. If you cast on 25 stitches this will give you four repeats of the pattern. The part you repeat is between the asterisks; so on row 1 you would begin with k1, then work a yfwd, k1, then work the decrease sk2po, k1, another yfwd, and then k1. The sk2po decreases the two stitches that you make by working the two yfwds. Go back to the asterisk and begin the repeat again with yfwd, k1, etc. Keep repeating the six stitches until you reach the end of the row. Count your stitches and make sure you still have 25; if you have more, you haven't worked the sk2po properly, if you have less you may have missed one of the yfwds. Row 2 is just a purl row. On row 3, begin with k1 and then work the repeat four times. Row 4 is a purl row. These four rows form the pattern and are repeated. So go back to row 1 and start again.

Shaping lace fabric

Placing markers for the lace pattern repeats is a good idea when you are shaping a piece of lace knitting for a garment. By marking the beginning of the first repeat and the end of the last repeat, you can increase stitches at the beginning and end of a row and keep the lace pattern correct. For more information on increasing into stitch patterns see page 76.

Blocking lace fabric

A lace pattern needs to be stretched slightly when blocking (see page 68). It needs to be opened out to show off the pattern of holes. By working decreases so often the fabric will be puckered. When working a gauge (tension) square, pull it out so that it lies flat and the holes are open. Do not over stretch it or it will be distorted.

FAIR ISLE

Authentic fair isle sweaters were worked as circular knitting so the right side of the knitting was always facing the knitter. This meant that the pattern was always visible and only knit stitches were used.

Because the knitting was circular there were no seams; armholes and the front openings of cardigans were cut after the knitting was finished. Extra stitches were added for this purpose and they were called steeks; the extra stitches were turned back after cutting and sewn down to prevent the stitches unravelling. Sleeves were picked up around the armholes and knitted down to the cuff, and shoulder seams were grafted.

Today the term fair isle knitting is used to describe the technique of knitting with two colours in one row and is used in flat as well as circular knitting.

Reading a chart

Fair isle patterns are worked from charts. One square represents one stitch and one line of squares represents one row. The rows will be numbered, knit rows (right side rows) will be odd numbers and are read from right to left; purl rows (wrong side rows) are even numbers and are read from left to right.

Start knitting from the bottom right-hand corner of the chart. The whole garment may not need to be charted; many fair isle patterns have a small repeat. The chart will tell you which stitches to repeat. On each side of the pattern repeat there may be extra stitches that are only worked once. These balance the pattern, to make sure that it is the same at both side seams.

Colour charts show the actual yarn colours whilst on black and white charts each colour is represented by a symbol. A key is given with the chart to show which symbol or colour represents which colour yarn.

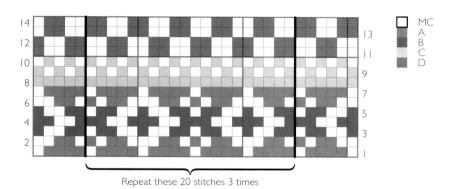

Repeat these 20 stitches 3 times

Knit Perfect

In fair isle, the unused colour is loosely carried along the back of the work between stitches. Carrying the yarn between stitches is called stranding and you can strand yarn across if the pattern is small and the colours are changed frequently. However, if the yarn is to be stranded over five stitches or more, the loop will be too long and it will get snagged and distort the fabric. You must catch the loop in on the centre stitch of a long strand to prevent this. This is called weaving in.

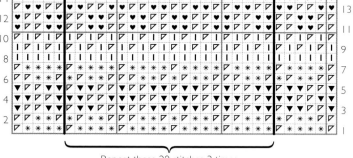

Repeat these 20 stitches 3 times

fair isle

Knit Perfect

Practise knitting with both hands, it really is the easiest and fastest way of working. If you find the Continental method too awkward, adapt it to suit yourself. For example, try holding the yarn between the thumb and index finger.

Gauge (tension)

It is important in either stranding or weaving in that the yarn carried across the back is not pulled up too tightly. If it is, the knitted fabric will pucker and not lie flat. Keep spreading the stitches out on the needle to maintain the correct gauge (tension).

Fair isle knitting is easier and faster if you can learn to use both the right and left hands to hold the yarns. To do this you must practise the unfamiliar technique of either the English or Continental methods of knitting and purling (see page 18). If you find two-handed knitting awkward you can also hold both yarns in one hand (see right). If you find both of these methods difficult, you can hold only the working yarn, letting it drop to pick up the new yarn when you need to change colour but this is a very slow method of working.

Stranding

The loops formed by carrying the yarn between areas of colour are called floats. To get the floats to lie neatly and without lumps where the colours are changed and to prevent the yarns from becoming twisted together and tangled, one colour always lies above the other on the wrong side of the work. By keeping the back of the work neat in this way, the stitches on the front of the work will lie flat without puckering and without holes appearing between the colour changes. Never strand yarns over more than five stitches. In stranding, one colour must always be above the other on the back of the work. If they constantly change position, the fabric will be bulky and the yarns will tangle.

Using both hands

Hold the most frequently used colour (usually the background colour) in the right hand and the second colour in the left hand (see page 18 for the position of hands and yarns in the English and Continental methods). Whilst knitting, the right-hand colour crosses over the left-hand colour and it will always lie above the left-hand (second) colour.

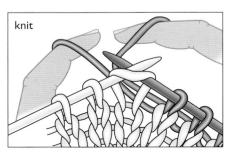
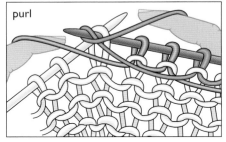

1 When knitting with the right-hand colour, keep the left-hand colour below the needle and out of the way of the working yarn.

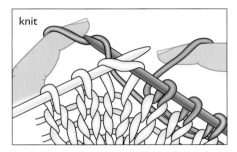
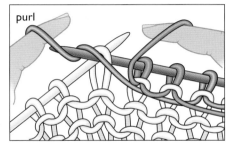

2 When knitting with the left-hand colour, keep the right-hand colour above the needle.

✓ Knit Perfect

✓ There is no need to make bobbins for each colour of yarn. Just use the yarn straight from the ball.

✓ Turn the work clockwise at the end of a knit row and anti-clockwise at the end of a purl row. This action will prevent the yarns becoming tangled.

✓ Always carry both yarns to the beginning and end of the each row by catching the unused yarn into the first and last stitch. If you don't, the fabric here will be thinner than where both yarns are stranded across the back.

✓ As you work across the row, keep easing out the fabric to its correct width on the needle, so the floats or weaving are not pulled too tightly.

Both yarns in one hand

Hold both yarns together in the right hand. Have the working yarn over the index finger, knit or purl the required stitches then drop it and pick up the other colour on to the index finger. The predominant colour will always be picked up over the second colour and the second colour will always be picked up below the predominant colour. This will ensure that the floats of the predominant colour will always be above those of the second colour.

One yarn at a time

Drop one colour and pick up the new colour, making sure they don't become twisted and the floats are lying correctly. The predominant colour is always picked up over the second colour and the second colour is always picked up from below the other colour.

Weaving in

You must weave the floats in if they are stranded over five stitches or more. This is the same technique used to weave in ends in intarsia (see page 51). Refer to the diagrams and remember to weave the yarn in loosely without pulling up the stitches.

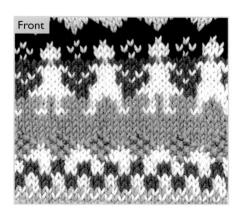

Front

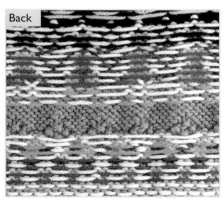

Back

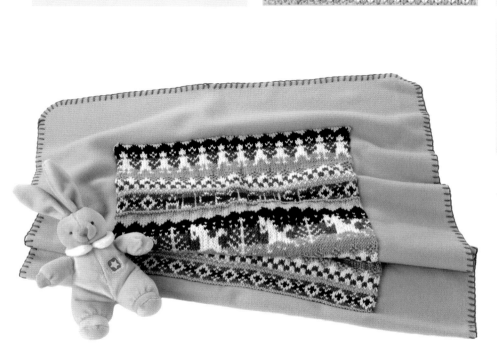

the result:

FAIR ISLE KNITTING

The knitting should be smooth on the front with the yarn floats lying neatly across the back with one colour always above the other.

KNIT SOMETHING NOW!

Using just two colours on each row does not limit the range of designs possible in traditional fair isle. This patch gives plenty of practise knitting with yarn held in both hands.

Fair isle baby blanket is knitted in a worsted (DK) wool/cotton yarn on size 6 (4mm/UK8) needles. See page 143 for pattern.

CABLES

Cables are simply a way of twisting two sets of stitches or carrying stitches across the fabric. There are two ways of moving the stitches; cabling and crossing. Stitches are cabled when all the stitches are knitted, but stitches are crossed when knit stitches are moved over a background of purl stitches. In patterns, cables are twisted to the back or front, while crossed stitches move right or left.

The two techniques to learn are moving the stitches at the back and moving them at the front. This is done by holding the stitches on a cable needle either at the back or the front of the work. This simple cable twists two sets of knit stitches, using four stitches.

Basic abbreviations for cables…

C4F	cable four front
C4B	cable four back
Cr4L	cross four left
Cr4R	cross four right

When following a pattern with cables, the designer will explain how to work the cables under special abbreviations at the start of the pattern.

Instead of twisting stitches to form cables, stitches can be crossed, carrying two knit stitches to the left or right, over a background of purl stitches.

Cable four front (C4F)

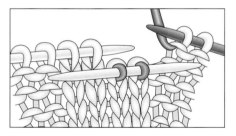

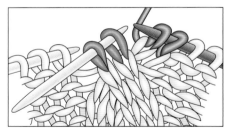

1 Slip the next two stitches from the left-hand needle on to a cable needle and hold at the front of the work.

2 Knit the next two stitches on the left-hand needle, then knit the two stitches from the cable needle.

Cable four back (C4B)

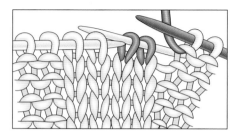

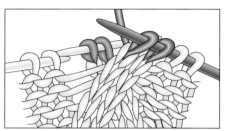

1 Slip the next two stitches from the left-hand needle on to a cable needle and hold at the back of the work.

2 Knit the next two stitches on the left-hand needle, then knit the two stitches from the cable needle.

More cables…

C6F or C6B is worked by slipping three stitches on to the cable needle and then knitting three stitches. C8F or C8B is worked with four stitches in each part of the cable. The more stitches there are in a cable, the more rows there are between twists. So C4F or C4B has three rows straight, C6F or C6B has five rows straight and so on. To make a looser cable, work more rows straight between twists.

Cross four left (Cr4L)

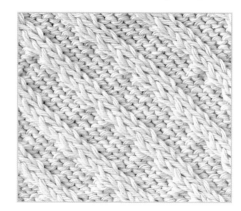

1 Slip the next two stitches from the left-hand needle on to a cable needle and hold at the front of the work.

2 Purl the next two stitches on the left-hand needle, then knit the 2 stitches from the cable needle.

Cross four right (Cr4R)

1 Slip the next two stitches from the left-hand needle on to a cable needle and hold at the back of the work.

2 Knit the next two stitches on the left-hand needle, then purl the two stitches from the cable needle.

the result:

CABLES AND CROSS STITCHES

The more stitches there are in a cable the more rows are worked between twists. Crossed stitches can move every right side row or with more rows worked between them.

More crossing cables...

Cr3L or Cr3R could be worked by moving the two knit stitches over one purl background stitch or by moving one knit stitch over two purl background stitches. Cr5L or Cr5R could be worked by moving two knit stitches over three purl background stitches or three knit stitches over two purl background stitches. In a pattern an explanation of the abbreviations used is given. Crossed stitches can be moved on every right side row or with straight rows in between.

✓ Knit Perfect

✓ Cable needles can be straight or they can have a kink in them to stop the stitches falling off. Try both kinds or, if you find the cable needle fiddly to work with because it is too short, try using a short double-pointed needle of the same size as those used for the main knitting. If you find working the stitches off the cable needle awkward, replace them on to the left-hand needle to work them.

✓ Use a row counter or make a mark for each row worked on a piece of paper to keep track of the rows between twists of the cable. To count the rows between twists of a cable, look for the row where you worked the twist; you will be able to identify this by following the path of the yarn from the last stitch of the cable to the first background stitch for a front cross cable or from the last background stitch to the first stitch of the cable for a back cross cable. On the row below this there will be no connecting strand of yarn between these same stitches. Count each strand for every row above the twist row.

▼ KNIT SOMETHING NOW!

This cable throw has each panel knitted separately so it is ideal for practising cables.

Cable throw knitted in four colours of a bulky (chunky) wool yarn on size 10½ (7mm/UK2) needles.
See page 134 for pattern.

43

EMBOSSED KNITTING

Embossed features are three dimensional, for example, popcorns and bobbles, both of which involve making extra stitches out of one stitch and are knitted independently of the background fabric. They also include bells and leaves, which are knitted into the background fabric.

Popcorn worked over four stitches

A popcorn is a small knot of stitches that are increased and immediately decreased.

1 To make four stitches from one stitch (knit into the front of the next stitch, then knit into the back of it) twice. Slip the original stitch from the left-hand needle.

2 With the tip of the left-hand needle, pull the second, third, and fourth stitches over the first stitch and off the needle. Work the stitch after the popcorn firmly to hold the popcorn in place at the front of the work.

Variations

Sometimes popcorn instructions will tell you to increase by (k1, p1) twice into the same stitch. Larger bobbles are made by increasing more stitches out of one stitch. You can work more or less rows of stockinette (stocking) stitch or work in reverse stockinette (stocking) stitch or garter stitch on these stitches. Decreases, too, can be worked in different ways, working a pair of decreases at each end of two rows or decreasing to three stitches and working a central decrease (see page 31).

Simple bobble of five stitches

A bobble is a round button of fabric, larger than a popcorn, made by increasing stitches and working a few rows on these stitches before decreasing. There are many ways to create a bobble and the pattern instructions will tell you the kind of bobble to work.

1 To make five stitches from one stitch (knit into the front of the next stitch, then knit into the back of it) twice, then knit into the front of the same stitch again. Slip the original stitch from the left-hand needle.

2 (Turn the work and purl these five stitches, turn the work and knit the same five stitches) twice.

3 To decrease the five stitches back to one stitch, with the tip of the left-hand needle, pull the second, third, fourth and fifth stitches over the first stitch and off the needle.

Bells

These small funnels of fabric, open at one end and knitted into the background fabric, look like small bells. Start by casting on stitches between two stitches of background fabric which is usually reverse stockinette (stocking) stitch and shape them by decreasing the cast on stitches over several rows.

Bell over 6 sts with 5 sts of rev st st each side.

Cast on 10 sts and work 2 rows in rev st st.
Row 1 (RS) P5, cast on 6 sts using the cable cast on method (see page 26), p5.
Row 2 K5, p the 6 sts just cast on, k5.
Row 3 P5, k6, p5.
Row 4 As row 2.
Row 5 P5, ssk, k2, k2tog, p5.
Row 6 K5, p4, k5.
Row 7 P5, ssk, k2tog, p5.
Row 8 K5, p2, k5.

Row 9 P5, k2tog, p5.
Row 10 K5, p1, k5.
Row 11 P4, p2tog (last st of bell and 1 st of rev st st), p5.
Row 12 K10.

The bell can be made bigger by casting on more stitches. Always shape the bell by working pairs of decreases (see pages 30–1). Bells can be worked singly, in rows or as an all-over pattern.

Leaves

Instead of the extra stitches being made all at once as for a bobble, two stitches at a time are increased on every right side row either side of a central stitch. They are usually created by a yarn over. The leaf is then decreased by working a pair of decreases on every right side row until three stitches remain, then a central decrease is worked to return to the original one stitch. The leaf is not worked separately but the extra stitches are worked into each row across the fabric. Leaves are usually worked on reverse stockinette (stocking) stitch or garter stitch.

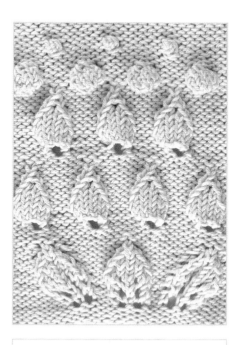

Simple leaf worked up to a width of 7 stitches with 5 sts of rev st st each side.

Cast on 11 sts and work 2 rows in rev st st.
Row 1 P5, yo, k1, yo, p5.
Row 2 K5, p3, k5.
Row 3 P5, k1, yo, k1, yo, k1, p5.
Row 4 K5, p5, k5.
Row 5 P5, k2, yo, k1, yo, k2, p5. The leaf now has 7 sts.
Row 6 K5, p7, k5.
Row 7 P5, ssk, k3, k2tog, p5.
Row 8 K5, p5, k5.

Row 9 P5, ssk, k1, k2tog, p5.
Row 10 K5, p3, k5.
Row 11 P5, sl2tog-k1-psso, p5.
Row 12 K to end.
Make a bigger leaf by working more increase rows. Make a more solid leaf by working M1 instead of yo. The leaf can be sloped to the right or left by working a decrease on one side in the rev st st and an increase on the other side in the rev st st.

the result:

EMBOSSED KNITTING

From the top the sample shows four stitch popcorns, five stitch bobbles, two rows of bells and a central leaf with leaves sloping to the left and right each side.

 ## Knit Perfect

Embossed features add great texture to a garment as an all-over pattern such as the Popcorn pattern on page 104 or the Boxed bobble pattern on page 105. Popcorns and bobbles are often added to cables, for example the Medallion bobble cable on page 111 and the Nosegay pattern on page 117. Combined with other stitches they contrast well with lace or knit and purl fabrics.

Here a single repeat of Norwegian fir lace from page 122 is used as a central panel between lines of popcorns on five stitches of stockinette (stocking) stitch and a panel of leaves worked on a background of seven stitches of reverse stockinette (stocking) stitch.

SHORT ROWS

Short rows are partially knitted rows; the work is turned before the row is completed and the same stitches are worked back across. This results in there being two more rows at one side of the fabric than at the other. Short row knitting is also called turning, or partial knitting.

The technique is commonly used for shaping sock heels, known as turning a heel. On each turning row one less stitch is worked and then, to turn the heel, you work one more stitch each turning row until you are back to your original number of stitches.

On a knit row

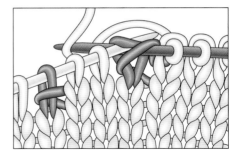

1 Knit to the turning point, slip the next stitch knitwise on to the right-hand needle and bring the yarn forward between the needles to the right side of the work.

2 Slip the slipped stitch back to the right-hand needle and take the yarn back to the knit position. Turn the work as though at the end of a row. The slipped stitch has been wrapped and it has a bar across it. Purl back across the row.

To hide the bar...
When you knit back over the turning point and the wrapped stitch you can knit it into the fabric to hide it. Work to the wrapped stitch. Insert the tip of the right-hand needle into the bar and the wrapped stitch, and knit them together. The bar will be knitted in and not show on the fabric. Alternatively you can leave the bar as it is.

Knit Perfect

✓ When you turn the work, a hole appears when all the stitches are worked over again. You can either leave this as a pattern feature or use the wrap method to cover it up.

✓ Wrapping the stitch does not work if you are only decreasing or increasing by one stitch on every turning row. To hide the hole in this case, slip the first stitch after the turn purlwise and then work the slip stitch together with the head of the stitch below when working back across the turn. This method can also be used instead of the wrap method.

On a purl row

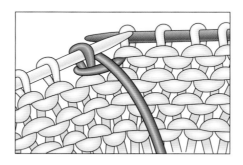

1 Purl to the turning point, slip the next stitch purlwise on to the right-hand needle and then take the yarn back between the needles to the right side of the work.

2 Slip the slipped stitch back to the right-hand needle and take the yarn back to the knit position. Turn the work as though at the end of a row. The slipped stitch has been wrapped and it has a bar across it. Purl back across the row.

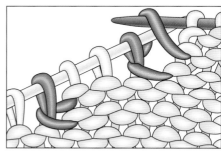

To hide the bar...
Insert the tip of the right-hand needle into the back of the loop and place it on to the left-hand needle. Purl it and the wrapped stitched together.

Horizontal darts can also be worked in short rows to add shape to a garment. Work from the side edge to the tip of the dart and turn, then work back to three or four stitches from the side edge. Continue in this way, working three or four stitches further from the side seam each time until the dart is the required depth. Then work across all stitches.

Shoulder shaping can also be done using short rows. Binding (casting) off the stitches produces a stepped edge. Instead, turn the work before the stitches that are to be bound (cast) off. Repeat this on each bind (cast) off row. You will then have all the stitches still on the needle to bind (cast) off in one go or to join the shoulder seam by the three-needle seam bind (cast) off method (see page 27).

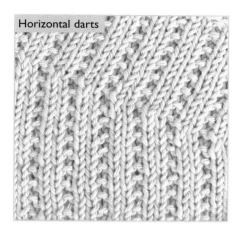
Horizontal darts

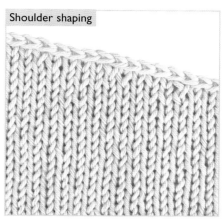
Shoulder shaping

Matching gauges (tensions) Short rows are also useful when knitting together two stitch patterns with different row gauges (tensions). For example, a garter stitch front border on a stockinette (stocking) stitch cardigan. You need to work six rows of garter stitch for every four rows of stockinette (stocking) stitch. Finish the row at the end of the garter stitch, turn and knit the garter stitches, turn and knit back across them. Then work across all stitches of the garment.

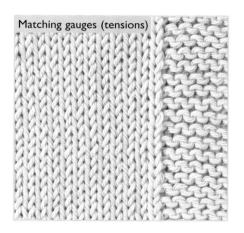
Matching gauges (tensions)

KNIT SOMETHING NOW! ▶

This sculptured cushion is worked in a pattern of points built up by short rows. The turns are not wrapped so the holes add a jagged edge to the points.

The short row cushion is knitted in a sport (4 ply) weight 100 per cent silk yarn on size 3 (3.25mm/UK10) needles. See page 138 for pattern.

TWISTED STITCHES

Single stitches can be twisted over each other without using a cable needle. As in cables, two knit stitches can be cabled to the right or the left. Twisted stitches can also be crossed (one knit stitch moving over a purl stitch) to the right or left.

Basic abbreviations for twisted stitches...

RT   twisted cables – right twist
LT   twisted cables – left twist
Cr2R   crossed stitches – cross right
Cr2L   crossed stitches – cross left

When following a pattern with twisted stitches, the designer will explain how to work the stitches under special abbreviations at the start of the pattern.

▲KNIT SOMETHING NOW!

A coaster featuring twisted stitches in the shape of hearts. Knit it together with a place mat with a pocket for cutlery – an ideal pair for outdoor eating.

Place mat and coaster knitted in a worsted (DK) wool yarn on size 6 (4mm/UK8) needles. See page 135 for pattern.

Twisted cables – right twist (RT)

1 Insert right-hand needle into second stitch on left-hand needle and knit it. Don't slip this stitch off the needle.

2 Knit the first stitch on the left-hand needle and slip both stitches on to the right-hand needle.

Twisted cables – left twist (LT)

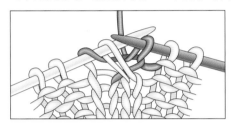
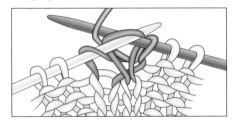

1 Insert right-hand needle into front of second stitch on left-hand needle, working behind the first stitch, and knit it. Don't slip this stitch off the needle.

2 Knit the first stitch on the left-hand needle and slip both stitches on to the right-hand needle.

Crossed stitches – cross right (Cr2R)

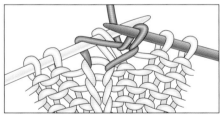
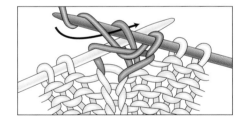

1 Insert right-hand needle into second stitch on the left-hand needle and knit it. Don't slip this stitch off the needle.

2 Purl the first stitch on the left-hand needle and slip both stitches on to the right-hand needle.

Crossed stitches – cross left (Cr2L)

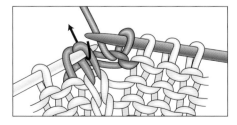

1 Insert right-hand needle into back of second stitch on left-hand needle, working behind first stitch, and purl it. Don't slip this stitch off the needle.

2 Knit the first stitch on the left-hand needle and slip both stitches on to the right-hand needle.

INTARSIA

Intarsia is a technique of colour knitting suitable for large areas of colour where several blocks of different colours are worked in the same row. Unlike fair isle knitting where two colours are carried along the row to form a repeating pattern, intarsia knitting is characterized by single motifs, geometric patterns or pictures.

Intarsia uses a separate ball of yarn for each block of colour. The yarns are twisted together to link the areas of colour and prevent a hole. Most colourwork designs are worked in stockinette (stocking) stitch and it is only suitable for flat knitting; in circular knitting the yarns will always be at the end of the colour block and must be cut off and rejoined at the beginning. Intarsia patterns are worked from charts and often the whole garment will be charted (see page 39).

Bobbins

Each area of colour needs its own bobbin of yarn. You should never knit straight from the ball because with all the twisting, the yarn will become horribly tangled and the knitting becomes a chore. Working with bobbins you can pull out sufficient yarn to knit the stitches and then leave it hanging at the back of the work out of the way of the other yarns.

You can buy plastic bobbins and wrap a small amount of yarn on to each one but it is easy to make your own and cheaper if the intarsia design requires a lot of separate areas of colour. Leaving a long end, wind the yarn in a figure of eight around your thumb and little finger. Cut the yarn and use this cut end to tie a knot around the middle of the bobbin. Use the long end to pull the yarn from the middle of the bobbin. If the knotted end becomes loose around the bobbin as you pull yarn out, keep tightening it otherwise the bobbin will unravel.

Plan your knitting before you start. Work out how many bobbins of each colour you will need. If there are only a small number of stitches to be worked, cut a sufficient length of yarn, there is no need to wind it into a bobbin. Allow three times the width of stitches for the yarn needed to work those stitches.

Joining in a new colour

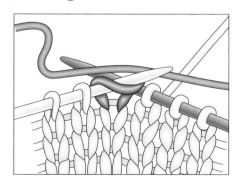 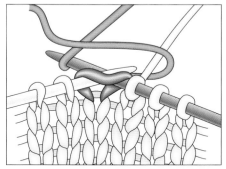

1 Insert the tip of the right-hand needle into the next stitch, place the cut end (4in/10cm from the end) of the new colour over the old colour and over the tip of the right-hand needle.

2 Take the working end of the new colour and knit the next stitch, pulling the cut end off the needle over the working end as the stitch is formed so it is not knitted in. Hold the cut end down against the back of the work.

To continue...
The old and new colours will be twisted together, preventing a hole and you can carry on using the new colour. Leave the cut end dangling to be sewn in later or continue weaving it in (see page 51).

On a purl row, join in a new colour in the same way, twisting the yarns together on the wrong side of the work.

---

intarsia

Twisting yarns together

Once you've joined in all the colours that you need across the row, on the return row the yarns should be twisted to join the blocks of colour together. When you change colour, always pick up the new colour from under the old yarn. This is particularly important when the colours are changed at the same place in two or more rows. A line of loops will be formed on the wrong side of the work; these should not show through to the right side. Pull the yarns up firmly for the first stitch after twisting.

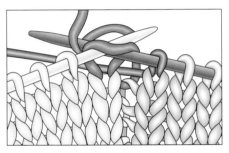

Twisting yarns on a knit row
Insert the tip of the right-hand needle into the next stitch, pull the old colour to the left, pick up the new colour and bring it up behind the old colour. Knit the next stitch. The two yarns are twisted together.

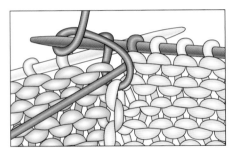

Twisting yarns on a purl row
Insert the tip of the right-hand needle into the next stitch, pull the old colour to the left, pick up the new colour and bring it up behind the old colour. Purl the next stitch. The two yarns are twisted together.

Carrying yarn

Sometimes you will need to begin a new colour several stitches before where you used it on the previous row. Work the next stitch with the new colour, twisting it with the old colour as before; do not pull the yarn too tightly across the back of the work, spread the stitches out to get the correct tension. This will result in a loop of the new colour laying across the back of the work. If it is only a couple of stitches, this will not be a problem. If it is over several stitches, and there is a long loop, you need to catch it into the knitting or it will snag during wear. If it is more than seven stitches, it is best to cut the yarn and join it in at the new position.

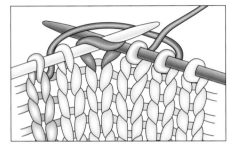

On a knit row
1 Knit two stitches in the new colour. Insert the tip of the right-hand needle into the next stitch, then pick up the long loop.

On a purl row
1 Purl two stitches in the new colour. Insert the tip of the right-hand needle into the next stitch, then pick up the long loop.

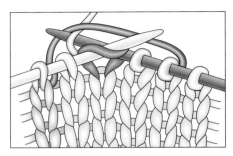

2 Wrap the yarn around as though to knit, then pull the long loop off the needle. Knit the stitch. The loop will be caught without appearing on the front of the work.

2 Wrap the yarn around as though to purl, then pull the long loop off the needle. Purl the stitch. The loop will be caught without appearing on the front of the work.

Using bobbins

Each area of colour on an intarsia chart needs a separate length of yarn. This simple block pattern shows the three bobbins needed to work the central square of each block using the intarsia method. Each bobbin is picked up in turn and used before being left to hang from a short length of yarn to prevent it becoming tangled with the others. When the centre square is completed, only one bobbin will be used to finish the block and the other two will be cut off and the ends sewn in neatly.

■ A   ■ C
■ B   ■ D

Weaving in yarn

In an intarsia design, you will get a lot of ends of yarn where areas of colour have begun or ended. It is important to weave in these ends either as you knit or stop knitting after every ten rows and sew them in. It gets rid of any ends that could tangle with working yarns, and if you leave it until the end it will seem a very long and arduous job. Sewing in the ends is neater but, if you have many yarn ends to finish, weaving them in as you go is faster.

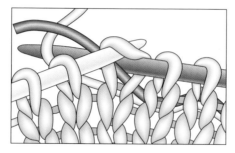

Weaving in ends on a knit row
1 Insert the tip of the right-hand needle into the next stitch, bring the cut end over the needle, wrap the yarn around the needle as though to knit.

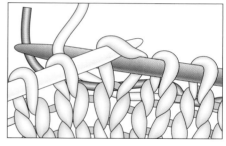

2 Pull the cut end off the needle and finish knitting the stitch. The cut end is caught into the knitted stitch.
Work the next stitch as normal then catch the cut end in as before. If you work alternately like this the cut end will lie above and below the row of stitches.

✓ Knit Perfect

Finish a piece of intarsia knitting by sewing in and cutting off any stray ends neatly. Where the two colours are twisted together, you will see a line of loops. Using a large-eyed tapestry needle, darn in the end along this line in one direction and then back again for a few stitches.

Block the piece (see page 68) and push any distorted stitches back into place with the end of a tapestry needle.

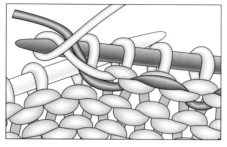

Weaving in ends on a purl row
1 Insert the tip of the right-hand needle into the next stitch, bring the cut end over the needle, wrap the yarn around the needle as though to purl.

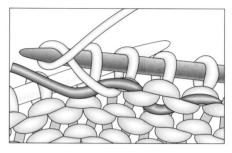

2 Pull the cut end off the needle and finish purling the stitch. The cut end is caught into the purled stitch.
Work the next stitch as normal then catch the cut end in as before. If you work alternately like this the cut end will lie above and below the row of stitches.

KNIT SOMETHING NOW! ▶

Practise using the intarsia method of colour knitting by making this colourful cushion.

Intarsia cushion knitted in a worsted (DK) wool yarn on size 6 (4mm/UK8) needles. See page 156 for pattern.

CIRCULAR KNITTING on double-pointed needles

Flat knitting is knitted in rows, working back and forth, moving the stitches from one needle to the other. Circular knitting is knitted in rounds, working round and round without turning the work.

✓ Knit Perfect

✓ The first round is awkward; the needles not being used dangle and get in the way. When you have worked a few rounds the fabric helps hold the needles in shape and knitting will become easier.

✓ For maximum control, always use the correct length of needle for what you are knitting; short needles for a small number of stitches such as for gloves, and longer needles for garments.

✓ To avoid a gap at the beginning of the first round, use the tail end of the yarn and the working yarn together to work the first few stitches. Or cast on one extra stitch at the end of the cast on, slip it on to the first needle and knit it together with the first stitch.

✓ Avoid gaps at the change over between needles by pulling the yarn up tightly, or work a couple of extra stitches from the next needle on each round. This will vary the position of the change over and avoid a ladder of looser stitches forming.

✓ Double-pointed needles are also used for knitting circles and squares (see page 54) or seamless garments. Use five needles to knit a square, with the stitches divided between the four sides.

Working on four needles

Use a set of four double-pointed needles, adding the stitches at one end and taking them off at the other. Cast the stitches on to one needle and then divide them evenly between three of the needles. For example, if you need to cast on 66 sts, there will be 22 sts on each needle; if you need to cast on 68 sts, there will be 23 sts on two of the needles and 22 on the third. The fourth needle is the working needle.

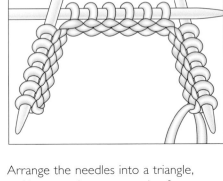

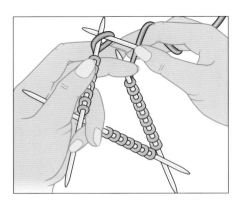

Arrange the needles into a triangle, making sure the cast on edge faces inwards and is not twisted. Place a marker between the last and first cast on stitches to identify the beginning of the round. Slip this marker on every round. Knit the first stitch, pulling up the yarn firmly so there is no gap between the third and first needle. Knit across the rest of the stitches on the first needle. As this needle is now empty, it becomes the working needle.

To continue...

Knit the stitches from the second needle, then use the new working needle to knit the stitches from the third needle. One round has been completed. Continue in this way, working in rounds and creating a tube of fabric. By knitting each round you will produce stockinette (stocking) stitch. To produce garter stitch, you will need to knit one round and then purl one round.

CIRCULAR KNITTING on circular needles

A circular needle can be used in place of double-pointed needles. The length of flexible nylon wire fixed between two short needles comes in several lengths. The longer ones are suitable for large garments and the shorter ones are ideal for small projects like hats.

Knit Perfect

✔ To uncoil circular needles, immerse them in hot water for a few minutes to straighten them out.

✔ Circular needles are also useful for knitting backwards and forwards for flat knitting. It is easier to work a large number of stitches (such as for a throw) on circular needles because all the weight of the fabric is held in front of you, on your lap, rather than at the end of long straight needles.

Cast on the required number of stitches on to one of the needle ends. Spread them evenly around the needle, making sure the cast on edge faces inwards and is not twisted. The stitches should lie closely together and not be pulled too far apart. If the stitches are stretched when the needles are joined, you will need to use a shorter needle.

To identify the beginning of the round, place a marker in a contrast colour yarn between the last and first cast on stitch and slip this on every row.
  Bring the two needles together and knit the first stitch, pulling up the yarn to prevent a gap. Continue knitting each cast on stitch to reach the marker. One round has been completed.

KNIT SOMETHING NOW!

The mittens are worked in one colour on four needles with the faces worked flat on two needles and sewn on after. Work pairs of tigers, bears, dogs or cats.

Fun children's mittens are knitted in a worsted (DK) wool yarn on size 3 (3.25mm/UK10) double-pointed needles for the rib and size 6 (4mm/UK8) double-pointed needles. See page 136 for pattern.

Exploring Choices

These advanced techniques will add excitement and individuality to your knitting. Three techniques – medallion knitting, entrelac and mitred squares – show you how to work creatively with shapes. Embellish your knitting using beads, looped knitting, smocking or embroidery stitches. Alter the knitted fabric by fulling. Sections guide you through reading a knitting pattern, explaining abbreviations and commonly used phrases. A sweater pattern is explained stage by stage, from the first stitches cast on, tips on shaping sleeves and neck, and how to alter a pattern to fit you. A section on making up includes various seams to professionally finish your garment. Finishing details include tassels and cords, flowers and leaves, how to make buttons and add an edging.

▼ KNIT SOMETHING NOW!

A textured throw worked in traditional Garden Plot squares sewn together to form larger squares.

The throw is knitted in a worsted (DK) weight cotton yarn on size 6 (4mm/UK8) needles. See page 140 for pattern.

MEDALLION KNITTING

Medallions are individually knitted patches, sewn together to form larger items like throws, cushions and bedspreads or garments. It is a form of patchwork knitting. Large single medallions can be used as the two sides of a bag, a small rug or the top of a beret. Most medallions, whether circles, ovals or squares, are knitted with five double-pointed needles from the centre out, with rows of increases arranged to form the shape. Circles have rows of at least eight increases evenly spaced, whilst a square will have eight increases worked in pairs at four corners. Increases are usually worked on every alternate row. Squares can also be worked on two needles by increasing from one corner and then decreasing to the opposite corner.

Basic circle (see sample opposite)

Cast on 8 sts and arrange on 4 needles.
Round 1 and every following alternate round Knit.
Round 2 (increase round) Knit into front and back of every st. 16 sts.
Round 4 (K1, knit into front and back of next st) 8 times. 24 sts.
Round 6 (K2, knit into front and back of next st) 8 times. 32 sts.
Continue in this way, working one more stitch between increases on every increase round. Keep laying the circle down as you work to make sure it is flat; too many increases over too few rounds will make the fabric wavy. To stop this work another knit round between increase rounds. When circle is the required size, cast off loosely.

✓ Knit Perfect

✓ Block the medallions to shape (see page 68).

✓ Use a multicoloured yarn to work medallions. In circular knitting, purl every alternate round for garter stitch. Mix garter stitch ridges with stockinette (stocking) stitch ridges. Use alternating ridges of stockinette (stocking) stitch and reverse stockinette (stocking) stitch or garter stitch for the square knitted on two needles.

✓ Work the increases in another way; as a yarn over or use an invisible increase like M1.

✓ Keep laying the medallion flat as you work to make sure it isn't becoming wavy. Add more straight rounds between increase rounds if it is.

Basic square

Cast on 8 sts and arrange on 4 needles.
Round 1 and every foll alt round Knit.
Round 2 (increase round) Knit into front and back of every st. 16 sts.
Round 4 (Knit into front and back of next st, k2, knit into back and front of next st) 4 times. 24 sts.
Round 6 (Knit into front and back of next st, k4, knit into back and front of next st) 4 times. 32 sts.
Continue in this way, working two more stitches between increases on every increase round. Check frequently to make sure the square is lying flat and if not work another knit round between increase rounds. When the square is the required size, cast off loosely. Knit two large squares for a bag or cushion. Work several small squares and join them together for a throw or bedspread.

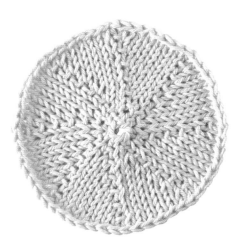

More circles...
A circle knitted like this can be used in different ways. A small circle makes the top of a beret. Continue working in rounds and make a small circular rug or join two circles together for a cushion or an unusual bag.

Because the eight increases are worked in the same place on each round, the shape will be octagonal rather than a true circle. The bigger you knit the circle, the more pronounced this shape will be. At this point, work 16 increases in the increase row by dividing the stitches between increases in two.

For example, after working the round (k14, knit into front and back of next st) 8 times, there will be 16 stitches between increases. The next round will be (k7, knit into front and back of next st) 16 times. Work three knit rounds between increase rows.

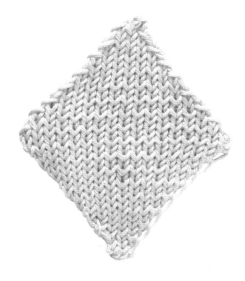

Square on two needles

An increase is worked before the first stitch on every row (see page 38).
Cast on 3 stitches.
Row 1 Purl.
Row 2 (RS) Yo, k3.
Row 3 Yo, p4.
Row 4 Yo, k5.
Row 5 Yo, p6.
Continue in this way until the side of the square is the required length, ending with a WS row. A decrease is now worked at the start of every row (see page 30–1)
Next row Ssk, k to end.
Next row P2tog, p to end.
Continue to decrease until 3 sts remain, sk2po. Fasten off.
Depending on the gauge (tension), the square may be more of a diamond. Block it to shape or work in a pattern that has more rows to the 4in (10cm). A traditional use of this square is called Garden Plot or Grandmother's Garden where several different patterns are worked. When the squares are sewn together, the diagonal patterns across the square form diamonds (see page 140).

BEADED KNITTING

In beaded knitting, beads (or sequins) are used on stockinette (stocking) stitch to form a pattern, or they are incorporated into a lace, cable or texture pattern. (It should not be confused with bead knitting, a technique that involves working different colour beads together to form a pattern, and where no knitted fabric is visible.)

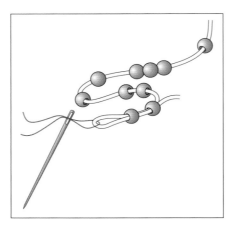

Thread the beads on to the ball of yarn before starting the knitting, the pattern instructions will tell you how many. To do this, choose a needle that will pass easily through the hole in the bead, and thread it with the two ends of a loop of sewing cotton. Thread the end of the yarn through the cotton loop. Now thread the beads on to the needle, pulling them down the sewing cotton and on to the yarn. Unwind sufficient yarn from the ball to accommodate the number of beads to be used and then rewind the ball to start knitting the item.

Knit Perfect

✔ Beads should have a large enough hole to slide on to the yarn without being forced. If the fit is too tight, the yarn will wear and fray.

✔ Match the beads to the yarn; use small, light beads with a delicate yarn and larger beads with a harder wearing, thicker yarn.

✔ The fabric should be knitted tightly enough so that the beads won't slip between the stitches to the wrong side. Always knit the stitches either side of the bead firmly.

The slip stitch method

Add the beads on a right side row so they hang horizontally. This is usually referred to in pattern instructions as place bead (PB).

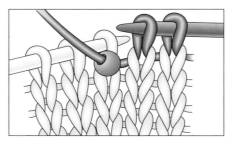

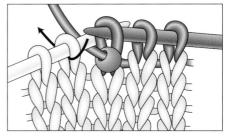

1 On a right side row, work to the position of the bead, knitting the last stitch worked firmly. Bring the yarn to the front of the work and push a bead down the yarn so that it rests next to the last stitch worked.

2 Slip the next stitch purlwise. Take the yarn back to the wrong side of the work and knit the next stitch firmly.

KNIT SOMETHING NOW! ▶

A stunning evening bag knitted in gold yarn is decorated with bronze beads. The simple lace pattern is enhanced with the beads used in a diamond pattern.

Beaded bag knitted in a sport (4ply) lurex yarn on size 3 (3.25mm/UK10) needles. See page 141 for pattern.

LOOPED KNITTING

A border of looped knitting makes a mock fur fabric for the collar and cuffs on a garment. As an all-over fabric, it can be used to make soft toys or, with the loops cut, a pile rug. The base fabric is garter stitch; a row of twisted knit stitches knitted through the back of the loop (k1 tbl) is followed by a row of loop stitches.

The pattern is a two row repeat with the loops made on the wrong side row and all the stitches are knitted through the back of the stitch on the right side row. Knitting the first and last stitches of the loop row through the back of the stitch makes the edges more stable for making up.

Row 1 Work a row of (k1tbl) twisted stitches.
Row 2 K1 tbl, then make loop as follows:

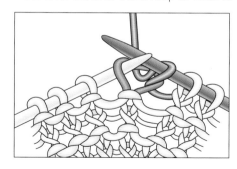

1 Knit into the back of the next stitch, do not slip stitch off the left-hand needle.

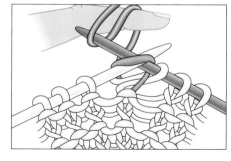

2 Insert the tip of the right-hand needle into the front of the same stitch and knit the stitch by passing the yarn anti-clockwise around the index finger of the left hand and then round the needle. Slip the stitch off the left-hand needle.

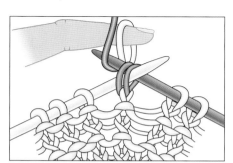

3 Insert the tip of the left-hand needle through the front of the two stitches just worked and knit them together. Pull the loop on the index finger gently to tighten the stitch. Remove finger. Repeat steps 1-3 for every stitch across the row to the last stitch, k1 tbl. These two rows form the pattern.

For flatter loops...
The fabric produced has loops on every alternate row and the loops will stand up. By adding more twisted knit rows between the loop rows the loops will lie flatter.

the result:

LOOPS AND CUT PILE
A sample of looped knitting showing half the loops intact and the other half cut to create a pile. The twisted stitches which prevent the loops or pile being pulled out show on the back of the fabric.

▶ KNIT SOMETHING NOW!

A really woolly sheep uses the loop stitch to great effect!

Sheep toy knitted in a worsted (DK) weight wool yarn on size 3 (3.25mm/UK10) needles. See page 142 for pattern.

ENTRELAC

Another way to work patchwork knitting is entrelac. In entrelac (a French word, which is pronounced on-tra-lak) the squares are knitted diagonally in rows; one row of squares being completed and the next row worked in the opposite direction on top. The knitted piece is started at the bottom from a cast-on edge and finished at the top. The squares can be worked in stockinette (stocking) stitch, as well as in lace, cable or textured stitches. If two colours are used, one for each alternate row, a woven effect is achieved, as shown here. In entrelac the stitches of all the squares in one row will be on the needles.

Each square has twice as many rows as stitches. The written instructions for entrelac can appear to be confusing so to learn how easy this technique is, work the following sample. The squares are eight stitches wide and the piece is three squares wide.

To begin, a foundation row of base triangles is worked. These are built up by short rows from the cast on stitches (see page 46). There is no need to work the wrapped stitch.

Base row of triangles

Cast on 24 sts loosely using the knitting on method (see page 26).

First base triangle
Rows 1 and 2 K2 and turn, p1, sl 1 purlwise (pwise) and turn.
Rows 3 and 4 K3 and turn, p2, sl 1 pwise and turn.
Rows 5 and 6 K4 and turn, p3, sl 1 pwise and turn.
Rows 7 and 8 K5 and turn, p4, sl 1 pwise and turn.
Rows 9 and 10 K6 and turn, p5, sl 1 pwise and turn.
Rows 11 and 12 K7 and turn, p6, sl 1 pwise and turn.
Row 13 K8 and do not turn.
The first triangle is completed.

right side

To continue...
Leave these eight stitches on the right-hand needle and work the second triangle over the next eight stitches. The third triangle is then worked over the following eight stitches. There will be 24 stitches on the right-hand needle. Turn at the end of this row of triangles to begin the return row of squares.

Purl row of squares

To make the sides of the piece straight, you need a side edge triangle.

** Left side edge triangle
Rows 1 and 2 P2 and turn, k2 and turn.
Rows 3 and 4 P into front and back of first st (to shape side edge), p2tog (last st of triangle and next st on right-hand needle to join the pieces together) and turn, k3 and turn.

wrong side

Rows 5 and 6 P into front and back of first st (p1 fb), p1, p2tog and turn, k4 and turn.
Rows 7 and 8 P1 fb, p2, p2tog and turn, k5 and turn.
Rows 9 and 10 P1 fb, p3, p2tog and turn, k6 and turn.
Rows 11 and 12 P1 fb, p4, p2tog and turn, k7 and turn.
Row 13 P1 fb, p5, p2tog and do not turn. All 8 sts of the base triangle have been used. Leave the 8 sts of the side triangle on the right-hand needle.

Square
With the right-hand needle and wrong side of the work facing, pick up and purl 8 sts evenly along the next edge of the base triangle and turn.
Rows 1 and 2 K7, sl 1 pwise and turn, p7 (including sl st of previous row), p2tog (last st of square and next st on right-hand needle to join pieces together) and turn.
Repeat these 2 rows 6 times more.
Rows 15 and 16 K7, sl 1 pwise and turn, p7, p2tog and do not turn. All 8 sts of the base triangle have been used. Leave the 8 sts of this square on the right-hand needle. Work the second square over the next 8 sts.
To make this side edge straight, you need to work a right side edge triangle.

Right side edge triangle

With the right-hand needle and wrong side of the work facing, pick up and purl 8 sts evenly along the next edge of the base triangle and turn.

Rows 1 and 2 K7, sl 1 pwise and turn, p6 (including sl st of previous row), p2tog (to shape side edge) and turn.
Rows 3 and 4 K6, sl 1 pwise and turn, p5, p2tog and turn.
Rows 5 and 6 K5, sl 1 pwise and turn, p4, p2tog and turn.
Rows 7 and 8 K4, sl 1 pwise and turn, p3, p2tog and turn.
Rows 9 and 10 K3, sl 1 pwise and turn, p2, p2tog and turn.
Rows 11 and 12 K2, sl 1 pwise and turn, p1, p2tog.
Rows 13 and 14 K1, sl 1 pwise and turn, p2tog and turn. All sts are on the left-hand needle ready for the next row of squares. **

Knit row of squares

On this row, there are no side triangles to work.

right side

First square

Slip the first st on to the right-hand needle then with the right side of the work facing, pick up and knit 7 sts evenly along the edge of the right side triangle and turn. 8 sts.

Rows 1 and 2 P7, sl 1 purlwise and turn, k7 (including sl st of previous row), ssk (last st of square and next st on left-hand needle to join pieces together) and turn.
Rep these 2 rows 6 times more.
Rows 15 and 16 P7, sl 1 purlwise and turn, k7, ssk and do not turn.
All sts of the square in the row below have been used.

Second and third squares

With right-hand needle and right side of work facing, pick up and knit 8 sts along edge of next square in row below and turn.
Work as given for first square. Then work a third square the same. Turn.
Work a purl row of squares from ** to ** again, working into the squares of the previous row instead of the base triangles. To finish the piece, a row of triangles has to be worked to give a straight top edge.

Top row of triangles

With right side of work facing, slip the first st on to the right-hand needle then pick up and knit 7 sts along edge of first square and turn. 8 sts.

Rows 1 and 2 P8 and turn, k7, ssk (last st of square and next st on right-hand needle to join the pieces) and turn.
Rows 3 and 4 P6, p2tog (to shape top edge) and turn, k6, ssk and turn.
Rows 5 and 6 P5, p2tog and turn, k5, ssk and turn.
Rows 7 and 8 P4, p2tog and turn, k4, ssk and turn.
Rows 9 and 10 P3, p2tog and turn, k3, ssk and turn.
Rows 11 and 12 P2, p2tog and turn, k2, ssk and turn.
Rows 13 and 14 P1, p2tog and turn, k1, ssk and turn.
Rows 15 and 16 P2tog and turn, ssk and do not turn. Leave this st on right-hand needle.
Repeat this top triangle twice more across the top of the piece. Cut yarn and thread through last stitch to fasten off.

Knit Perfect

✓ The number of stitches to cast on equals the number of stitches in each square multiplied by the number of squares. Cast on more or less stitches to make the squares bigger or smaller.

✓ Always start with the base row of triangles, then repeat the purl row of squares and the knit row of squares to form the main fabric, ending with a purl row to work the top triangles across.

✓ The woven effect of entrelac can be emphasised by working in two colours; work the knit rows of squares in one colour and the purl rows of squares in another. The squares can also be worked in any stitch; try knitting them in cable patterns, textured stitch patterns like moss or garter stitch, or a lace pattern.

✓ Slipping the edge stitches purlwise makes it easier to pick up stitches; pick them up through both loops of the edge stitch. Edge stitches are explained more fully in mitred squares, see page 60.

MITRED SQUARES

Another patchwork knitting technique is mitred squares (also known as domino knitting). Each square is worked individually and the stitches for the next square are picked up from any side of the first square. It requires little or no sewing up. The shape of the squares is achieved by decreasing into the centre, hence the name of mitred squares. In mitred squares only the stitches of one square will be on the needles at any time.

This is a technique best learnt by working it and this example is a group of four basic garter stitch squares.

Basic mitred square

Cast on 19 sts loosely using the knitting on method (see page 26).

Row 1 and every foll WS row K to last st, sl 1 purlwise with yarn in front of the work (wyif).

Row 2 (RS) K8, sl 1-k2tog-psso, k7, sl 1 pwise wyif. 17 sts.

Row 4 K7, sl 1-k2tog-psso, k6, sl 1 pwise wyif. 15 sts.

Row 6 K6, sl 1-k2tog-psso, k5, sl 1 pwise wyif. 13 sts.

Row 8 K5, sl 1-k2tog-psso, k4, sl 1 pwise wyif. 11 sts.

Row 10 K4, sl 1-k2tog-psso, k3, sl 1 pwise wyif. 9 sts.

Row 12 K3, sl 1-k2tog-psso, k2, sl 1 pwise wyif. 7 sts.

Row 14 K2, sl 1-k2tog-psso, k1, sl 1 pwise wyif. 5 sts.

Row 16 K1, sl 1-k2tog-psso, sl 1 pwise wyif. 3 sts.

Row 18 Sl 1-k2tog-psso. Cut yarn and thread through last st to fasten off.

One square is completed. By slipping the last stitch of every row, a line of edge stitches is created along two sides of the square. These make it much easier to pick up stitches for the next square.

Second square

To work the next square, with the right-hand needle and right side of work facing, pick up and knit 9 sts along the side of the first square through both loops of the edge stitches, pick up 1 st at the corner then cast on 9 sts (using knitting on method). 19 sts. Complete as given for basic mitred square.

Third square

Cast on 9 sts, then pick up and knit 10 sts (1 corner st and 9 other sts) along edge of first square through both loops of the edge stitches. Complete as given for basic mitred square.

Fourth square

With the right-hand needle, pick up and knit 9 sts along side of square three, pick up and knit 1 st at corner then pick up and knit 9 sts along side of second square. 19 sts. Complete as given for basic mitred square.

the result:

MITRED SQUARE

This sample knitted in garter stitch shows all the techniques needed to work mitred squares and to join them together. The basic square can be any number of stitches, as long as it is an odd number. Work the squares in stockinette (stocking) stitch by working the WS rows as purl rows. Moss stitch works well over the odd number of stitches; just repeat k1, p1 across all rows. Whichever stitch you use, always remember to keep working the edge stitches in the same way; slip the last stitch purlwise with the yarn at the front of the work and knit the slipped stitch on the return row.

fourth square

second square

third square

first square

Designing with mitred squares

The basic square forms a mitred corner, work two together and a rectangle is formed. Work three together and an L shape is made; work four together and a complete mitred square is made. For a rectangle, cast on twice the number of stitches for the basic square (2 x 19 sts = 38 sts), for an L shape cast on three times the stitches and for a complete square cast on four times the stitches. Place a slip marker every 19 stitches to show you where one square ends and the next begins. Work each 19 stitches as a basic square; do not work a slip stitch on the inside edges of the individual squares; work it to match the main fabric.

To complete the square, either sew it closed or pick up stitches along each edge towards the middle and use the three needle seam bind (cast) off (see page 27).

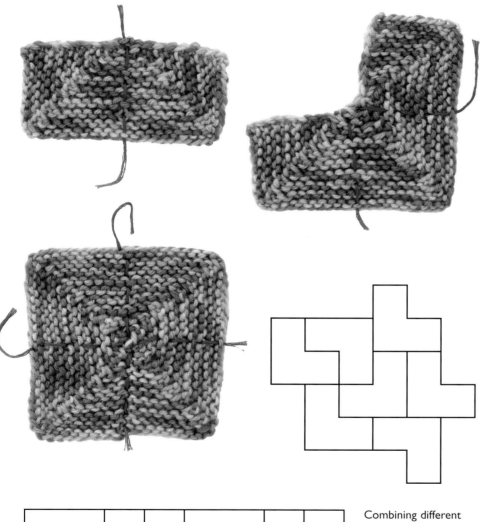

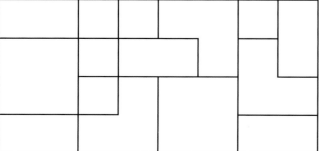

Combining different shapes together in various ways (above and left, for example) can make interesting patchwork patterns. You can plan it on paper first or just start knitting.

Knit Perfect

✔ The edge stitches are important; whatever fabric you are working, slip the last stitch purlwise with the yarn at the front of the work and knit the slipped stitch on the return row. If the penultimate stitch is a knit, you will have to bring the yarn forward between the needles. If it is a purl stitch, the yarn will be in the correct position. Always knit the slipped stitch on the next row, the yarn will be in the knit position to remind you.

✔ Mitred squares look best when worked in many colours. Either choose a multi-coloured yarn or make your own by tying yard (metre) lengths of different coloured yarns together. It is a great way to use up leftover yarn.

✔ With a multi-coloured yarn it is unnecessary to cut the yarn between each square. Use the last stitch of one square as the first stitch of the next. Keeping one yarn going makes the placement of the squares more random and your knitted piece will grow organically rather than in a planned manner.

✔ Weave any ends in as you go (see page 51).

✔ Try a different decrease, instead of sl 1-k2tog-psso work sk2po or, for an unbroken chain stitch running up the centre, sl2tog-k1-psso.

FULLING

Fulling is the process of washing woollen fabric to produce a felt-like fabric. It is often mistakenly called felting, which is worked on carded unspun wool, whilst fulling is worked on a finished fabric. Fulled fabric is soft, spongy and has a brushed appearance; any garment that is fulled will be more dense and warmer than one that is not.

Fulling can only be worked on yarns that are 100 per cent wool; it doesn't work on synthetics, cotton or wools that have been treated to be machine washable. The treatment withstands exactly the changes that are needed to full a garment. During fulling, the wool expands, fibres mesh together and individual stitches close up so it is hard to see fulled stitches. The finished fabric will also shrink by up to 10 per cent in length and width.

Hand or machine fulling?
The two methods for fulling a fabric are by hand or washing machine. By hand offers the most control, you can stop and check the fabric at every stage. By machine is less hard work, and you can full a number of items together, but it is not as easy to control. There is no single recipe for fulling, each yarn reacts differently and may be easier or harder to full. To experiment, knit several identical samples in the yarn you are using making a note of needle size and gauge (tension). Keep one sample aside to compare with the fulled samples.

Hand fulling

Fulling depends on extremes of temperature, from hot to cold, agitation by kneading and the use of laundry soap or soap flakes. Do not use detergent or washing powder. Dissolve the soap flakes in hot water and immerse one of the samples.

Start kneading the fabric without pulling, stretching or rubbing the knitting together. Remove the sample from the water frequently to check the fulling process. Rinse the soap out in cold water and pull the sample gently. If the stitches still move apart easily, continue the fulling. Keep up the temperature of the hot water. Stop when the fabric is dense and has a fuzzy appearance. Rinse the soap out and squeeze to remove excess water. Roll the sample up in a towel to soak up any remaining moisture and then lay it out flat, away from direct heat, to dry. Make a note of how long it took.

Try another sample but rinse it more often in cold water or knead it in hotter water. These things will make a difference to how quickly the sample fulls. Overwork one of the samples until it is matted and distorted to see the difference between correct fulling and matting. Keep notes of everything you do as you do it.

✔ Knit Perfect

✔ Always test samples of coloured knitting such as fair isle and intarsia to make sure all the yarns are colourfast.

✔ Fulling only works on 100 per cent wool; work a sample before you knit your project to make sure your yarn will full.

✔ Fulled fabric can be cut and sewn like a woven fabric. The stitches will not fray or unravel. Garments that are too large can be taken in with darts or tucks or shortened by cutting off the bottom edge and finishing it with blanket stitch.

✔ Start by hand fulling, it is easier to control. It will be more work but you will not run the risk of ruining your project in the washing machine. Wear gloves to protect your hands from the hot water and soap.

✔ Brush the surface of the knitting when dry with a stiff brush; use a gently pulling or lifting action rather than a vigorous back and forwards motion.

Machine fulling

Wash the samples with soap in a full load. They need friction to be fulled correctly so add towels to fill the machine. Run them through on the shortest hot wash/cold rinse cycle but do not spin dry. Remove from the machine whenever possible during the cycle to check their progress. If they haven't fulled correctly, take one sample out and put the others through the same cycle again. Repeat until you have achieved the effect you want. By removing samples at each stage, you have a record of when the perfect fulling moment happens.

Fulling garments

Garments will not behave in exactly the same way as the samples. There is more fabric and there are seams, both factors will alter the fulling process. Use your sample results as a guide only and check at every stage of the process because fulling is irreversible.

When the garment has fulled correctly, lay it out flat and pull it into shape, straightening the seams. Fulled garments are usually more figure hugging so try it on when it is almost dry. Gently pull the armhole seams so the sleeves sit correctly and arrange the neckband. Pull evenly around the edge of the body and sleeves for the correct length. Remove carefully and lay out flat to dry.

the result:

TEST SAMPLES

These three samples were all knitted in stockinette (stocking) stitch over the same number of stitches and rows. The first one (1) has not been fulled, the second (2) has been fulled the correct amount and the third (3) has been distorted and matted rather than fulled.

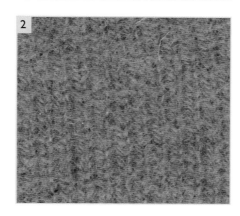

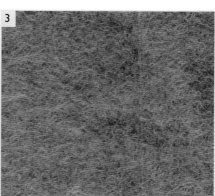

KNIT SOMETHING NOW! ▼

The lavender sachets and covered clothes hanger are ideal for your first fulling projects.

The **scented sachets** and **hanger cover** are knitted in a 2ply jumper weight 100 per cent shetland wool yarn on size 3 (3.25mm/UK10) needles. See page 144 for pattern.

SMOCKING

Smocking can be worked very successfully on ribbed fabric. Like smocking on a woven fabric, it pulls in the knitted fabric in a decorative manner. The smocking stitches can be worked in the same yarn as the main fabric, in a contrasting colour or in embroidery threads which have a larger range of colours for coloured smocking patterns. Make sure the smocking thread is colourfast and washes to the same instructions as the knitted yarn.

The rib should not be too wide or the resulting bunching of fabric will be too bulky, especially in thick yarns. A (p3, k1) rib or (p4, k1) rib is ideal.

Smocking stitch on (p3, k1) rib

Work from left to right and in a zigzag manner. The smocking stitches should be equally spaced on every 4th row. (Note: the artwork shows the stitches not tightened so the path of the needle can clearly be seen.)

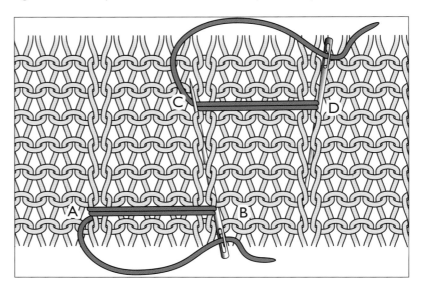

1 Bring the needle with the smocking thread up at A, having secured it on the wrong side by running it through the edge of the knit rib with a few backstitches. Follow the row across and take it under the stitch at B from right to left. Take the needle across the front of the work between the knit stitches and take it under the knit stitch at A from left to right. Pull the stitch tight so the ribs lie next to each other without distorting them and work two more stitches the same, finishing with the needle down at B.

2 Count 4 rows up from B and bring the needle up at C. Follow the row across and take it under the knit stitch at D from right to left. Work two more stitches the same, pulling them tight as before and finishing with the needle down at D. Take the needle back down to the previous smocking row, 4 rows below. Repeat these two smocking rows across the rib fabric and up to the top of the piece.

Ribbed fabrics for smocking

(p3, k1) rib
Cast on a multiple of 4 sts plus 3 sts.
Row 1 P3, * k1, p3; rep from * to end.
Row 2 K3, * p1, k3; rep from * to end.
These 2 rows form the rib pattern and are repeated.

(p4, k1) rib
Cast on a multiple of 5 sts plus 4 sts.
Row 1 P4, * k1, p4; rep from * to end.
Row 2 K4, * p1, k4; rep from * to end.
These 2 rows form the rib pattern and are repeated.

the result:

SMOCKED RIB

The embroidery thread can be a contrast colour as shown here, or the same colour as the knitting. Careful counting of the stitches and rows is essential for the smocking to look even.

✓ Knit Perfect

When the knitted fabric is smocked it will loose some of its elasticity, so is not suitable for close-fitting cuffs and lower edge ribs on garments.

There are also honeycomb stitches that are smocked while being knitted (see Stitch library page 104–5).

READING KNITTING PATTERNS

A knitting pattern tells you how to knit and make up a knitted project. There are two styles of instructions; a pattern that tells you what to do row by row, and a pattern that has shorter written instructions with a chart. If each row of a garment was written down row by row the knitting pattern would probably fill a small book, so the instructions use shorthand phrases and abbreviations. The abbreviations are listed on the pattern with an explanation of what they mean. Many are commonly used, such as k and p (see page 35). Others refer to special stitches, like C4F, and these are explained in the technique or patterns.

Common shorthand phrases

cont as set/cont as established
instead of repeating the same instructions over and over, you must continue to work as previously told. For example: **Row 1** K. **Row 2** P. Cont in st st as set.

keeping patt correct
continue with a stitch pattern, keeping it correctly worked over the correct amount of stitches, whilst doing something that may interfere with the stitch pattern (see page 76).

at the same time
two things must be done at the same time. For example, decreasing at an armhole edge and decreasing at a neck edge.

work straight/work even
continue without increasing or decreasing.

work as given for
to avoid repeating instructions. For example, the front is often worked as given for the back up to a certain point.

reversing all shaping
shaping is given for one piece and the other piece must be shaped to be a mirror image of it. For example, the left and right side of the neck, or the left and right front of a cardigan.

Sizes

Knitting patterns are usually written in more than one size, with the smallest size first (outside the brackets) and the remaining sizes inside square brackets, separated by colons. The largest size is at the end. For example, if the sizes are S [M:L:XL], the chest measurements could be 30 [32:34:36] in (76 [82:87:92] cm). Your size will always appear in the same place in the bracket; instructions for the first size will always be first, for the second size they will be second, etc. If a pattern is written in both imperial and metric measurements, stick to one or the other; some imperial to metric measurements are not exact conversions.

Reading size instructions

Square brackets are used within the instructions to indicate the number of stitches and rows to be worked, or how many times a pattern is repeated, for each size. For example, cast on 90 [92:94:96] sts, or work patt 1 [2:3:4] times. If a zero appears for your size do not work the instruction it is referring to. For example, dec 3 [0:1:2] sts. If only one figure appears then it refers to all sizes. Read through the pattern and underline or highlight your size in the square brackets.

Size diagrams

Knitting patterns should have a drawing of the knitted pieces with their finished measurements. These help to decide which size is best for you or if you need to alter things like body or sleeve length. They also show the shape of the pieces and make the written instructions clearer. If your pattern does not have size diagrams, it is a good idea to draw your own, using the finished measurements given and adding any others by using the gauge (tension) information.

Reading a stitch chart

A knitting pattern may contain a stitch chart which is similar to a colour pattern. A stitch chart is an illustration of a cable, a lace pattern or a texture pattern with each stitch being represented by a symbol, which usually reflects the texture of the stitch. A knit stitch often appears as a blank square, whilst a purl stitch is a dot or horizontal dash. The key tells you what each symbol means. Imagine looking at the right side of a knitted piece; each symbol represents the stitch as it appears on the right side of the work. A whole garment may be charted like this or just one repeat of the stitch pattern. Each square is one stitch on your needle. Decreases are shown after they have been worked and so appear as one square. Yarn overs are shown as a new stitch and so occupy one square. Beginning at the bottom right-hand corner, right side rows are read from right to left and wrong side rows from left to right. Colour charts are covered on page 39.

Stitch chart with symbols

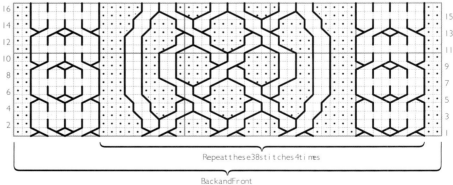

Repeat these 38 stitches 4 times

Back and Front

C4F		Cr3L
C4B		Cr3R
Cr4L	·	p on RS rows, k on WS rows
Cr4R	☐	k on RS rows, p on WS rows

Cable abbreviations…
See pages 42–43 for Cables and a guide to the abbreviations.

KNITTING A GARMENT

Reading through a knitting pattern for the first time can seem a bit daunting. There's a lot of information given but it also assumes you know a lot, too. Use this pattern as a guide to knitting a garment, from choosing the yarn to sewing it up. This is a pattern for a close-fitting stockinette (stocking) stitch sweater with waist shaping, set in sleeves and a turtleneck. The instructions as they would appear in a knitting pattern are set in boxes, the text below explains what is meant.

Order of knitting...
The written instructions take you through the construction of a garment piece by piece. Garments are usually knitted in the same order, back, front and sleeves, and often one piece will contain cross-references to another which has already been knitted, if they are both worked the same. For example, for a front it might say work in rib as given for back. When the main pieces have been worked, the finishing is done. The pieces are blocked and the garment is made up with any other details like neckband, pockets or button bands added.

Sizes

To fit bust	30/32 [34/36:38/40]in (76/82 [87/92:97/102] cm)
Actual size	36 [40:44]in (92 [102:112]cm)
Length	22½ [23:23½]in (57 [58.5:60]cm)
Sleeve length	20½ [21:21½]in (52 [53.5:54.5]cm)

First decide which size you are going to make. The important measurement is the actual size, measured as the finished width under the arm. Different designers add different amounts of ease to the bust/chest measurement, depending on the style of the garment. So look at the actual size rather than the size ranges which are often there only as a guide. Refer to the size diagrams that are a sketch of the finished pieces needed to make up the garment. Check that the sleeve and body lengths are right for you. If they are too long or too short, make alterations to the body or sleeve shaping (see page 74). Go through the pattern and underline or highlight all the instructions in the brackets for your size.

Materials

Debbie Bliss Merino DK (100% Merino Wool – 109yds/100m per 1¾oz /50g ball)
10 [11:12] × 1¾oz/50g balls in colour 213 Light Blue

Always try to use the yarn recommended by the designer, especially novelty yarns which sometimes have a gauge (tension) all of their own. However, if the spinner discontinues a yarn, or it is a standard thickness, then another yarn can be substituted (see page 130).

The type of yarn used to knit the projects in this book are given in the pattern, together with the yardages and tension. The actual yarn used is given on page 312 with suppliers listed on page 315.

Needles

1 pair size 3 (3.25mm/UK10) needles.
1 pair size 6 (4mm/UK8) needles.

These are the recommended sizes of needles to use. They will give you the gauge (tension) that the garment has been calculated from.

Gauge (tension)

22 sts and 28 rows to 4in (10cm) measured over stockinette (stocking) stitch on size 6 (4mm/UK8) needles.

Work a gauge (tension) square before you begin knitting (see page 33).

Back

Using size 3 (3.25mm/UK10) needles, cast on 101 [113:123] sts.
Row 1 (RS) K1, * p1, k1; rep from * to end.
Row 2 P1, * k1, p1; rep from * to end.
Rep these 2 rows until rib measures 2in (5cm) from beg, ending with a WS row.
Change to size 6 (4mm/UK8) needles and work 10 rows in st st.

Patterns vary, some have an increase row worked evenly over the last rib row. When the rib is complete, pick up one of the larger needles and knit the stitches off the smaller needle. Remember to discard both the smaller needles when you pick up the other larger needle. If the pattern does not tell you, always start stockinette (stocking) stitch (1 row k, 1 row p) with a knit (right side) row.

Side shaping

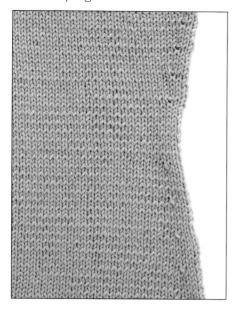

Working in st st, dec 1 st at each end of next and every foll 8th row to 91 [103:113] sts.

From the size diagrams, you can see that the side edges are shaped into the waist. One stitch is decreased at each side on the next row, then work seven rows without shaping and decrease on the next row, work another seven rows and decrease on the next row until you reach the stitch total for your size. You can decrease by working two stitches together at the edge or you could work the decreases as full fashioning. These decorative decreases will add an elegant finish to the garment (see page 30–1). A full fashioning decrease row would be k3, ssk, k to last 5 sts, k2tog, k3.

Work straight until back measures 10in (25cm) from beg, ending with a p row.
Inc 1 st at each end of next and every foll 6th row to 99 [111:121] sts.

Several rows are worked at the waist without shaping and then the back is increased out again for the bust measurement. One stitch is increased at each end of the next row, then work five rows without shaping and increase on the next row, work another five rows

straight and increase on the next row until you reach the stitch total for your size. You can full fashion the increases to match the decreases (see page 29). A full fashioning increase row would be k2, knit into front and back of next st, k to last 4 sts, knit into front and back of next st, k3.

Work straight until back measures 14in (35.5cm) from beg, ending with a p row.

Lay the work on a flat smooth surface, not on your lap or the carpet as they can cling to the knitting and you won't get a true measurement. Use a tape measure and place it vertically slightly in from the edge of the piece to get an accurate measurement. Measure from the cast on edge to the needles.

Shape armholes

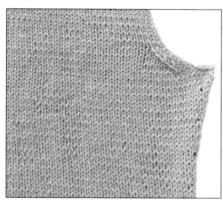

Bind (cast) off 5 [6:7] sts at beg of next 2 rows. Dec 1 st at each end of every row to 79 [85:91] sts.

Use the same method to decrease as you used for the shaping to the waist.

Work straight until armhole measures 7½ [8:8½]in (19 [20.5:21.5]cm), ending with a p row.

Shape shoulders

Bind (cast) off 6 [7:8] sts at beg of next 4 rows then 6 sts at beg of next 2 rows. Bind (cast) off rem 43 [45:47] sts.

Front

Work as given for back until front is 16 rows less than back to shoulder shaping, ending with a p row.

Instead of repeating all the same instructions, work exactly as you did for the back, using the same methods of decreasing and increasing. In many patterns this is given as a measurement. Make sure you work the same number of straight rows at the waist and below the underarm. On the back, place a marker 16 rows down from the first row of bind (cast) off stitches at the shoulders. Count the number of rows from the last decrease at the armhole to this marker, and work the same number of rows on the front. Sewing the garment together is made much easier if the side and armhole seams have the same number of rows.

Shape neck

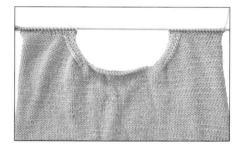

Next row K29 [31:33] sts, join in a 2nd ball of yarn and bind (cast) off centre 21 [23:25] sts, k to end. Working both sides at the same time, dec 1 st at neck edge on foll 11 rows. 18 [20:22] sts at each side. Work 4 rows straight, ending at armhole edge (work 1 row more on left side of neck).

Patterns vary on how they tell you to work the neck shaping. This pattern tells you to work both sides at the same time, by joining in a second ball of yarn. Working both sides at once ensures that they will be the same. In some other patterns, the left side is worked first and the right side is worked as a mirror image of it. Use the same method as before to decrease.

knitting a garment

Shape shoulders

Bind (cast) off 6[7:8] sts at beg of next and foll alt row. Work 1 row then cast off rem 6 sts.

Sleeves

Using size 3 (3.25mm/UK10) needles, cast on 45 [47:49] sts and work 2in (5cm) in rib as given for back.

You can work the sleeves one at a time. But you can also work both sleeves at the same time on the same needles, like the neck shaping. By doing this, you will know that you have worked all the shaping in exactly the same way. Cast on two sets of stitches, with a ball of yarn for each, and work across the first sleeve, pick up the new yarn and work the same row across the second sleeve.

Change to size 6 (4mm/UK8) needles and work in st st, inc 1 st at each end of 5th and every foll 11th [10th:9th] row to 67 [71:77] sts.

Work 4 rows straight in st st and then increase 1 st at each end of next row. Work 10 [9:8] rows straight and then increase on the next row. Use the same method for the increases as before.

Work straight until sleeve measures 20½ [21:21½] in (52 [53.5:54.5] cm), ending with a p row.

Shape cap

Bind (cast) off 5 [6:7] sts at beg of next 2 rows. Dec 1 st at each end of next 3 rows, then on foll 3 alt rows, and then on every foll 4th row to 41 [41:45] sts. Dec 1 st at each end of every foll alt row to 25 sts, and then on foll 2 rows, ending with a p row. Bind (cast) off 4 sts at beg of next 2 rows, then rem 13 sts.

The top of a set-in sleeve is shaped in a curve to fit into the armhole. Read the instructions carefully and use a pencil and paper to keep a tally of the straight rows and decreases. Use the same method to decrease as before.

Finishing

Sew in all ends of yarn, by weaving up the edges of the pieces. Block pieces to measurements.

Blocking is the process of pinning out the garment pieces to their finished measurements and then setting the fabric shape by steam or wet pressing. Fair isle and intarsia designs can look crumpled when they come off the needle and improve immensely with careful pressing. Lace is stretched out to reveal its full glory and heavy cabled fabrics lie flatter. Always refer to the washing and pressing instructions on the ball band to help you decide which method to use. Blocking is done on a soft surface that you can stick pins into and that won't spoil if it gets damp. Ironing boards are ideal for small pieces, but large garment pieces need more room to lie flat. You can make a blocking board from a folded blanket covered with a towel or sheet.

Using rust proof pins, pin the knitted pieces out, wrong side up, on the blocking board, using the measurements given on the size diagrams. Pin out the width and length first and then the other measurements. Place a pin every 1in (2.5cm) or so to hold the edges straight. Do not pin out the ribs. If you press these they will loose their elasticity.

Wet pressing Wet a clean cloth and wring out the excess water until it is just damp. Place it over the pinned out piece (avoiding the ribs) and leave to dry away from direct heat. When the cloth is completely dry, remove it. Make sure the knitted pieces are also dry before you take out the pins and remove them from the board.

Steam pressing Lay a clean cloth over the pinned out piece to protect it. Set the steam iron on an appropriate heat setting for the yarn. Hold the iron close to the surface of the knitting without touching it. Do not press the iron on to the knitted fabric or steam the ribs. Let the steam penetrate the fabric. Remove the cloth and allow the fabric to dry before unpinning. Some yarns will not stand the high temperature needed for steaming so always check the ball band first. Synthetic yarns should never be steamed.

Making up

Join right shoulder seam.

For a neat finish, use mattress stitch to join all the seams (see page 72).

Neckband

Using size 3 (3.25mm/UK10) needles, pick up and k22 sts down left side of neck, 21 [23:25] sts across front neck, 22 sts up right side of neck and 42 [44:46] sts across back neck. 107 [111:115] sts. Work 5in (12.5cm) rib as given for back. Bind (cast) off loosely in rib.

To pick up stitches neatly see page 70.

Join shoulder and neckband seam. Set in sleeves. Join side and sleeve seams.

To set the sleeve into the armhole, pin the centre of the sleeve cap to the shoulder seam and each end to the beginning of the armhole shaping. Sew both sets of bound (cast) off stitches together at the beginning of the sleeve and armhole shaping. Pin the remaining sleeve cap around the armhole, easing any fullness in evenly.

Size diagrams

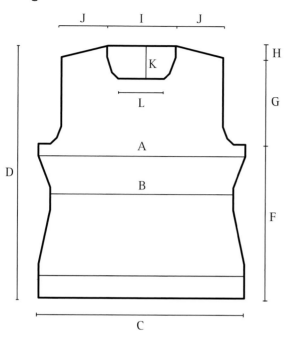

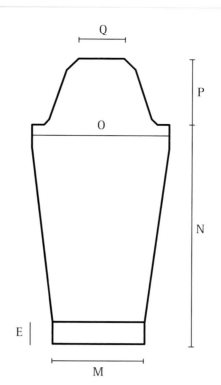

Size diagram measurements

A   18 [20:22]in (46 [51:56]cm)
B   16½ [18½:20½]in (42 [47:52]cm)
C   18½ [20½:22½]in (47 [52:57]cm)
D   22½ [23:23½]in 57 [58.5:60]cm)
E   2in (5cm)
F   14in (35.5cm)
G   7½ [8:8½]in (19 [20.5:21.5]cm)
H   1in (2.5cm)
I   8 [8¼:8½]in (20.5 [21:21.5] cm)
J   3¼ [3½:4]in (8.5 [9:10]cm)
K   3in (7.5cm)
L   4 [4¼:4½]in (10 [11:11.5]cm)
M   8 [8½:9]in (20.5 [21.5:23.5]cm)
N   20½ [21:21½]in (52 [53.5:54.5]cm)
O   12 [13:14]in (30.5 [33:35.5]cm)
P   5½ [6:6½]in (14 [15:16.5]cm)
Q   4in (10cm)

KNIT SOMETHING NOW! ▶

This basic sweater pattern can be used as the basis for various adaptations such as adding a central lace or cable panel.

Turtleneck fitted sweater knitted in worsted (DK) weight merino wool on size 6 (4mm/UK8) needles. See pages 66–9 for pattern.

OTHER GARMENT DETAILS

It is the finishing details which can make all the difference to the look of a garment – picking up stitches evenly, sewing up invisibly and making the correct size buttonholes all give the final professional touch.

✓ Knit Perfect

Knitting patterns will usually tell you how many stitches to pick up. You must pick up the stitches evenly; begin and end at the edges and space the remaining stitches equally along the edge.

Using a tape measure and with the work laid out flat, place a marker (length of yarn or a safety pin) in the centre of the edge, divide each half in half again and place a marker, and then halve each quarter and place a marker, dividing the edge into eight equal sections. Divide the number of stitches to be picked up by eight. Count the number of rows or stitches in each section and work the picked up stitches evenly between them.

For example, each section has ten rows and you have to pick up eight stitches. Pick up a stitch in each of the first four rows, miss a row then pick up a stitch in each of the next four rows, miss a row, then go on to the next section.

Work the stitches in the last section so that there is a stitch picked up in each of the last four rows, for example, one stitch in each of first two rows, miss a row, one stitch in each of next two rows, miss a row, one stitch in each of last four rows.

Picking up stitches

When you add a neckband, button band or any type of border to another knitted piece, you pick up the stitches for it evenly along the edge using one needle. With the right side of the work facing, the needle is held in the right hand and inserted through the edge stitches, the left hand holding the work. A new ball of yarn is joined and is wrapped around the needle and a loop is pulled through. One stitch has been knitted on to the needle. Use a size smaller needle than that used for the main piece.

On a horizontal bound (cast) off edge

Hold the work in your left hand. With a needle and the yarn in your right hand, insert the needle into the centre of the first stitch in the row below the bound (cast) off edge. Wrap the yarn knitwise around the needle and draw through a loop. Continue in this way, inserting the needle through the centre of the stitch.

On a vertical edge
(for example, the front of a cardigan)

Hold the work in your left hand. With a needle and the yarn in your right hand, insert the needle between the first and second stitches at the beginning of the first row, wrap the yarn around knitwise and pull through a stitch. Continue up the edge, inserting the needle between the stitches on each row, taking in one stitch. If you are using a thick yarn, where one stitch may measure ½in (1.5cm) or more, insert the needle through the centre of the edge stitch, taking in only half a stitch to reduce bulk.

On a shaped edge
(for example, neck shaping)

Use the above methods for picking up stitches along the straight edges of the neck. On the shaped part, insert the needle into the centre of the stitches one row below the decreasing. Do not pick up along the edge as this will result in holes. If you have to pick up extra stitches to cover a gap, for example, between the bind (cast) off stitches and the shaping, decrease these stitches on the next row.

Buttonholes

A knitting pattern will tell you to work the button band before the buttonhole band. This is because you can use the button band to work out how many buttons you need and how they will be spaced. Lie the piece flat and place a pin at the position of the top and bottom buttons. These should be ½in (1.5cm) from the ends. Using a tape measure, place pins to mark the positions of the remaining buttons. Make sure they are spaced evenly by counting the rows or stitches between the pins. To decide on the size of buttonhole to use, work a few samples of different buttonholes on a sample of the border stitch. Small garments like lacy cardigans or summer tops will look better with several small buttons than a few large ones, while a heavy cabled garment is better with fewer, larger buttons.

For small buttons

Make the buttonhole using a yarn over with a corresponding decrease. On a band worked in rib or moss stitch, try to space the buttonholes so that the yarn over is worked in place of the purl stitch and the decrease is worked with the knit stitch on top. For example, opposite the button marker, on a right side row, work a k1, yo, k2tog. This will give a neater finish.

For large buttons

Work the buttonhole by binding (casting) off two or three stitches on a right side row and then casting them back on in the next row.

For example, on a band picked up and worked horizontally along the edge of a cardigan, you would work to one stitch before the marker, bind (cast) off three stitches, work to one stitch before the next marker and work another buttonhole and so on to the end of the row. The marker marks the centre of the buttonhole, so by working to one stitch before the marker, the centre of the buttonhole will be in the right position. On the next row, work to the bound (cast) off stitches, turn the work and cast on three stitches using the cable cast on method (see page 26). Before placing the final stitch on the left-hand needle, bring the yarn to the front between the needles; this stops a loop being formed which makes the buttonhole look untidy. Don't cast on too tightly, the stitches need to be as elastic and as wide as those on the bound (cast) off edge. Turn the work back and continue across the row to the next buttonhole. It looks neater if you plan to work the buttonholes in the same place in the rib. For example, bind (cast) off three stitches over k1, p1, k1 each time.

To sew on buttons, either use the same yarn, if it is thin enough to go through the button, or use a strong sewing thread in a matching colour.

Knit Perfect

✔ If the knitting pattern does *not* tell you how many stitches to pick up, measure the length of the edge and multiply it by the stitch gauge (tension) of the border to be knitted. You can get this from measuring the border if it has already been used on the garment, or by knitting a piece of the border as though it were for a gauge (tension) sample. Place markers every 1in (2.5cm) along the edge and pick up the number of stitches in 1in (2.5cm) of the border.

Practise by picking up stitches along the edge of the gauge (tension) square worked for the main fabric.

For example, if the edge measures 10in (25cm) and the stitch gauge (tension) of the border is 4 stitches to 1in (2.5cm), you would place markers every 1in (2.5cm) and pick up 4 stitches between them for a total of 40 stitches.

✔ If you pick up too few stitches for a neckband, button band or border, it will pull or gather up the main fabric. If you have too many stitches, the neckband, button band or border will be fluted and will not lie flat. Work out your stitches carefully before you begin and always unravel and start again if it does not look right.

A badly knitted border will spoil a well-knitted garment.

Sewing up

Whenever possible sew the pieces together with the yarn they are knitted from. If the yarn is something that will break easily or has a pile, like chenille, use a plain yarn in a matching colour. Check that it will wash the same as the knitting yarn. Do not use the long ends left after knitting the pieces; always sew these in before seaming. If you have to unpick the garment for any reason, the ends may start to unravel the knitting. Use a tapestry needle and an 18in (45cm) length of yarn. The action of taking the yarn through the work too frequently can fray it.

Mattress stitch

To get an invisible seam use mattress stitch. This is worked from the right side, making it easier to match patterns such as fair isle, and shaping details, like on a sleeve. Place the two pieces to be joined side by side on a flat surface.

Secure the yarn by weaving it down the edge of one of the pieces, bringing it to the front on the first row between the corner stitch and the second stitch. On the opposite edge, insert the needle from back to front on the first row between the corner stitch and the second stitch. Take the needle back to the first edge and insert it from back to front through the same hole. Pull the yarn up tight to draw the pieces together.

Joining two pieces of stockinette (stocking) stitch

Work row by row and use for vertical seams like side and sleeve seams. Secure the yarn as given above. Take the needle across to the opposite side and insert it into the first row again from front to back, take it under the horizontal strand of the row above and pull the yarn through. Take the needle across to the other edge, insert the needle into the first row again from front to back and take it under the horizontal strands of the two rows above. Pull the yarn through. Insert the needle into the first edge again, in the same hole that the yarn came out of and take it under the horizontal strands of the two rows above. Continue zigzagging between the edges, working under two rows each time. Pull the yarn up every few stitches to draw the seam together; not too tightly, the seam should not pucker the fabric.

Joining ribs

This is worked row by row. In k1, p1 rib work through the centre of the first stitch so that half a stitch is taken up on each side. Work under one row at a time. Pull the seam together and a whole stitch will be formed, so the rib is not interrupted by the seam. In k2, p2 rib work as given for st st, taking up a whole stitch to keep the rib correct.

Joining two pieces of reverse stockinette (stocking) stitch

Work row by row and use for vertical seams like side and sleeve seams. Join the lower edges and work as above but instead of working under two strands, work under one strand only. Insert the needle from front to back under the horizontal strand of the row above and pull the yarn through. Take the needle across to the other edge and insert it from front to back under the top loop of the second stitch. Take the needle back to the other edge and work under the strand of the row above. Continue in this way, inserting the needle under the top loop of the second stitch on one edge and under the horizontal strand between the first and second stitches on the other edge. One side of the seam takes in one and half stitches and the other takes in one stitch but this weaves the rev st st together so the seam is invisible.

Joining two pieces of garter stitch

This is worked row by row the same way as for reverse stockinette (stocking) stitch, working under the top loop of a stitch on one side and the horizontal strand between stitches on the other side.

Joining two bound (cast) off edges

Work stitch by stitch and use for shoulder seams. Lay the two pieces, one above the other, with the bound (cast) off edges together. Weave the yarn through a few stitches on the bottom piece to secure it. Bring the needle to the front through the centre of the first stitch of the row below the bound (cast) off edge. Take the needle up to the top piece and insert the needle through the centre of the first stitch and bring it out in the centre of the next stitch. Take the needle back down to the bottom piece and insert it into the same hole, and bring it up in the centre of the next stitch. Take the needle back to the top piece and insert the needle into the same hole and bring it out in the centre of the next stitch. Pull the yarn up tight to hide the bound (cast) off edges. Continue in this way, and the seam will resemble a new row of stitches.

Joining bound (cast) off stitches to rows

Use for sewing a sleeve into an armhole. Lay the pieces flat with the edges together. Secure the end of the yarn to the bound (cast) off edge. Bring the needle out through the centre of the first stitch of the row below the bound (cast) off edge. Take the needle up to the row piece and insert it under one horizontal strand between the first and second stitches. Insert the needle into the same place on the bound (cast) off piece and bring it out through the centre of the next stitch. Continue in this way, pulling the yarn tight to close the seam. There are usually more rows than stitches so one stitch cannot always be sewn to one row. Pin the pieces together carefully and pick up two horizontal strands every so often to take in the extras rows.

Sewing in a sleeve

Whatever style of sleeve a garment has, it is sewn in after joining shoulder seams but before joining side and sleeve seams.

Dropped shoulders

Dropped shoulders On garments with dropped shoulders there is no armhole shaping to sew the sleeve into. Bind (cast) off the sleeve top in one row. Lay the joined front and back pieces flat, measure half of the top of the sleeve measurement (information found on the size diagrams) down from the shoulder seam on each side edge and place a marker. Pin the centre of the bound (cast) off edge of the sleeve to the shoulder seam. Pin each end of the top of the sleeve to the markers. Pin the rest of the sleeve top between the markers and sew evenly in position, making sure the seam is straight.

Square set-in sleeves

Square set-in sleeves The sleeve top is bound (cast) off in one row like a dropped shoulder, but a square armhole is created by casting off a few stitches. Match the centre of the sleeve top to the shoulder seam. Pin each end into the corner of the armhole and sew the sleeve top into place. Then sew the ends of the sleeve horizontally against the bound (cast) off edges of the armhole.

ADAPTING A PATTERN

Not everyone is a standard size but knitting patterns assume they are and that by following the instructions slavishly the garment will fit perfectly. It is disappointing to spend time knitting a sweater which you never wear because the sleeves are too long or the body just that bit too short to be comfortable. Many patterns provide a diagram of the knitted pieces with measurements. Check these carefully against your own measurements to ensure a perfect fit. If the pattern doesn't have a diagram you will need to draw your own. It is worth the effort for a sweater that fits.

✓ Knit Perfect

✓ To work out the stitches and rows per inch (cm), divide the gauge (tension) by 4 (10). For example, 18 sts and 24 rows to 4in (10cm) = 4.5 sts and 6 rows to 1in (1.8 sts and 2.4 rows to 1cm).

✓ It is important to work in only imperial or metric measurements, do not use both together.

✓ If you find the maths too daunting, chart the garment on to graph paper. Chart the sleeve as per the instructions and then you will be able to see how many increases are made up each side. Chart any side shaping on the front or back. It is always easier to see the shape of the garment rather than try to visualize it from written instructions.

Sleeve length

The important measurement is from the centre of the back of your neck to your wrist (or where you want the cuff to end). Place one end of a tape measure on the bone at the back of your neck, extend your arm and measure to your wrist bone. On the garment diagram add the measurements for the back neck and both shoulders together and then divide this by two. This is the measurement from the centre back neck to the top of the sleeve. Take this measurement from your neck to wrist measurement and this will be the sleeve length. For example, the back neck plus shoulders = 18in (46cm), divide by 2 = 9in (23cm). Your neck to wrist measurement is 30in (76cm), so 30in (76cm) minus 9in (23cm) = 21in (53cm) sleeve length. Compare this to the sleeve length measurement given on the diagram.

To make the sleeve longer…
simply work more rows after the shaping until the sleeve measures the correct length.

To make the sleeve shorter…
is trickier. A sleeve is increased evenly up its length to get to the required width at the top to fit into the armhole. If you follow the instructions but stop when you reach your required sleeve length you may not have increased enough stitches and your sleeve will be too narrow to fit into the armhole.
Calculate the required increases as described below.

Charting a shorter sleeve

Chart your sleeve on graph paper to work out how to space the increases to fit them into your shorter length. On graph paper, one square represents one stitch. Draw a line centrally at the bottom of the sheet, the number of stitches after you have worked the cuff and any increase row. Mark the centre. To work out how many rows you have to work the increases over, take

the length of the cuff from the sleeve length and multiply this by the number of rows per inch (cm). For example, if your sleeve length is 21in (53.5cm) with a cuff of 2in (5cm) the length of the sleeve without the cuff is 19in (48.5cm). Multiply this by the row tension, for example, 6 rows to 1in (2.4 rows to 1cm) = 114 rows (115.2 rows). Round any fractions down to an even number. Count 114 rows from the cuff line and draw a line for the top of the sleeve. Draw a vertical line from the centre of the cuff line to the top line. Count out half the number of stitches after all the increases each side from this central line.

Take the number of cuff stitches (56) from the sleeve top stitches (98) making 42 stitches which means 21 stitches have to be increased at each side of the sleeve. Divide the number of rows by the number of increases, 114 divided by 21 = 5.4, rounded down to 5.

Mark the first increase on the fifth row and then on every following fifth row until the width is reached. Then draw a straight line from the last increase to the top. There should be at least 1in (2.5cm) straight after the last increase. Work from this chart to knit the new shorter sleeve length.

Garment length

If there is no armhole shaping, just work the length that you require to the shoulder shaping. For a garment with armhole shaping, you need to alter the length before reaching the armhole. The armhole length must remain as in the instructions as the sleeve shaping has been worked out to fit into that armhole. If the garment has shaping from the waist to the bust, draw a chart to work out the increases as described for working out a shorter sleeve.

Adding colour motifs

Using the instructions for the plain sweater, chart the main pieces of the garment on graph paper. Use the same outline for both the back and front, with the neck shaping drawn in for the front, and chart one sleeve. It is now easy to draw in any colour motifs or fair isle patterns that you want to add.

Adding a cable panel

You can add a cable panel to the plain sweater pattern on page 146. To be in proportion, a cable panel should measure about one third of the width of the front. Any smaller than this and it will look lost and have no impact. Any bigger and it will dominate and become an all-over fabric instead of a panel.

Designing the panel

To design your panel choose cables from the Stitch library (see pages 110–18). Start with a central feature cable, something bold or intricate, and then add complimentary but smaller cables each side. For example, the centre cable may have three stitches in each of the strands and uses C6F and C6B to cross the strands so it would look better with six stitch cables each side rather than thinner four stitch cables.

Chart the cables on graph paper with two stitches of reverse stockinette (stocking) stitch each side of the cables.

For example, the sweater shown here is a size 38in (96.5cm) with an actual chest measurement of 44in (112cm). The front measures 22in (56cm) therefore the panel should be about 7in (18cm).

Knitting the garment

Knit the back of the garment. Using the same needles you used to get the stockinette (stocking) stitch tension, cast on the required number of stitches for the cable panel you have designed plus at least three stitches each side for stockinette (stocking) stitch. Knit a gauge (tension) square of the cable panel. Lay it out flat and measure the cables and the reverse stockinette (stocking)

stitch each side. Do not include the stockinette (stocking) stitch. If it is over a third of the width of the back, use fewer stitches between the cables, but no less than two because each cable should have room to lie against reverse stockinette (stocking) stitch. If it is too narrow, add another smaller cable on each side.

When you were knitting the cable panel gauge (tension) piece you will have noticed that you need more stitches to get a panel which is the same width of stockinette (stocking) stitch. Cables pull the knitted fabric together and the reverse stockinette (stocking) stitch acts a bit like a rib, rolling under the edges of the cables.

Lay the back of the garment flat on a table with the right side towards you. Using a ruler, measure the width of the cable panel in the middle of the fabric along one row and place a pin at each side. Count the number of stitches across the row between the pins. This is the number of stitches of stockinette (stocking) stitch that will be replaced by the stitches of the cable panel.

For this example, the cable panel measures 7½in (19cm) and has 58 stitches (see sample below). The same width of stockinette (stocking) stitch has 33 stitches.

To calculate the number of stitches needed for the front of the sweater, subtract the number of stockinette (stocking) stitches and add on the number of cable panel stitches. Take away the number of stitches cast on for

▲ KNIT SOMETHING NOW!

Add a cable panel or colour motifs to this simple sweater.

Cable panel sweater knitted in fisherman (aran) merino wool on size 6 (4mm/UK8) and size 8 (5mm/UK6) needles. See page 147 for pattern.

the rib (this must stay the same as the back) to work out how many stitches to increase evenly on the last rib row.

For example, the back of the sweater has 99 stitches; to place the panel in the middle, 99 sts minus 33 sts to be removed = 66 sts, so there will be 33 sts of stockinette (stocking) stitch each side of the cable panel of 58 sts. For the front, there needs to be a total of 66 sts + 58 sts = 124 sts. The rib of the sweater is worked on 99 sts. The number of increase stitches from the rib to the front stitches is 124 sts minus 99 sts = 25 sts. These increase sts are usually worked into the last row of the rib.

To place increases (M1) evenly in a row, calculate as follows: divide the number of increases minus one, into the number of stitches in the row for the number of stitches between increases.

In this example, 25 incs minus 1 = 24 incs, then 99 sts divided by 24 incs = 4.125 sts, round down to 4 sts, which will leave 3 sts to be worked at the sides. The increase row is rib 2, M1, (rib 4, M1) 24 times, rib 1. 124 sts.

Measure the cable panel and the reverse stockinette (stocking) stitch each side.

KNITTING A PATTERNED GARMENT

Increasing and decreasing to shape a piece of stockinette (stocking) stitch is straightforward. Each stitch is either knitted or purled. In stitch patterns with a repeat of two or more stitches, an increased stitch must be worked in pattern to keep the pattern correct.

To shape a sleeve, a knitting pattern will instruct you to increase one stitch into pattern at each end of every, say, 6th row but will not tell you how to work the stitch you have made. The increases are worked at the ends of the rows using inc 1, but not the full fashioning method (see page 28). There are two ways to keep track of increases, working them into pattern successfully: charting, which is the easiest, and using markers.

Charting

Chart the outline of the sleeve on to graph paper (see below). Beginning at the bottom right-hand corner, plot the rows of the stitch pattern as given in the knitting instructions, using symbols to represent the stitches (see page 65 and the Stitch library). This helps you identify the pattern repeat. The lace cardigan on this page is knitted in a pattern with a six stitch repeat, plus one stitch at the end to balance it.

Lace pattern

Row 1 K1, * yfwd, k1, sk2po, k1, yfwd, k1; rep from * to end.
Row 2 P to end.
Row 3 K2, * yfwd, sk2po, yfwd, k3; rep from * to end, ending last rep with k2.
Row 4 P to end.
These 4 rows form the lace pattern.
Plot the lace pattern across the bottom of the sleeve and the first and last repeats up to the top of the sleeve. Now fill in what pattern stitches you can in the increased stitches at each side. Use this method for cables, texture stitches as well as lace stitches but remember that in a lace pattern, a yarn over increase must be accompanied by a decrease. If there are not sufficient stitches to work both, wait until you have increased enough stitches to do so. Rather than work a long panel of stockinette (stocking) stitch before you can work a complete pattern repeat, it is sometimes possible to change the decrease. There is a double decrease in this pattern and by changing it to a single decrease, like ssk, half a pattern repeat can be worked. Use the same method for cables or texture stitches.

Decreases can be charted in the same way. For example, a neck is shaped by decreasing on every row. Chart the outline of the front of the garment with the neck shaping and plot in the stitch pattern. The knitting pattern will tell you which stitch pattern row you should finish before beginning to shape the neck.

✓ Knit Perfect

A good knitting pattern should be written so that any shaping into the stitch pattern will look well designed. Some instructions, however, can result in half a cable or an incomplete lace stitch repeat being worked at each side of the neck or armhole. If this looks like it is going to happen, add or take off one stitch more than instructed to get the pattern lying nicely into the shaping.

Don't alter it by more than one stitch in bulky (chunky) yarn or a couple of stitches in worsted (DK) yarn. At the neck shaping, make a note of what you have done, so more or less stitches are picked up for the neckband.

Chart for lace pattern on sleeve showing increases

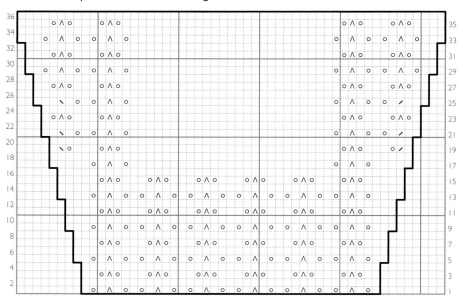

Chart for cable pattern on sleeve showing increases

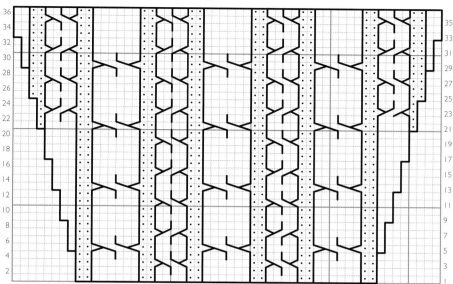

Chart for lace pattern on front showing neck and shoulder shaping

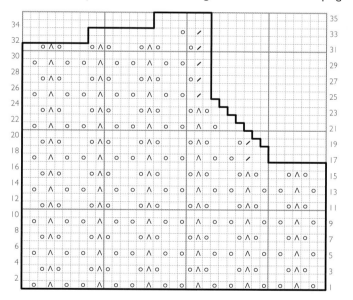

Working with markers

Work the first increases at each end of the row, placing markers between the new stitches and the original stitches. Continue in pattern, slipping the markers on every row and working the increases into stockinette (stocking) stitch. Wait until you have sufficient new stitches next to the marker to work a complete pattern repeat. A half pattern repeat could be worked if the pattern will allow (see charting method left). When a whole repeat has been worked, move the marker out to begin a new pattern repeat.

Before working the first decreases place a marker one pattern repeat in from the edges to be shaped. Work this pattern repeat until there are insufficient stitches to work it correctly. Work the remaining stitches in stockinette (stocking) stitches until they, too, are decreased. Move the marker one pattern repeat in and continue to decrease over these stitches.

KNIT SOMETHING NOW! ▶

Knit this cardigan to practise shaping over a lace pattern. Draw your own chart and plot the pattern before you start any shaping.

Lace cardigan knitted in worsted (DK) weight merino wool on size 6 (4mm/UK8) needles. See page 148 for pattern.

TASSELS, FRINGES AND CORDS

Adding fringing and cords made from complementary yarns to your garments and soft furnishings provides the finishing touch. They are quick and easy to make.

Tassels

Wrap the yarn loosely around a piece of card the required length of the tassel. Thread a long length of yarn under the strands at the top, fold in half and secure tightly with a knot, leaving two long ends. Cut the wrapped strands at the bottom and remove the cardboard. Thread one long end on to a tapestry needle, insert it through the top of the strands and bring out 1 in (2.5cm) below. Wrap the yarn several times around the tassel. Pass the needle through the middle of the wrapped strands to secure the long end, then insert the needle again and pull it back through the top. Use these ends to sew the tassel in place. Trim the bottom of the tassel neatly.

Plain fringe

Wrap yarn loosely around a piece of cardboard the required length of the fringe. Cut the wrapped strands at the bottom and remove the cardboard. Fold several lengths in half and, using a crochet or rug hook, pull the strands through the edge of the knitted piece from front to back by catching the fold with the hook. Pass the ends through the folded loop and pull to tighten the knot. Space each bunch of strands evenly along the edge. Trim the bottom of the fringe neatly to the finished length required.

Knotted fringe

Work the fringe as given left with an even number of strands in each bunch. Take half the strands from one bunch and half the strands from the next and tie them together. Continue across the fringe, making sure the knots are in line. The extra knot will take up yarn so make the strands longer than the desired finished length. Try working another row of knots below, combining the original bunches again.

Knitted cord

This long tube, sometimes called an I-cord, is knitted on two double-pointed needles, using two sizes smaller than normally used for the yarn.

Cast on four stitches and knit one row. Do not turn the work but instead push the stitches to the other end of the needle. Swap the right-hand needle with the left-hand needle, pull up the yarn and knit the four stitches again. Repeat for every row. By pulling the yarn up at the end of the row, the edges of the knitting are pulled together and a tube is formed. Cast on three stitches for a finer cord, and five stitches for a thicker one. Piping cord can be threaded through the knitted cord for a firmer edging for cushions or as the handle for a bag.

The intarsia cushion (see page 156) uses a knitted cord to trim the edges.

Twisted cord

Strands of yarn twisted together will form a cord. The more strands you use, the thicker the cord will be. Cut lengths of yarn three times the finished length required and tie them together with a knot at each end. Hook one end over a doorknob or hook, and holding the other knotted end, stand back so that the strands are taut. Insert a pencil into the end and wind it to twist the strands. Keep the strands taut as you wind, twisting until the cord starts to fold up and twist around itself. Keeping the cord taut, remove the end from the doorknob and bring both knotted ends together. The cord will twist around itself. Ask someone to hold the middle or hang a weight from a hook on the middle of the cord to hold it taut as it twists. Small tassels can be made at either end by knotting the strands, cutting the looped end and then untying the knots from the other end. A textured cord is made by combining different yarns or colours.

The heart sachet (see page 144) is hung up by a twisted cord loop.

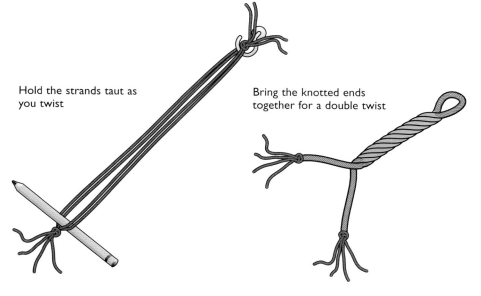

Hold the strands taut as you twist

Bring the knotted ends together for a double twist

EDGINGS

Edgings can be added to garments instead of ribs or added to knitted items like throws (see page 140). They can be knitted separately, worked from the cast-on edge with the main fabric worked up from them or added to an edge by picking up stitches from a finished piece. Knitted edgings can also trim woven fabric garments, or used on household items. See the stitch library page 127–9 for more edgings.

✓ Knit Perfect

✓ For a simple delicate edging which looks great around collars, work a picot bind (cast) off (see page 27) or pick up and knit sts along an edge and then bind (cast) off.

✓ Have a look in antique shops for old garments, table linen and bed linen. A lot of these will have knitted lace edgings. White cotton lace edgings add a romantic look to ordinary bed linen. Choose one from the Stitch library (see page 127–9). Use a yarn with the same washing instructions as the bed linen. Wash both to make sure they don't shrink before sewing the edging on. Add edgings around ready-made cushions and throws.

✓ Lengths of knitted lace were traditionally used to decorate shelf edges. Soften the bottom edge of roller blinds by sewing on a picot point or frilled edging.

✓ Add the ruffled or frilled edging to the ends of a plain scarf. Use the same colour yarn or a contrasting one.

Ruffled edging worked first

Cast on a number of sts divisible by 6 plus 5 close to the finished number of sts required plus 10 sts for every 6 sts. For example, if 50 is the finished number of sts required, cast on 53 sts (8 × 6 + 5) plus 80 sts (8 × 10). The three extra stitches will be decreased evenly across the first row of the main fabric after knitting the ruffle.

Row 1 (WS) K5, * p11, k5; rep from * to end.
Row 2 P5, * k2tog, k7, ssk, p5; rep from * to end.
Row 3 K5, * p9, k5; rep from * to end.
Row 4 P5, * k2tog, k5, ssk, p5; rep from * to end.

Cont in this way, dec 1 st at each side of knit sts on every RS row and work 2 purl sts less in each repeat on every WS row until 3 knit sts remain for each ruffle, ending with a WS row.

Next row P5, * sl2tog-k1-psso, p5; rep from * to end.
Next row K5, * p1, k5; rep from * to end.

Cont in main fabric, dec 3 sts evenly for required number of sts on first row.

Ruffled edging worked at the end

Work before binding (casting) off the stitches of main piece or pick up and knit stitches along the edge of the main piece (see page 70). A multiple of 6 stitches plus 5 is required so increase stitches to get patt rep. The M1 stitches are made to the right and left (see page 29).

Row 1 (RS) P5, * k1, p5; rep from * to end.
Row 2 K5, * p1, k5; rep from * to end.
Row 3 P5, * M1R, k1, M1L, p5; rep from * to end.
Row 4 K5, * p3, k5; rep from * to end.
Row 5 P5, * M1R, k3, M1L, p5; rep from * to end.

Cont in this way, inc 1 st at each side of k sts on RS rows and work the extras sts as p sts on WS rows until there are 11 knit sts for each ruffle, ending with a WS row. Bind (cast) off loosely in patt.

Frilled edging

This edging is always worked first or as
a separate border and sewn on.
Cast on four times the finished number
of stitches required.
Row 1 * K2, lift first of these 2 sts over
second and off the needle; rep from *
to end. (Half the number of sts remain.)
Row 2 * P2tog; rep from * to end.
(Finished number of sts.)
Cont in main fabric of garment or cast off.

Double frill

You will need three needles. Work a frilled
edging as above followed by 8 rows of
st st (ending with a WS row), leave sts
on the needle. On another needle, work
a second frill followed by 2 rows of st st
(ending with a WS row). Place the two
needles together with the short frill over
the longer frill and both right sides facing
the front. Join together by knitting through
both sets of sts (see page 27).

points of equal size

**two sizes of points, one increased
to 18 sts and the other to 12 sts**

Picot point edging

Each point is worked separately, the
stitches left on a spare needle and then
joined together at the top by working
across all stitches. They can be any size and
different sizes worked alternately make
for a wave effect. Work in moss stitch or
a stitch pattern instead of garter stitch.
Sew beads or tassels on to the points.
Cast on 2 sts.
Row 1 K2.
Row 2 Yo, k2.
Row 3 Yo, k3.
Row 4 Yo, k4.

Cont in this way until the required even
number of sts is reached, having worked
an even number of incs. Cut yarn and
push the sts to the end of the needle.
Cast on 2 sts on to the other needle
and work another point. Continue in this
way until there are the required number
of points. Do not cut the yarn after the
last point, use it to knit across all the
points. Either work a few rows of garter
stitch and cast off or continue into the
main fabric.

Cable edging

Work as a separate border and sew
on to main piece or pick up and knit
stitches from edging for main fabric.
Add 2 sts and 2 plain rows more for a
six stitch cable version.
Cast on 8 sts.
Row 1 (RS) P3, k4, p1.
Row 2 K1, p4, k3.
Row 3 P3, C4F, p1.
Row 4 K1, p4, k3.
Rep these 4 rows until edging is
required length.

BUTTONS

Finishing a knitted project by making your own buttons will make it really individual. You can cover buttons in knitted fabric using the same yarn as the main piece and then embroider them or stitch on some beads. Make bobble buttons by running a gathering thread around a circle of fabric and stuff. Dorset buttons are a traditional thread button; work in yarn or use embroidery threads for their range of colours.

Covered buttons

You can use self-cover buttons, which are available in kits, or a plain flat button with a shank. Self-cover buttons are made from metal or plastic and come in two pieces, the part you cover and the back plate to secure the covering fabric. There will also be a pattern outline of a circle to use as a guide for the size of the fabric. If you are using an ordinary button, cut a pattern in thin card by drawing a circle with a diameter of twice the width of the button. For example, a 1in (2.5cm) diameter button would have a pattern 2in (5cm) in diameter. For the knitted cover, use a worsted (DK) yarn or finer, otherwise the fabric will be too bulky to fit around the button. The fabric has to be tight and firm so use needles two or three sizes smaller than normal.

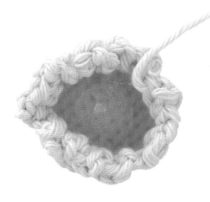

Tension square

Work a small gauge (tension) square using the smaller needles. Lay the button pattern on to the square and place pins on all four sides so you can count the number of stitches and rows. Divide the number of rows by three. Working in stockinette (stocking) stitch, cast on half the number of stitches and work one third of the rows, increasing into the first and last stitch of every second row until all the stitches for the required width have been added. Work straight for a third of the rows and then decrease over the same number of rows back to the original number of stitches. Bind (cast) off and leave a long end for gathering. Use the card pattern as a guide while you are knitting. The cover will be octagonal rather than a true circle.

Embellishing and finishing

The fabric can be embroidered or beaded at this point but do not add anything too close to the edges which will be folded under and not seen. Don't make the fabric too lumpy on the wrong side. Run a gathering thread around the edge, place the button in the middle and pull the thread up tightly. (If the covered button shows through the knitting, cover the top with a circle of thin fabric.) Adjust the folds of fabric and make a few extra stitches through the folds to sew them together. Secure the end of the thread. The back plate of the self-cover button is unnecessary and probably will not fit unless the knitting is very fine.

Bobble buttons

Work the fabric shape in the same way as the covered buttons. Run a gathering thread around the edge, pull up and stuff firmly with toy stuffing. Gather up tightly and secure the end of the thread.

Dorset thread buttons

These buttons are worked in yarn around a metal or plastic ring. The ring is covered with closely worked blanket stitch (see page 86) and weaving through crossing spokes fills the centre. Use sport (4ply) yarn, crochet thread or embroidery threads to make the buttons in one colour or in a different colour for each stage. The button is attached by working stitches through the centre at the back.

1 Thread a tapestry needle with a long length of yarn, and work blanket stitch around the ring, covering the end of the yarn with the first few stitches to secure it. Make sure the stitches lie close together and that the ring is entirely covered. Work a small stitch into the top of the first stitch to join. Twist the blanket stitch around so that the horizontal loops face towards the centre.

2 Put the ring on to a piece of paper and divide it into six sections by placing a mark opposite the last stitch worked and spacing another four marks evenly around the ring. Starting at the last stitch worked, where the thread is still joined, number the marks from 1 to 6. Make a spoke by taking the thread across the centre of the ring to 4 and inserting the needle into the horizontal loop from front to back. Take the thread across the back of the ring to 5 and insert the needle from back to front. Take the thread across the ring to 2 and insert it from front to back. Take the thread up at 3 and then down at 6 for the final spoke.

3 Bring the yarn at the back of the ring to the centre where the spokes meet. Work a small cross to bind them together. Working clockwise, take the needle under the first two spokes, back over the second spoke and then under the second and third spokes, forming a small backstitch on the second spoke. Take the needle under the third and fourth, then under the fourth and fifth and so on. As you work out from the centre, pull the backstitches gently to tighten the weaving. Continue weaving until the centre is completely filled. Secure the thread and cut off neatly.

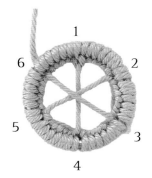

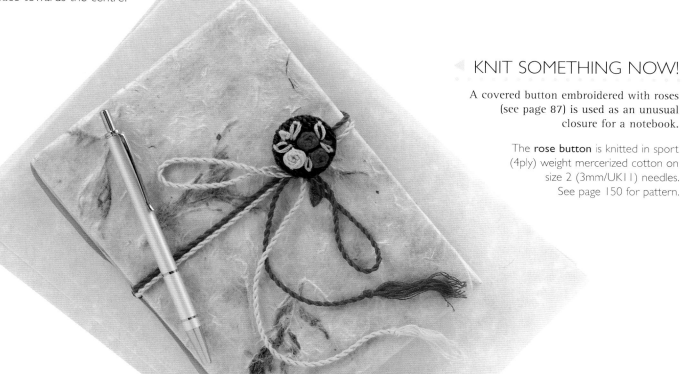

KNIT SOMETHING NOW!

A covered button embroidered with roses (see page 87) is used as an unusual closure for a notebook.

The **rose button** is knitted in sport (4ply) weight mercerized cotton on size 2 (3mm/UK11) needles. See page 150 for pattern.

FLOWERS AND LEAVES

Knitted flowers and leaves are great for adding to plain garments or for scattering across a throw or cushion. Work in fine silky yarns for glamour, velvet chenille for luxury, or crisp cotton yarns that hold their shape well. If knitted in 100 per cent wool, the fabric can be fulled (see page 62). Embellish the edges of the leaves or petals with beads or embroidery.

Rose

Use a worsted (DK) yarn or thinner and a size smaller needle than normal, 3 (3.25mm/UK10), to make a firm fabric. Cast on 80 sts and knit 1 row.
Work 1in (2.5cm) st st, beg with a k row.
Dec row (K2tog) 40 times. 40 sts.
Dec row (P2tog) 20 times. 20 sts.
Dec row (K2tog) 10 times. 10 sts.
Cut yarn, leaving a long length. Thread yarn on to a tapestry needle and thread through sts on needle, taking them off the needle one by one. Pull up into gathers. Form the rose by twisting it round and round from the centre with right side of fabric facing outwards. Pull the rose into shape as you go, letting the fabric roll over in some places. Work a few stitches through all layers at the bottom to hold them in place.

For a smaller rose, cast on fewer stitches and work less straight rows before decreasing as above.

Basic leaf

Cast on 3 sts and purl 1 row.
Row 1 (RS) K1, yfwd, k1, yfwd, k1. 5 sts.
Row 2 and every foll WS row Purl.
Row 3 K2, yfwd, k1, yfwd, k2. 7 sts.
Row 5 K3, yfwd, k1, yfwd, k3. 9 sts.
Row 7 K4, yfwd, k1, yfwd, k4. 11 sts.
Row 9 Ssk, k7, k2tog. 9 sts.
Row 11 Ssk, k5, k2tog. 7 sts.
Row 13 Ssk, k3, k2tog. 5 sts.
Row 15 Ssk, k1, k2tog. 3 sts.
Row 17 Sk2po.
Cut yarn and pull through last st. Make the leaf larger by adding extra increase rows. If you want a more solid leaf, work M1 instead of yfwd. Work the leaf in garter stitch instead of stockinette (stocking) stitch by working each WS row as a knit row. Make five leaves and arrange them in a circle with cast on points together at the centre to make a flower.

▼ KNIT SOMETHING NOW!

A rose with two leaves has been fulled after knitting and makes an attractive brooch. The lavender sachet below right is trimmed with a leaf edging.

The **brooch** is knitted in 2ply jumper weight shetland wool and the leaf edging is knitted in sport (4ply) weight mercerized cotton. See page 150 for pattern.

Daisy

These flowers look great worked in 4ply cotton yarn using size 2(3mm/UK11) needles, although they can be worked in any thickness or texture of yarn. Try a mohair or brushed yarn for a soft flower, or metallic or rayon yarns for a funky flower. Fill the centre with French knots (see page 86) or a button.
Cast on 2 sts.
** Row 1 Knit into front and back of first st, k1.
Row 2 and every foll WS row K to end.
Row 3 Knit into front and back of first st, k2.
Cont in g st, inc into first st of every RS row until there are 6 sts, ending with a WS row.
Next row Bind (cast) off 4 sts, k2.
Next row K to end. ******
One petal completed.
Work from ** to ** four more times.
Bind (cast) off rem 2 sts.
Run a gathering thread along the straight edge. Join the first petal to the last at cast on and bind (cast) off edges, forming a circle. Pull up the gathers until the daisy lies flat. Secure the thread. Make the petals bigger by working more increase rows. Make more petals and form into a spiral with two or more layers of petals.

EMBROIDERY

Embroidery should be done when the knitting has been completed and the pieces blocked but before the garment has been made up. You can use decorative stitches to add embellishments to any knitted fabric, although stockinette (stocking) stitch is the ideal base. The knitted stitches form a grid to work over and act as a guide for spacing embroidery stitches.

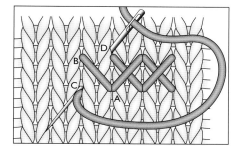

Cross stitch

Stockinette (stocking) stitch forms the grid for working cross stitch. They are worked over one stitch and one row, or on a fine knitted fabric, two stitches and two rows. Insert the needle between the stitches and make sure the top diagonal always goes in the same direction.

Bring the needle up at A then down at B, back up at C and then down at D. One stitch completed. Use this method for individual stitches or different colours.

For a horizontal or vertical line of cross stitches, work one diagonal of each stitch and then work back to complete the cross.

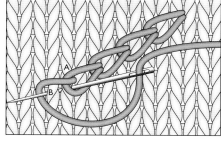

Chain stitch

Bring the needle out at A. In one movement, push the needle down in the same place and bring it out at B for the next stitch, looping the thread under the needle tip.

▼ KNIT SOMETHING NOW!

These drawstring bags are worked in knit and purl stitches. The bag on the right is embroidered using cross stitch (see above), and the other has delicate ribbon roses sewn on (see page 87).

Drawstring bags knitted in worsted (DK) cotton yarn on size 6 (4mm/UK8) needles and embroidered with DMC Stranded Cotton. See page 151 for pattern.

embroidery

Knit Perfect

✓ Use embroidery threads, tapestry wools or knitting yarn. The thread should be the same or slightly thicker than the knitted yarn. Too thin and it will sink into the fabric; too thick and it will distort the knitting. Check the threads are colourfast and will not shrink when washed. Work an embroidered sample and wash it if you are not certain.

✓ To transfer a pattern to the knitted fabric, draw it on tissue paper and tack into place on the knitted piece. Stitch through the paper and the knitted fabric. When completed, carefully cut or tear away the paper. On lightweight knitted fabric tack a piece of sew-on interfacing on to the wrong side and use it as a backing for the embroidery. Do not use iron-on interfacing as this may ruin the knitted fabric.

✓ Use a large-eyed blunt tapestry needle for embroidery. Work the embroidery stitches loosely, don't pull too tightly or the knitted fabric will pucker. Keep laying the piece flat to check for stretching or pulling. To begin the embroidery, weave the end of the thread through a few knitted stitches on the back of the fabric, working back through the thread to secure it; if you start with a knot, it may come undone during wear and knots make the wrong side lumpy.

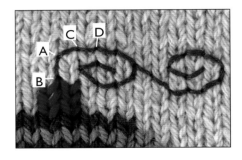

Backstitch

A continuous line used for outlining, for flower stems or for adding details.

To begin bring the needle up at A. Take the needle down at B and then up at C, down at A and up at D.

Lazy daisy stitch

Individual chain stitches worked around a centre to create the petals of a flower. The loops are fastened with a small stitch.

Bring the needle out at A. In one movement, push the needle down in the same place and bring it out at B, looping the thread under the needle tip. Take the needle back down at B, working over the loop, and bring it up at A for the next stitch.

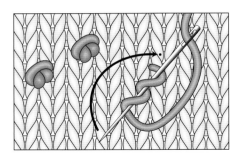

French knot

Can be worked as the centre of lazy daisy stitch.

Bring the needle up and wind the yarn twice around the needle. Take the needle back down half a stitch away. Hold the loops around the needle with your finger tip to keep them in place whilst pulling the thread through to the back.

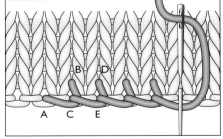

Blanket stitch

Use as a decorative edging along a garment, to sew on a patch pocket or appliqué shape, or to reinforce buttonholes. Often used to neaten raw edges, it can be worked from left to right or from right to left.

Bring the needle out at A. In one movement, take it down at B and back up at C, looping the thread under the needle tip. The next stitch is worked to the right, down at D and up at E. The horizontal threads should lie on the edge of the fabric.

Swiss darning or duplicate stitch

This stitch looks as though it has been knitted into the fabric; it follows the line of the yarn for the knit stitch on the right side of stockinette (stocking) stitch. It is used to embroider small areas of colour that would be tedious to knit, or to work a colour pattern instead of using fair isle or intarsia techniques. It is also useful for correcting mistakes in fair isle or intarsia. Use the same thickness of yarn used for the knitting. Take care to insert the needle between the strands and not to split the knitted stitches. The stitches will appear slightly raised on the surface of the knitting.

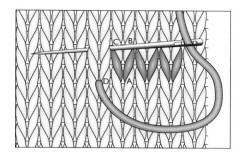

Horizontal stitches

Work from right to left, bringing the needle out at the base of the stitch (A). In one movement, take the thread around the top of the stitch by taking the needle down at B and up at C. In one movement, take the needle down at the base of the stitch (A) and up at the base of the next stitch (D). Continue across the row.

Vertical stitches

Work from bottom to top, bringing the needle out at the base of the stitch (A). Take the thread around the top of the stitch (B and C) and back down at the base (A). This time bring the needle up at the base of the stitch above and continue up the line of knitted stitches.

Rose stitch

Use a thin yarn or embroidery thread for the straight stitches and a thicker yarn or ribbon for the weaving through them that will cover the straight stitches.

Work five straight stitches in a circle the size of the rose required, all radiating from the central point. Thread the needle with the ribbon (or thick yarn) and bring it up through the centre hole. Going round and round from the centre outwards weave under and over the straight stitches until they are completely covered.

KNIT SOMETHING NOW! ▷

Mounted on ready-made greetings cards, these simple knitted patches are swiss darned with a heart for Valentine's Day and a tree for Christmas.

Valentine and **Christmas tree card** knitted in sport (4ply) mercerized cotton yarn on size 2 (3mm/UK11) needles and swiss darned with 12ply silk embroidery thread. See page 153 for pattern.

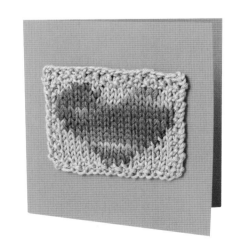

CORRECTING MISTAKES

When you are a beginner or are knitting fast, it is easy to work stitches incorrectly; splitting the yarn, dropping stitches off the needle, or not completing the stitch properly are common mistakes that are easily rectified. Twisting a cable the wrong way or working a colour pattern incorrectly are more serious errors. This is why it is important to inspect your knitting every few rows to save yourself the trouble of unpicking and re-knitting.

Dropped stitches

The sooner you spot that you have dropped a stitch the easier it is to rectify the mistake. Get into the habit of checking your knitting every few rows.

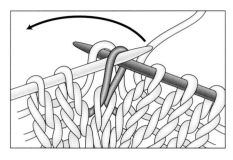

Knit stitch one row below
Insert the right needle through the front of the dropped stitch and then pick up the strand of yarn behind it. With the tip of the left needle, pass the stitch over the strand and off the needle.

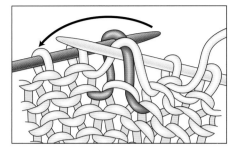

Purl stitch one row below
Insert the right needle through the back of the dropped stitch and then pick up the yarn strand in front of it. With the left needle, pass the stitch over the loop and off the needle.

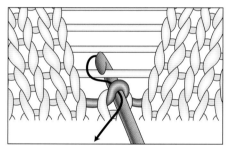

Stitch several rows below
If the stitch has run down a few rows, but no more than 4 rows, either repeat the instructions given for each row (making sure that you use the correct yarn strand for each row), or use a crochet hook. Insert the hook through the front of the dropped stitch, catch the yarn strand and pull through the stitch. Repeat for all the rows. For a purl stitch, work a knit stitch on the opposite side. If more than one stitch has been dropped, slip the others on to a safety pin to stop them running any further, while you pick them up one by one.
If you dropped a stitch and did not notice it until quite a few rows later, the only solution is to unravel your work back to that point. If you try to pick it up, the yarn strands will not be long enough to work the stitches to the correct tension. The picked up stitches will be tight and will show up badly.

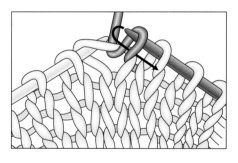

Unravelling one row
If the error occurred in stitches that you have just worked on the right needle. There is no need to take the work off the needle, just unravel, stitch-by-stitch, back to the error.
Insert the left needle into the stitch below from the front, drop the stitch off the right needle and pull the yarn. Repeat this for each stitch back to the error. Work in the same way for purl stitches.

✓ Knit Perfect

✔ When you spot an error quite a few rows back, mark the row with a coloured thread.

✔ If you are pulling back a complicated pattern, make a note of how many rows are pulled back and mark it on your pattern. Then you will start with the correct pattern row when you resume knitting.

✔ Put stitches back on to a size smaller needle, it will slip through the stitches easier. Remember to pick up the correct size needle when you start knitting.

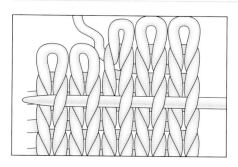

Unravelling several rows

Take the work off the needles, gather it up into one hand and unravel each row carefully to the row above the error. Do not be tempted to lay the work out flat to do this as the stitches are more likely to unravel beyond the row you are unravelling. Replace the stitches on to the needle and then unravel the last row as given left.

If you are using a slippery yarn or one that will not unravel easily, such as a hairy yarn, or if you are nervous about dropping stitches, you can pick up stitches in the row below the error before unravelling, as follows. Take a spare needle smaller than that used for the knitting and weave it through the first loop and over the second loop of each stitch on the row below the mistake (shown above).

If you are working a cable or lace pattern, pick the nearest row without too much patterning and where you can see the stitches clearly. Pull back the stitches above the spare needle. Slip the stitches back on to the correct size needles, making sure they are not twisted and lie correctly for the next row.

Split yarn

If you have split the yarn while working a stitch, go back and re-work it. The split yarn will show up on the surface of the work. Unravel the stitch by inserting the left-hand needle through the front, drop the stitch off the right-hand needle and pull the yarn. Rework the stitch with the yarn strand as given for dropped stitches.

Incomplete stitches

These occur where you have wrapped the yarn around the needle but it has not been pulled through the old stitch to form a new stitch. The yarn strand will be on the needle next to the unworked stitch. Work the stitch properly with the yarn strand as given for dropped stitches.

Colour patterns

If you have missed a few stitches or part of the pattern in a fair isle, use duplicate stitch to correct the errors (see page 87). If you have missed out a few rows or a whole section of pattern, either unravel the work back to the row before the error, or use the grafting method given right, and below in the Knit Perfect box.

Cables

It is easy to twist a cable the wrong way. If it was done in the previous few rows, unravel the cable stitches only and reknit by using the long loops of yarn released by unravelling. If the error is a long way down the piece or if by correcting it as above, it becomes really noticeable, it can only really be solved satisfactorily by unravelling the work back and reworking the whole piece again.

Grafting

Grafting is joining two sets of stitches by imitating a row of knitted stitches. It is often used in place of a seam, where a seam would show or be too bulky. It is easiest to work on stockinette (stocking) stitch. Use a tapestry needle and matching yarn. Two sets of stitches are left on needles.

1 Lay them edge to edge, and working from right to left, insert the tapestry needle from the back of the work through the first st on the lower edge.
2 Insert the tapestry needle from the back through the first stitch of the other edge and pull the yarn through.
3 Insert the tapestry needle into the first stitch of the lower edge again from front to back this time and then through the next stitch from back to front. Pull the yarn through.
4 Insert the tapestry needle into the first stitch of the upper edge again from front to back and then through the next stitch from back to front. Pull the yarn through. Continue as set, forming a row of new stitches, pulling the yarn through at the same gauge (tension) as the rest of the knitting.

 ## Knit Perfect

A mistake made in a fair isle panel can be altered through grafting, by reknitting the rows with the mistake. Thread a size smaller needle through the stitches of a one colour row above the mistake and another needle through the stitches of a one colour row below the mistake. Cut the yarn in the middle of the mistake row and pull back the knitting to the two needles. Your knitting will be in two pieces with the stitches caught on two needles. Knit the fair isle pattern rows up and the two sets of stitches can now be grafted together.

Stitch Library

This library of over 100 different stitches is presented in seven sections. The first section shows the great variety of fabrics that can be made simply by working knit and purl stitches (pages 91–98), beginning with moss stitch and including basketweave and check patterns, and on to stars and hearts. Next is a selection of traditional gansey or guernsey stitches (pages 99–102), which combine in panels to produce the famous fishermen's sweaters of the British Isles. Texture stitches follow (pages 103–7) to make your knitting three dimensional. The section on rib stitches (pages 108–9) presents lace ribs as well as ribs suitable for aran sweaters and brioche stitch which produces a thick, cosy fabric. A wide variety of cables is next (pages 110–18), ranging from simple four stitch cables to the more elaborate celtic cable and twisting vine cables. The next section of lace stitches (pages 119–26) includes traditional stitches used in Shetland shawls like Horseshoe lace and Crest of the Wave, as well as openwork leaves and diamonds. The final section is a selection of edgings (pages 127–9) from small delicate trims through to the wider and more open Cobweb frill, all of which can add a special finish to your knitting. Many of these stitches have been used in the projects but you can substitute others when you gain in experience.

KNIT SOMETHING NOW! ▷

Combine a variety of stitches from the stitch library to create a sampler cushion cover.

The **patchwork cushion** is knitted in worsted (DK) weight cotton yarn on size 6 (4mm/UK8) needles. See page 152 for pattern.

KNIT AND PURL STITCHES

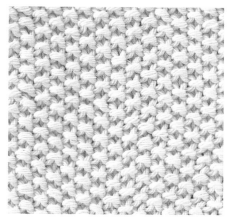

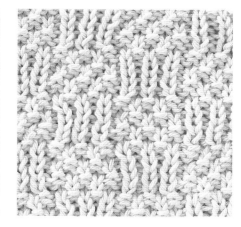

Moss Stitch (reversible)

On an odd number of stitches.
Row I K1, * p1, k1; rep from * to end.
Repeat this row.

On an even number of stitches.
Row I * K1, p1; rep from * to end.
Row 2 * P1, k1; rep from * to end.
Repeat these 2 rows.

Double Moss Stitch
(reversible)

On an odd number of stitches.
Row I K1, * p1, k1; rep from * to end.
Row 2 P1, * k1, p1; rep from * to end.
Row 3 As row 2.
Row 4 As row 1.
Repeat these 4 rows.

On an even number of stitches.
Row I * K1, p1; rep from * to end.
Row 2 As row 1.
Row 3 * P1, k1; rep from * to end.
Row 4 As row 3.
Repeat these 4 rows.

Double Moss Stitch and Rib Check (reversible)

Multiple of 12 sts plus 7.
Row I * (P1, k1) 3 times, p2, (k1, p1) twice; rep from * to last 7 sts, (p1, k1) 3 times, p1.
Row 2 K1, (p1, k1) 3 times, * (k1, p1) twice, k2, (p1, k1) 3 times; rep from * to end.
Row 3 P1, * k1, p1; rep from * to end.
Row 4 K1, * p1, k1; rep from * to end.
Row 5 As row 1.
Row 6 As row 2.
Row 7 * P2, k1, p1, k1, p2, (k1, p1) twice, k1; rep from * to last 7 sts, p2, k1, p1, k1, p2.
Row 8 K2, p1, k1, p1, k2, * (p1, k1) twice, p1, k2, p1, k1, p1, k2; rep from * to end.
Row 9 As row 3.
Row 10 As row 4.
Row II As row 7.
Row 12 As row 8.
Repeat these 12 rows.

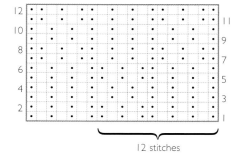

12 stitches

KEY

- · p on RS rows, k on WS rows
- ☐ k on RS rows, p on WS rows

Stitch library charts

Stitch charts have been included for most of the stitches in the library, apart from those where increasing and decreasing a number of stitches makes a chart difficult to follow.

You can use the stitch charts to design your own garments,w work out increases and decreases in pattern (see page 76-7), design your own cable panels (see page 75) or put together gansey sweater designs. See page 65 for how to read charts.

KNIT AND PURL STITCHES

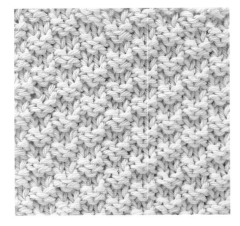

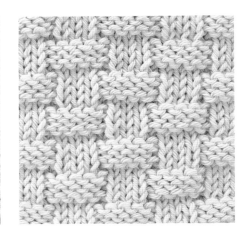

Two Stitch Check

(reversible)

Multiple of 4 sts plus 2.
Row 1 K2, * p2, k2; rep from * to end.
Row 2 P2, * k2, p2; rep from * to end.
Row 3 As row 2.
Row 4 As row 1.
Repeat these 4 rows.

Four Stitch Check

(reversible)

Multiple of 8 sts.
Rows 1, 2, 3 and 4 * K4, p4; rep from * to end.
Rows 5, 6, 7 and 8 * P4, k4; rep from * to end.
Repeat these 8 rows.

Basketweave

Multiple of 8 sts plus 5.
Row 1 (RS) Knit.
Row 2 * K5, p3; rep from * to last 5 sts, k5.
Row 3 P5, * k3, p5; rep from * to end.
Row 4 As row 2.
Row 5 Knit.
Row 6 K1, p3, k1, * k4, p3, k1; rep from * to end.
Row 7 * P1, k3, p4; rep from * to last 5 sts, p1, k3, p1.
Row 8 As row 6.
Repeat these 8 rows.

4 stitches

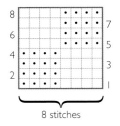

8 stitches

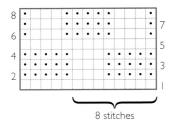

8 stitches

KNIT AND PURL STITCHES

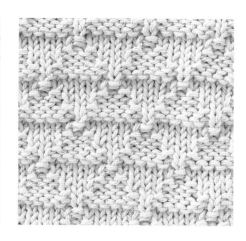

Double Basketweave

Multiple of 18 sts plus 10.
Row 1 (RS) Knit.
Row 2 P10, * p1, k2, p2, k2, p11; rep from * to end.
Row 3 * K1, p8, (k2, p2) twice, k1; rep from * to last 10 sts, k1, p8, k1.
Row 4 P1, k8, p1, * p1, (k2, p2) twice, k8, p1; rep from * to end.
Row 5 * K11, p2, k2, p2, k1; rep from * to last 10 sts, k10.
Row 6 As row 2.
Row 7 As row 3.
Row 8 As row 4.
Row 9 As row 5.
Row 10 Purl.
Row 11 * (K2, p2) twice, k10; rep from * to last 10 sts, k2, (p2, k2) twice.
Row 12 P2, (k2, p2) twice, * k8, p2, (k2, p2) twice; rep from * to end.
Row 13 * K2, (p2, k2) twice, p8; rep from * to last 10 sts, k2, (p2, k2) twice.
Row 14 P2, (k2, p2) twice, * p10, (k2, p2) twice; rep from * to end.
Row 15 As row 11.
Row 16 As row 12.
Row 17 As row 13.
Row 18 As row 14.
Repeat these 18 rows.

Pennant

Multiple of 7 sts plus 1.
Row 1 (RS) K1, * p1, k6; rep from * to end.
Row 2 * P5, k2; rep from * to last st, p1.
Row 3 K1, * p3, k4; rep from * to end.
Row 4 * P3, k4; rep from * to last st, p1.
Row 5 K1, * p5, k2; rep from * to end.
Row 6 P1, * k6, p1; rep from * to end.
Repeat these 6 rows.

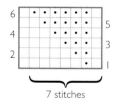

7 stitches

Pyramid

Multiple of 6 sts plus 1.
Row 1 (RS) * K1, p5; rep from * to last st, k1.
Row 2 P1, * k5, p1; rep from * to end.
Row 3 * K2, p3, k1; rep from * to last st, k1.
Row 4 P1, * p1, k3, p2; rep from * to end.
Row 5 * K3, p1, k2; rep from * to last st, k1.
Row 6 P1, * p2, k1, p3; rep from * to end.
Row 7 * P3, k1, p2; rep from * to last st, p1.
Row 8 K1, * k2, p1, k3; rep from * to end.
Row 9 * P2, k3, p1; rep from * to last st, p1.
Row 10 K1, * k1, p3, k2; rep from * to end.
Row 11 * P1, k5; rep from * to last st, p1.
Row 12 K1, * p5, k1; rep from * to end.
Repeat these 12 rows.

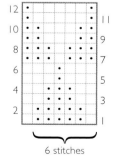

6 stitches

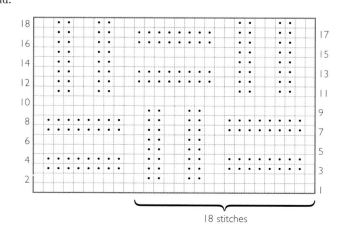

18 stitches

KEY

- p on RS rows, k on WS rows
- □ k on RS rows, p on WS rows

KNIT AND PURL STITCHES

Moss Stitch Diamonds

Multiple of 6 sts plus 1.
Row 1 (RS) * K3, p1, k2; rep from * to last st, k1.
Row 2 P1, * (p1, k1) twice, p2; rep from * to end.
Rows 3, 4 and 5 * K1, p1; rep from * to last st, k1.
Row 6 As row 2.
Repeat these 6 rows.

Moss Stitch Rib

Multiple of 10 sts plus 1.
Row 1 (RS) * K4, p1, k1, p1, k3; rep from * to last st, k1.
Row 2 P1, * p2, (k1, p3) twice; rep from * to end.
Row 3 * K2, (p1, k1) 4 times; rep from * to last st, k1.
Row 4 P1, * k1, p1, k1, p3, (k1, p1) twice; rep from * to end.
Row 5 As row 3.
Row 6 As row 2.
Repeat these 6 rows.

King Charles Brocade

Multiple of 12 sts plus 1.
Row 1 (RS) *K1, p1, k9, p1; rep from * to last st, k1.
Row 2 K1, * p1, k1, p7, k1, p1, k1; rep from * to end.
Row 3 * (K1, p1) twice, k5, p1, k1, p1; rep from * to last st, k1.
Row 4 P1, * (p1, k1) twice, p3, k1, p1, k1, p2; rep from * to end.
Row 5 * K3, p1, (k1, p1) 3 times, k2; rep from * to last st, k1.
Row 6 P1, * p3, k1, (p1, k1) twice, p4; rep from * to end.
Row 7 * K5, p1, k1, p1, k4; rep from * to last st, k1.
Row 8 As row 6.
Row 9 As row 5.
Row 10 As row 4.
Row 11 As row 3.
Row 12 As row 2.
Repeat these 12 rows.

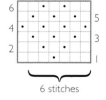

6 stitches

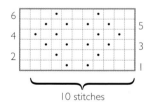

10 stitches

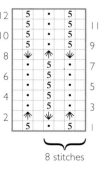

8 stitches

KEY
- • p on RS rows, k on WS rows
- ☐ k on RS rows, p on WS rows

KNIT AND PURL STITCHES

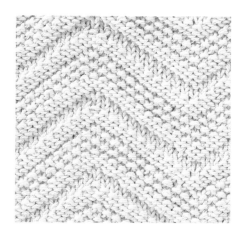

Stepped Diamonds

Multiple of 12 sts plus 2.
Row 1 (RS) * P2, k10; rep from * to last 2 sts, p2.
Row 2 K2, * p10, k2; rep from * to end.
Row 3 * K2, p2, k6, p2; rep from * to last 2 sts, k2.
Row 4 P2, * k2, p6, k2, p2; rep from * to end.
Row 5 * K4, p2, k2, p2, k2; rep from * to last 2 sts, k2.
Row 6 P2, * (p2, k2) twice, p4; rep from * to end.
Row 7 * K6, p2, k4; rep from * to last 2 sts, k2.
Row 8 P2, * p4, k2, p6; rep from * to end.
Row 9 As row 5.
Row 10 As row 6.
Row 11 As row 3.
Row 12 As row 4.
Repeat these 12 rows.

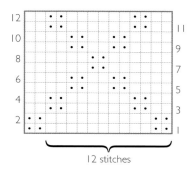

12 stitches

Mock Cable

(reversible)

Multiple of 10 sts.
Row 1 * P4, k1, p1, k4; rep from * to end.
Row 2 *P3, k2, p2, k3; rep from * to end.
Row 3 * P2, k2, p1, k1, p2, k2; rep from * to end.
Row 4 * P1, (k2, p2) twice, k1; rep from * to end.
Row 5 * K2, p3, k3, p2; rep from * to end.
Row 6 * K1, p4, k4, p1; rep from * to end.
Repeat these 6 rows.

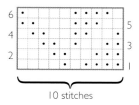

10 stitches

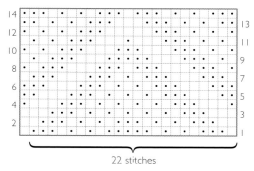

22 stitches

Moss Stitch Chevron

Multiple of 22 sts plus 1.
Row 1 (RS) * K1, p3, k1, (p1, k1) twice, p5, k1, (p1, k1) twice, p3; rep from * to last st, k1.
Row 2 P1, * p1, k3, p1, (k1, p1) twice, k3, p1, (k1, p1) twice, k3, p2; rep from * to end.
Row 3 * K3, p3, k1, (p1, k1) 5 times, p3, k2; rep from * to last st, k1.
Row 4 K1, * p3, k3, p1, (k1, p1) 4 times, k3, p3, k1; rep from * to end.
Row 5 * P2, k3, p3, k1, (p1, k1) 3 times, p3, k3, p1; rep from * to last st, p1.
Row 6 K1, * k2, p3, k3, p1, (k1, p1) twice, k3, p3, k3; rep from * to end.
Row 7 * K1, p3, k3, p3, k1, p1, k1, p3, k3, p3; rep from * to last st, k1.
Row 8 K1, * p1, k3, p3, k3, p1, k3, p3, k3, p1, k1; rep from * to end.
Row 9 * K1, p1, k1, p3, k3, p5, k3, p3, k1, p1; rep from * to last st, k1.
Row 10 K1, * p1, k1, p1, (k3, p3) twice, k3, (p1, k1) twice; rep from * to end.
Row 11 * K1, (p1, k1) twice, p3, k3, p1, k3, p3, (k1, p1) twice; rep from * to last st, k1.
Row 12 K1, * p1, (k1, p1) twice, k3, p5, k3, (p1, k1) 3 times; rep from * to end.
Row 13 * P2, k1, (p1, k1) twice, p3, k3, p3, (k1, p1) 3 times; rep from * to last st, p1.
Row 14 K1, * k2, p1, (k1, p1) twice, k3, p1, k3, p1, (k1, p1) twice, k3; rep from * to end.
Repeat these 14 rows.

KEY

- • p on RS rows, k on WS rows
- ☐ k on RS rows, p on WS rows

KNIT AND PURL STITCHES

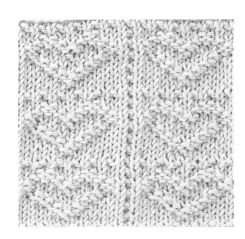

Small Gingham

(reversible)

Multiple of 10 sts plus 5.
Row 1 * P5, k1, (p1, k1) twice; rep from * to last 5 sts, p5.
Row 2 K5, * (k1, p1) twice, k6; rep from * to end.
Rows 3 to 6 Repeat rows 1 and 2 twice more.
Row 7 P1, (k1, p1) twice, * p6, (k1, p1) twice; rep from * to end.
Row 8 * P1, (k1, p1) twice, k5; rep from * to last 5 sts, p1, (k1, p1) twice.
Rows 9 to 12 Repeat rows 7 and 8 twice more.
Repeat these 12 rows.

Gingham Check

Multiple of 14 sts plus 9.
Row 1 (RS) * (K1, p1) 4 times, k1, p5; rep from * to last 9 sts, (k1, p1) 4 times, k1.
Row 2 (K1, p1) 4 times, k1, * k6, (p1, k1) 4 times; rep from * to end.
Rows 3 to 5 Repeat rows 1 and 2 once more then row 1 again.
Row 6 P9, * (p1, k1) twice, p10; rep from * to end.
Row 7 * K9, (p1, k1) twice, p1; rep from * to last 9 sts, k9.
Rows 8 to 15 Repeat rows 6 and 7 four times more.
Row 16 As row 6.
Repeat these 16 rows.

Heart Squares

Multiple of 14 sts plus 1.
Row 1 (RS) * P1, k1; rep from * to last st, p1.
Row 2 Purl.
Row 3 * P1, k6; rep from * to last st, p1.
Row 4 P1, * p5, k3, p6; rep from * to end.
Row 5 * P1, k4, p2, k1, p2, k4; rep from * to last st, p1.
Row 6 P1, * (p3, k2) twice, p4; rep from * to end.
Row 7 * P1, k2, p2, k5, p2, k2; rep from * to last st, p1.
Row 8 P1, * p1, k2, p3, k1, p3, k2, p2; rep from * to end.
Row 9 * P1, k1, p2, k2, p3, k2, p2, k1; rep from * to last st, p1.
Row 10 P1, * p2, k4, p1, k4, p3; rep from * to end.
Row 11 * P1, (k3, p2) twice, k3; rep from * to last st, p1.
Row 12 Purl.
Repeat these 12 rows.

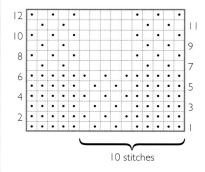

10 stitches

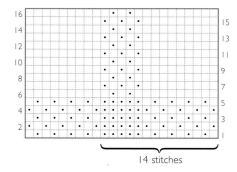

14 stitches

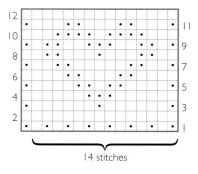

14 stitches

KEY

· p on RS rows, k on WS rows
□ k on RS rows, p on WS rows

KNIT AND PURL STITCHES

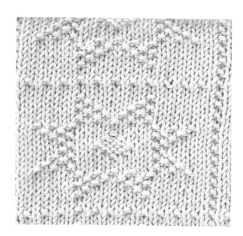

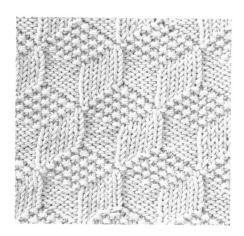

Star in a Square

Multiple of 24 sts plus 1.
Row 1 (RS) * P1, k1; rep from * to last st, p1.
Row 2 Purl.
Row 3 * P1, k23; rep from * to last st, p1.
Row 4 P1, * (p7, k1) twice, p8; rep from * to end.
Row 5 * P1, k8, p1, k5, p1, k8; rep from * to last st, p1.
Row 6 P1, * p7, k1, p1, k1, p3, k1, p1, k1, p8; rep from * to end.
Row 7 * P1, k8, p1, (k1, p1) 3 times, k8; rep from * to last st, p1.
Row 8 P1, * p7, k1, (p1, k1) 4 times, p8; rep from * to end.

Row 9 * P1, k2, p1, (k1, p1) twice, k9, p1, (k1, p1) twice, k2; rep from * to last st, p1.
Row 10 P1, * p3, k1, p1, k1, p11, k1, p1, k1, p4; rep from * to end.
Row 11 * P1, k4, p1, k1, (p1, k4) twice, p1, k1, p1, k4; rep from * to last st, p1.
Row 12 P1, * p5, k1, p4, k3, p4, k1, p6; rep from * to end.
Row 13 * P1, k6, p1, k2, p5, k2, p1, k6; rep from * to last st, p1.
Row 14 As row 12.
Row 15 As row 11.
Rows 16 to 23 Work from row 10 back to row 3.
Row 24 Purl.
Repeat these 24 rows.

Tumbling Blocks

Multiple of 10 sts.
Row 1 * K1, p1; rep from * to end.
Row 2 * P1, k1, p1, k2, p2, k1, p1, k1; rep from * to end.
Row 3 * K1, p1, k3, p3, k1, p1; rep from * to end.
Row 4 * P1, k4, p4, k1; rep from * to end.
Row 5 * K5, p5; rep from * to end.
Rows 6 to 8 Repeat row 5, 3 times more.
Row 9 * K4, p1, k1, p4; rep from * to end.
Row 10 * K3, (p1, k1) twice, p3; rep from * to end.
Row 11 * K2, (p1, k1) 3 times, p2; rep from * to end.
Row 12 * K1, p1; rep from * to end.
Row 13 * P1, k1; rep from * to end.
Row 14 * P2, (k1, p1) 3 times, k2; rep from * to end.
Row 15 * P3, (k1, p1) twice, k3; rep from * to end.
Row 16 * P4, k1, p1, k4; rep from * to end.
Row 17 * P5, k5; rep from * to end.
Rows 18 to 20 Repeat row 17, 3 times more.
Row 21 * K1, p4, k4, p1; rep from * to end.

Row 22 * P1, k1, p3, k3, p1, k1; rep from * to end.
Row 23 * K1, p1, k1, p2, k2, p1, k1, p1; rep from * to end.
Row 24 * P1, k1; rep from * to end.
Repeat these 24 rows.

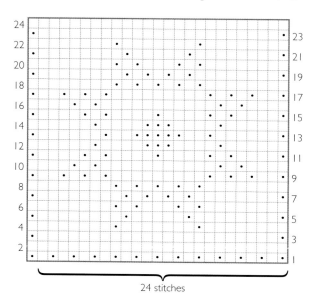

24 stitches

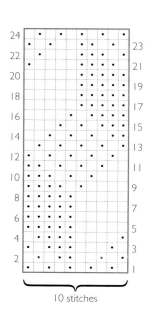

10 stitches

KNIT AND PURL STITCHES

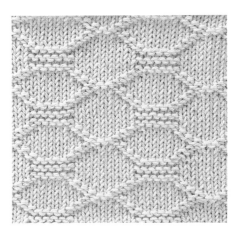

Star in a Diamond

Multiple of 32 sts plus 1.

Row 1 (RS) * P1, (k1, p1) 3 times, k9, p1, k9, (p1, k1) 3 times; rep from * to last st, p1.

Row 2 P1, * k1, (p1, k1) 3 times, p7, k1, p1, k1, p7, (k1, p1) 4 times; rep from * to end.

Row 3 * P1, (k1, p1) 4 times, k5, p1, k3, p1, k5, (p1, k1) 4 times; rep from * to last st, p1.

Row 4 P1, * k1, (p1, k1) 4 times, p3, k1, p5, k1, p3, (k1, p1) 5 times; rep from * to end.

Row 5 * P1, (k1, p1) 6 times, k7, (p1, k1) 6 times; rep from * to last st, p1.

Row 6 P1, * k1, p1, k1, p7, k1, p9, k1, p7, (k1, p1) twice; rep from * to end.

Row 7 * P1, (k1, p1) twice, k5, p1, k1, p1, k7, p1, k1, p1, k5, (p1, k1) twice; rep from * to last st, p1.

Row 8 P1, * k1, p1, k1, p5, k1, p3, k1, p5, k1, p3, k1, p5, (k1, p1) twice; rep from * to end.

Row 9 * K2, p1, k1, p1, (k3, p1) twice, k1,

p1, k3, p1, k1, (p1, k3) twice, (p1, k1) twice; rep from * to last st, k1.

Row 10 P1, * p2, k1, p3, k1, p5, (k1, p1) 3 times, k1, p5, (k1, p3) twice; rep from * to end.

Row 11 K4, p1, k1, p1, k5, p1, (k1, p1) 4 times, k5, p1, k1, p1, k3; rep from * to last st, k1.

Row 12 P1, * p4, k1, p7, k1, (p1, k1) 3 times, p7, k1, p5; rep from * to end.

Row 13 * K4, p1, (k1, p1) 12 times, k3; rep from * to last st, k1.

Row 14 P1, * p2, k1, p3, k1, (p1, k1) 9 times, p3, k1, p3; rep from * to end.

Row 15 * K2, p1, k5, p1, (k1, p1) 8 times, k5, p1, k1; rep from * to last st, k1.

Row 16 P1, * k1, p7, k1, (p1, k1) 7 times, p7, k1, p1; rep from * to end.

Row 17 * P1, k9, p1, (k1, p1) 6 times, k9; rep from * to last st, p1.

Row 18 As row 16.

Row 19 As row 15.

Rows 20 to 32 Work from row 14 back to row 2.

Block Quilting

Multiple of 14 sts.

Row 1 (RS) * K4, p6, k4; rep from * to end.

Row 2 Purl.

Rows 3 and 4 Repeat rows 1 and 2 once more.

Row 5 As row 1.

Row 6 * P3, k2, p4, k2, p3; rep from * to end.

Row 7 * K2, p2, k6, p2, k2; rep from * to end.

Row 8 * P1, k2, p8, k2, p1; rep from * to end.

Row 9 * P2, k10, p2; rep from * to end.

Row 10 As row 8.

Row 11 As row 7.

Row 12 As row 6.

Repeat these 12 rows.

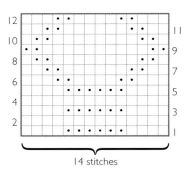

14 stitches

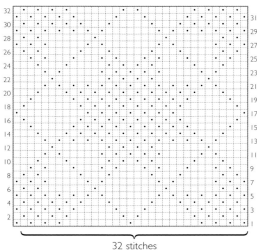

32 stitches

KEY

·   p on RS rows, k on WS rows

☐   k on RS rows, p on WS rows

GANSEY PATTERNS

Moss Stitch Ladder

Panel of 5 sts.
Row 1 (RS) P1, (k1, p1) twice.
Row 2 K5.
Repeat these 2 rows.

Two Stitch Ladder

Panel of 8 sts.
Row 1 (RS) P1, k1, p1, k2, p1, k1, p1.
Row 2 K1, p1, k1, p2, k1, p1, k1.
Row 3 P1, k1, p4, k1, p1.
Row 4 K1, p1, k4, p1, k1.
Repeat these 4 rows.

Ladder Stitch

Panel of 10 sts.
Row 1 (RS) P1, k8, p1.
Row 2 K1, p8, k1.
Row 3 P10.
Row 4 As row 2.
Repeat these 4 rows.

Panel of 5 stitches

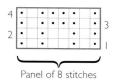

Panel of 8 stitches

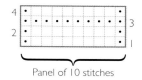

Panel of 10 stitches

Using gansey patterns

Gansey, Guernsey and Jersey are all names for the traditional sweater of fishermen of the British Isles. The stitches are worked in panels, either beginning above the rib or halfway up the body to form a yoke.

Simple ganseys have a repeat pattern of one wide panel, such as Inverness Diamond (page 102), and one narrow panel, such as Two Stitch Ladder (above).

More complicated patterns can be made by adding more narrow and wide panels to the repeat. Often ganseys will have a panel of a single four stitch cable to add more texture.

Patterns like Anchor (page 100), Tree (page 101) and Humber Star (page 102) can be separated by ridges of reverse stockinette (stocking) stitch to form squares.

KEY

• p on RS rows, k on WS rows

☐ k on RS rows, p on WS rows

GANSEY PATTERNS

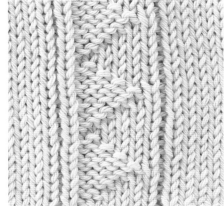

Anchor

Panel of 17 sts.
Row 1 (RS) K8, p1, k8.
Row 2 P7, k1, p1, k1, p7.
Row 3 K6, (p1, k1) twice, p1, k6.
Row 4 (P5, k1) twice, p5.
Row 5 K4, (p1, k3) twice, p1, k4.
Row 6 P3, k1, p9, k1, p3.
Row 7 K2, (p1, k5) twice, p1, k2.
Row 8 (P1, k1) twice, p9, (k1, p1) twice.
Row 9 K2, (p1, k5) twice, p1, k2.
Row 10 P1, k1, p13, k1, p1.
Row 11 K8, p1, k8.
Row 12 Purl.
Rows 13 and 14 Repeat rows 11 and 12 once more.
Row 15 K4, (p1, k1) 4 times, p1, k4.
Row 16 Purl.
Row 17 As row 1.
Row 18 As row 2.
Row 19 As row 1.
Row 20 Purl.
Row 21 Knit.
Row 22 Purl.
Repeat these 22 rows or work rows 1 to 20 for single motif.

Flags

Panel of 7 sts.
Row 1 (RS) K5, p1, k1.
Row 2 P1, k2, p4.
Row 3 K3, p3, k1.
Row 4 P1, k4, p2.
Row 5 K1, p5, k1.
Row 6 As row 4.
Row 7 As row 3.
Row 8 As row 2.
Repeat these 8 rows.

Lightning

Panel of 8 sts.
Row 1 (RS) K1, p2, k5.
Row 2 P4, k2, p2.
Row 3 K3, p2, k3.
Row 4 P2, k2, p4.
Row 5 K5, p2, k1.
Row 6 As row 4.
Row 7 As row 3.
Row 8 As row 2.
Repeat these 8 rows.

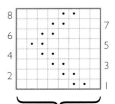

Panel of 8 stitches

Panel of 7 stitches

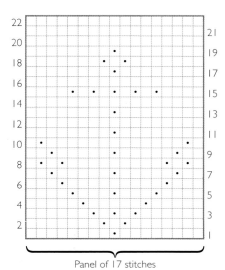

Panel of 17 stitches

KEY

- · p on RS rows, k on WS rows
- ☐ k on RS rows, p on WS rows

GANSEY PATTERNS

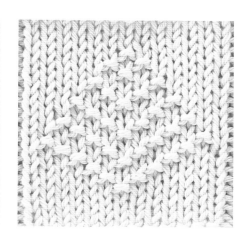

Marriage Lines

Panel of 11 sts.
Row 1 (RS) (K1, p1) twice, k7.
Row 2 P6, k1, p1, k1, p2.
Row 3 K3, p1, k1, p1, k5.
Row 4 P4, k1, p1, k1, p4.
Row 5 K5, p1, k1, p1, k3.
Row 6 P2, k1, p1, k1, p6.
Row 7 K7, (p1, k1) twice.
Row 8 As row 6.
Row 9 As row 5.
Row 10 As row 4.
Row 11 As row 3.
Row 12 As row 2.
Repeat these 12 rows.

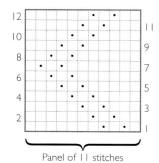

Panel of 11 stitches

Full Diamonds

Panel of 15 sts.
Row 1 (RS) K6, p3, k6.
Row 2 P5, k5, p5.
Row 3 K4, p7, k4.
Row 4 P3, k9, p3.
Row 5 K2, p11, k2.
Row 6 P1, k13, p1.
Row 7 As row 5.
Row 8 As row 4.
Row 9 As row 3.
Row 10 As row 2.
Repeat these 10 rows.

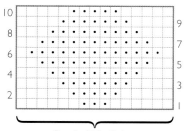

Panel of 15 stitches

Tree

Panel of 13 sts.
Row 1 (RS) K6, p1, k6.
Row 2 P5, k1, p1, k1, p5.
Row 3 K4, p1, k3, p1, k4.
Row 4 P3, (k1, p2) twice, k1, p3.
Row 5 (K2, p1) twice, k1, (p1, k2) twice.
Row 6 P1, k1, p2, k1, p3, k1, p2, k1, p1.
Row 7 K3, (p1, k2) twice, p1, k3.
Row 8 (P2, k1) twice, p1, (k1, p2) twice.
Row 9 As row 3.
Row 10 As row 4.
Row 11 K5, p1, k1, p1, k5.
Row 12 P4, k1, p3, k1, p4.
Row 13 As row 1.
Row 14 As row 2.
Row 15 As row 1.
Row 16 Purl.
Row 17 Knit.
Row 18 Purl.
Repeat these 18 rows or work rows 1 to 16 for single motif.

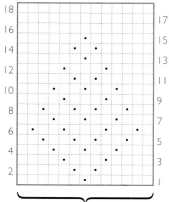

Panel of 13 stitches

GANSEY PATTERNS

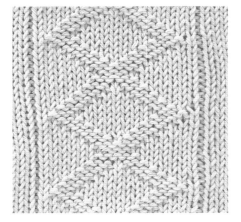

Inverness Diamonds

Panel of 17 sts.
Row 1 (RS) K7, p3, k7.
Row 2 P6, k5, p6.
Row 3 K5, p3, k1, p3, k5.
Row 4 P4, k3, p3, k3, p4.
Row 5 K3, p3, k5, p3, k3.
Row 6 P2, k3, p7, k3, p2.
Row 7 K1, p3, k9, p3, k1.
Rows 8 to 12 Work from row 6 back to row 2.
Repeat these 12 rows.

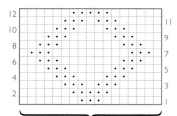

Panel of 17 stitches

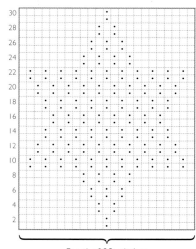

Panel of 23 stitches

Humber Star

Panel of 23 sts.
Row 1 (RS) K11, p1, k11.
Row 2 P11, k1, p11.
Row 3 K10, p1, k1, p1, k10.
Row 4 P10, k1, p1, k1, p10.
Row 5 K9, p1, (k1, p1) twice, k9.
Row 6 P9, k1, (p1, k1) twice, p9.
Row 7 K8, p1, (k1, p1) 3 times, k8.
Row 8 P8, k1, (p1, k1) 3 times, p8.
Row 9 K1, (p1, k1) 11 times.
Row 10 P1, (k1, p1) 11 times.
Row 11 K2, p1, (k1, p1) 9 times, k2.
Row 12 P2, k1, (p1, k1) 9 times, p2.
Row 13 K3, p1, (k1, p1) 8 times, k3.
Row 14 P3, k1, (p1, k1) 8 times, p3.
Row 15 K4, p1, (k1, p1) 7 times, k4.
Row 16 P4, k1, (p1, k1) 7 times, p4.
Row 17 As row 13.
Row 18 As row 14.
Row 19 As row 11.
Row 20 As row 12.
Row 21 As row 9.
Row 22 As row 10.
Row 23 As row 7.
Row 24 As row 8.
Row 25 As row 5.
Row 26 As row 6.
Row 27 As row 3.
Row 28 As row 4.
Row 29 As row 1.
Row 30 As row 2.
Repeat these 30 rows.

KEY

- · p on RS rows, k on WS rows
- □ k on RS rows, p on WS rows

Double Moss Stitch Diamond

Panel of 13 sts.
Row 1 (RS) K6, p1, k6.
Row 2 P6, k1, p6.
Row 3 K5, p1, k1, p1, k5.
Row 4 P5, k1, p1, k1, p5.
Row 5 K4, p1, (k1, p1) twice, k4.
Row 6 P4, k1, (p1, k1) twice, p4.
Row 7 K3, p1, (k1, p1) 3 times, k3.
Row 8 P3, k1, (p1, k1) 3 times, p3.
Row 9 K2, p1, k1, p1, k3, p1, k1, p1, k2.
Row 10 P2, k1, p1, k1, p3, k1, p1, k1, p2.
Row 11 (K1, p1) twice, k5, (p1, k1) twice.
Row 12 (P1, k1) twice, p5, (k1, p1) twice.
Row 13 As row 9.
Row 14 As row 10.
Row 15 As row 7.
Row 16 As row 8.
Row 17 As row 5.
Row 18 As row 6.
Row 19 As row 3.
Row 20 As row 4.
Repeat these 20 rows.

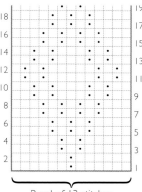

Panel of 13 stitches

TEXTURE STITCHES

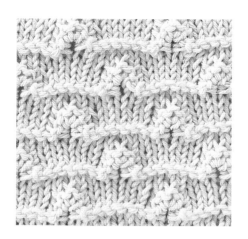

Ruching

On an odd number of stitches.
Row 1 (RS) Knit.
Row 2 Purl.
Rows 3 and 4 Repeat rows 1 and 2 once more.
Row 5 K1, * k into front and back of next st, k1; rep from * to end.
Row 6 Knit.
Row 7 Purl.
Rows 8 to 12 Repeat rows 6 and 7 twice more, then row 6 again.
Row 13 P1, * p2tog, p1; rep from * to end.
Row 14 Knit.
Repeat these 14 rows.

Bubble Pattern

Multiple of 10 sts plus 2.
Row 1 (RS) Knit.
Row 2 Purl.
Row 3 K1, * (k5, turn, p5, turn) 3 times, k10; rep from * to end, ending last rep with k1.
Row 4 Purl.
Row 5 Knit.
Row 6 Purl.
Row 7 K6, * (k5, turn, p5, turn) 3 times, k10; rep from * to last st, k1.
Row 8 Purl.
Repeat these 8 rows.

Textured Picot Stripe

Abbreviation:
M7 – (k1, yfwd, k1, yfwd, k1, yfwd, k1) all into next st.

Multiple of 8 sts plus 5 (stitch count varies).
Row 1 (RS) K2, * M7, k7; rep from * to last 3 sts, M7, k2.
Row 2 Knit.
Row 3 K1, * k2tog, k5, ssk, k5; rep from * to last 10 sts, k2tog, k5, ssk, k1.
Row 4 P1, * ssp, p1, sl 1 wyif, p1, p2tog, p5; rep from * to last 8 sts, ssp, p1, sl 1 wyif, p1, p2tog, p1.
Row 5 K1, * k2tog, sl 1 wyib, ssk, k5; rep from * to last 6 sts, k2tog, sl 1 wyib, ssk, k1.
Row 6 Purl.
Row 7 K2, * k4, M7, k3; rep from * to last 3 sts, k3.
Row 8 Knit.
Row 9 K2, * k3, k2tog, k5, ssk, k2; rep from * to last 3 sts, k3.
Row 10 P3, * p2, ssp, p1, sl 1 wyif, p1, p2tog, p3; rep from * to last 2 sts, p2.
Row 11 K2, * k3, k2tog, sl 1 wyib, ssk, k2; rep from * to last 3 sts, k3.
Row 12 Purl.
Repeat these 12 rows.

TEXTURE STITCHES

Popcorn Pattern

Abbreviations:

MK – purl next 3 sts then pass 2nd and 3rd sts over first st.

MS – (k1, p1, k1) all into next st.

Multiple of 4 sts plus 3 (stitch count varies).
Row 1 (RS) Knit.
Row 2 P1, MS, p1, * p2, MS, p1; rep from * to end.
Row 3 * K1, MK, k2; rep from * to last 5 sts, k1, MK, k1.
Row 4 Purl.
Row 5 Knit.
Row 6 P3, * MS, p3; rep from * to end.
Row 7 * K3, MK; rep from * to last 3 sts, k3.
Row 8 Purl.
Repeat these 8 rows.

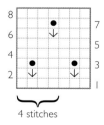

4 stitches

Bramble Stitch

Abbreviation:

MS – (k1, p1, k1) all into next st.

Multiple of 4 sts plus 2.
Row 1 (RS) Purl.
Row 2 K1, * MS, p3tog; rep from * to last st, k1.
Row 3 Purl.
Row 4 K1, * p3tog, MS; rep from * to last st, k1.
Repeat these 4 rows.

4 stitches

Smocking

Abbreviation:

smocking st – insert RH needle from front between 6th and 7th sts, wrap yarn around needle and draw through a loop, sl this loop on to LH needle and k tog with first st on LH needle.

Multiple of 16 sts plus 2.
Row 1 (RS) P2, * k2, p2; rep from * to end.
Row 2 * K2, p2; rep from * to last 2 sts, k2.
Row 3 P2, * smocking st, k1, p2, k2, p2; rep from * to end.
Rows 4 and 6 As row 2.
Row 5 As row 1.
Row 7 P2, k2, p2, * smocking st, k1, p2, k2, p2; rep from * to last 4 sts, k2, p2.
Row 8 As row 2.
Repeat these 8 rows.

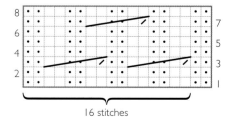

16 stitches

KEY

●	MK
↓	MS
·	p on RS rows, k on WS rows
□	k on RS rows, p on WS rows

KEY

↑	p3tog
↓	MS
·	p on RS rows, k on WS rows

KEY

·	p on RS rows, k on WS rows
□	k on RS rows, p on WS rows
╱	k2tog
╱	smocking stitch

TEXTURE STITCHES

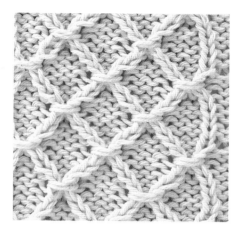

Smocked Honeycomb

Abbreviation:
tie st – sl next 5 sts on to cable needle, wrap yarn around these 5 sts twice, then k1, p3, k1 from cable needle.

Multiple of 16 sts plus 3.
Row 1 (RS) P3, * k1, p3; rep from * to end.
Row 2 * K3, p1; rep from * to last 3 sts, k3.
Row 3 P3, * tie st, p3; rep from * to end.
Rows 4 and 6 As row 2.
Row 5 As row 1.
Row 7 P3, k1, * p3, tie st; rep from * to end, ending last rep with k1, p3.
Row 8 As row 2.
Repeat these 8 rows.

Boxed Bobble

Abbreviation:
MB – k into front, back and front of next st and turn, k3 and turn, p3 and pass 2nd and 3rd sts over first st.

Multiple of 6 sts plus 1.
Row 1 (RS) Purl.
Row 2 and every foll alt row Purl.
Row 3 P1, * k5, p1; rep from * to end.
Row 5 P1, * k2, MB, k2, p1; rep from * to end.
Row 7 As row 3.
Row 8 Purl.
Repeat these 8 rows.

Gooseberry Stitch

Abbreviation:
M5 – (p1, yo, p1, yo, p1) all into next st.

Multiple of 4 sts plus 1.
Row 1 (RS) Knit.
Row 2 K1, * M5, k1; rep from * to end.
Row 3 Purl.
Row 4 K1, * sl 2 wyif, p3tog, psso, k1; rep from * to end.
Row 5 Knit.
Row 6 K1, * k1, M5, k1; rep from * to last st, k1.
Row 7 Purl.
Row 8 K1, * k1, sl 2 wyif, p3tog, psso, k1; rep from * to last st, k1.
Repeat these 8 rows.

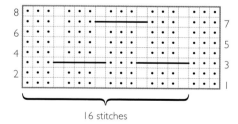

16 stitches

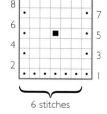

6 stitches

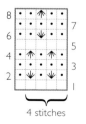

4 stitches

KEY

·	p on RS rows, k on WS rows
☐	k on RS rows, p on WS rows
—	tie stitch

KEY

■	MB
·	p on RS rows, k on WS rows
☐	k on RS rows, p on WS rows

KEY

↑	sl 2 wyif, p3tog, psso
↓	M5
·	p on RS rows, k on WS rows
☐	k on RS rows, p on WS rows

TEXTURE STITCHES

Dimple Stitch

Abbreviation:

gathering st – take yarn to back of work as though to knit, insert needle from below under 3 strands, k the next st, bring the st out under the strands.

Multiple of 6 sts plus 5.
Row 1 (RS) Knit.
Row 2 P1, * sl 3 wyif, p3; rep from * to end, ending last rep with p1.
Row 3 K1, * sl 3 wyib, k3; rep from * to end, ending last rep with k1.

Row 4 As row 2.
Rows 5 and 7 Knit.
Row 6 Purl.
Row 8 P2, * gathering st, p5; rep from * to end, ending last rep with p2.
Row 9 Knit.
Row 10 P1, * p3, sl 3 wyif; rep from * to last 4 sts, p4.
Row 11 K4, * sl 3 wyif, k3; rep from * to last st, k1.
Row 12 As row 10.
Rows 13 and 15 Knit.
Row 14 Purl.
Row 16 P5, * gathering st, p5; rep from * to end.
Repeat these 16 rows.

Bobble Circle Pattern

Abbreviation:

MS – (k1, p1, k1) all into next st.

Multiple of 12 sts plus 3.
Row 1 (RS) Knit.
Row 2 * P6, MS, p1, MS, p3; rep from * to last 3 sts, p3.
Row 3 K3, * k3, p3, k1, p3, k6; rep from * to end.
Row 4 * P4, MS, (p1, p3tog) twice, p1, MS, p1; rep from * to last 3 sts, p3.
Row 5 K3, * k1, p3, k5, p3, k4; rep from * to end.
Row 6 * P3, MS, p3tog, p5, p3tog, MS; rep from * to last 3 sts, p3.

Row 7 K3, * p3, k7, p3, k3; rep from * to end.
Row 8 * P3, p3tog, p7, p3tog; rep from * to last 3 sts, p3.
Row 9 Knit.
Row 10 * P3, MS, p7, MS; rep from * to last 3 sts, p3.
Row 11 As row 7.
Row 12 * P3, p3tog, MS, p5, MS, p3tog; rep from * to last 3 sts, p3.
Row 13 As row 5.
Row 14 * P4, p3tog, (p1, MS) twice, p1, p3tog, p1; rep from * to last 3 sts, p3.
Row 15 As row 3.
Row 16 * P6, p3tog, p1, p3tog, p3; rep from * to last 3 sts, p3.
Row 17 Knit.
Row 18 Purl.
Repeat these 18 rows.

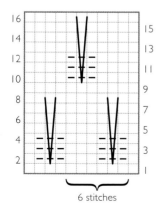

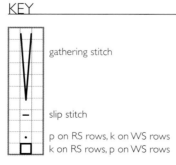

KEY

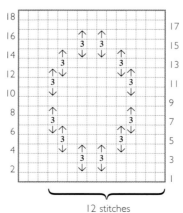

gathering stitch

— slip stitch

. p on RS rows, k on WS rows
☐ k on RS rows, p on WS rows

KEY

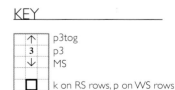

↑ p3tog
3 p3
↓ MS
☐ k on RS rows, p on WS rows

12 stitches

TEXTURE STITCHES

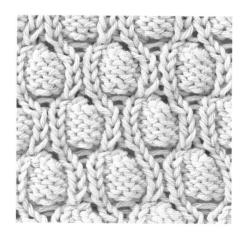

Cocoon Stitch

Abbreviation:
M5 – (p1, yo, p1, yo, p1) all into next st.

Multiple of 8 sts plus 7.
Row 1 (RS) * K1, p5, k1, p1; rep from *
to last 7 sts, k1, p5, k1.
Row 2 P1, sl 2 wyif, p3tog, psso, p1, *
M5, p1, sl 2 wyif, p3tog, psso, p1; rep
from * to end.
Rows 3, 5 and 7 * K1, p1, k1, p5; rep
from * to last 3 sts, k1, p1, k1.
Rows 4 and 6 P1, k1, p1, * k5, p1, k1,
p1; rep from * to end.
Row 8 P1, M5, p1, * sl 2 wyif, p3tog,
psso, p1, M5, p1; rep from * to end.
Row 9 As row 1.
Row 10 P1, k5, p1, * k1, p1, k5, p1; rep
from * to end.
Row 11 As row 1.
Row 12 As row 10.
Repeat these 12 rows.

Blind Buttonhole Stitch

Multiple of 8 sts plus 6.
Row 1 (WS) Knit.
Row 2 Purl.
Rep these 2 rows once more then row 1
again.
Row 6 K1, * sl 4 wyib, k4; rep from * to
last 5 sts, sl 4 wyib, k1.
Row 7 P1, sl 4 wyif, * p4, sl 4 wyif; rep
from * to last st, p1.
Rep these 2 rows once more then row 6
again.
Row 11 Knit.
Row 12 Purl.
Rep these 2 rows once more then row 11
again.
Row 16 K5, * sl 4 wyib, k4; rep from * to
last st, k1.
Row 17 P5, * sl 4 wyif, p4; rep from * to
last st, p1.
Rep these 2 rows once more.
Row 20 As row 16.
Repeat these 20 rows.

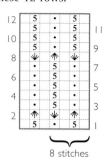

KEY

5	p5 on RS rows, k5 on WS rows
↑	sl 2 wyif, p3tog, psso
↓	M5
•	p on RS rows, k on WS rows
☐	k on RS rows, p on WS rows

RIB STITCHES

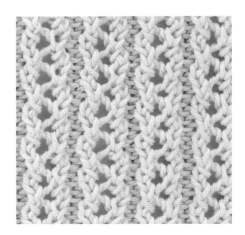

Mistake Rib

Multiple of 4 sts plus 3.
Row 1 * K2, p2; rep from * to last 3 sts, k2, p1.
Repeat this row.

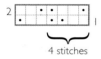

4 stitches

KEY

- · p on RS rows, k on WS rows
- ☐ k on RS rows, p on WS rows

Rick Rack Rib

Abbreviations:
twist k – take RH needle behind first st and k into back of second st, k first st, slip both sts off LH needle.
twist p – with yarn in front, miss first st and p into second st, p first st, sl both sts off LH needle together.

Multiple of 5 sts plus 1.
Row 1 (RS) K1, * p1, twist k, p1, k1; rep from * to end.
Row 2 * P1, k1, twist p, k1; rep from * to last st, p1.
Repeat these 2 rows.

5 stitches

KEY

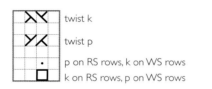

✕✕	twist k
⅄⅄	twist p
·	p on RS rows, k on WS rows
☐	k on RS rows, p on WS rows

Openwork Rib

Multiple of 5 sts plus 2.
Row 1 (RS) P2, * k1, yo, ssk, p2; rep from * to end.
Row 2 * K2, p3; rep from * to last 2 sts, k2.
Row 3 P2, * k2tog, yo, k1, p2; rep from * to end.
Row 4 As row 2.
Repeat these 4 rows.

5 stitches

KEY

o	yo
╱	k2tog
╲	ssk
·	p on RS rows, k on WS rows
☐	k on RS rows, p on WS rows

RIB STITCHES

Brioche Stitch

Even number of sts.
Foundation row * Yo, sl 1 wyib, k1; rep from * to end.
Row 1 * Yo, sl 1 wyib, k2tog (sl st and yo of previous row); rep from * to end.
Repeat row 1.

Aran Rib 1

Abbreviation:
Cr3L – slip 1 st on to cable needle at front, k1 tbl, p1, then k1 tbl from cable needle.

Multiple of 8 sts plus 3.
Row 1 (RS) * K3, (p1, k1 tbl) twice, p1; rep from * to last 3 sts, k3.
Row 2 P3, * (k1, p1 tbl) twice, k1; rep from * to end.
Row 3 * K3, p1, Cr3L, p1; rep from * to last 3 sts, k3.
Row 5 As row 1.
Row 6 As row 2.
Repeat these 6 rows.

KEY

Cr3L

· p on RS rows, k on WS rows
☐ k on RS rows, p on WS rows

Aran Rib 2

Abbreviations:
Cr2L – slip 1 st on to cable needle at front, p1, k1 tbl from cable needle.
Cr2R – slip 1 st on to cable needle at back, k1 tbl, p1 from cable needle.

Multiple of 7 sts plus 4.
Row 1 (RS) * K4, Cr2L, p1; rep from * to last 4 sts, k4.
Row 2 P4, * k1, p1 tbl, k1, p4; rep from * to end.
Row 3 * K4, p1, Cr2L; rep from * to last 4 sts, k4.
Row 4 P4, * p1 tbl, k2, p4; rep from * to end.
Row 5 * K4, p1, Cr2R; rep from * to last 4 sts, k4.
Row 6 As row 2.
Row 7 * K4, Cr2R, p1; rep from * to last 4 sts, k4.
Row 8 P4, * k2, p1 tbl, p4; rep from * to end.
Repeat these 8 rows.

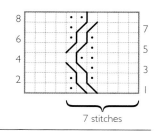

7 stitches

KEY

Cr2R

Cr2L

· p on RS rows, k on WS rows
☐ k on RS rows, p on WS rows

CABLE STITCHES

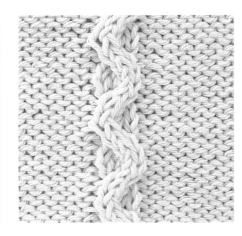

Four Stitch Cable

(crossed every 4th row)

Abbreviation:
C4F – sl 2 sts on to cable needle at front, k2, k2 from cable needle.

Panel of 4 sts on rev st st.
Row 1 (RS) K4.
Row 2 P4.
Row 3 C4F.
Row 4 P4.
Repeat these 4 rows.

Four Stitch Cable

(crossed every 6th row)

Abbreviation: C4F – sl 2 sts on to cable needle at front, k2, k2 from cable needle.

Panel of 4 sts on rev st st.
Rows 1 and 3 (RS) K4.
Rows 2 and 4 P4.
Row 5 C4F.
Row 6 P4.
Repeat these 6 rows.

To cross the cable to the right work C4B instead of C4F.
Abbreviation:
C4B – sl 2 sts on to cable needle at back, k2, k2 from cable needle.

Six Stitch Cable

(crossed every 6th row)

Abbreviation:
C6F – sl 3 sts on to cable needle at front, k3, k3 from cable needle.

Panel of 6 sts on rev st st.
Rows 1 and 3 (RS) K6.
Row 2 and every foll WS row P6.
Row 5 C6F.
Row 6 P6.
Repeat these 6 rows.

Six Stitch Cable

(crossed every 8th row)

Abbreviation:
C6F – sl 3 sts on to cable needle at front, k3, k3 from cable needle.

Panel of 6 sts on rev st st.
Rows 1, 3 and 5 (RS) K6.
Row 2 and every foll WS row P6.
Row 7 C6F.
Row 8 P6.
Repeat these 8 rows.

To cross the cable to the right work C6B instead of C6F.
Abbreviation:
C6B – sl 3 sts on to cable needle at back, k3, k3 from cable needle.

Four Stitch Wave Cable

Abbreviations:
C4F – sl 2 sts on to cable needle at front, k2, k2 from cable needle.
C4B – sl 2 sts on to cable needle at back, k2, k2 from cable needle.

Panel of 4 sts on rev st st.
Rows 1 and 5 (RS) K4.
Row 2 and every foll WS row P4.
Row 3 C4F.
Row 7 C4B.
Row 8 P4.
Repeat these 8 rows.

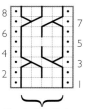

Panel of 4 stitches

KEY

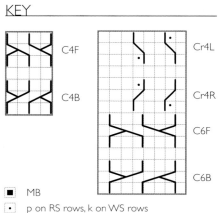

C4F
C4B
Cr4L
Cr4R
C6F
C6B

■ MB
· p on RS rows, k on WS rows
□ k on RS rows, p on WS rows

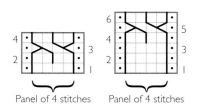

Panel of 4 stitches   Panel of 4 stitches

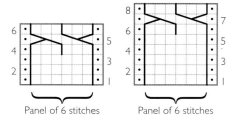

Panel of 6 stitches   Panel of 6 stitches

CABLE STITCHES

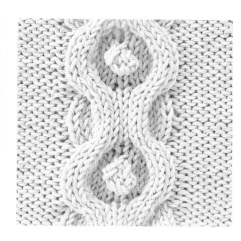

Ensign's Braid

Abbreviations:
Cr4L – sl 3 sts on to cable needle at front, p1, k3 from cable needle.
Cr4R – sl 1 st on to cable needle at back, k3, p1 from cable needle.
C6F – sl 3 sts on to cable needle at front, k3, k3 from cable needle.
C6B – sl 3 sts on to cable needle at back, k3, k3 from cable needle.

Panel of 20 sts on rev st st.
Row 1 (RS) K3, p4, C6B, p4, k3.
Row 2 and every foll WS row K all k sts and p all p sts.
Row 3 (Cr4L, p2, Cr4R) twice.
Row 5 (P1, Cr4L, Cr4R, p1) twice.
Row 7 P2, C6F, p4, C6B, p2.
Row 9 (P1, Cr4R, Cr4L, p1) twice.
Row 11 (Cr4R, p2, Cr4L) twice.
Row 13 K3, p4, C6F, p4, k3.
Row 15 As row 3.
Row 17 As row 5.
Row 19 P2, C6B, p4, C6F, p2.
Row 21 As row 9.
Row 23 As row 11.
Row 24 (P3, k4, p3) twice.
Repeat these 24 rows.

Oxo Cable

Abbreviations:
C4F – sl 2 sts on to cable needle at front, k2, k2 from cable needle.
C4B – sl 2 sts on to cable needle at back, k2, k2 from cable needle.

Panel of 8 sts on rev st st.
Row 1 (RS) K8.
Row 2 P8.
Row 3 C4B, C4F.
Row 4 P8.
Rows 5 to 8 As rows 1 to 4.
Row 9 K8.
Row 10 P8.
Row 11 C4F, C4B.
Row 12 P8.
Rows 13 to 16 As rows 9 to 12.
Repeat these 16 rows.

Medallion Bobble Cable

Abbreviation:
MB – (k1, p1) twice into next st and turn, p4 and turn, k4 and turn, (p2tog) twice and turn, k2tog.
C6F – sl 3 sts on to cable needle at front, k3, k3 from cable needle.
C6B – sl 3 sts on to cable needle at back, k3, k3 from cable needle.

Panel of 15 sts.
Rows 1, 3, 7, 11 and 15 (RS) P1, k13, p1.
Row 2 and every foll WS row K1, p13, k1.
Row 5 P1, C6B, k1, C6F, p1.
Row 9 P1, k6, MB, k6, p1.
Row 13 P1, C6F, k1, C6B, p1.
Row 16 As row 2.
Repeat these 16 rows.

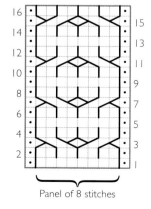

Panel of 8 stitches

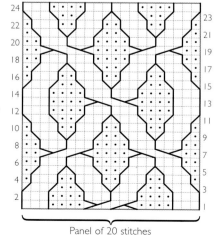

Panel of 20 stitches

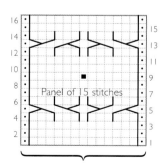

Panel of 15 stitches

CABLE STITCHES

Five Rib Braid

Abbreviations:

C5F – sl 3 sts on to cable needle at front, k2, sl p st back on to LH needle and p it, k2 from cable needle.

C5B – sl 3 sts on to cable needle at back, k2, sl p st back on to LH needle and p it, k2 from cable needle.

Panel of 18 sts on rev st st.
Row 1 (RS) P2, (k2, p1) 5 times, p1.
Row 2 and every foll WS row K2, (p2, k1) 5 times, k1.
Row 3 P2, k2, (p1, C5F) twice, p2.
Row 5 As row 1.
Row 7 P2, (C5B, p1) twice, k2, p2.
Row 8 As row 2.
Repeat these 8 rows.

Celtic Cable

Abbreviations:

Cr3L – sl 2 sts on to cable needle at front, p1, k2 from cable needle.

Cr3R – sl 1 st on to cable needle at back, k2, p1 from cable needle.

Cr4L – sl 2 sts on to cable needle at front, p2, k2 from cable needle.

Cr4R – sl 2 sts on to cable needle at back, k2, p2 from cable needle.

C4F – sl 2 sts on to cable needle at front, k2, k2 from cable needle.

C4B – sl 2 sts on to cable needle at back, k2, k2 from cable needle.

Panel of 24 sts on rev st st.
Row 1 (RS) (P2, C4B, p2) 3 times.
Row 2 and every foll WS row K all k sts and p all p sts.
Row 3 P1, Cr3R, (Cr4L, Cr4R) twice, Cr3L, p1.
Row 5 Cr3R, p1, (p2, C4F, p2) twice, p1, Cr3L.
Row 7 K2, p2, (Cr4R, Cr4L) twice, p2, k2.
Row 9 (K2, p2) twice, p2, C4B, p2, (p2, k2) twice.
Row 11 K2, p2, (Cr4L, Cr4R) twice, p2, k2.
Row 13 Cr3L, p1, (p2, C4F, p2) twice, p1, Cr3R.
Row 15 P1, Cr3L, (Cr4R, Cr4L) twice, Cr3R, p1.
Row 16 (K2, p4, k2) 3 times.
Repeat these 16 rows.

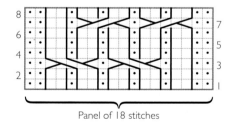

Panel of 18 stitches

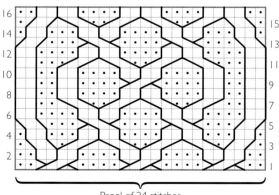

Panel of 24 stitches

CABLE STITCHES

Triple Twist Cable

Abbreviations:

Cr4L – sl 2 sts on to cable needle at front, p2, k2 from cable needle.
Cr4R – sl 2 sts on to cable needle at back, k2, p2 from cable needle.
C4F – sl 2 sts on to cable needle at front, k2, k2 from cable needle.
C4B – sl 2 sts on to cable needle at back, k2, k2 from cable needle.

Panel of 24 sts on rev st st.
Row 1 (RS) (P2, C4B, p2) 3 times.
Row 2 and every foll WS row K all k sts and p all p sts.
Row 3 Cr4R, Cr4L, p2, k4, p2, Cr4R, Cr4L.
Row 5 K2, p4, k2, p2, C4B, p2, k2, p4, k2.
Row 7 Cr4L, Cr4R, p2, k4, p2, Cr4L, Cr4R.
Row 9 As row 1.
Row 11 (Cr4R, Cr4L) 3 times.
Row 13 K2, (p4, C4F) twice, p4, k2.
Row 15 (Cr4L, Cr4R) 3 times.
Row 16 (K2, p4, k2) 3 times.
Repeat these 16 rows.

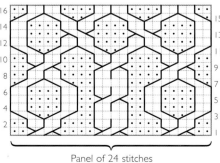

Panel of 24 stitches

Hollow Oak

Abbreviations:

MB – (k1, k1 tbl, k1, k1 tbl, k1) all into next st, pass 2nd, 3rd, 4th and 5th sts over first.
Cr3L – sl 2 sts on to cable needle at front, p1, k2 from cable needle.
Cr3R – sl 1 st on to cable needle at back, k2, p1 from cable needle.
C3F – sl 2 sts on to cable needle at front, k1, k2 from cable needle.
C3B – sl 1 st on to cable needle at back, k2, k1 from cable needle.

Panel of 11 sts on rev st st.
Row 1 (RS) P3, k2, MB, k2, p3.
Rows 2, 4 and 6 K3, p5, k3.
Row 3 P3, MB, k3, MB, p3.
Row 5 As row 1.
Row 7 P2, C3B, p1, C3F, p2.
Row 8 K2, p2, k1, p1, k1, p2, k2.
Row 9 P1, Cr3R, k1, p1, k1, Cr3L, p1.
Row 10 K1, p3, k1, p1, k1, p3, k1.
Row 11 C3B, (p1, k1) twice, p1, C3F.
Row 12 P2, (k1, p1) 4 times, p1.
Row 13 K3, (p1, k1) 3 times, k2.
Row 14 As row 12.
Row 15 Cr3L, (p1, k1) twice, p1, Cr3R.
Row 16 As row 10.
Row 17 P1, Cr3L, k1, p1, k1, Cr3R, p1.
Row 18 As row 8.
Row 19 P2, Cr3L, p1, Cr3R, p2.
Row 20 As row 2.
Repeat these 20 rows.

KEY

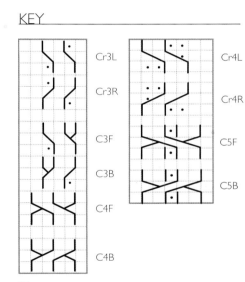

Cr3L
Cr3R
C3F
C3B
C4F
C4B

Cr4L
Cr4R
C5F
C5B

■ MB

· p on RS rows, k on WS rows

☐ k on RS rows, p on WS rows

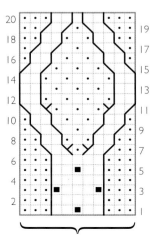

Panel of 11 stitches

CABLE STITCHES

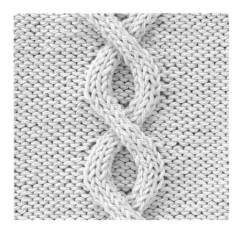

Circle Cable

Abbreviations:
Cr4L – sl 3 sts on to cable needle at front, p1, k3 from cable needle.
Cr4R – sl 1 st on to cable needle at back, k3, p1 from cable needle.
Cr5L – sl 3 sts on to cable needle at front, p2, k3 from cable needle.
Cr5R – sl 2 sts on to cable needle at back, k3, p2 from cable needle.
C6F – sl 3 sts on to cable needle at front, k3, k3 from cable needle.

Panel of 12 sts on rev st st.
Row 1 (RS) P1, Cr5R, Cr5L, p1.
Row 2 and every foll WS row K all k sts and p all p sts.
Row 3 Cr4R, p4, Cr4L.
Row 5 K3, p6, k3.
Row 7 Cr4L, p4, Cr4R.
Row 9 P1, Cr5L, Cr5R, p1.
Row 11 P3, C6F, p3.
Row 12 K3, p6, k3.
Repeat these 12 rows.

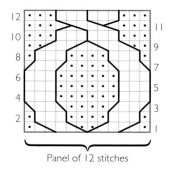

Panel of 12 stitches

Ripple and Rock

Abbreviations:
MB – (k1, yfwd, k1, yfwd, k1) all into next st, turn and p5, turn and k5, turn and p2tog, p1, p2tog, turn and k3tog.
Cr3L – sl 2 sts on to cable needle at front, p1, k2 from cable needle.
Cr3R – sl 1 st on to cable needle at back, k2, p1 from cable needle.

Panel of 13 sts on rev st st.
Row 1 (RS) P3, Cr3R, p1, Cr3L, p3.
Row 2 and every foll WS row K all k sts and p all p sts.
Row 3 P2, Cr3R, p3, Cr3L, p2.
Row 5 P1, Cr3R, p5, Cr3L, p1.
Row 7 Cr3R, p7, Cr3L.
Row 9 Cr3L, p7, Cr3R.
Row 11 P1, Cr3L, p5, Cr3R, p1.
Row 13 P2, Cr3L, p3, Cr3R, p2.
Row 15 P3, Cr3L, p1, Cr3R, p3.
Row 17 As row 1.
Row 19 As row 3.
Row 21 P2, k2, p2, MB, p2, k2, p2.
Row 23 As row 13.
Row 25 As row 15.
Row 26 K4, p2, k1, p2, k4.
Repeat these 26 rows.

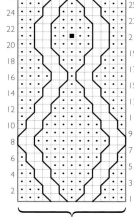

Panel of 13 stitches

Braid Cable

Abbreviations:
Cr3L – sl 2 sts on to cable needle at front, p1, k2 from cable needle.
Cr3R – sl 1 st on to cable needle at back, k2, p1 from cable needle.
C4F – sl 2 sts on to cable needle at front, k2, k2 from cable needle.
C4B – sl 2 sts on to cable needle at back, k2, k2 from cable needle.

Panel of 9 sts on rev st st.
Row 1 (RS) Cr3L, Cr3R, Cr3L.
Row 2 and every foll WS row K all k sts and p all p sts.
Row 3 P1, C4B, p2, k2.
Row 5 Cr3R, Cr3L, Cr3R.
Row 7 K2, p2, C4F, p1.
Row 8 K1, p4, k2, p2.
Repeat these 8 rows.

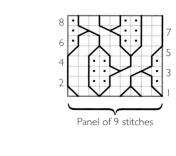

Panel of 9 stitches

CABLE STITCHES

Trellis Diamond

Abbreviations:

Cr2L – sl 1 st on to cable needle at front, p1, k1 from cable needle.

Cr2R – sl 1 st on to cable needle at back, k1, p1 from cable needle.

Cr3L – sl 2 sts on to cable needle at front, p1, k2 from cable needle.

Cr3R – sl 1 st on to cable needle at back, k2, p1 from cable needle.

Cr4L – sl 3 sts on to cable needle at front, p1, k3 from cable needle.

Cr4R – sl 1 st on to cable needle at back, k3, p1 from cable needle.

C2FP – sl 1 st on to cable needle at WS, p1, p1 from cable needle.

C2BP – sl 1 st on to cable needle at RS, p1, p1 from cable needle.

C6F – sl 3 sts on to cable needle at front, k3, k3 from cable needle.

Panel of 18 sts on rev st st.

Row 1 (RS) P5, Cr4R, Cr4L, p5.

Row 2 and every foll WS row except rows 10, 14 and 18 K all k sts and p all p sts.

Row 3 P4, Cr4R, p2, Cr4L, p4.

Row 5 P3, Cr3R, k1, p4, k1, Cr3L, p3.

Row 7 P2, Cr3R, p1, Cr2L, p2, Cr2R, p1, Cr3L, p2.

Row 9 P1, Cr2R, k1, p3, Cr2L, Cr2R, p3, k1, Cr2L, p1.

Row 10 (K1, p1) twice, k4, C2FP, k4, (p1, k1) twice.

Row 11 Cr2R, p1, (Cr2L, p2, Cr2R) twice, p1, Cr2L.

Row 13 K1, p3, (Cr2L, Cr2R, p2) twice, p1, k1.

Row 14 P1, (k4, C2BP) twice, k4, p1.

Row 15 K1, p3, (Cr2R, Cr2L, p2) twice, p1, k1.

Row 17 Cr2L, p1, (Cr2R, p2, Cr2L) twice, p1, Cr2R.

Row 18 As row 10.

Row 19 P1, Cr2L, k1, p3, Cr2R, Cr2L, p3, k1, Cr2R, p1.

Row 21 P2, Cr3L, p1, Cr2R, p2, Cr2L, p1, Cr3R, p2.

Row 23 P3, Cr3L, k1, p4, k1, Cr3R, p3.

Row 25 P4, Cr4L, p2, Cr4R, p4.

Row 27 P5, Cr4L, Cr4R, p5.

Row 29 P6, C6F, p6.

Row 30 K6, p6, k6.

Repeat these 30 rows.

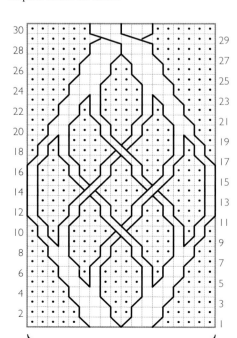

Panel of 18 stitches

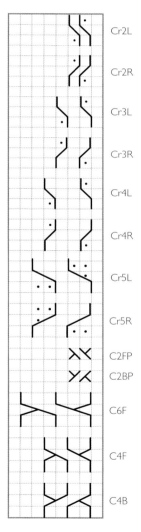

Cr2L
Cr2R
Cr3L
Cr3R
Cr4L
Cr4R
Cr5L
Cr5R
C2FP
C2BP
C6F
C4F
C4B

■ MB

· p on RS rows, k on WS rows

☐ k on RS rows, p on WS rows

CABLE STITCHES

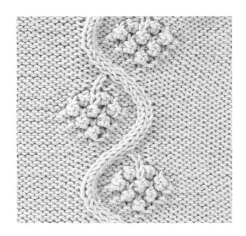

Grapes on the Vine

Abbreviations:

MS – (k1, p1, k1) all into next st.

Cr2L – sl 1 st on to cable needle at front, p1, k1 from cable needle.

Cr2R – sl 1 st on to cable needle at back, k1, p1 from cable needle.

Cr3L – sl 2 sts on to cable needle at front, p1, k2 from cable needle.

Cr3R – sl 1 st on to cable needle at back, k2, p1 from cable needle.

Cr4L – sl 2 sts on to cable needle at front, p2, k2 from cable needle.

Cr4R – sl 2 sts on to cable needle at back, k2, p2 from cable needle.

Panel of 14 sts on rev st st (stitch count varies on some rows).

Row 1 (RS) P3, Cr3L, p4, k1, p3.

Rows 2, 4, 16 and 18 K all k sts and p all p sts.

Row 3 P4, Cr4L, p1, Cr2R, p3.

Row 5 P3, k1, p2, Cr4L, p4.

Row 6 K4, p2, k4, MS, k3. 16 sts.

Row 7 P2, (k1, p3) twice, Cr3L, p3.

Row 8 K3, p2, k4, MS, p3tog, MS, k2. 18 sts.

Row 9 P1, (k1, p3) 3 times, Cr3L, p2.

Row 10 K2, p2, k4, MS, (p3tog, MS) twice, k1. 20 sts.

Row 11 (K1, p3) 4 times, k2, p2.

Row 12 K2, p2, k4, p3tog, (MS, p3tog) twice, k1. 18 sts.

Row 13 P1, (k1, p3) 3 times, Cr3R, p2.

Row 14 K3, p2, k4, p3tog, p1, p3tog, k2. 14 sts.

Row 15 P3, k1, p4, Cr3R, p3.

Row 17 P3, Cr2L, p1, Cr4R, p4.

Row 19 P4, Cr4R, p2, k1, p3.

Row 20 K3, MS, k4, p2, k4. 16 sts.

Row 21 P3, Cr3R, (p3, k1) twice, p2.

Row 22 K2, MS, p3tog, MS, k4, p2, k3. 18 sts.

Row 23 P2, Cr3R, (p3, k1) 3 times, p1.

Row 24 K1, MS, (p3tog, MS) twice, k4, p2, k2. 20 sts.

Row 25 P2, k2, (p3, k1) 4 times.

Row 26 K1, p3tog, (MS, p3tog) twice, k4, p2, k2. 18 sts.

Row 27 P2, Cr3L, (p3, k1) 3 times, p1.

Row 28 K2, p3tog, p1, p3tog, k4, p2, k3. 14 sts.

Repeat these 28 rows.

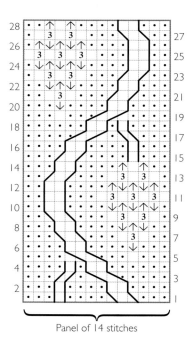

Panel of 14 stitches

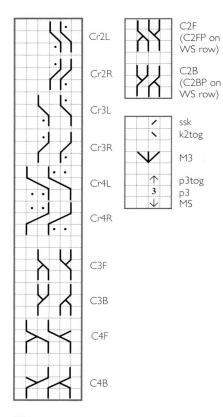

KEY

Cr2L, Cr2R, Cr3L, Cr3R, Cr4L, Cr4R, C3F, C3B, C4F, C4B

C2F (C2FP on WS row)
C2B (C2BP on WS row)

ssk, k2tog, M3, p3tog, p3, MS

■ MB
· p on RS rows, k on WS rows
□ k on RS rows, p on WS rows

CABLE STITCHES

Heart Cable

Abbreviations:

M3 – (k1 tbl, k1) into next st, pick up vertical strand between these 2 sts and k into back of it.

Cr3L – sl 2 sts on to cable needle at front, p1, k2 from cable needle.

Cr3R – sl 1 st on to cable needle at back, k2, p1 from cable needle.

Cr4L – sl 2 sts on to cable needle at front, p2, k2 from cable needle.

Cr4R – sl 2 sts on to cable needle at back, k2, p2 from cable needle.

C3F – sl 2 sts on to cable needle at front, k1, k2 from cable needle.

C3B – sl 1 st on to cable needle at back, k2, k1 from cable needle.

C4F – sl 2 sts on to cable needle at front, k2, k2 from cable needle.

C4B – sl 2 sts on to cable needle at back, k2, k2 from cable needle.

Panel of 21 sts.

Row 1 (RS) P1, k3, (p1, k1) twice, ssk, M3, k2tog, (k1, p1) twice, k3, p1.

Row 2 K1, p2, (k1, p1) 3 times, p3, (p1, k1) 3 times, p2, k1.

Row 3 P1, Cr3L, p1, k1, p1, ssk, k1, M3, k1, k2tog, p1, k1, p1, Cr3R, p1.

Row 4 K2, p3, k1, p1, k1, p5, k1, p1, k1, p3, k2.

Row 5 P2, Cr4L, C4B, p1, C4F, Cr4R, p2.

Row 6 K4, p5, k1, p1, k1, p5, k4.

Row 7 P4, C4B, (p1, k1) twice, p1, C4F, p4.

Row 8 K4, p3, (k1, p1) 4 times, p2, k4.

Row 9 P2, C4B, (p1, k1) 4 times, p1, C4F, p2.

Row 10 K2, p3, (k1, p1) 6 times, p2, k2.

Row 11 P1, C3B, (p1, k1) 6 times, p1, C3F, p1.

Row 12 K1, p2, (k1, p1) 7 times, k1, p2, k1.

Repeat these 12 rows.

Nosegay Pattern

Abbreviations:

MB – (k1, p1) twice into next st and turn, p4 and turn, k4 and turn, (p2tog) twice and turn, k2tog.

Cr2L – sl 1 st on to cable needle at front, p1, k1 from cable needle.

Cr2R – sl 1 st on to cable needle at back, k1, p1 from cable needle.

C2F – sl 1 st on to cable needle at front, k1, k1 from cable needle.

C2B – sl 1 st on to cable needle at back, k1, k1 from cable needle.

C2FP – sl 1 st on to cable needle at WS, p1, p1 from cable needle.

C2BP – sl 1 st on to cable needle at RS, p1, p1 from cable needle.

Panel of 16 sts on rev st st.

Row 1 (RS) P6, C2B, C2F, p6.

Row 2 K5, C2FP, p2, C2BP, k5.

Row 3 P4, Cr2R, C2B, C2F, Cr2L, p4.

Row 4 K3, Cr2L, k1, p4, k1, Cr2R, k3.

Row 5 P2, Cr2R, p1, Cr2R, k2, Cr2L, p1, Cr2L, p2.

Row 6 (K2, p1) twice, k1, p2, k1, (p1, k2) twice.

Row 7 P2, MB, p1, Cr2R, p1, k2, p1, Cr2L, p1, MB, p2.

Row 8 K4, p1, k2, p2, k2, p1, k4.

Row 9 P4, MB, p2, k2, p2, MB, p4.

Row 10 K7, p2, k7

Repeat these 10 rows.

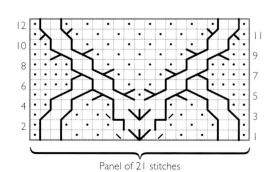

Panel of 21 stitches

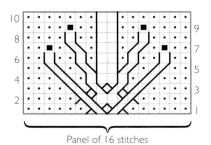

Panel of 16 stitches

CABLE STITCHES

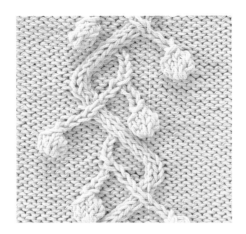

Twisted Vine

Abbreviations:

MB – (k1, p1, k1, p1, k1) all into next st
and turn, p5 and turn, k5 and turn, p2tog,
p1, p2tog and turn, k3tog. P st above
bobble on next row.

Cr2L – sl 1 st on to cable needle at front,
p1, k1 from cable needle.

Cr2R – sl 1 st on to cable needle at back,
k1, p1 from cable needle.

Cr3L – sl 1 st on to cable needle at front,
p2, k1 from cable needle.

Cr3R – sl 2 sts on to cable needle at back,
k1, p2 from cable needle.

Cr4L – sl 2 sts on to cable needle at front,
p2, k2 from cable needle.

Cr4R – sl 2 sts on to cable needle at back,
k2, p2 from cable needle.

C3F – sl 1 st on to cable needle at front,
k2, k1 from cable needle.

C3B – sl 2 sts on to cable needle at back,
k1, k2 from cable needle.

Panel of 17 sts on rev st st.
Row 1 (RS) P6, k1, p4, Cr4R, p2.
Row 2 and every foll WS row K all k sts
and p all p sts.
Row 3 MB, p5, Cr2L, p1, Cr4R, p4.
Row 5 Cr3L, p4, Cr4R, p6.
Row 7 P2, Cr3L, Cr4R, p3, MB, p4.
Row 9 P4, C3F, p4, Cr2R, p4.
Row 11 P2, Cr4R, Cr3L, p1, Cr2R, p5.
Row 13 P2, k2, p4, Cr3L, p6.
Row 15 P2, Cr4L, p4, k1, p6.
Row 17 P4, Cr4L, p1, Cr2R, p5, MB.
Row 19 P6, Cr4L, p4, Cr3R.
Row 21 P4, MB, p3, Cr4L, Cr3R, p2.
Row 23 P4, Cr2L, p4, C3B, p4.
Row 25 P5, Cr2L, p1, Cr3R, Cr4L, p2.
Row 27 P6, Cr3R, p4, k2, p2.
Row 28 K2, p2, k6, p1, k6.
Repeat these 28 rows.

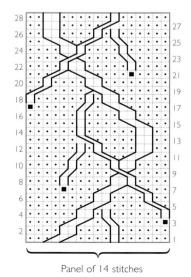

Panel of 14 stitches

KEY

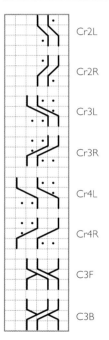

Cr2L

Cr2R

Cr3L

Cr3R

Cr4L

Cr4R

C3F

C3B

■ MB

• p on RS rows, k on WS rows

□ k on RS rows, p on WS rows

LACE STITCHES

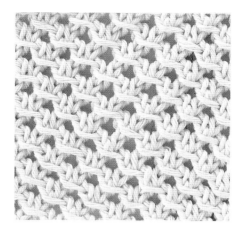

Lace Mesh

Multiple of 3 sts (cast on a minimum of 6 sts).
Row 1 K2, * yo, sl 1, k2, psso the 2 k sts; rep from * to last st, k1.
Row 2 Purl.
Row 3 K1, * sl 1, k2, psso the 2 k sts, yo; rep from * to last 2 sts, k2.
Row 4 Purl.
Repeat these 4 rows.

Zig Zag Lace

Multiple of 10 sts.
Row 1 (RS) * K2, p3, k2tog, yo, k3; rep from * to end.
Row 2 and every WS row Purl.
Row 3 * K1, p3, k2tog, yo, k4; rep from * to end.
Row 5 * P3, k2tog, yo, k5; rep from * to end.
Row 7 * K3, yo, ssk, p3, k2; rep from * to end.
Row 9 * K4, yo, ssk, p3, k1; rep from * to end.
Row 11 * K5, yo, ssk, p3; rep from * to end.
Row 12 Purl.
Repeat these 12 rows.

Vine Lace Zig Zag

Multiple of 10 sts plus 1.
Row 1 (RS) K1, * k2tog, k4, yo, k1, yo, ssk, k1; rep from * to end.
Row 2 and every foll WS row Purl.
Row 3 K1, * k2tog, k3, (yo, k1) twice, ssk, k1; rep from * to end.
Row 5 K1, * k2tog, k2, yo, k1, yo, k2, ssk, k1; rep from * to end.
Row 7 K1, * k2tog, (k1, yo) twice, k3, ssk, k1; rep from * to end.
Row 9 K1, * k2tog, yo, k1, yo, k4, ssk, k1; rep from * to end.
Row 11 K1, * k2tog, (k1, yo) twice, k3, ssk, k1; rep from * to end.
Row 13 K1, * k2tog, k2, yo, k1, yo, k2, ssk, k1; rep from * to end.
Row 15 K1, * k2tog, k3, (yo, k1) twice, ssk, k1; rep from * to end.
Row 16 Purl.
Repeat these 16 rows.

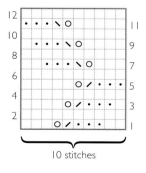

10 stitches

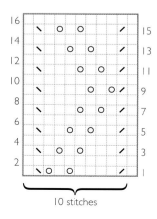

10 stitches

KEY

o	yo
╱	k2tog
╲	ssk
•	p on RS rows, k on WS rows
☐	k on RS rows, p on WS rows

LACE STITCHES

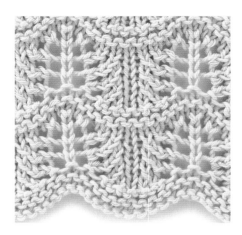

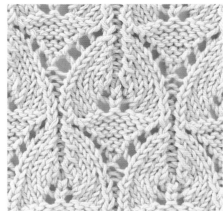

Crest of the Wave

Multiple of 12 sts plus 1.
Rows 1 to 4 Knit.
Rows 5, 7, 9 and 11 K1, * (k2tog) twice, (yo, k1) 3 times, yo, (ssk) twice, k1; rep from * to end.
Rows 6, 8, 10 and 12 Purl.
Repeat these 12 rows.

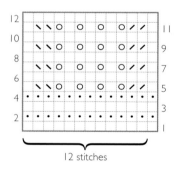

12 stitches

Gothic Window

Multiple of 12 sts plus 1.
Row 1 (RS) P1, * ssk, k3, yo, k1, yo, k3, k2tog, p1; rep from * to end.
Row 2 * K1, p11; rep from * to last st, k1.
Rows 3 to 6 Rep rows 1 and 2 twice more.
Row 7 P1, * yo, k3, ssk, p1, k2tog, k3, yo, p1; rep from * to end.
Row 8 * K1, p5; rep from * to last st, k1.
Row 9 P1, * p1, yo, k2, ssk, p1, k2tog, k2, yo, p2; rep from * to end.
Row 10 * K2, (p4, k1) twice; rep from * to last st, k1.
Row 11 P1, * p2, yo, k1, ssk, p1, k2tog, k1, yo, p3; rep from * to end.
Row 12 * K3, p3, k1, p3, k2; rep from * to last st, k1.
Row 13 P1, * p3, yo, ssk, p1, k2tog, yo, p4; rep from * to end.
Row 14 * K4, p2, k1, p2, k3; rep from * to last st, k1.
Row 15 K1, * yo, k3, k2tog, p1, ssk, k3, yo, k1; rep from * to end.
Row 16 * P6, k1, p5; rep from * to last st, p1.
Rows 17 to 20 Repeat rows 15 and 16 twice more.
Row 21 P1, * k2tog, k3, yo, p1, yo, k3, ssk, p1; rep from * to end.
Row 22 As row 8.
Row 23 P1, * k2tog, k2, yo, p3, yo, k2, ssk, p1; rep from * to end.

Row 24 * K1, p4, k3, p4; rep from * to last st, k1.
Row 25 P1, * k2tog, k1, yo, p5, yo, k1, ssk, p1; rep from * to end.
Row 26 * K1, p3, k5, p3; rep from * to last st, k1.
Row 27 P1, * k2tog, yo, p7, yo, ssk, p1; rep from * to end.
Row 28 * K1, p2, k7, p2; rep from * to last st, k1.
Repeat these 28 rows.

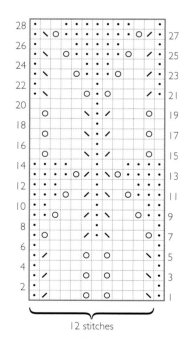

12 stitches

KEY

O	yo
/	k2tog
\	ssk
•	p on RS rows, k on WS rows
☐	k on RS rows, p on WS rows

LACE STITCHES

Quatrefoil Eyelets

Multiple of 8 sts plus 7.
Row I (RS) K2, * k1, yo, ssk, k5; rep from * to last 5 sts, k1, yo, ssk, k2.
Row 2 and every foll WS row Purl.
Row 3 K1, k2tog, * yo, k1, yo, ssk, k3, k2tog; rep from * to last 5 sts, yo, k1, yo, ssk, k1.
Row 5 As row 1.
Row 7 Knit.
Row 9 K2, * k5, yo, ssk, k1; rep from * to last 5 sts, k5.
Row II K2, * k3, k2tog, yo, k1, yo, ssk; rep from * to last 5 sts, k5.
Row 13 As row 9.
Row 15 Knit.
Row 16 Purl.
Repeat these 16 rows.

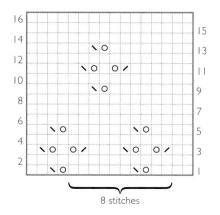

8 stitches

Quatrefoil Eyelets in Diamonds

Multiple of 12 sts plus 3.
Row I (RS) K1, * k1, yo, ssk, k3, p1, k3, k2tog, yo; rep from * to last 2 sts, k2.
Row 2 P2, * p4, k1, p1, k1, p5; rep from * to last st, p1.
Row 3 K1, * yo, ssk, k2, p1, k3 (twice); rep from * to last 2 sts, yo, ssk.
Row 4 P2, * p2, k1, p5, k1, p3; rep from * to last st, p1.
Row 5 K1, * k2, p1, k2, k2tog, yo, k3, p1, k1; rep from * to last 2 sts, k2.
Row 6 P2, * k1, p9, k1, p1; rep from * to last st, p1.
Row 7 K1, * p1, k3, k2tog, yo, k1, yo, ssk, k3; rep from * to last 2 sts, p1, k1.
Row 8 As row 6.
Row 9 K1, * k2, p1, k3, yo, ssk, k2, p1, k1; rep from * to last 2 sts, k2.
Row 10 As row 4.
Row II K2tog, * yo, (k3, p1) twice, k2, k2tog; rep from * to last st, yo, k1.
Row 12 As row 2.
Repeat these 12 rows.

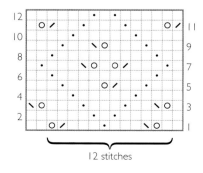

12 stitches

Lace Rib

Multiple of 4 sts plus 1.
Row I (RS) * P1, k3; rep from * to last st, p1.
Row 2 K1, * p1, yo, p2tog, k1; rep from * to end.
Row 3 As row 1.
Row 4 Knit.
Repeat these 4 rows.

4 stitches

LACE STITCHES

Ridged Feather Stitch

Multiple of 11 sts.
Row 1 (RS) Knit.
Row 2 Purl.
Row 3 (P2tog) twice, (yo, k1) 3 times, yo, (p2tog) twice.
Row 4 Purl.
Repeat these 4 rows.

Norwegian Fir

Multiple of 12 sts plus 1.
Row 1 (RS) P1, * p3, k5, p4; rep from * to end.
Row 2 and every foll WS row Purl.
Row 3 P2tog, * p2, k2, yo, k1, yo, k2, p2, p3tog; rep from * to end, ending last rep with p2tog.
Row 5 P2tog, * p1, k2, yo, k3, yo, k2, p1, p3tog; rep from * to end, ending last rep with p2tog.
Row 7 P2tog, * k2, yo, k5, yo, k2, p3tog; rep from * to end, ending last rep with p2tog.
Row 8 Purl.
Repeat these 8 rows.

Dainty Chevron

Multiple of 8 sts plus 1.
Row 1 (RS) K1, * ssk, (k1, yo) twice, k1, k2tog, k1; rep from * to end.
Row 2 and every foll WS row Purl.
Row 3 As row 1.
Row 5 K1, * yo, ssk, k3, k2tog, yo, k1; rep from * end.
Row 7 K1, * k1, yo, ssk, k1, k2tog, yo, k2; rep from * to end.
Row 9 K1, * k2, yo, sl2tog-k1-psso, yo, k3; rep from * to end.
Row 10 Purl.
Repeat these 10 rows.

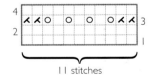

11 stitches

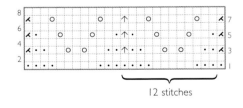

12 stitches

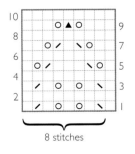

8 stitches

KEY

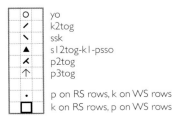

O	yo
/	k2tog
\	ssk
▲	sl2tog-k1-psso
⊀	p2tog
↑	p3tog
·	p on RS rows, k on WS rows
□	k on RS rows, p on WS rows

LACE STITCHES

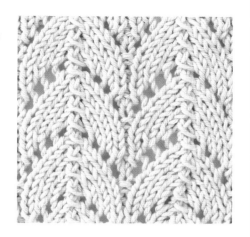

Snowflake Eyelets

Multiple of 8 sts plus 5.
Row 1 (RS) K1, * k3, ssk, yo, k1, yo, k2tog; rep from * to last 4 sts, k4.
Row 2 and every foll WS row Purl.
Row 3 K1, * k4, yo, sl2tog-k1-psso, yo, k1; rep from * to last 4 sts, k4.
Row 5 As row 1.
Row 7 Ssk, * yo, k1, yo, k2tog, k3, ssk; rep from * to last 3 sts, yo, k1, yo, k2tog.
Row 9 K1, * yo, sl2tog-k1-psso, yo, k5; rep from * to last 4 sts, yo, sl2tog-k1-p2sso, yo, k1.
Row 11 As row 7.
Row 12 Purl.
Repeat these 12 rows.

Mini Horseshoe Lace

Multiple of 6 sts plus 1.
Row 1 (RS) K1, * yo, k1, sk2po, k1, yo, k1; rep from * to end.
Row 2 Purl.
Row 3 K1, * k1, yo, sk2po, yo, k2; rep from * to end.
Row 4 Purl.
Repeat these 4 rows.

Horseshoe Lace

Multiple of 10 sts plus 1.
Row 1 (RS) K1, * yo, k3, sl 1, k2tog, psso, k3, yo, k1; rep from * to end.
Row 2 Purl.
Row 3 P1, * k1, yo, k2, sl 1, k2tog, psso, k2, yo, k1, p1; rep from * to end.
Row 4 K1, * p9, k1; rep from * to end.
Row 5 P1, * k2, yo, k1, sl 1, k2tog, psso, k1, yo, k2, p1; rep from * to end.
Row 6 As row 4.
Row 7 P1, * k3, yo, sl 1, k2tog, psso, yo, k3, p1; rep from * to end.
Row 8 Purl.
Repeat these 8 rows.

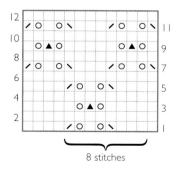

8 stitches

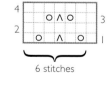

6 stitches

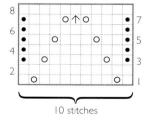

10 stitches

KEY

○	yo
╱	k2tog
╲	ssk
∧	sk2po
·	p on RS rows, k on WS rows
□	k on RS rows, p on WS rows

LACE STITCHES

Diamonds

Multiple of 8 sts plus 1.
Row 1 (RS) K1, * k1, k2tog, yo, k1, yo, ssk, k2; rep from * to end.
Row 2 and every foll WS row Purl.
Row 3 K1, * k2tog, yo, k3, yo, ssk, k1; rep from * to end.
Row 5 K2tog, * yo, k5, yo, sk2po; rep from * to end, ending last rep with ssk.
Row 7 K1, * yo, ssk, k3, k2tog, yo, k1; rep from * to end.
Row 9 K1, * k1, yo, ssk, k1, k2tog, yo, k2; rep from * to end.
Row 11 K1, * k2, yo, sk2po, yo, k3; rep from * to end.
Row 12 Purl.
Repeat these 12 rows.

Leaf Patterned Lace

Multiple of 10 sts plus 1.
Row 1 (RS) K1, * k2, k2tog, yo, k1, yo, ssk, k3; rep from * to end.
Row 2 and every foll WS row Purl.
Row 3 K1, * k1, k2tog, (k1, yo) twice, k1, ssk, k2; rep from * to end.
Row 5 K1, * k2tog, k2, yo, k1, yo, k2, ssk, k1; rep from * to end.
Row 7 K2tog, * k3, yo, k1, yo, k3, sk2po; rep from * to end, ending last rep with ssk.
Row 9 K1, * yo, ssk, k5, k2tog, yo, k1; rep from * to end.
Row 11 K1, * yo, k1, ssk, k3, k2tog, k1, yo, k1; rep from * to end.
Row 13 K1, * yo, k2, ssk, k1, k2tog, k2, yo, k1; rep from * to end.
Row 15 K1, * yo, k3, sk2po, k3, yo, k1; rep from * to end.
Row 16 Purl.
Repeat these 16 rows.

Ladder Lace

Multiple of 14 sts plus 11.
Row 1 (RS) K2tog, k3, yo, * k1, yo, k3, ssk, yo, sk2po, yo, k2tog, k3, yo; rep from * to last 6 sts, k1, yo, k3, ssk.
Row 2 Purl.
Repeat these 2 rows.

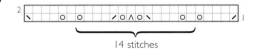

14 stitches

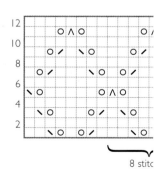

8 stitches

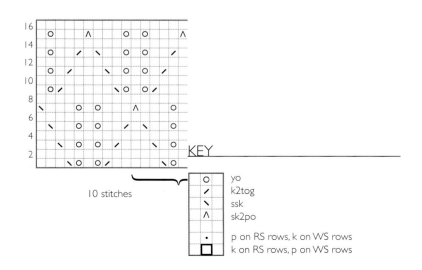

10 stitches

KEY

O	yo
⁄	k2tog
\	ssk
∧	sk2po
•	p on RS rows, k on WS rows
☐	k on RS rows, p on WS rows

LACE STITCHES

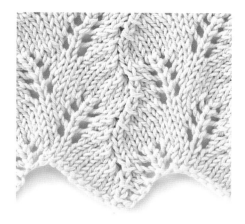

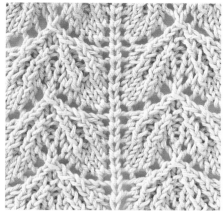

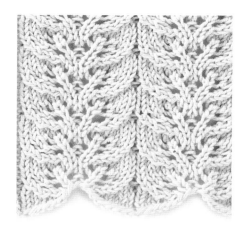

Fern Lace

Multiple of 16 sts.
Row 1 (RS) * K9, yo, k1, yo, k3, sk2po;
rep from * to end.
Row 2 and every foll WS row Purl.
Row 3 * K10, yo, k1, yo, k2, sk2po; rep
from * to end.
Row 5 * K3tog, k4, yo, k1, yo, k3,
(yo, k1) twice, sk2po; rep from * to end.
Row 7 * K3tog, k3, yo, k1, yo, k9; rep
from * to end.
Row 9 * K3tog, k2, yo, k1, yo, k10; rep
from * to end.
Row 11 * K3tog, (k1, yo) twice, k3, yo,
k1, yo, k4, sk2po; rep from * to end.
Row 12 Purl.
Repeat these 12 rows.

Beech Leaf Lace

Multiple of 14 sts plus 1 (stitch count
varies).
Row 1 (RS) K1, * yo, k5, yo, sk2po, yo,
k5, yo, k1; rep from * to end. 16 sts.
Row 2 Purl.
Row 3 K1, * yo, k1, k2tog, p1, ssk, k1,
yo, p1, yo, k1, k2tog, p1, ssk, k1, yo, k1;
rep from * to end.
Row 4 * P4, (k1, p3) 3 times; rep from *
to last st, p1.
Row 5 K1, * yo, k1, k2tog, p1, ssk, k1,
p1, k1, k2tog, p1, ssk, k1, yo, k1; rep
from * to end. 14 sts.
Row 6 * P4, k1, p2, k1, p2, k1, p3; rep
from * to last st, p1.
Row 7 K1, * yo, k1, yo, k2tog, p1, ssk,
p1, k2tog, p1, ssk, (yo, k1) twice; rep
from * to end.
Row 8 * P5, (k1, p1) twice, k1, p4; rep
from * to last st, p1.
Row 9 K1, * yo, k3, yo, sk2po, k1, k3tog,
yo, k3, yo, k1; rep from * to end.
Row 10 Purl.
Repeat these 10 rows.

Twin Leaf Lace

Multiple of 18 sts plus 1.
Row 1 (RS) P1, * k4, k3tog, yo, k1, yo,
p1, yo, k1, yo, k1, yo, sk2po, k4, p1; rep from *
to end.
Row 2 and every foll WS row * K1, p8;
rep from * to last st, k1.
Row 3 P1, * k2, k3tog, (k1, yo) twice, k1,
p1, k1, (yo, k1) twice, sk2po, k2, p1; rep
from * to end.
Row 5 P1, * k3tog, k2, yo, k1, yo, k2, p1,
k2, yo, k1, yo, k2, sk2po, p1; rep from *
to end.
Row 6 As row 2.
Repeat these 6 rows.

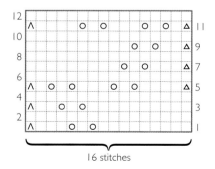

16 stitches

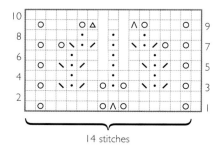

14 stitches

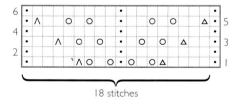

18 stitches

KEY

○	yo
╱	k2tog
╲	ssk
△	k3tog
⋀	sk2po
•	p on RS rows, k on WS rows
☐	k on RS rows, p on WS rows

LACE STITCHES

Diamond Lace with Rosettes

Multiple of 14 sts plus 3.

Row 1 (RS) K1, yo, * k3tog, yo, k9, yo, ssk, yo; rep from * to last 2 sts, k2tog.
Row 2 and every foll WS row Purl.
Row 3 K1, k2tog, * yo, k11, yo, sk2po; rep from * to end, ending last rep with ssk, k1.
Row 5 K2, * (yo, ssk) twice, k5, (k2tog, yo) twice, k1; rep from * to last st, k1.
Row 7 K2, * k1, (yo, ssk) twice, k3, (k2tog, yo) twice, k2; rep from * to last st, k1.
Row 9 K2, * k2, (yo, ssk) twice, k1, (k2tog, yo) twice, k3; rep from * to last st, k1.

Row 11 K2, * k3, yo, ssk, yo, sk2po, yo, k2tog, yo, k4; rep from * to last st, k1.
Row 13 K2, * k4, k2tog, yo, k1, yo, ssk, k5; rep from * to last st, k1.
Row 15 K2, * k3, k2tog, yo, k3, yo, ssk, k4; rep from * to last st, k1.
Row 17 K2, * k4, yo, ssk, yo, k3tog, yo, k5; rep from * to last st, k1.
Row 19 K2, * k5, yo, sk2po, yo, k6; rep from * to last st, k1.
Row 21 K2, * k2, (k2tog, yo) twice, k1, (yo, ssk) twice, k3; rep from * to last st, k1.
Row 23 K2, * k1, (k2tog, yo) twice, k3, (yo, ssk) twice, k2; rep from * to last st, k1.

Row 25 K2, * (k2tog, yo) twice, k5, (yo, ssk) twice, k1; rep from * to last st, k1.
Row 27 K1, k2tog, * yo, k2tog, yo, k7, yo, ssk, yo, sk2po; rep from * to end, ending last rep with ssk, k1.
Row 29 K2, * yo, ssk, k9, k2tog, yo, k1; rep from * to last st, k1.
Row 31 K2, * k1, yo, ssk, k7, k2tog, yo, k2; rep from * to last st, k1.
Row 32 Purl.
Repeat these 32 rows.

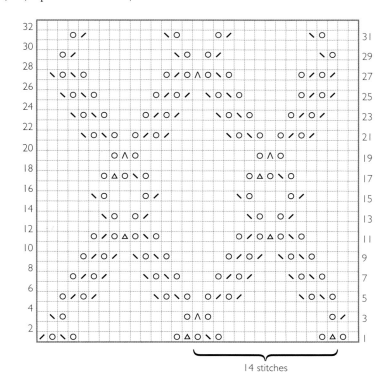

14 stitches

KEY

O	yo
╱	k2tog
╲	ssk
△	k3tog
∧	sk2po
·	p on RS rows, k on WS rows
□	k on RS rows, p on WS rows

EDGINGS

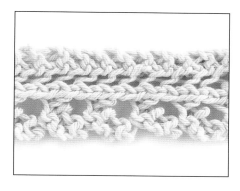

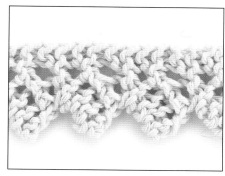

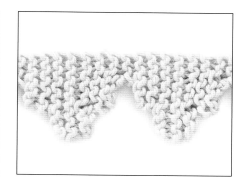

Loop Edging

Cast on 6 sts.
Row 1 (RS) K1, k2tog, yo, k2, (yo) twice, k1.
Row 2 K1, (k1, p1) into double yo, k3.
Row 3 K1, k2tog, yo, k5.
Row 4 Bind (cast) off 2 sts, p2tog, yo, k3.
Repeat these 4 rows.

Openwork Garter Stitch

Cast on 4 sts.
Row 1 (RS) K2, yfwd, k2.
Row 2 and every foll WS row Knit.
Row 3 K3, yfwd, k2.
Row 5 K2, yfwd, k2tog, yfwd, k2.
Row 7 K3, yfwd, k2tog, yfwd, k2.
Row 8 Bind (cast) off 4 sts, k to end.
Repeat these 8 rows.

Turret Edging

Cast on 3 sts.
Rows 1 to 3 Knit.
Row 4 Cast on 3 sts, k to end.
Rows 5 to 7 Knit.
Row 8 Cast on 3 sts, k to end.
Rows 9 to 11 Knit.
Row 12 Bind (cast) off 3 sts, k to end.
Rows 13 to 15 Knit.
Row 16 Bind (cast) off 3 sts, k to end.
Repeat these 16 rows.

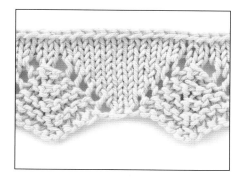

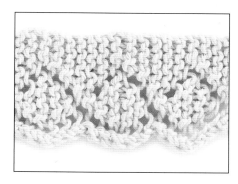

Scallop Border

Multiple of 13 sts.
Row 1 (RS) * K1, yo, k4, sk2po, k4, yo, k1; rep from * to end.
Row 2 * P2, k9, p2; rep from * to end.
Row 3 * K2, yo, k3, sk2po, k3, yo, k2; rep from * to end.
Row 4 * P3, k7, p3; rep from * to end.
Row 5 * K3, yo, k2, sk2po, k2, yo, k3; rep from * to end.
Row 6 * P4, k5, p4; rep from * to end.
Row 7 * K4, yo, k1, sk2po, k1, yo, k4; rep from * to end.
Row 8 * P5, k3, p5; rep from * to end.
Row 9 * K5, yo, sk2po, yo, k5; rep from * to end.
Row 10 Purl. Repeat these 10 rows.

Openwork Edging

Cast on 5 sts.
Row 1 (RS) Sl 1, yo, k2tog, yo, k2.
Row 2 and every foll WS row Knit.
Row 3 Sl 1, (yo, k2tog) twice, yo, k1.
Row 5 Sl 1, (yo, k2tog) twice, yo, k2.

Row 7 Sl 1, (yo, k2tog) 3 times, yo, k1.
Row 9 Sl 1, (yo, k2tog) 3 times, yo, k2.
Row 11 Bind (cast) off 6 sts, yo, k2tog, k1.
Row 12 Knit.
Repeat these 12 rows.

Garter Stitch Diamond

Cast on 10 sts.
Row 1 (RS) K5, k2tog, yo, k3tog.
Row 2 and every foll WS row Yo, k to end.
Row 3 K4, k2tog, yo, k1, yo, k2tog.

Row 5 K3, k2tog, yo, k3, yo, k2tog.
Row 7 K2, k2tog, yo, k5, yo, k2tog.
Row 9 K4, yo, k2tog, k1, k2tog, yo, k3tog.
Row 11 K5, yo, k3tog, yo, k3tog.
Row 12 Yo, k to end.
Repeat these 12 rows.

EDGINGS

Zig Zag Edging

Cast on 11 sts.
Row 1 (RS) K3, yo, k2tog, k2, yo, k2tog, yo, k2.
Row 2 Yo, k2tog, p8, k2.
Row 3 K2, (yo, k2tog) twice, k2, yo, k2tog, yo, k2.
Row 4 Yo, k2tog, p9, k2.
Row 5 K3, (yo, k2tog) twice, k2, yo, k2tog, yo, k2.
Row 6 Yo, k2tog, p10, k2.
Row 7 K2, (yo, k2tog) 3 times, k2, yo, k2tog, yo, k2.
Row 8 Yo, k2tog, p11, k2.
Row 9 K2, (ssk, yo) twice, k2, (ssk, yo) twice, k2tog, k1.
Row 10 Yo, k2tog, p10, k2.
Row 11 K1, (ssk, yo) twice, k2, (ssk, yo) twice, k2tog, k1.
Row 12 Yo, k2tog, p9, k2.
Row 13 K2, ssk, yo, k2, (ssk, yo) twice, k2tog, k1.
Row 14 Yo, k2tog, p8, k2.
Row 15 K1, ssk, yo, k2, (ssk, yo) twice, k2tog, k1.
Row 16 Yo, k2tog, p7, k2.
Repeat these 16 rows.

Leaf Edging

Abbreviation:
k-fb – knit into front and back of next st.

Cast on 6 sts.
Row 1 (RS) K3, yfwd, k1, yfwd, k2.
Row 2 P6, k-fb, k1.
Row 3 K2, p1, k2, yfwd, k1, yfwd, k3.
Row 4 P8, k-fb, k2.
Row 5 K2, p2, k3, yfwd, k1, yfwd, k4.
Row 6 P10, k-fb, k3.
Row 7 K2, p3, ssk, k5, k2tog, k1.
Row 8 P8, k-fb, p1, k3.
Row 9 K2, p1, k1, p2, ssk, k3, k2tog, k1.
Row 10 P6, k-fb, k1, p1, k3.
Row 11 K2, p1, k1, p3, ssk, k1, k2tog, k1.
Row 12 P4, k-fb, k2, p1, k3.
Row 13 K2, p1, k1, p4, sk2po, k1.
Row 14 P2tog, bind (cast) off 3 sts, k1, p1, k3.
Repeat these 14 rows.

Tassel Border

Multiple of 13 sts.
Row 1 (RS) * P2, (k1, p1) 4 times, k1, p2; rep from * to end.
Row 2 * K2, (p1, k1) 4 times, p1, k2; rep from * to end.
Rows 3 and 4 Repeat rows 1 and 2 once more.
Row 5 * P2, k1, p1, ssk, k1, k2tog, p1, k1, p2; rep from * to end.
Row 6 * K2, p1, k1, p3, k1, p1, k2; rep from * to end.
Row 7 * P2, k1, p1, sl2tog-k1-psso, p1, k1, p2; rep from * to end.
Row 8 * K2, (p1, k1) twice, p1, k2; rep from * to end.
Row 9 * P2, ssk, k1, k2tog, p2; rep from * to end.
Row 10 * K2, p3, k2; rep from * to end.
Row 11 * P2, sl next 3 sts on to cable needle, wrap yarn around them twice, k3 from cable needle, p2; rep from * to end.
Row 12 * K2, p3, k2; rep from * to end.
Row 13 * P1, sl2tog-k1-psso, p2; rep from * to end.
Row 14 Purl.
Repeat these 14 rows.

EDGINGS

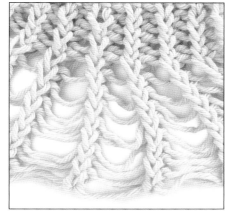

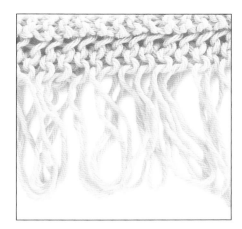

Welted Ruffle

Cast on 9 sts.
Row 1 Knit.
Row 2 P6 and turn, k6.
Row 3 P6, k3.
Row 4 K3, p6.
Row 5 K6 and turn, p6.
Row 6 Knit.
Repeat these 6 rows.

Cobweb Frill

Multiple of 3 sts plus 1.
Row 1 (RS) K1 tbl, * p1, p1 tbl, k1 tbl; rep from * to end.
Row 2 P1 tbl, * k1 tbl, k1, p1 tbl; rep from * to end.
Rows 3 to 8 Repeat rows 1 and 2 three times more.
Row 9 K1 tbl, * drop next st off needle, p1 tbl, k1 tbl; rep from * to end.
Row 10 P1 tbl, * k1 tbl, p1 tbl; rep from * to end.
Row 11 K1 tbl, * p1 tbl, k1 tbl; rep from * to end.
Rows 12 and 13 Repeat rows 10 and 11 once more.
Unravel dropped sts down to cast on edge.

Fringe

Cast on 8 sts.
Row 1 (RS) K2, yo, k2tog, k4.
Row 2 P3, k2, yo, k2tog, k1.
Repeat these 2 rows for required length, ending with a WS row.
Last row Bind (cast) off 4 sts, draw yarn through next st and fasten off.
Slip rem 3 sts off needle and unravel.

Projects

The projects given in this book use the techniques described in the earlier sections. Full instructions are given to create each item and the introduction to each project refers you back to any specific techniques used to create it. If a stitch pattern or motif forms part of the design you will find references to the Stitch library or the Motif section and suggestions are given for when you can substitute an alternative pattern or design to the one used.

The yarns specified are widely available in yarn shops, by mail order or from the internet. If the recommended yarn is unavailable then a substitute yarn of the same thickness or weight can be used. The replacement yarn must knit up to the same gauge (tension) and this information can be found on the ball band.

Substituting yarns

All the information you need to calculate yarn amounts is on the yarn's ball band. To work out how much replacement yarn you need follow these simple steps.

1 Take the number of balls of the recommended yarn from the Materials section of the pattern and multiply them by the number of yards/metres per ball. For example, 10 x 1¾oz (50g) balls of worsted (DK) 100% cotton yarn – 125yd/115m per ball would give a total length of 10 x 125yd = 1250yd (10 x 115m = 1150m).

2 Look at the ball band of the replacement yarn to find the number of yards/metres per 1¾oz (50g). For example, 154yd/140m.

3 Divide the total length required by the length of the replacement ball to give the number of balls of replacement yarn needed. For example 1250yd ÷ 154 = 8.1 (1150m ÷ 140 = 8.2) rounded up to 9 balls.

If the project uses more than one colour yarn, repeat these steps for each colour.

◀ KNIT SOMETHING NOW!

This Shaker-style sampler hangs on a wire quilt hanger and is embroidered in swiss darning with details added in backstitch.

The **house sampler** is knitted in a sport (4ply) weight tweed yarn using size 6 (4mm/UK8) needles and embroidered in tapestry wool. See page 155 for pattern.

GARTER STITCH SCARF

This cosy scarf is easy to knit using only three simple techniques, casting on, garter stitch and binding (casting) off (see pages 19–22). Use the recommended yarns, and follow the basic instructions, to knit either a plain or striped version. To substitute the yarns see Substituting yarns left and below. If you want to add a tasselled fringe (see page 78), you will need extra yarn.

■ Scarf measures 6in (15cm) wide by 62in (158cm) long

STRIPED SCARF

you will need

MATERIALS
Aran merino wool yarn –
90yd/82m per ball
1 x 1¾oz/50g ball each in colours:
A purple
B dark lilac
C lilac
D cream

NEEDLES
Size 7 (4.5mm/UK7) needles

■ **Gauge (Tension)**
19 sts to 4in (10cm) measured over garter stitch on size 7 (4.5mm/UK7) needles

Using size 7 (4.5mm/UK7) needles and A, cast on 28 sts. Working in g st (k every row), work in stripe patt of 10 rows A, 10 rows B, 10 rows C, 10 rows D, until scarf measures 62in (158cm) or length required. Bind (cast) off. Sew in yarn ends (see page 32).

PLAIN SCARF

you will need

MATERIALS
Chunky wool yarn (wool/alpaca mix) – 109yd/100m per ball
2 x 3½oz/100g balls in lilac

If you want a scarf longer than 62in (158cm) add another ball of yarn.

NEEDLES
Size 11 (8mm/UK0) needles

■ **Gauge (Tension)**
12 sts to 4in (10cm) measured over garter stitch on size 11 (8mm/UK0) needles

Using size 11 (8mm/UK0) needles, cast on 18 sts and work as given for striped version using one colour throughout.

Choosing a different yarn

If you want to use a different yarn than those given choose a thick one like aran, bulky (chunky) or thicker. The scarf will grow quickly and you may even finish it in a day.

All the information you need to knit the scarf is on the yarn's ball band. The number of stitches to cast on is determined by the gauge (tension), which is given to 4in (10cm). For a scarf 6in (15cm) wide you will need to cast on 1½ times the number of stitches to 4in (10cm).

For example, a worsted (DK) weight yarn has a gauge (tension) of 22 sts to 4in (10cm) using size 6 (4mm/UK8) needles. You would cast on 33 sts and use size 6 (4mm/UK8) needles. For a bulky weight yarn with a gauge (tension) of 14 sts to 4in (10cm) on size 8 (5mm/UK6) needles you would cast on 21 sts and use size 8 (5mm/UK6) needles. To calculate how many balls you will need see page 130.

FLOWER TOP

This simple T-shaped top has a pretty frilled bottom edge made by decreasing stitches (see page 30). The simple three colour motif is knitted from the chart on page 158 and outlined in chain stitch (see page 85). It fastens at the back of the neck.

To fit age 6–12 [12-18] months
Actual chest measurement 18 [21] in (46 [54] cm)

you will need

MATERIALS

Worsted (DK) yarn (wool/cotton mix) – 123yd/113m per ball
1 x 1¾oz (50g) each in colour:
A green
B aqua blue
C pale lilac

2 buttons

NEEDLES

Size 3 (3.25mm/UK10) needles
Size 6 (4mm/UK8) needles

3 stitch holders

Gauge (Tension)

22 sts and 28 rows to 4in (10cm) measured over stockinette (stocking) stitch on size 6 (4mm/UK8) needles

FRONT

Using size 6 (4mm/UK8) needles and B, cast on 123[143] sts.
Row 1 (RS) P3, * k7, p3; rep from * to end.
Row 2 K3, * p7, k3; rep from * to end.
Row 3 P3, * skpo, k3, k2tog, p3; rep from * to end.
Row 4 K3, * p5, k3; rep from * to end.
Row 5 P3, * skpo, k1, k2tog, p3; rep from * to end.
Row 6 K3, * p3, k3; rep from * to end.
Row 7 P3, *sk2po, p3; rep from * to end. 51[59] sts.
Change to A.
Work 3[4]in (9[10] cm) in st st, beginning and ending with a p row.
Start colour pattern.
Next row K17[21]A, work first row of chart, k17[21]A.
Next row P17[21]A, work 2nd row of chart, p17[21]A.
Cont in this way until 18th row of chart has been completed.
Using A only, work 2 rows in st st.
SHAPE NECK
Next row K22[25] and turn, leaving rem sts on a stitch holder.
Dec 1 st at neck edge on next and every foll row to 17[19] sts.
Work straight until front measures 8[9]in (20.5[23]cm) from beg, ending with a p row.
Bind (cast) off.
With RS of work facing, slip centre 7[9] sts on to a stitch holder, rejoin A and k to end.
Dec 1 st at neck edge on next and every foll row to 17[19] sts.
Work straight until work measures same as other side of neck, ending with a p row.
Bind (cast) off.

BACK

Work as given for Front (omitting chart) until back measures 5[6]in (12.5[15]cm), ending with a p row.
BACK NECK OPENING
Next row K25[29] and turn, leaving rem sts on a stitch holder.
Work straight on these 25[29] sts until back measures same as front, ending with a p row.
Bind (cast) off 17[19] sts, leave rem 8[10] sts on a stitch holder.
With RS of work facing, rejoin yarn to rem 26[30] sts and bind (cast) off 1 st, k to end. 25[29] sts.
Work straight to match first side, ending with a p row.
Next row K8[10], bind (cast) off 17[19] sts.
Slip these 8[10] sts on to a stitch holder.

SLEEVES (BOTH ALIKE)

Using size 6 (4mm/UK8) needles and B, cast on 29[35] sts.
Knit 3 rows.
Change to C and cont in st st, starting with a k row. Inc 1 st at each end of 3rd and every foll 4th row to 41[55] sts.
Work straight until sleeve measures 5[7]in (12.5[18]cm), ending with a p row.
Bind (cast) off.

FINISHING
NECKBAND
Join shoulder seams. With RS facing, using size 3(3.25mm/UK10) needles and B, k across 8[10] sts at left back neck, pick up and k 9[11] sts down left side of front neck, k across 7[9] sts at centre front, pick

up and k 9[11] sts up right side of neck, k across 8[10] sts at right back neck. 41[51] sts.
Knit 2 rows. Bind (cast) off.

BUTTON BAND
With RS of work facing, using size 3 (3.25mm/UK10) needles and B, pick up and k 20 sts up left side of back neck opening.
Knit 1 row.
Buttonhole row (K8, yo, k2tog) twice.
Knit 1 row.
Bind (cast) off.

BUTTONHOLE BAND
With RS of work facing, using size 3 (3.25mm/ UK10) needles and B, pick up and k 20 sts down right side of back neck opening.
Knit 2 rows.
Bind (cast) off.

CHAIN STITCH
Using A, work chain stitch (page 85) around the flower. Outline the centre with B.

FINISHING
Place markers 4[5]in (10[12.5]cm) from shoulder seam on armhole edges.
Sew in sleeves between markers.
Join side and sleeve seams.
Sew on buttons.

STRIPED BAG

The back and front of this simple yet eye-catching bag are knitted in one piece in stockinette (stocking) stitch (see page 25). It is then sewn up and the handles and lining attached.

■ Bag measures 6¾in (17cm) wide by 7in (18cm) long, excluding handles

you will need

MATERIALS
Mercerized sport weight (4ply) cotton yarn – 125yd/115m per ball
1 x 1¾oz (50g) each in colour:
A wine
B pale pink
C rose pink
D white
E leaf green

15in (37cm) x 8in (19.5cm) calico or closely woven cotton fabric for lining

Sewing thread to match lining

NEEDLES
Size 3 (3.25mm/UK10) needles

Gauge (Tension)
23 sts and 32 rows to 4in (10cm) measured over st st on size 3 (3.25mm/UK10) needles

BACK AND FRONT
Using size 3 (3.25mm/UK10) needles and A, cast on 80 sts.
Working in st st, work in stripe patt of
* 6 rows A, 2 rows B, 4 rows C, 2 rows B, 2 rows D, 2 rows A, 2 rows C, 4 rows E, 6 rows B *, 2 rows D, 2 rows C, 2 rows E.
Work another 30 rows in stripe patt from * to *.
Using B, bind (cast) off.

HANDLES (MAKE 2 ALIKE)
Using size 3 (3.25mm/UK10) needles and A, cast on 60 sts.
Working in st st, work in stripe patt of 2 rows A, 2 rows C, 2 rows E, 6 rows B.
Using B, bind (cast) off.

FINISHING
Block the piece to measurements.
Fold front and back in half with RS together and sew side and bottom seams. Fold the 6 rows of B to the inside to form a facing and sew into place. Fold handles along their length and slipstitch cast on edge to bound (cast) off edge. Place markers for handles 1½in (4cm) from the sides along the top edge. Sew handles to bag, through facing only.

LINING
Neaten the edges of the fabric. Fold in half and sew side seams, using a seam allowance of ⅝in (1.5cm). Fold over the seam allowance along top edge and press. Push lining into bag with wrong sides together and sew along the facing.

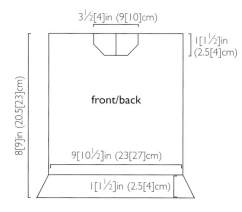

3½[4]in (9[10]cm)
1[1½]in (2.5[4]cm)
8[9]in (20.5[23]cm)
front/back
9[10½]in (23[27]cm)
1[1½]in (2.5[4]cm)

8[10]in (20.3[25.5]cm)
5[7]in (12.5[18]cm)
sleeve
5[6]in (12.5[15]cm)

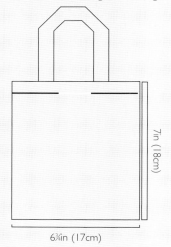

7in (18cm)
6¾in (17cm)

CABLE THROW

Each cable panel is knitted separately so this throw is quick and easy to knit (see page 42). All the cable designs used are included in the Stitch library (see pages 110–18) so simply follow the instructions for each one to make the panels. There are additional cable patterns in the library so you could substitute your own choice of pattern but make sure you choose a mix of large and small cables. The throw can be knitted in stripes as shown or all in one colour.

Throw measures approx 46in (117cm) wide by 50in (127cm) long

you will need

MATERIALS
Chunky tweed-effect wool yarn – 142yd/130m per ball as follows:
3 x 3½oz/100g hanks each in colours:
A oatmeal
B blue green
C moss green

2 x 3½oz/100g hanks in colour:
D grey

To make the throw in one colour you will need 11 hanks

NEEDLES
Size 10½ (7mm/UK2) needles
Cable needle

Gauge (Tension)
12 sts and 17 rows to 4in (10cm) measured over stockinette (stocking) stitch on size 10½ (7mm/UK2) needles

BASIC CABLE PANEL
Using size 10½ (7mm/UK2) needles cast on number of stitches required for cable pattern plus 3 sts of rev st st and 3 sts of st st each side (cable pattern sts plus 12 sts).
Knit 3 rows.
Row 1 (RS) K3, p3, work first row of cable pattern, p3, k3.
Row 2 P3, k3, work 2nd row of cable pattern, k3, p3.
Cont in patt as set until cable panel measures 50in (127cm) from beg, ending with a RS row.
Knit 3 rows.
Bind (cast) off.

Celtic cable, panel 3

Triple twist cable, panel 5

Use these instructions to work the following cable panels.
PANEL 1
Ripple and rock (see page 114) using C.
PANEL 2
Oxo cable (see page 111) using B.
PANEL 3
Celtic cable (see page 112) using A.
PANEL 4
Four stitch wave cable (see page 110) using D.
PANEL 5
Triple twist cable (see page 113) using B.
PANEL 6
Six stitch cable – crosses every eighth row (see page 110) using C.
PANEL 7
Hollow oak cable (see page 113) using D.
PANEL 8
Braid cable (see page 114) using A.

FINISHING
Work as many panels as required. Block the pieces to length measurement. Lay the pieces out side by side and sew together (see page 72).

1	2	3	4	5	6	7	8

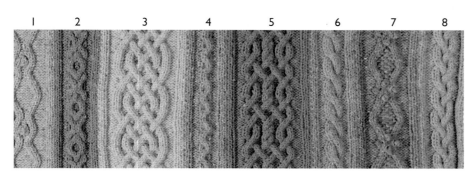

PLACE MAT AND COASTER

The place mat is made up of panels of stitches twisted symmetrically to the left and right forming heart-shaped outlines in the stocking stitch (see page 48). The panels are separated by columns of moss stitch, which is also used to give a firm edge round the mats. A single heart-shaped panel is used on the moss stitch coaster. A final touch is a handy pocket at the side to hold cutlery.

Mat measures 13in (33cm) wide by 10in (25.5cm) side
Coaster measures 4in (10cm) square

you will need

MATERIALS
Worsted (DK) weight cotton (92yd/84m per ball) as follows:
3 x 1¾oz/50g balls in bright green

NEEDLES
Size 6 (4mm/UK8) needles
Spare needle

Gauge (Tension)
22 sts and 29 rows to 4in (10cm) measured over stockinette (stocking) stitch on size 6 (4mm/UK8) needles

PLACE MAT

POCKET LINING
Using size 6 (4mm/UK8) needles cast on 12 sts.
Row 1 P1, k3, RT, LT, k3, p1.
Row 2 P to end.
Row 3 P1, LT, RT, k2, LT, RT, p1.
Row 4 P1, k1, p8, k1, p1.
Row 5 P1, k1, RT, k4, LT, k1, p1.
Row 6 As row 4.
Row 7 P1, RT, k6, LT, p1.
Row 8 P to end.
Rep these 8 rows twice more, then rows 1 and 2 again.
Leave these 12 sts on a spare needle.

MAT
Using 6 (4mm/UK8) needles cast on 63 sts.
Row 1 P1, * k1, p1; rep from * to end.
This row forms moss st. Rep this row twice more.
Inc row Moss st 7 sts, M1 knitwise, (moss st 12 sts, M1 knitwise) 4 times, moss st to end. 68 sts.
Start patt.
Row 1 P1, k1, p1, * k3, RT, LT, k3, p1, k1, p1; rep from * to end.
Row 2 P1, k1, * p12, k1; rep from * to last st, p1.
Row 3 P1, k1, p1, * LT, RT, k2, LT, RT, p1, k1, p1; rep from * to end.
Row 4 (P1, k1) twice, * p8, (k1, p1) twice, k1; rep from * to last 12 sts, p8, (k1, p1) twice.
Row 5 (P1, k1) twice, * RT, k4, LT, (k1, p1) twice, k1; rep from * to last 12 sts, RT, k4, LT, (k1, p1) twice.
Row 6 As row 4.
Row 7 P1, k1, p1, * RT, k6, LT, p1, k1, p1; rep from * to end.
Row 8 As row 2.
Rep these 8 rows twice more, then rows 1 to 5 again.

POCKET BORDER
Next row (WS) Patt to last 17 sts, (k1, p1) twice, k1, p2tog, (k1, p1) 5 times.

Next row (P1, k1) 7 times, p1, patt to end.
Next row Patt to last 15 sts, (p1, k1) 7 times, p1.
Next row (P1, k1) 7 times, p1, patt to end.
Next row Patt to last 13 sts, cast off 11 sts in patt, patt to end.

JOIN IN POCKET LINING
Next row P1, k1, patt across 12 sts of pocket lining, patt to end.
Cont in patt until piece measures approx 10in (25cm) from beg, ending with row 5.
Dec row (P1, k1) twice, p2tog, * (k1, p1) 5 times, k1, p2tog; rep from * 4 times, (k1, p1) 5 times.
Moss st 3 rows.
Bind (cast) off in patt.

COASTER

Using size 6 (4mm/UK8) needles cast on 19 sts and work 3 rows in moss st as given for mat.
Inc row Moss st 9 sts, M1 knitwise, moss st to end. 20 sts.
Row 1 (P1, k1) twice, p1, k3, RT, LT, k3, (p1, k1) twice, p1.
Row 2 (P1, k1) twice, p12, (k1, p1) twice.
Row 3 (P1, k1) twice, p1, LT, RT, k2, RT, LT, (p1, k1) twice, p1.
Row 4 (P1, k1) 3 times, p8, (k1, p1) 3 times.
Row 5 (P1, k1) 3 times, RT, k4, LT, (k1, p1) 3 times.
Row 6 As row 4.
Row 7 (P1, k1) twice, p1, RT, k6, LT, (p1, k1) twice, p1.
Row 8 (P1, k1) twice, p12, (k1, p1) twice.
Rep these 8 rows once more, then rows 1 to 5 again.
Dec row (P1, k1) 3 times, p2tog, (k1, p1) 6 times.
Moss st 3 rows.
Bind (cast) off in patt.

FINISHING
Block pieces to measurements. Sew pocket lining to mat.

FUN CHILDREN'S MITTENS

Bear   Tiger

These brightly coloured mittens with their animal faces are fun to knit and introduce the technique of circular knitting using a set of double-pointed needles (see page 52). The faces are knitted and embroidered separately and stitched on to the backs of the mittens in pairs (see page 87).

Mittens measure 3½ [4]in (9 [10]cm) across palm and are 5 [5½]in (12.5 [14]cm) long

you will need

MATERIALS
Worsted (DK) weight wool yarn (131yd/120m per ball)
1 x 1¾oz/50g ball each in colours:

Tiger

MC orange
A black
B cream
oddment of pink for nose

Bear

MC dark brown
A light brown
oddment of black for face

Dog

MC light brown
A beige
oddment of black for face

Cat

MC ginger
A cream
oddments of pink for nose and black for face

Note: oddments mean that only a small amount is needed;, use tapestry wool with an equivalent thickness to a worsted (DK) or leftover yarn

NEEDLES
Set of 4 size 3 (3.25mm/UK10) double-pointed needles
Set of 4 size 6 (4mm/UK8) double-pointed needles

Stitch holder

Gauge (Tension)
22 sts and 28 rows to 4in (10cm) measured over stockinette (stocking) stitch on size 6 (4mm/ UK8) needles

TIGER MITTENS
(make 2)
Using size 3 (3.25mm/UK10) needles and MC, cast on 30[36] sts and divide between 3 needles.
Round 1 K1, * p1, k1; rep from * to end. Rep this round 12 times more.
Change to size 6 (4mm/UK8) needles and, working in st st and stripe pattern of 4 rows MC and 2 rows A, knit 2[4] rows.
START THUMB GUSSET
Round 1 K14[17], M1, k2, M1, k14[17]. Knit 2 rounds straight.
Round 4 K14[17], M1, k4, M1, k14[17]. Knit 2 rounds straight.
Round 7 K14[17], M1, k6, M1, k14[17]. Knit 2 rounds straight.
Round 10 K14[17], M1, k8, M1, k14[17]. Knit 2 rounds straight.
Round 13 K14[17], slip next 10 sts on to st holder, cast on 2 sts, k to end. 30[36] sts. Knit 8[12] rows straight.
SHAPE TOP
Dec round (K4, k2tog) 5[6] times. Knit 2 rounds straight.
Dec round (K3, k2tog) 5[6] times. Knit 2 rounds straight.
Dec round (K2, k2tog) 5[6] times. Bind (cast) off rem 15[18] sts.
THUMB
Slip 10 sts from stitch holder on to 3 needles, rejoin yarn and k10 then pick up and k 2 sts from those bound (cast) off previously. 12 sts.
Knit 7[9] rounds straight.
Dec round (K1, k2tog) 4 times.
Dec round (K2tog) 4 times.
Cut yarn, thread through rem 4 sts and pull up.
FACE (MAKE 1 FOR EACH MITTEN)
Using 2 size 3 (3.25mm/UK10) needles and B, cast on 9[11] sts. Turn the work at the end of each row for flat knitting. Working in st st, starting with a k row, inc 1 st at each end of 2nd and foll 2 rows. 15[17] sts.
Work 4[6] rows without shaping.
Dec 1 st at each end of next 3 rows.
Bind (cast) off.

EYES (MAKE 2 FOR EACH MITTEN)
Using 2 size 3 (3.25mm/UK10) needles and A, cast on 2 sts.
P 1 row.
Cont in st st, starting with a k row, inc 1 st at each end of next row.
Work 2 rows.
Dec 1 st at each end of next row.
Bind (cast) off.
NOSE (MAKE 1 FOR EACH MITTEN)
Using 2 size 3 (3.25mm/UK10) needles and pink, cast on 3 sts.
P 1 row.
Cont in st st, starting with a k row, inc 1 st at each end of next and foll alt row.
P 1 row.
Bind (cast) off.
OUTER EARS (MAKE 2 FOR EACH MITTEN)
Using 2 size 3 (3.25mm/UK10) needles and MC, cast on 10 sts.
Knit 2 rows.
Cont in g st, dec 1 st at each end of next and every foll alt row to 2 sts.
K2tog, cut yarn and pull through rem st.
INNER EARS (MAKE 2 FOR EACH MITTEN)
Using 2 size 3 (3.25mm/UK10) needles and B, cast on 6 sts.
P 1 row.
Cont in st st, starting with a k row, dec 1 st at each end of next and foll alt row.
Work 1 row.
K2tog, cut yarn and pull through rem st.

FINISHING
Sew nose on face, matching bind (cast) off edges. Using black, and referring to the picture, backstitch the mouth and use long straight stitches for the whiskers. Sew the face on to the mitten. Sew the eyes on to the mitten above the face. Sew the inner ear to the outer ear, matching cast on edges and points. Sew the ears either side of the mitten at the top.

BEAR MITTENS

Using MC only, work two mittens as given for Tiger.

FACE, NOSE AND EYES

Work as given for Tiger, using A for the face and black for the nose and eyes.

OUTER EARS (MAKE 2 FOR EACH MITTEN)

Using 2 size 3 (3.25mm/UK10) needles and A, cast on 12 sts.

Knit 4 rows.

Cont in g st, dec 1 st at each end of every row to 4 sts.

Bind (cast) off.

INNER EARS (MAKE 2 FOR EACH MITTEN)

Using 2 size 3 (3.25mm/UK10) needles and MC, cast on 6 sts.

Work 3 rows in st st, starting with a k row.

Dec 1 st at each end of next row.

Bind (cast) off.

FINISHING

Finish as given for Tiger (omit whiskers).

CAT MITTENS

Using MC only, work two mittens as given for Tiger.

FACE, NOSE, EYES AND EARS

Work as given for Tiger, using A for the face, pink for the nose, black for the eyes, MC for the outer ear and A for the inner ear. Finish as given for Tiger.

DOG MITTENS

Using MC only, work two mittens as given for Tiger.

FACE, NOSE, EYES AND OUTER EARS

Work as given for Tiger, using A for the face and outer ears, and black for the nose, mouth and eyes. Finish as given for Tiger (omitting inner ears and whiskers).

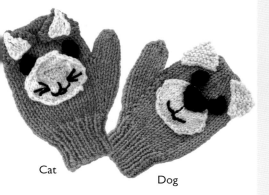

Cat

Dog

RIB STITCH SCARF

This warm sampler scarf is worked in blocks of six different rib patterns and is ideal for practising knitting ribs (see page 32). The first stitch of every row is slipped to give a neat edge (see page 34).

■ Scarf measures approx 6in (15cm) wide by 64in (162cm) long

you will need

MATERIALS

Chunky tweed-effect wool yarn (142yd/130m per ball):
2 x 3½oz/100g balls in colour dark red

NEEDLES

Size 10½ (6.5mm/UK3)

Gauge (Tension)

18 sts and 18 rows to 4in (10cm) measured over k2, p2 rib (slightly stretched) on size 10½ (6.5mm/UK3) needles

SCARF

Using size 10½ (6.5mm/UK3) needles cast on 27 sts.

Row 1 (RS) Sl 1, k1, (p3, k2) 5 times.

Row 2 Sl 1, p1, (k3, p2) 5 times.

Rep these 2 rows 8 times more.

Row 19 Sl 1, k1, (p2, k1) 8 times, k1.

Row 20 Sl 1, p1, (k2, p1) 8 times, p1.

Rep these 2 rows 8 times more.

Row 37 Sl 1, k1, (p2, k3) 5 times.

Row 38 Sl 1, p2, k2, (p3, k2) 4 times, p2.

Rep these 2 rows 8 times more.

Row 55 Sl 1, k1, (p2, k2) 6 times, k1.

Row 56 Sl 1, p2, (k2, p2) 6 times.

Rep these 2 rows 8 times more.

Row 73 Sl 1, k1, (p3, k1) 6 times, k1.

Row 74 Sl 1, p1, (k3, p1) 6 times, p1.

Rep these 2 rows 8 times more.

Row 91 Sl 1, k2, (p4, k4) 3 times.

Row 92 Sl 1, p3, (k4, p4) twice, k4, p3.

Rep these 2 rows 8 times more.

These 108 rows form the patt.

Cont in patt, beg with row 1, until scarf measures 64in (162cm) or length required, ending with the last row of a rib stripe.

Bind (cast) off in patt.

FINISHING

Block scarf to measurements, without overstretching the ribs.

SHORT ROW CUSHION

Knitted in a luxurious multicoloured silk yarn this elegant cushion has V-shaped points which are worked individually along one row of knitting. Each point is finished with a pair of beads and the rows are set alternately to give a tiled effect. The finished cushion is unusual and gives practise in the technique of knitting short rows (see page 46).

■ Cushion measures 15in (38cm) square

you will need

MATERIALS
Sport (4ply) weight silk yarn:
2 x 1¾oz/50g skeins in shades of blue

Fabric for back of cushion

15in (38cm) square cushion pad

36 large beads and 72 small beads in shades of blue and green

NEEDLES
Size 3 (3.25mm/UK10) needles

Gauge (Tension)
26 sts and 32 rows to 4in (10cm) measured over stockinette (stocking) stitch on size 3 (3.25mm/UK10) needles

Special Abbreviation
MAKE A POINT
Row 1 P14 and turn.
Row 2 K13 and turn.
Row 3 P12 and turn.
Row 4 K11 and turn.
Row 5 P10 and turn.
Row 6 K9 and turn.
Row 7 P8 and turn.
Row 8 K7 and turn.
Row 9 P6 and turn.
Row 10 K5 and turn.
Row 11 P4 and turn.
Row 12 K3 and turn.
Row 13 P4 and turn.
Row 14 K5 and turn.
Row 15 P6 and turn.
Row 16 K7 and turn.
Row 17 P8 and turn.
Row 18 K9 and turn.
Row 19 P10 and turn.
Row 20 K11 and turn.
Row 21 P12 and turn.
Row 22 K13 and turn.
Row 23 P14 and turn.

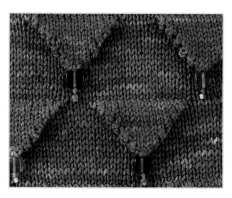

FRONT
Using size 3 (3.25mm/UK10) needles, cast on 97 sts and work 16 rows in st st, beg with a k row.
** Work a row of 5 points as follows: K20 and turn, make a point, (k33 and turn, make a point) 4 times, k20 (end of row).
Working across all sts, work 13 rows in st st, beg with a p row.
Work a row of 4 points as follows: K29 and turn, make a point, (k33 and turn, make a point) 3 times, k29 (end of row). **
Working across all sts, work 13 rows in st st, beg with a p row. ***
Work from ** to *** 3 times more, ending with 5 rows of st st, instead of 13 rows. Bind (cast) off.

FINISHING
Sew all the points closed at the top by joining the first and last rows. Block the front to 15in (38cm) square, pulling the points into shape. To sew on the beads, secure strong thread behind the point, put one large bead and then two small beads on to the needle, pull the thread through. Take the thread back through the small bead next to the large bead and through the large bead. Secure the thread behind the point. Cut a 17in (43cm) square from fabric and neaten the edges to prevent fraying. With RS together, pin the knitting to the fabric, taking care not to stretch the knitting. Sew around three sides, leaving the bottom edge open. Turn right side out and insert cushion pad. Sew the bottom seam closed.

BERET

This pretty beret is knitted in three sizes to fit a child and a small and average size for a woman. Knit it in an attractive tweedy wool for winter or make a fun striped version. All the shaping is done by increasing and decreasing stitches (see page 28–31).

To fit head circumference 18 [20:22]in (45.5 [51:56]cm)

STRIPED BERET

you will need

MATERIALS
Worsted (DK) weight wool yarn (131yd/120m per ball):
1 × 1¾oz/50g balls each in colour:
A pale rose
B purple

NEEDLES
Size 3 (3.25mm/UK10) needles
Size 6 (4mm/UK8) needles

Gauge (Tension)
22 sts and 28 rows to 4in (10cm) measured over stockinette (stocking) stitch on size 6 (4mm/UK8) needles

Using size 3 (3.25mm/UK10) needles and A, cast on 91[101:111] sts.
Row 1 (RS) K1, * p1, k1; rep from * to end.
Row 2 P1, * k1, p1; rep from * to end.
Rep these 2 rows twice more.
Change to size 6 (4mm/UK8) needles and B. Work in stripe patt of 4 rows B, 4 rows A throughout.
Inc row (K5[5:6], M1, k4[5:5], M1) 10 times, k1. 111[121:131] sts.
Work 11 rows in st st, beg with a p row.
Inc row (K6[6:7], M1, k5[6:6], M1) 10 times, k1. 131[141:151] sts.
Work 9[11:13] rows in st st.
3rd size only
Dec row (K13, k2tog) 10 times, k1. 141 sts.
Work 3 rows in st st.
2nd and 3rd sizes only
Dec row (K12, k2tog) 10 times, k1. 131 sts.
Work 3 rows in st st.
All sizes
Dec row (K11, k2tog) 10 times, k1. 121 sts.
Work 3[3:1] rows.
Dec row (K10, k2tog) 10 times, k1. 111 sts.
Work 3[1:1] rows.
Dec row (K9, k2tog) 10 times, k1. 101 sts.
P 1 row.
Dec row (K8, k2tog) 10 times, k1. 91 sts.
P 1 row.
Dec row (K7, k2tog) 10 times, k1. 81 sts.
P 1 row.
Dec row (K6, k2tog) 10 times, k1. 71 sts.
P 1 row.
Dec row (K5, k2tog) 10 times, k1. 61 sts.
P 1 row.
Dec row (K4, k2tog) 10 times, k1. 51 sts.
P 1 row.
Dec row (K3, k2tog) 10 times, k1. 41 sts.
Dec row P1, (p2tog, p2) 10 times. 31 sts.
Dec row (K1, k2tog) 10 times, k1. 21 sts.
Dec row P1, (p2tog) 9 times, p2. 12 sts.
Cut yarn and draw through rem 12 sts.

FINISHING
Sew up seam (see page 72).

PLAIN BERET

you will need

MATERIALS
Sport (4ply) weight tweed wool yarn (123yd/113m per ball)
1[2:2] × 1¾oz/50g balls in colour green

NEEDLES
Size 3 (3.25mm/UK10) needles
Size 6 (4mm/UK8) needles

Gauge (Tension)
22 sts and 28 rows to 4in (10cm) measured over stockinette (stocking) stitch on size 6 (4mm/UK8) needles

Work as given for striped beret using one colour throughout.

GARDEN PLOT SQUARES THROW

The medallion square used here is adapted from a traditional pattern called the Garden plot square or great-grandmother's bedspread. The square is knitted from corner to corner (see page 55) with a single leaf at the beginning and a line of smaller leaves across the middle at the widest point (see page 45). They are joined with the four single leaves placed together. Because it is knitted in squares, the work can be any size required, either to be used as a throw or made to fit a bed.

Throw measures 56in (142cm) square. A quarter of the throw is shown left
Each square measures approximately 8½in (21.5cm)
Border measures 2½in (6.5cm) wide

you will need

MATERIALS
Worsted (DK) weight cotton yarn (93yd/85m per ball):
34 x 1¾oz/50g balls in colour pale grey

NEEDLES
Size 6 (4mm/UK8) needles

Gauge (Tension)
19 sts and 28 rows to 4in (10cm) measured over stockinette (stocking) stitch on size 6 (4mm/UK8) needles

Special Abbreviation
MB (make a bobble) – (k1, k1tbl) twice, k1 all into next st, pass 2nd, 3rd, 4th and 5th sts over first st (see page 44)

SQUARE (MAKE 36)
Using size 6 (4mm/UK8) needles cast on 3 sts.
Row 1 Yo, k3.
Row 2 Yo, k4.
Row 3 Yo, k2, yo, k1, yo, k2.
Row 4 Yo, k2, p3, k3.
Row 5 Yo, k4, yo, k1, yo, k4.
Row 6 Yo, k3, p5, k4.
Row 7 Yo, k6, yo, k1, yo, k6.
Row 8 Yo, k4, p7, k5.
Row 9 Yo, k8, yo, k1, yo, k8.
Row 10 Yo, k5, p9, k6.
Row 11 Yo, k10, yo, k1, yo, k10.
Row 12 Yo, k6, p11, k7.
Row 13 Yo, k7, ssk, k7, k2tog, k7.
Row 14 Yo, k7, p9, k8.
Row 15 Yo, k8, ssk, k5, k2tog, k8.
Row 16 Yo, k8, p7, k9.
Row 17 Yo, k9, ssk, k3, k2tog, k9.
Row 18 Yo, k9, p5, k10.
Row 19 Yo, k10, ssk, k1, k2tog, k10.
Row 20 Yo, k10, p3, k11.
Row 21 Yo, k11, sl2tog-k1-psso, k11. 24 sts.
Rows 22 and 23 Yo, k to end.
Row 24 Yo, p to end.
Rows 25 and 26 Yo, k to end.
Row 27 Yo, p2, * yo, p2tog, p1; rep from * to end.
Rep rows 22 to 27 twice more, then rows 22 to 26 once more. 47 sts.
Row 45 Yo, k3, yo, k1, yo, (k7, yo, k1, yo) 5 times, k3.
Row 46 Yo, k3, p3, (k7, p3) 5 times, k4.
Row 47 Yo, k5, yo, k1, yo, (k9, yo, k1, yo) 5 times, k5.
Row 48 Yo, k4, p5, (k7, p5) 5 times, k5.
Row 49 Yo, k7, yo, k1, yo, (k11, yo, k1, yo) 5 times, k7.
Row 50 Yo, k5, p7, (k7, p7) 5 times, k6. (Place a marker here for corner of square. The square now begins to decrease.)

Row 51 Ssk, k4, ssk, k3, k2tog, (k7, ssk, k3, k2tog) 5 times, k4, k2tog.
Row 52 K5, p5, (k7, p5) 5 times, k5.
Row 53 Ssk, k3, ssk, k1, k2tog, (k7, ssk, k1, k2tog) 5 times, k3, k2tog.
Row 54 K4, p3, (k7, p3) 5 times, k4.
Row 55 Ssk, k2, sl2tog-k1-psso, (k7, sl2tog-k1-psso) 5 times, k2, k2tog. 47 sts.
Row 56 K to end.
Row 57 Ssk, k43, k2tog.
Row 58 P to end.
Row 59 Ssk, k4, yo, ssk, (k6, yo, ssk) 4 times, k3, k2tog.
Row 60 P to end.
Row 61 Ssk, k1, k2tog, yo, k1, yo, ssk, (k3, k2tog, yo, k1, yo, ssk) 4 times, k1, k2tog.
Row 62 P to end.
Row 63 Ssk, k2, MB, (k7, MB) 4 times, k2, k2tog.
Row 64 P to end. 39 sts.
Row 65 Ssk, k to last 2 sts, k2tog.
Row 66 K to end.
Row 67 P2tog, p to last 2 sts, ssp.
Row 68 K to end.
Row 69 Ssk, k to last 2 sts, k2tog.
Row 70 P to end.
Rep rows 65 to 70 twice more. 21 sts.
Row 83 Ssk, k8, yo, ssk, k7, k2tog.
Row 84 P to end.
Row 85 Ssk, k5, k2tog, yo, k1, yo, ssk, k5, k2tog.
Row 86 P to end.
Row 87 Ssk, k6, MB, k6, k2tog.
Row 88 P to end. 15 sts.
Row 89 Ssk, k to last 2 sts, k2tog.
Row 90 K to end.
Rep rows 89 and 90 until 3 sts remain.
Row 99 Sk2po.
Cut yarn and draw through rem st.

FINISHING

Block each medallion square to 8¹/2in (21.5cm), making sure the corners are square. Join together with single leaves meeting in the middle.

BORDER

The number of sts increases by one on every RS row until row 14 where the extra sts are bound (cast) off.
Using size 6 (4mm/UK8) needles cast on 7 sts.
Row 1 (RS) K3, yfwd, k2tog, yfwd, k2.
Rows 2, 4, 6, 8, 10 and 12 K to end.
Row 3 K4, yfwd, k2tog, yfwd, k2.
Row 5 K5, yfwd, k2tog, yfwd, k2.
Row 7 K6, yfwd, k2tog, yfwd, k2.
Row 9 K7, yfwd, k2tog, yfwd, k2.
Row 11 K8, yfwd, k2tog, yfwd, k2.
Row 13 K9, yfwd, k2tog, yfwd, k2.
Row 14 Bind (cast) off 7 sts, k to end.
7 sts.
Rep these 14 rows until border is long enough to fit around throw.
Sew on border, easing it around corners.

MAKING A LARGER BEDSPREAD

You can knit more squares to make a larger throw or a bedspread. For a bedspread, measure the width and length of the bed or an existing bedspread of the required size. Your bedspread will look best if it is an even number of squares wide and long. Each square is 8¹/2in (21.5cm). Divide the width and length by 8¹/2in (21.5cm) and round the results up or down to an even number and then add 5in (13cm) for the border.

For example, to make a single bedspread measuring 83in (211cm) x 100in (254cm):
The width 83in (211cm) is divided by 8¹/2in (21.5cm) = 9.8 squares.
Round up to 10.
The length 100in (254cm) is divided by 8¹/2in (21.5cm) = 11.8 squares. Round up to 12. A total of 120 squares.

Yarn Amounts

⁴/5 (0.8) of a ball will knit 1 square.
1 ball will knit approx 52in (132cm) of border.
For a bedspread of 120 squares multiply 120 by ⁴/5 (0.8) = 96 balls.
Border measures 2 x 90in (228cm) + 2 x 107in (271cm) = 394in (998cm) divided by 52in (132cm) = 7.5 balls.
Total number of balls required = 103.5 rounded up to 104 balls.

BEADED BAG

This shimmering evening bag is knitted in lurex and for added glitz tiny bronze beads are set around the eyelet holes of the lace pattern. The beads are threaded on to the yarn before starting to knit and added in as instructed (see page 56).

Bag measures 6in (17cm) wide by 7in (18cm) long, excluding handles

you will need

MATERIALS

Sport (4ply) weight lurex yarn (80% viscose/20% polyester – 104 yd/95m)

2 x 1¾oz/50g balls in colour gold

About 500 bronze beads

Fabric for handle and lining

NEEDLES

Size 3 (3.25mm/UK10) needles

Gauge (Tension)

29 sts and 41 rows to 4in (10cm) measured over lace pattern on size 3 (3.25mm/UK10) needles

Beads

Before beginning to knit, divide the beads in half and thread one half on to one ball and the rest of the beads on to the other ball.

BACK AND FRONT (MAKE 2)

Using size 3 (3.25mm/UK10) needles cast on 51 sts.
Start lace and bead patt.
Row 1 and every foll WS row P to end.
Row 2 (RS) K2, * yfwd, ssk, k5, PB, k5, k2tog, yfwd, k1; rep from * to last st, k1.
Row 4 K1, * yfwd, ssk, k4, PB, k3, PB, k5; rep from * to last 2 sts, yfwd, ssk.
Row 6 K5, PB, * k7, PB; rep from * to last 5 sts, k5.
Row 8 K3, * PB, k4, k2tog, yfwd, k5, PB, k3; rep from * to end.
Row 10 K1, PB, * k5, k2tog, yfwd, k1, yfwd, ssk, k5, PB; rep from * to last st, k1.
Row 12 K3, * PB, k5, yfwd, ssk, k4, PB, k3; rep from * to end.
Row 14 As row 5.
Row 16 * K2tog, yfwd, k5, PB, k3, PB, k4; rep from * to last 3 sts, k2tog, yfwd, k1.
Rep these 16 rows 4 times more, then rows 1 to 3 again.
Bind (cast) off loosely.

FINISHING

Block the back and front to 7in (18cm) wide by 8in (20.5cm) long. Join together along bottom and side edges. From the lining fabric, cut a piece 15¹/4in (39cm) wide by 9¹/4in (23.5cm) long. Neaten the edges to prevent fraying. With RS facing, fold in half and join the side seams with a ⁵/8in (1.5cm) seam allowance. Fold ⁵/8in (1.5cm) over at the top to the wrong side.

For the handle, cut two pieces of fabric 3in (7.5cm) wide and 13in (33cm) long. Fold in half and press, open out and then fold each edge into the middle and press. Fold in half again, along first fold line, to make a handle of four fabric thicknesses. Topstitch close to each edge.

Attach the handle firmly to the wrong side of the bag lining at the side seam and on the fold opposite. Push lining into bag with wrong sides together and sew into place around top edge.

SHEEP TOY

A great way to try the looped knitting technique (see page 57), this charming sheep has the fleece for its back and head knitted in one piece, with another piece for the underbelly. It isn't a suitable toy for babies and very young children to play with but will be treasured for future years.

■ Sheep's height is 5in (13cm)

you will need

MATERIALS
Worsted (DK) weight wool yarn (131yd/120m)
1 x 1¾oz/50g ball each in colours:
A white
B black

White toy stuffing

NEEDLES
Size 3 (3.25mm/UK10) needles

Gauge (Tension)
26 sts and 32 rows to 4in (10cm) measured over stockinette (stocking) stitch on size 3 (3.25mm/UK10) needles

BODY
Using size 3 (3.25mm/UK10) needles and A, cast on 42 sts, placing markers between sts 11 and 12 and between sts 30 and 31. Do not slip markers as you knit, leave them on the first row to use when sewing up.
** **Row 1** K1 tbl into each st to end.
Row 2 K1 tbl, loop st into each st to last st, k1 tbl.
Rep these 2 rows 4 times more.

SHAPE BACK LEGS
Next row Cast off 6 sts, k1 tbl into each st to end.
Next row Cast off 6 sts, loop st into each st to last st, k1 tbl.
Patt 8 rows.

SHAPE FRONT LEGS
Next row Cast on 6 sts, k1 tbl into each st to end.
Next row Cast on 6 sts, k1 tbl into first st, loop st into each st to last st, k1 tbl.
Patt 8 rows.
Next row Cast off 6 sts, k1 tbl into each st to end.
Next row Cast off 6 sts, loop st into each st to last st, k1 tbl. *** 20 sts.

SHAPE HEAD
Dec 1 st at each end of next and foll alt row. 16 sts.
Patt 12 rows.
Bind (cast) off loosely by k1 tbl into each st.

UNDERBELLY
Using size 3 (3.25mm/UK10) needles and A, cast on 22 sts and place a marker between sts 11 and 12.
Work as given for body from ** to ***.
10 sts.
Bind (cast) off these 10 sts loosely by k1 tbl into each st.

HEAD
Using size 3 (3.25mm/UK10) needles and B, cast on 18 sts and work 2 rows in st st, starting with a k row.
Inc row K4, M1, (k1, M1) twice, k6, M1, (k1, M1) twice, k4. 24 sts.
P 1 row.
Inc row K5, M1, k3, M1, k8, M1, k3, M1,
k5. 28 sts.
P 1 row.
Inc row K6, M1, k3, M1, k10, M1, k3, M1, k6. 32 sts.
P 1 row.
Inc row K7, M1, k3, M1, k12, M1, k3, M1, k7. 36 sts.
Work 11 rows in st st, starting with a p row.
Dec row K7, k2tog, k1, ssk, k12, k2tog, k1, ssk, k7. 32 sts.
Work 3 rows in st st.
Dec row K6, k2tog, k1, ssk, k10, k2tog, k1, ssk, k6. 28 sts.
P 1 row.
Dec row K5, k2tog, k1, ssk, k8, k2tog, k1, ssk, k5. 24 sts.
P 1 row.
Dec row K3, (k2tog, k2) 5 times, k1. 14 sts.
P1 row.
Bind (cast) off.

EARS (MAKE 2)
Using size 3 (3.25mm/UK10) needles and B, cast on 10 sts and work 2 rows in st st, starting with a k row.
Inc row K1, M1, k8, M1, k1. 12 sts.
P 1 row.
Inc row K1, M1, k12, M1, k1. 14 sts.
Work 3 rows in st st.
Dec 1 st at each end of next and every foll alt row to 8 sts.
P 1 row.
Cut yarn and thread through rem sts.

BACK LEGS (MAKE 2)
Join the body to the underbelly at back leg seams by matching markers. Join rem centre back seam.
With RS of work facing and using size 3 (3.25mm/UK10) needles and A, pick up and knit 20 sts evenly around back leg of body.
** **Dec row** K4, k2tog, k8, k2tog, k4. 18 sts.
Change to B and work 8 rows in st st, starting with a k row.
Dec row K1, (k2tog) 8 times, k1. 10 sts.
Dec row P1, (p2tog) 4 times, p1. 6 sts.
Cut yarn and thread through rem sts. ***

Join back leg seams. Join underbelly seam from top of back leg to bottom of front leg.

FRONT LEGS (MAKE 2)

With RS of work facing and using A, pick up and knit 20 sts evenly around front leg of body.
Work as given for back legs from ** to ***.
Join front leg seams, leaving neck open.

FINISHING

Stuff the body making sure the legs are firm. Join centre back head seam. Join head at cast on edge, making sure the back seam is in the middle. Stuff the head firmly and join top seam. Fold the ears in half and join the seam. Attach to each side of the head at the beginning of the head decreases. Attach the loop stitch head piece to front of black head by sewing cast off edge between ears. Position the head into the neck opening and sew loop stitch fabric around head. Embroider two eyes using A.

FAIR ISLE BABY BLANKET

For a first fair isle project this pretty patch is ideal. Knitted in the traditional way with only two colours used on each row it gives practise in holding the yarn in both hands and weaving the yarns in as you knit (see page 39-41). Colour charts for each of the pattern bands are given (see page 159) and the finished patch is sewn on to a piece of cosy fleece, edged in blanket stitch (see page 86). You can personalize the patch by inserting the baby's name using the alphabet given on page 158.

Patch measures 16in (40.5cm) wide by 23in (58.5cm) long
Blanket measures 26in (66cm) wide by 33in (84cm) long

you will need

MATERIALS

Worsted (DK) weight wool/cotton mix yarn (123yd/113m per ball):
1 x 1¾oz/50g ball each in colours:
MC cream
A light blue violet
B blue violet
C dark blue
D pale lilac
E mauve
F dark mauve
G light pink

26in (66cm) wide by 33in (84cm) long piece of fleece fabric in a complementary colour

NEEDLES

Size 6 (4mm/UK8) needles

Gauge (Tension)

24 sts and 24 rows to 4in (10cm) measured over fair isle pattern on size 6 (4mm/UK8) needles

FAIR ISLE PATCH

When working from the charts read RS rows (odd numbers) from right to left and WS rows (even numbers) from left to right.
Using size 6 (4mm/UK8) needles and D, cast on 97 sts and work 2 rows in st st, starting with a k row.
Work 10 rows from chart A.
Work 12 rows from chart B.
Work 14 rows from chart C.
Work 8 rows from chart D.
Work 10 rows from chart A.
Work 12 rows from chart B.
Work 18 rows from chart E.
Work 8 rows from chart D.
Work 10 rows from chart A. Insert baby's name if required on rows 2 to 8 using the alphabet given on page 158. Chart the name on to graph paper. If there is more than one name, use the small four-stitch motifs to separate them. Make sure the name is centred on the panel and that the fair isle pattern is the same each side. Use MC to work the name.
Work 12 rows from chart B.
Work 14 rows from chart F.
Work rows 1 to 4 from chart D.
Using G, bind (cast) off.

FINISHING

Block the knitted piece to 16in (40.5cm) wide by 23in (58.5cm) long. Sew it on to the centre of the fleece fabric. Using one of the yarn colours to contrast with the fleece, work blanket stitch around the edge of the fleece.

SCENTED SACHETS AND COVER

Fulling makes a denser knitted fabric (see page 62), which makes it ideal for these scented sachets and coat hanger cover. The attractive gingham pattern and the heart motif worked from a chart from the motif library (page 158) both use the fair isle method of stranding yarns (see page 40).

Envelope sachet about 4in (10cm) square
Heart sachet about 4in (10in) square
Hanger cover 2in (5cm) wide by 14in (35.5cm) long

you will need

MATERIALS
Sport (4ply) weight shetland wool yarn (129yd/118m per ball)
1 x 1oz/25g ball each in colours:
A cream
B lilac
C purple

Lavender or similar to fill heart and envelope sachets

Envelope sachet: button, fabric for sachet 4in x 8in (10cm x 20cm)

Coat hanger cover: wadding

NEEDLES
Size 3 (3.25mm/UK10) needles

Gauge (Tension)
Before fulling: 30 sts and 30 rows to 4in (10cm) measured over gingham pattern on size 3 (3.25mm/UK10) needles
After fulling: 38 sts and 38 rows to 4in (10 cm) measured over gingham pattern

ENVELOPE SACHET
Using size 3 (3.25mm/UK10) needles and C, cast on 26 sts and work 4 rows in st st, beg with a k row.

START HEART MOTIF
Work from the chart given on page 158 of the Motif library.
Next row K5, work 16 sts of first row of chart from right to left, k to end.
Next row P5, work 16 sts of 2nd row of chart from left to right, p to end.
Cont as set until the 14th row of chart has been completed.
Work 80 rows in st st.
Bind (cast) off loosely.

FULLING
The piece is fulled until it measures approximately 4in (10cm) wide. Steam press flat.

FINISHING
Place markers to divide the length into three sections, making the heart motif end 1in (2.5cm) shorter than the other two sections. Fold the opposite end to the heart motif up at the marker and join the side seams to form an envelope. Fold the heart motif flap over. Make a 2in (5cm) twisted cord (see page 79) using two strands of purple wool. Sew on button. Make a small bag to contain the lavender by folding the fabric in half and joining the side seams. Fill with lavender and sew the top closed. Put lavender sachet into envelope.

HEART SACHET
(MAKE 2)
This is worked from the top down, the two top sections are worked separately, then joined to continue the heart shape. Carry yarn not in use loosely up the edge. Use the fair isle method of stranding.

FIRST SECTION
Using size 3 (3.25mm/UK10) needles and A, cast on 6 sts.
* **Row 1** (RS) K2B, k2A, k2B.
Row 2 Using A, cast on and p 2 sts, p2B, p2A, p2B. 8 sts.
Row 3 Using B, cast on and k 2 sts, k2C, k2B, k2C, k2B. 10 sts.
Row 4 Using B, p into front and back of first st, p1B, p2C, p2B, p2C, p1B, using B, p into front and back of last st. 12 sts.
Row 5 Using B, k into front and back of first st, (k2A, k2B) twice, k2A, using B, k into front and back of last st. 14 sts.
Row 6 Using B, p into front and back of first st, p1B, (p2A, p2B) twice, p2A, p1B, using B, p into front and back of last st. 16 sts. *
Cut yarns and push these 16 sts to the end of the needle.

SECOND SECTION
Using A, cast on 6 sts on to the same needle and work from * to *.
Row 7 K1B, (k2C, k2B) 7 times (working across first section as well), k2C, k1B. 32 sts.
Row 8 Using B, p into front and back of first st, (p2C, p2B) 7 times, p2C, using B, p into front and back of last st. 34 sts.
Row 9 K2A, * k2B, k2A; rep from * to end.
Row 10 P2A, * p2B, p2A; rep from * to end.
Row 11 K2B, * k2C, k2B; rep from * to end.
Row 12 P2B, * p2C, p2B; rep from * to end.
These 4 rows form the gingham check patt. Rep these 4 rows once more.
Keeping gingham patt correct as set, dec 1 st at each end of next and foll 2 alt rows, then at each end of every foll row to 2 sts. Bind (cast) off loosely.

LACE BAGS

Knitted in a 4ply mercerized cotton, these dainty lace bags can be filled with lavender, dried roses or pot pourri. The techniques required to create the lace pattern are yarn over (see page 37) and decreasing (see page 30).

▌Bag measures approximately 3in (7.5cm) wide by 4in (10cm) long

FULLING

The pieces are fulled until they measure approximately 4in (10cm) wide. Steam press each piece flat.

FINISHING

Join the two heart shapes together, leaving a gap at the top. Fill with lavender and sew gap closed. Make a twisted cord, 8in (20cm) long using two strands of purple yarn (see page 79) and sew to the top as a hanging loop.

COAT HANGER COVER

Using size 3 (3.25mm/UK10) needles and A, cast on 30 sts and work 142 rows in gingham check patt as given for heart sachet.
Bind (cast) off loosely.

FULLING

The piece is fulled until it measures approximately 4in (10cm) wide. Steam press flat.

FINISHING

Wrap wadding neatly around the hanger until it is covered. Fold the knitted cover in half along its length. Mark the centre of the long fold and push the hook of the coat hanger carefully through the fabric from the WS at this point. Pull the cover around the wadding and pin the ends together and the long seam at the bottom. Adjust the wadding if necessary. Sew the seams closed. Tie a piece of ribbon or twisted cord around the base of the hook and sew in place.

you will need

MATERIALS
Sport (4ply) weight mercerized cotton yarn (153yd/140m per ball)

Light Pink Bag
1 x 1¾oz/50g ball in light pink

Dark Pink Bag
1 x 1¾oz/50g ball in dark pink

Dark Purple Bag
1 x 1¾oz/50g ball in dark purple

20in (51cm) of ¼in (7mm) wide ribbon in a colour to match your chosen cotton yarn

White voile or organza for lining

Lavender, dried rose petals, pot pourri or similar

NEEDLES
Size 2 (3mm/UK11) needles

Gauge (Tension)
28 sts and 30 rows to 4in (10cm) measured over stockinette (stocking) stitch on size 2 (3mm/UK11) needles

LIGHT PINK BAG
Using size 2 (3mm/UK11) needles and A, cast on 41 sts and purl 1 row.
Work 40 rows in Dainty Chevron stitch (see Stitch library page 122), ending with a p row.

PICOT BIND (CAST) OFF
Next row Bind (cast) off 2 sts, * slip st back on to left-hand needle, cast on 2 sts using cable cast on method (see page 26), bind (cast) off 5 sts; rep from * to end. Cut yarn and draw through last st.

DARK PINK BAG
Using size 2 (3mm/UK11) needles and B, cast on 41 sts and purl 1 row.
Work 32 rows in Horseshoe Lace (see Stitch library page 123), ending with a p row.
Work the picot bind (cast) off as given for light pink bag.

DARK PURPLE BAG
Using size 2 (3mm/UK11) needles and C, cast on 45 sts and purl 1 row.
Work 36 rows in Snowflake Eyelets (see Stitch library page 123), ending with a p row.
Work the picot bind (cast) off as given for light pink bag.

FINISHING
Block bag to measurements, pinning each picot point separately. When dry remove pins and fold in half, wrong sides together, and join side and bottom seams. Cut a piece of lining fabric 7in (18cm) wide by 4in (10cm) long. Fold in half and join side and bottom seams. Finish the top edge to prevent fraying. Fill with lavender or chosen filling. Put filled lining into bag. Thread ribbon through holes in lace, approximately 1in (2.5cm) from top, beginning and ending at centre front. Pull up and tie securely with a bow.

FUNNEL NECK SWEATER

Knitted in stockinette (stocking) stitch, this sweater has square set in sleeves and a funnel neck. Because there's no neck shaping, a cable panel can easily be added to the front (see left). The instructions are for a plain sweater with suggestions on where to alter the length of the sleeves and body (see page 74). Separate instructions are given for the cable panel sweater (see page 75). Sizes are given for women, men and children.

ADULT'S PLAIN SWEATER

To fit bust/chest measurement 32/34[36/38:40/42:44/46]in (81.5/86.5[91.5/96.5:101.5/106.5:112/117]cm)

BACK AND FRONT (BOTH ALIKE)
Using size 6 (4mm/UK8) needles, cast on 91[99:109:117] sts.
Row 1 (RS) K1, * p1, k1; rep from * to end.
Row 2 P1, * k1, p1; rep from * to end.
Rep these 2 rows until rib measures 3in (7.5cm), ending with a WS row.
Change to size 8 (5mm/UK6) needles and work in st st (beg with a k row) until piece measures 13½[13½:14:14]in (34.5[34.5:35.5:35.5]cm) from beg, ending with a p row. (Alter this measurement to lengthen or shorten the sweater.)
SHAPE ARMHOLES
Cast off 5 sts at beg of next 2 rows. 81[89:99:107] sts.
Cont without shaping until armhole measures 9[10:10½:11]in (23[25.5:26.5:28]cm), ending with a p row.
SHAPE SHOULDERS
Cast off 7[8:9:0] sts at beg of next 4 rows then 5[6:8:9] sts at beg of next 2 rows. 43[45:47:49] sts.
SHAPE NECK
Dec 1 st at each end of next and foll alt row. Work straight on rem 39[41:43:45] sts until neck measures 2½in (6cm), ending with a k row. Knit 4 rows. Bind (cast) off loosely knitwise.

SLEEVES (BOTH ALIKE)
Using size 6 (4mm/UK8) needles, cast on 53[57:61:65] sts and work 3in (7.5cm) in rib as given for back, ending with a WS row.
Change to size 8 (5mm/UK6) needles and work in st st (beg with a k row), inc 1 st at each end of 3rd[5th:5th:3rd] and every foll 6th[6th:6th:7th] row to 85[91:95:99] sts. Work straight until piece measures 19[21.5:23:24]in (48.5[54½:58.5:61]cm) from beg, ending with a p row. (Alter this measurement to lengthen or shorten sleeve; if making the sleeve shorter you will need to increase more frequently – see page 74.)
Bind (cast) off.

FINISHING
Block pieces to measurements. Join shoulder and neck seams. Place a marker at the centre of the sleeve top and match to shoulder seam. Using the square set in method (see page 73), sew in sleeve. Join side seams and underarm seams.

MATERIALS
Fisherman (aran) weight merino wool yarn (85yd/78m per ball): 15[16:17:18] × 1¾oz/50g balls in colour denim blue

NEEDLES
Size 6 (4mm/UK8) needles
Size 8 (5mm/UK6) needles

Gauge (Tension)
18 sts and 24 rows to 4in (10cm) measured over stockinette (stocking) stitch on size 8 (5mm/UK6) needles

Adult's sweater size diagram measurements
A 20 [22:24:26]in (51 [56:61:66]cm)
B 3in (7.5cm)
C 23½ [24½:25½:26]in (59.5 [62:65:66]cm)
D 2½in (6cm)
E 1in (2.5cm)
F 9 [10:10½:11]in (23 [25.5:26.5:28]cm)
G 13½ [13½:14:14]in (34.5 [34.5:35.5:35.5]cm)
H 8½ [9:9½:10]in (21.5 [23:24:25.5]cm)
I 5¾ [6½:7¼:8]in (14.5 [16.5:18.5:20.5]cm)
J 18 [20:21:22]in (46 [51:54:56]cm)
K 19 [21½:23:24]in (48.5 [54.5:58.5:61]cm)
L 11¾ [12½:13½:14½]in (30 [32:34.5:37]cm)

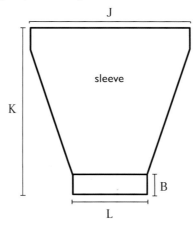
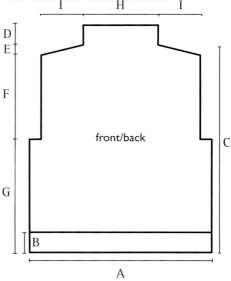

you will need

MATERIALS
Fisherman (aran) weight merino wool yarn (85yd/78m per ball): 12[12:13:13] × 1¾oz/50g balls in colour denim blue

NEEDLES
Size 6 (4mm/UK8) needles
Size 8 (5mm/UK6) needles

Gauge (Tension)
18 sts and 24 rows to 4in (10cm) measured over stockinette (stocking) stitch on size 8 (5mm/UK6) needles

Child's sweater size diagram measurements

A 14 [15:16:17]in (36 [38:41:43]cm)

B 2in (5cm)

C 15 [16½:18:19½]in (37 [42:46:50]cm)

D 1¼in (3cm)

E 1in (2.5cm)

F 6 [6½:7:7½]in (15 [16.5:18:19]cm

G 8 [9:10:11]in (20.5 [23:25.5:28]cm)

H 6 [6:6½:7]in (15 [15:16.5:18]cm)

I 4 [4½:4¾:5]in (10 [11.5:12:12.5]cm)

J 12 [13:14:15]in (30.5 [33:35.5:38]cm)

K 13 [14:15:16]in (33 [35.5:38:40.5]cm)

L 6 [6½:6¾:7¾]in (15 [16.5:17:19.5]cm)

Back view of sweater

CHILD'S PLAIN SWEATER

Child's sweater for age 5-6[7-8:9-10:11-12] years
To fit chest measurement 24[26:28:30]in (61 [66:71:76]cm)

BACK AND FRONT (BOTH ALIKE)
Using size 6 (4mm/UK8) needles, cast on 63[67:73:77] sts.
Row 1 (RS) K1, * p1, k1; rep from * to end.
Row 2 P1, * k1, p1; rep from * to end.
Rep these 2 rows until rib measures 2in (5cm), ending with a WS row.
Change to size 8 (5mm/UK6) needles and work in st st (beg with a k row), until piece measures 8[9:10:11]in (20.5[23:25.5:28]cm) from beg, ending with a p row. (Alter this measurement to lengthen or shorten the sweater.)
SHAPE ARMHOLES
Cast off 5 sts at beg of next 2 rows. 53[57:63:67] sts.
Cont without shaping until armhole measures 6[6½:7:7.½]in (15[16.5:18:19]cm), ending with a p row.
SHAPE SHOULDERS
Cast off 4[5:5:6] sts at beg of next 4 rows then 3[3:5:4] sts at beg of next 2 rows. 31[31:33:35] sts.
SHAPE NECK
Dec 1 st at each end of next and foll alt row. Work straight on rem 27[27:29:31] sts until neck measures 1¼in (3cm),

ending with a k row. Knit 4 rows.
Bind (cast) off loosely knitwise.
SLEEVES (BOTH ALIKE)
Using size 6 (4mm/UK8) needles, cast on 27[29:31:35] sts and work 2in (5cm) in rib as given for back, ending with a WS row.
Change to size 8 (5mm/UK6) needles and work in st st (beg with a k row), inc 1 st at each end of 3rd and every foll 4th[4th:4th:5th] row to 55[59:63:67] sts. Cont without shaping until piece measures 13[14:15:16]in (33[35.5:38:40.5]cm) from beg, ending with a p row. (Alter this measurement to lengthen or shorten sleeve; if making the sleeve shorter you will need to increase more frequently – see page 74.)
Bind (cast) off.

FINISHING
Block pieces to measurements given on size diagrams. Join shoulder and neck seams. Place a marker at the centre of the sleeve top and match to shoulder seam. Using the square set in method (see page 73), sew in sleeve. Join side seams and underarm seams.

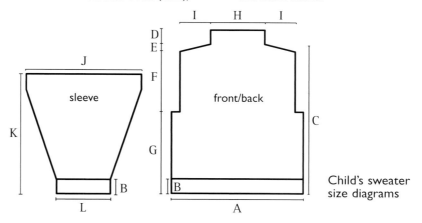

Child's sweater size diagrams

CABLE PANEL SWEATER (see main picture, facing page)

BACK
Work as given for back of plain sweater.

FRONT
Work 1 row less in rib as given for back.
Inc row Rib to end, including increases required for cable panel (see page 75).
Change to size 8 (5mm/UK6) needles.
START CABLE PANEL
Row 1 K to first stitch of cable panel, work first row of cable panel, k to end.

Row 2 P to cable panel, work second row of cable panel, p to end.
These 2 rows set st st panels and cable panel.
Complete front to match back.

SLEEVES (BOTH ALIKE)
Work as given for plain sweater.

FINISHING
Work as given for plain sweater.

LACE CARDIGAN

This pretty cardigan, knitted in a simple four row lace pattern, is ideal for learning how to shape knitting while keeping the pattern correct (see page 76). The neck edge has eyelet holes through which a ribbon is threaded and the moss stitch button and buttonhole bands use the technique of picking up stitches evenly down the fronts (see page 70) and making buttonholes (see page 71).

To fit bust/chest 30/32[34/36:38/40]in (76/81.5[86.5/91.5:96.5/101.5]cm)

you will need

MATERIALS

Worsted (DK) weight merino wool yarn (109yd/100m per ball): 8[9:10] x 1¾oz/50g balls in colour lilac

8[8:9] buttons

34in (86cm) of ¼in (0.6cm) wide ribbon in colour to match

NEEDLES

Size 3 (3.25mm/UK10) needles
Size 6 (4mm/UK8) needles

Gauge (Tension)

22 sts and 28 rows to 4in (10cm) measured over lace pattern on size 6 (4mm/UK8) needles

Lace pattern for gauge (tension) square

Using size 6 (4mm/UK8) needles, cast on 31 sts.
Row 1 (RS) K1, * yfwd, k1, sk2po, k1, yfwd, k1; rep from * to end.
Row 2 P to end.
Row 3 K1, * k1, yfwd, sk2po, yfwd, k2; rep from * to end.
Row 4 P to end.
Rep these 4 rows for at least 6in (15cm).
Bind (cast) off.
Measure your gauge (tension) (see page 33).

BACK

Using size 3 (3.25mm/UK10) needles, cast on 85[97:109] sts.
Row 1 K1, * p1, k1; rep from * to end.
This forms moss st.
Rep this row 3 times more.
Change to size 6 (4mm/UK8) needles.
Start lace patt.
Row 1 (RS) K1, * yfwd, k1, sk2po, k1, yfwd, k1; rep from * to end.
Row 2 P to end.
Row 3 K1, * k1, yfwd, sk2po, yfwd, k2; rep from * to end.
Row 4 P to end.
These 4 rows form the lace patt and are repeated.

SHAPE SIDE EDGES

Cont in lace patt as set, and working extra sts into patt, inc 1 st at each end of next and every foll 8th row to 97[109:121] sts. Cont without shaping until back measures 8[8½:9]in (20.5[21.5:23]cm) from beg, ending with a WS row.

SHAPE ARMHOLES

Keeping patt correct, bind (cast) off 5[7:9] sts at beg of next 2 rows.
Dec 1 st at each end of next 7[7:9] rows. 73[81:85] sts.
Cont in patt without shaping until armhole measures 8[8½:9]in (20.5[21.5:23]cm), ending with a WS row.

SHAPE SHOULDERS

Bind (cast) off 7[7:8] sts at beg of next 4 rows then cast off 5[7:7] sts at beg of next 2 rows.
Bind (cast) off rem 35[39:39] sts.

LEFT FRONT

Using size 3 (3.25mm/UK10) needles, cast on 43[49:55] sts and work 4 rows in moss st as given for back.
Change to size 6 (4mm/UK8) needles and work 4 rows in lace patt as given for back.

SHAPE SIDE EDGE

Cont in lace patt as set, and working extra sts into patt, inc 1 st at beg of next

and on same edge of every following 8th row to 49[55:61] sts.
Cont in patt without shaping until front measures same as back to armhole shaping, ending at side edge.

SHAPE ARMHOLE

Bind (cast) off 5[7:9] sts at beg of next row. Work 1 row.
Dec 1 st at armhole edge on foll 7[7:9] rows. 37[41:43] sts.
Cont in patt without shaping until armhole is 21 rows less than back to shoulder shaping, ending at front edge.

SHAPE NECK

Next row Bind (cast) off 7[8:8] sts, patt to end.
Patt 1 row.
Next row Bind (cast) off 4[5:5] sts, patt to end. 26[28:30] sts.
Dec 1 st at neck edge on foll 7 rows. 19[21:23] sts.
Cont in patt without shaping until front measures same as back to shoulder shaping, ending at armhole edge.

SHAPE SHOULDER

Bind (cast) off 7[7:8] sts at beg of next and foll alt row.
Patt 1 row.
Bind (cast) off rem 5 [7:7] sts.

RIGHT FRONT

Work as given for left front reversing all shapings.

SLEEVES (BOTH ALIKE)

Using size 3 (3.25mm/UK10) needles, cast on 43[49:55] sts and work 4 rows in moss st.
Change to size 6 (4mm/UK8) needles and work 4 rows in lace patt as given for back.
Cont in patt as set, and working extra sts into patt, inc 1 st at each end of next and every foll 6th row to 67[69:71] sts, then at each end of every foll 8th row to 75[81:87] sts.
Cont in patt without shaping until sleeve measures 17[18:19]in (43[45.5:48.5]cm), ending with a WS row.

SHAPE TOP

Bind (cast) off 5[7:9] sts at beg of next 2 rows.

Dec 1 st at each end of foll 5 rows, then at each end of foll 2 alt rows. 51[53:55] sts.

Dec 1 st at each end of every foll 4th row to 43 sts, then at each end of every foll alt row to 35 sts, and then at each end of every foll row to 29 sts.

Bind (cast) off 4 sts at beg of next 2 rows.

Bind (cast) off rem 21 sts.

FINISHING

Block pieces to measurements given on size diagram. Join shoulder seams.

NECKBAND

With RS of work facing and using size 3 (3.25mm/UK10) needles, pick up and k 11 sts across bound (cast) off sts at right front neck, 22 sts up right side of neck, 35[39:39] sts at back neck, 22 sts down left side of neck, and 11 sts across bound (cast) off sts at left front neck. 101[105:105] sts.

Work 1 row in moss st.

Eyelet row K1, yfwd, k2tog, patt 2[4:4] sts, yfwd, k2tog, * patt 4 sts, yfwd, k2tog; rep from * to last 4[6:6] sts, patt 2[4:4] sts, yfwd, k2tog.

Work 2 rows in moss st.

Bind (cast) off in moss st.

BUTTON BAND

Using size 3 (3.25mm/UK10) needles, pick up and k 73[77:83] sts evenly down left front edge, and work 4 rows in moss st.

Bind (cast) off in moss st.

BUTTONHOLE BAND

Using size 3 (3.25mm/UK10) needles, pick up and k 73[77:83] sts evenly up right front edge, and work 1 row in moss st.

Buttonhole row K1[3:1], (yfwd, k2tog, patt 8 sts) 7[7:8] times, yfwd, k2tog, patt 0[2:0] sts.

Work 2 rows in moss st.

Bind (cast) off in moss st.

Join side and sleeve seams. Sew sleeves into armholes using set in sleeve method (see page 73). Sew on buttons. Thread ribbon through eyelets around neckband.

BABY BOOTEES

These delightful bootees with roll top edges will keep a baby's toes cosy and show how easy it is to knit three-dimensional shapes. The techniques used include M1 to make a stitch between stitches (see page 29) and decreasing stitches (see page 30).

To fit ages 0-3 months and 3-6 months
Foot length 3½in (9cm) and 4¼in (10.5cm)

you will need

MATERIALS

Worsted (DK) weight merino wool yarn (131yd/120m)
1 x 1¾oz/50g ball in colour lilac

NEEDLES

Size 6 (4mm/UK8) needles

Gauge (Tension)

22 sts and 30 rows to 4in (10cm) measured over stockinette (stocking) stitch on size 6 (4mm/UK8) needles

BOOTEE (MAKE 2)

Using size 6 (4mm/UK8) needles cast on 30[36] sts and purl 1 row.

Inc row K2, M1, k12[15], M1, k2, M1, k12[15], M1, k2. 34[40] sts.

Purl 1 row.

Inc row K2, M1, k14[17], M1, k2, M1, k14[17], M1, k2. 38[44] sts.

Purl 1 row.

Inc row K2, M1, k16[19], M1, k2, M1, k16[19], M1, k2. 42[48] sts.

Beg with p row, work 7 rows in st st.

Dec row K14[17], (k2tog) 3 times, k2, (skpo) 3 times, k14[17]. 36[42] sts.

SHAPE TOP

Next row P21[24], p2tog and turn work as though at the end of the row, leaving the unworked sts on the RH needle.

Next row K7, skpo and turn, leaving unworked sts on the RH needle.

Next row P7, p2tog and turn.

Rep the last 2 rows once more.

Next row K7, skpo and turn.

Next row P7, p2tog, p across all unworked sts on LH needle to end of row.

Next row K17, skpo, k across all unworked sts on LH needle to end of row. 28[34] sts.

Beg with a p row, work 7 rows in st st.

Bind (cast) off.

FINISHING

Join seam along sole and at back of bootee.

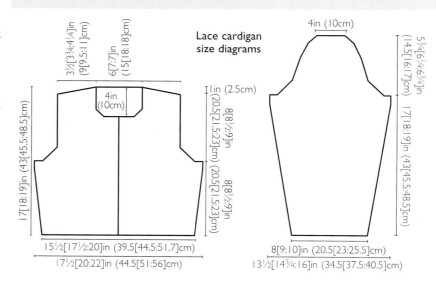

Lace cardigan size diagrams

3½[3¾:4¼]in (9[9.5:11]cm)

6[7:7]in (15[18:18]cm)

4in (10cm)

17[18:19]in (43[45.5:48.5]cm)

15½[17½:20]in (39.5[44.5:51.7]cm)

17½[20:22]in (44.5[51:56]cm)

1in (2.5cm)

8[8½:9]in (20.5[21.5:23]cm)

8[8½:9]in (20.5[21.5:23]cm)

4in (10cm)

5¾[6¼:6¾]in (14.5[16:17]cm)

17[18:19]in (43[45.5:48.5]cm)

8[9:10]in (20.5[23:25.5]cm)

13½[14¾:16]in (34.5[37.5:40.5]cm)

DAINTY KNITTED TRIMS

Use these trims to add a finishing touch to a piece of knitting, or decorate an item to make it special. The knitted rose brooch has been fulled to give it body (see page 62); a book is fastened by a button with an embroidered knitted cover and a matching twisted cord (see pages 82, 87 and 79); and a lacy leaf trim is the perfect edging to a scented sachet.

ROSE BROOCH

you will need

MATERIALS
Sport (4ply) weight shetland wool yarn (129yd/118m per ball):
1 × 1oz/25g ball each in colours:
A rose red
B green

Small amount of dark green embroidery thread

Brooch pin

NEEDLES
Size 3 (3.25mm/UK10) needles

Gauge (Tension)
28 sts and 36 rows to 4in (10cm) measured over stockinette (stocking) stitch on size 3 (3.25mm/UK10) needles

Using size 3 (3.25mm/UK10) needles and A, work a rose as given on page 84, bind (cast) off the stitches instead of threading the yarn through them.
Using B, work two leaves as given on page 84, working the increases as M1 instead of yarn over (see page 29).
The rose and leaves are fulled following the instructions on page 62.

FINISHING

Run a gathering thread through the base of the rose and pull up. Form the rose by twisting it round and round from the centre with right side of fabric facing outwards. Pull the rose into shape as you go. Work a few stitches through the base to secure it. Embroider veins on to the leaves. Sew the leaves either side of the rose. Sew the brooch pin on securely.

ROSE BUTTON FASTENING

you will need

MATERIALS
Sport (4ply) weight mercerized cotton yarn (53yd/140m per ball):
1 × 1¾oz/50g ball in dark purple

Stranded cotton embroidery threads:
1 hank in each of the colours dark rose, light pink and green

1in (2.5cm) button or button covering kit

Notebook

Ribbon the width to fit down spine of book and three times the length of the spine

NEEDLES
Size 2 (3mm/UK11) needles

Using size 2 (3mm/UK11) needles and 4ply yarn, work a covered button as given on page 82. Using embroidery threads, work a group of roses (rose stitch) and french knots. Work single chain stitches for the leaves. (See embroidery stitches, page 85–7.) Finish the button. Thread the ribbon through the spine of the book and tie the ends together and hide the knot in the spine. Make twisted cords in each of the light pink and dark rose embroidery threads, using two strands (see page 79). Sew one end of each on to the base of the button. Place the button on the front of the book, close to the edge. Wrap the twisted cords around the book, passing under the ribbon on the spine. Secure the cords to the ribbon with a few neat stitches. To close the book, tie the cords around the button in a bow.

LEAF EDGED SACHET

you will need

MATERIALS
Sport (4ply) weight mercerized cotton yarn (153yd/140m per ball):
1 × 1¾oz/50g ball in colour light pink

Fabric sachet with rose petal filling

Large bead

NEEDLES
Size 2 (3mm/UK11) needles

Measure the edge of the sachet where the edging will be stitched. Using size 2 (3mm/UK11) needles and 4ply yarn, work this length of leaf edging as given on page 128. Sew on to the sachet. If required, make a fastening loop from a short twisted cord, using two strands of the yarn (see page 79) and sew behind the edging. Sew on the bead.

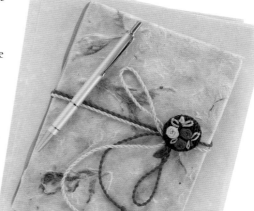

DRAWSTRING BAGS

These dainty drawstring bags have knitted background fabrics taken from patterns in the Stitch library. The ones chosen are particularly suitable for further embellishment with embroidery, whether you choose simple ribbon roses or cross stitch motifs. Add a swiss darned initial to make the bag truly personal (see page 85–87).

Bags measure 8in (20.5cm) wide by 9in (23cm) long

GINGHAM CHECK BAG

you will need

MATERIALS
Worsted (DK) weight cotton yarn (92yd/82m per ball):
2 x 1¾oz/50g balls in white

Oddments of blue yarn for embroidery

NEEDLES
Size 6 (4mm/UK8) needles

Gauge (Tension)
20 sts and 28 rows to 4in (10cm) measured over stockinette (stocking) stitch on size 6 (4mm/UK8) needles

BACK AND FRONT (MAKE 2 THE SAME)
Using size 6 (4mm/UK8) needles cast on 37 sts and work in gingham check pattern from Stitch library, page 96 until work measures approx 7½in (19cm), ending with row 5 of pattern.
** Work 5 rows in st st, beg with a p row.
Next row P to end. (Turning row for drawstring channel).
Work 5 rows in st st, beg with p row. Bind (cast) off.

FINISHING
Block pieces to 8in (20.5cm) wide and 10in (25.5cm) long. Embroider bag with initial using duplicate stitch. Fill other squares with motifs worked in cross stitch (see page 158). Join back and front together along bottom seam. Join side seams, leaving a small gap for drawstring in first 5 rows of st st. Turn hem over to the inside and slipstitch in place. Make two twisted cords the same length and thread through gaps from each side.

ROSE BROCADE BAG

you will need

MATERIALS
Worsted (DK) weight cotton yarn (92yd/82m per ball):
2 x 1¾oz/50g balls in mauve

Embroidery threads for roses

NEEDLES
Size 6 (4mm/UK8) needles

Gauge (Tension)
20 sts and 28 rows to 4in (10cm) measured over stockinette (stocking) stitch on size 6 (4mm/UK8) needles

BACK AND FRONT (MAKE 2 THE SAME)
Using size 6 (4mm/UK8) needles cast on 37 sts and work in King Charles brocade from Stitch library, page 94, until work measures approx 8in (20cm) from beg, ending with row 7 of pattern.
Work as given for gingham check bag from **.

FINISHING
Block pieces to 8in (20.5cm) wide and 10in (25.5cm) long. Embroider bag with roses (see page 87). Finish as given for gingham check bag.

PATCHWORK CUSHION

This sampler cushion cover uses squares knitted in a range of stitch patterns taken from the Stitch library including cables, bobbles and twisted stitches (see pages 42, 44 and 48). They give it a rich texture, and dividing up some of the squares into smaller patches further enhances the visual interest.

Cushion measures approximately 16in (40.5cm) square

you will need

MATERIALS

Worsted (DK) weight cotton yarn (93yd/85m per ball):
1 × 1¾oz/50g ball in colour
A pale grey

Worsted (DK) weight wool/cotton mix yarn (123yd/113m per ball):
1 × 1¾oz/50g ball each in colours:
B light blue violet
C pale lilac
D light pink

Worsted (DK) weight cotton yarn (92yd/84m per ball)
2 × 1¾oz/50g balls in colour:
E bright green

Backing fabric

16in (40.5cm) square cushion pad

NEEDLES

Size 6 (4mm/UK8) needles

Gauge (Tension)

20 sts and 28 rows to 4in (10cm) measured over stockinette (stocking) stitch on size 6 (4mm/UK8) needles using A

			3a	3b
1		2	3c	3d
4a	4b			
4c	4d	5		6
7		8		9

SQUARE 1
Using size 6 (4mm/UK8) needles and D, cast on 27 sts and work 36 rows in Bobble circle pattern (see page 106). Bind (cast) off in patt.

SQUARE 2
Using size 6 (4mm/UK8) needles and E, cast on 30 sts and work 36 rows in Bramble stitch (see page 104). Bind (cast) off in patt.

SQUARE 3
This is made up of four smaller squares.
SQUARE 3A
Using size 6 (4mm/UK8) needles and A, cast on 15 sts and work 20 rows of Medallion bobble cable (see page 111). Bind (cast) off in patt.
SQUARE 3B
Using size 6 (4mm/UK8) needles and B, cast on 15 sts and work 20 rows in Moss stitch (see page 91). Bind (cast) off in patt.
SQUARE 3C
Using size 6 (4mm/UK8) needles and D, cast on 19 sts and work 20 rows in Boxed bobble pattern (see page 105). Bind (cast) off in patt.
SQUARE 3D
Using size 6 (4mm/UK8) needles and E, cast on 18 sts and work 20 rows in Five rib braid (see page 112). Bind (cast) off in patt.

SQUARE 4
This is made up of four smaller squares.
SQUARE 4A
Using size 6 (4mm/UK8) needles and E, cast on 16 sts and work 20 rows in Nosegay pattern (see page 117). Bind (cast) off in patt.
SQUARE 4B
Using size 6 (4mm/UK8) needles and B, cast on 18 sts and work 20 rows in Two stitch check (see page 92). Bind (cast) off in patt.

SQUARE 4C
Using size 6 (4mm/UK8) needles and C, cast on 15 sts and work 20 rows in Mistake rib (see page 108). Bind (cast) off in patt.
SQUARE 4D
Using size 6 (4mm/UK8) needles and A, cast on 21 sts and work 20 rows in Heart cable (see page 117). Bind (cast) off in patt.

SQUARE 5
Using size 6 (4mm/UK8) needles and C, cast on 26 sts and work 36 rows in Stepped diamonds pattern (see page 95). Bind (cast) off in patt.

SQUARE 6
Using size 6 (4mm/UK8) needles and A, cast on 31 sts and work 36 rows in Double moss stitch and Rib check (see page 91). Bind (cast) off in patt.

SQUARE 7
Using size 6 (4mm/UK8) needles and A, cast on 29 sts and work 36 rows in Basketweave stitch (see page 92). Bind (cast) off in patt.

SQUARE 8
Using size 6 (4mm/UK8) needles and D, cast on 30 sts and work 36 rows in Mock cable (see page 95). Bind (cast) off in patt.

SQUARE 9
Using size 6 (4mm/UK8) needles and E, cast on 29 sts and work 36 rows in Heart squares pattern (see page 96). Bind (cast) off in patt.

FINISHING
Block the large squares to about 5½in (14cm) square and the smaller ones to about 3in (7.5cm). These measures are a guide only; some of the smaller squares are slightly longer or narrower. The squares are sewn together using E with the seam on the outside; use a small neat running stitch.
SQUARE 3
With WS together, sew 3A to 3C, and 3B

to 3D. Sew the two strips together.

SQUARE 4

With WS together, sew 4A to 4C, and 4B to 4D. Sew the two strips together. Sew squares 1, 4 and 7 together, 2, 5 and 8 together, and then 3, 6 and 9 together. Sew the three strips together. Block the whole piece to about 16in (40.5cm) square. Cut a piece of backing fabric to 17¼in (43.5cm) square. Neaten the edges and press a seam allowance of ⅝in (1.5cm) to the wrong side on all edges. With WS facing, place the front and back together and sew around three sides using a small neat running stitch. Insert the cushion pad and sew the remaining side closed.

GREETINGS CARDS

Knit these delightful patches in stocking stitch with a moss stitch frame. Then use embroidery silks to swiss darn an appropriate motif in the centre (see page 87). You can use the charts in this book or create your own on graph paper.

you will need

MATERIALS
Sport (4ply) weight mercerized cotton yarn (153yd/140m per ball):
1 × 1¾oz/50g ball in colour light pink

1 skein of 12ply silk embroidery thread in shades of pinks and reds

Card blank 4in (10cm) square

NEEDLES
Size 2 (3mm/UK11) needles

Gauge (Tension)
28 sts and 38 rows to 4in (10cm) measured over stockinette (stocking) stitch on size 2 (3mm/UK11) needles

you will need

MATERIALS
Sport (4ply) weight mercerized cotton yarn (153yd/140m per ball):
1 × 1¾oz/50g ball in colour dark purple

1 skein of 12ply silk embroidery thread in shades of green

Card blank 4in (10cm) square

VALENTINE CARD

Using size 2 (3mm/UK11) needles and 4ply yarn, cast on 20 sts.
Row 1 * K1, p1; rep from * to end.
Row 2 * P1, k1; rep from * to end. (These 2 rows form moss st).
Row 3 K1, p1, k to last st, p1.
Row 4 P1, k1, p to last st, k1.
Rep rows 3 and 4, six times more.
Work 2 rows in moss st.
Bind (cast) off.

FINISHING
Block the piece. Using all the strands of the 12ply embroidery thread, swiss darn the heart from the chart on page 158 on to the st st in the centre of the patch. Using double-sided tape, stick patch on to card.

CHRISTMAS TREE CARD

Using size 2 (3mm/UK11) needles and 4ply yarn, cast on 17 sts.
Row 1 K1, * p1, k1; rep from * to end. (This row forms moss st).
Rep this row once more.
Row 3 K1, p1, k to last 2 sts, p1, k1.
Row 4 K1, p to last st, k1.
Rep rows 3 and 4, six times more.
Work 2 rows in moss st.
Bind (cast) off.

FINISHING
Block the piece. Using all the strands of the 12ply embroidery thread, swiss darn the tree from the chart on page 158 on to the st st in the centre of the patch. Using double-sided tape, stick patch on to card.

GIFT BAGS

These small bags are a great way to practise the basic knitting techniques of casting on, stockinette (stocking) stitch, binding (casting) off, blocking and making up (see pages 19–25, 68, 72). And if you are using a novelty yarn they give an idea of how it will look knitted up. Measuring 4in (10cm) square, they can be decorated with ribbons, trims, buttons, beads, flowers or jewels. Make them for presenting small gifts at Christmas, birthdays or just as a thank-you gift. The bags are also shown on pages 14–15.

you will need

MATERIALS
1 x ball of a novelty yarn such as fun fur, metallic, fleece, mohair, ribbon, boucle or chenille. Yarns with a gauge (tension) of less than 15 stitches to 4in (10cm) will be too bulky and are unsuitable. Check the ball band first.
The yarns used to knit the bags illustrated are given with each pattern.

NEEDLES
The ball band gives the needle size that you will need.

BALL BAND
All the information you need to knit a bag is on the yarn's ball band. The number of stitches to cast on is determined by the gauge (tension) information.

For example, a worsted (DK) yarn has a gauge (tension) of 22 sts and 28 rows to 4in (10cm) using size 6 (4mm/UK8) needles. You would cast on 22 sts using this size needles.

A metallic yarn may have a gauge (tension) of 29 sts and 41 rows to 4in (10cm) on size 3 (3.25mm/UK10) needles. You would cast on 29 sts using these needles.

BASIC BAG PATTERN (MAKE 2)
Using the recommended size of needles, cast on number of stitches to 4in (10cm). Beginning with a knit row, work in stockinette (stocking) stitch until piece measures 4in (10cm) from beg, ending with a knit row.
Knit 2 rows.
Bind (cast) off knitwise.

OPTIONAL KNITTED HANDLES
Cast on 1½ times the number of stitches cast on for the bag and knit four rows.
Bind (cast) off knitwise.

FINISHING
Block the pieces to measure 4in (10cm) square, according to the information on the ball band. Some novelty yarns require careful pressing. Place the two bag pieces together with wrong sides facing. Work a neat running stitch around three sides, leaving top edge open. If the bag is knitted in fun fur or brushed yarn, use a smooth yarn or thread in a close colour match. Attach knitted handles (if made) to the inside on the side seams. Alternatively, use ribbon or felt cut to length. Add trims as required.

GOLD STAR RIBBON BAG
Yarn Jaeger Albany (cotton ribbon) in colour 270.
Trimming 29in (74cm) length of ½in (1.5cm) wide gold ribbon.
Using size 8 (5mm/UK6) needles cast on 22 sts and knit two squares.
Cut a 7in (18cm) length of the ribbon for the handle. Divide the remaining ribbon into five equal lengths with a tape measure, marking with

pins. Fold the ribbon into points, one by one, bringing the pins and the ribbon ends into the centre. Secure with a few stitches in the centre through all thicknesses. Attach to one square of the bag. Sew bag together and attach a ribbon handle to the inside of the side seams.

ROSEBUD BAG
Yarn Rowan Kidsilk Haze in colour 597 used double.
Trimming 10 ready-made ½in (1.5cm) roses, 7in (18cm) of ½in (7mm) wide ribbon to match roses.
Using size 5 (3.75mm/UK9) needles cast on 23 sts and knit two squares.
Sew on the roses in alternating lines of 3, 2, 3 and 2, on one square. Sew bag together and attach the ribbon handle to the inside of the side seams.

HEART AND BIRD BAG
(this page, top left)
Yarn Sirdar Snowflake Chunky (fleece effect) in colour 376.
Trimming felt, wooden bird button or similar and embroidery thread.
Using size 9 (5.5mm/UK5) needles cast on 14 sts and knit two squares.
Draw a heart shape on a 2½in (6cm) square of felt and cut it out. Cut a 7in (18cm) long by ¾in (2cm) wide handle from the felt. Using embroidery thread, work blanket stitch around the edges of the heart and handle (see page 86). Sew the heart on to one of the bag pieces and sew the button in the centre. Sew the bag together and attach the handle to the inside of the side seams.

HOUSE SAMPLER

Knit this sampler for someone who has moved into a new home. The house is swiss darned once the knitting is complete (see page 87).

Sampler measures 7in (18cm) square

DENIM HEART BAG

Yarn Rowan All Seasons Cotton in colour 160.
Trimming ready-made denim heart-shaped patch or similar.
Using size 7 (4.5mm/UK7) needles, cast on 18 sts and knit two squares. Knit a handle on 27 sts.

HOLOGRAM DAISY BAG

(opposite page, top right)
Yarn Rowan Lurex Shimmer in colour 336.
Trimming three ready-made hologram effect daisy patches or similar.
Using size 3 (3.25mm/UK10) needles cast on 29 sts and knit two squares. Knit a handle on 43 sts.

FLUFFY PINK RIBBON BAG

Yarn Sirdar Funky Fur in colour 536.
Trimming 24in (61cm) length of ¹/₂in (1.5cm) wide pink ribbon.
Using size 6 (4mm/UK8) needles cast on 20 sts and knit two squares.
Cut a 7in (18cm) length of ribbon for the handle. Tie the remaining ribbon into a bow and attach to one bag piece.
Sew the bag together and attach the handle to the inside of the side seams.

SNOWFLAKE BAG

Yarn Patons Tapestry (boucle) in colour 5000.
Trimming ready-made star, snowflake or similar.
Using size 6 (4mm/UK8) needles cast on 22 sts and knit two squares. Knit a handle on 33 sts.

you will need

MATERIALS

Sport (4ply) weight tweed wool yarn (120yd/110m per ball):
2 x 25g balls of colour oatmeal

Tapestry Wool (100% wool – 8.7yd/8m per skein):
1 skein each of:
dark red
red
light red
dark blue
blue
gold
dark green
green

Stranded cotton
1 x dark brown

Wire hanger

NEEDLES
Size 6 (4mm/UK8) needles

Gauge (Tension)
20 sts and 28 rows to 4in (10cm) over stockinette (stocking) stitch using 2 strands of sport (4ply) together and size 6 (4mm/UK8) needles

SAMPLER
Using size 6 (4mm/UK8) needles and 2 strands of sport (4ply) together, cast on 35 sts.
Row 1 P1, * k1, p1; rep from * to end. This row forms moss st.
Rep this row 3 times more.
Row 5 P1, k1, p1, k29, p1, k1, p1.
Row 6 P1, k1, p31, k1, p1.
Rep these 2 rows 20 times more, then row 5 again.
Work 4 rows in moss st.
Next row Bind (cast) off 5 sts in patt, patt 7 sts (including last st used in binding (casting) off), bind (cast) off 11 sts in patt, patt 7 sts (including last st used in binding (casting) off), bind (cast) off rem 5 sts in patt.

TABS (MAKE 2)
With RS of work facing, rejoin yarn to first set of 7 sts and work 12 rows in moss st. Bind (cast) off in patt.

FINISHING
Block the piece to 7in (18cm) square. Use 1 strand of tapestry wool to swiss darn the design on to the knitted piece, following the chart on page 158.
Use 6 strands of the stranded cotton to backstitch the smoke and use 2 long straight stitches for each window.
Sew the tabs over the wire hanger to the wrong side of the knitted piece.

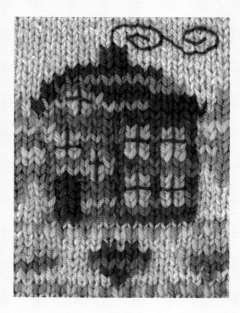

INTARSIA CUSHION

This cushion was inspired by the colours and forms of Jacobean crewel work and uses the intarsia method (see page 49). The back is worked in two halves to insert the cushion pad. It is fastened with buttonholes and four buttons covered with knitted fabric (see page 71 and 82). The contrast trim round the edge is a simple cord, knitted with double-pointed needles (see page 79).

■ Cushion front measures 15in (38cm) square

you will need

MATERIALS

Worsted (DK) weight wool yarn (131yd/120m):
3 × 1¾oz/50g balls in colour
MC natural:
1 × 1¾oz/50g ball each in colours:
A dark green
B green
C red
D light red
E purple
F pink
G light pink

4 self-cover buttons

15in (38cm) square cushion pad

NEEDLES

Size 6 (4mm/UK8) needles
2 size 6 (4mm/UK8) double-pointed needles

Gauge (Tension)

22 sts and 30 rows to 4in (10cm) measured over stockinette (stocking) stitch on size 6 (4mm/UK8) needles

FRONT

Using size 6 (4mm/UK8) needles and MC, cast on 83 sts.
Work 4 rows in st st, beg with a k row.

START CHART

Using the intarsia method work from the chart on page 157, starting at the bottom right-hand corner and reading the odd rows (k rows) from right to left and the even rows (p rows) from left to right.
Cont until all 104 rows of chart have been completed.
Using MC only, work 4 rows in st st, beg with a k row.
Bind (cast) off.

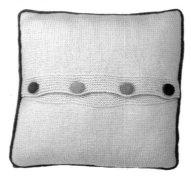

BACK (IN TWO SECTIONS)

BUTTON SECTION

Using size 6 (4mm/UK8) needles and MC, cast on 83 sts.
Work 51 rows in st st, ending with a k row. **
Knit 14 rows.
Bind (cast) off.

BUTTONHOLE SECTION

Work as given for button section to **.
Knit 7 rows.
Buttonhole row 1 K11, * bind (cast) off 2 sts, k18 (including last st used in bind (cast) off); rep from * twice more, bind (cast) off 2 sts, k to end.
Buttonhole row 2 K to end, casting on 2 sts over those bound (cast) off in previous row.
Knit 5 rows.
Bind (cast) off.

FINISHING

Block pieces to measurements. Lay buttonhole border over button border and join together at the sides. Join front to backs.

PIPING CORD

Using 2 size 6 (4mm/UK8) double-pointed needles and F, cast on 4 sts.
Work a tubular cord to fit around outside of cushion. Sew it over the seam.

COVERED BUTTONS

Cover four buttons using colours A, B, C and D. Sew into place on button border. Insert cushion pad.

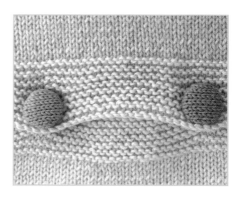

Fair Isle Baby Blanket — pattern rows (page 143)

Chart A

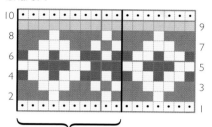

Repeat these 10 sts 9 times

Chart B

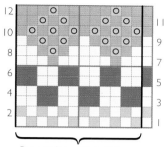

Repeat these 12 sts 8 times

Chart C

Repeat these 18 sts 5 times

Chart D

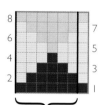

Repeat these 6 sts 16 times

Chart E

Repeat these 25 sts 3 times

Chart F

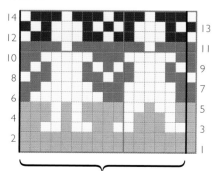

Repeat these 16 sts 6 times

k on RS rows, p on WS rows

- MC
- A
- B
- C
- D
- E
- F
- G

p on RS rows, k on WS rows

- ○ A
- • D

Introduction to crochet

Crochet is fun, it's versatile, and it's quick to learn – it's nowhere near as difficult as many people think! With the help of this book, you can learn to crochet even if you've never picked up a hook before. Or, if you already know the basics, this book will help you to improve your skills and learn new ones.

How to use this section

This section is divided into three main sub-sections.

The **Techniques** section (pages 166–237) gives you all the basic information you need. Complete with diagrams, photographs and helpful hints, the Techniques section will take you step by step through the basic stitches and techniques you need to start to crochet – from choosing yarns and selecting hooks, to how to work the basic crochet stitches that form the foundation of all crochet work. The Techniques section then takes you on to the next stage, giving you details of how to combine the stitches and skills you now have to create your very own crochet masterpieces. Fully illustrated throughout with diagrams, photographs and tips, this section will show you how to combine basic stitches to make exciting new combinations, how to work the more unusual stitches, such as Solomon's knots and bullion stitches, and how to complete your work to obtain a truly professional finish.

The **Stitch Library** (pages 238–55) contains full instructions, both written and diagrammatic, for some of the basic 'old favourite' stitches, and for some new and exciting stitches you can try out to create your own unique crochet items.

In the **Projects** section (pages 256–311) you will find the patterns to make the items that are featured within the other sections. Some are simple, some are more complex – but you will find all the techniques you need to complete the projects within this book. If you want to make a quick and easy project to try out a new technique, why not try the little Pot Pourri Sachets (pages 300–301) or the Corsage (page 272)? Or, if you want to create your very own heirloom, you could make the exquisite Heirloom Bedspread (pages 310–311). Among the 24 projects, there is bound to be something you would simply love to try out – for you, your home or your family! Finally, on pages 312–316, we detail the exact yarns that we used to create all the projects in the book, and provide a list of international suppliers of yarn and crochet equipment.

Whatever your skill level or whatever you want to make, this book will become an invaluable reference book to keep by your side whenever you decide to crochet.

So what's stopping you? Get some yarn and a hook and start crocheting now!

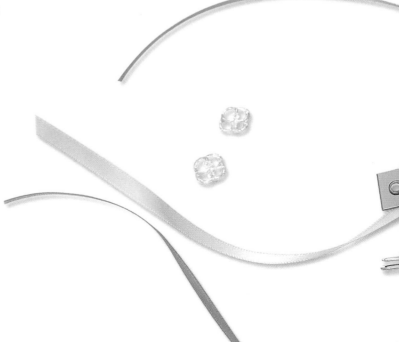

Equipment

Crochet uses surprisingly little equipment, which makes it a wonderfully portable craft – for the main bulk of the work, you basically just need a crochet hook, some yarn and a pattern! When it comes to finishing a project, you will need some other essential items, such as scissors, a tape measure and some pins. None of this equipment is expensive, and all is easy to get hold of – although you will probably need a useful box or tin to keep all your tools together.

Crochet hooks

These come in a range of sizes and can be made from a variety of materials – most commonly metal, plastic, wood and bamboo.

The size of hook needed is directly related to the thickness of yarn being used: a fine yarn will use a small hook, while a thick yarn will need a much chunkier hook. There are two basic sizing schemes for crochet hooks: the metric system and the American system. (There is also an old imperial sizing system that is now very rarely used, and we don't mention it in this book.) Throughout this book, you will find metric sizes quoted first, with American sizes given in brackets. Consult the chart shown right to convert between the systems.

Other equipment

Apart from the essential crochet hook, there will be a selection of other items that you may need to complete your crochet project.

- Scissors – to cut the yarn.
- Tape measure – to check that the work is the correct size.

- Ruler – this is useful to measure smaller pieces, such as tension swatches.
- Pins (large glass-headed or decorative-headed) – to secure pieces together before joining them. As ordinary pins can easily be lost in the surface of crochet, use large pins instead – these will be much easier to find later.
- Darning needle – to sew your crochet item together. It is best to use a blunt-pointed needle with an eye large enough to easily thread the yarn through – like those designed for sewing up knitting and for tapestry and cross stitch. The blunt point means that the fibres of the yarn are eased apart, rather than pierced and broken, which can weaken and damage the yarn.
- Notions – if the project you are making needs any ribbons, buttons or other fastenings, your pattern will give you details of exactly what you need to buy. It is a good idea to collect everything together before you start a project.

Crochet hook conversion chart

METRIC SIZES	AMERICAN SIZES
2.00mm	B1
2.25mm	B1
2.50mm	C2
3.00mm	D3
3.25mm	D3
3.50mm	E4
3.75mm	F5
4.00mm	G6
4.50mm	7
5.00mm	H8
5.50mm	I9
6.00mm	J10
6.50mm	K10½
7.00mm	–
8.00mm	L11
9.00mm	M13
10.00mm	N15

Yarn textures

There are three aspects that make up any crochet yarn: its texture, its fibre (natural or synthetic; plant- or animal-derived), and its thickness. Almost any hand-knitting yarn is also suitable for crochet. On these pages we explore yarn texture. The best yarns to use for crochet are usually those that are fairly smooth, such as classic wool, cotton or mixed yarns. More exotic or fancy yarns may be a little trickier to work with, but don't let that put you off experimenting with them.

Bouclé A bouclé yarn consists of loops of fibre held in place by a core thread. These loops can be quite large or very small, and the yarn can be difficult to crochet with – the larger the bouclé loops, the more difficult it will be to place the stitches in the correct place. However, if you can manage the snarls, this yarn produces a fascinating loopy, bubbly texture.

Chenille A chenille yarn is made by securing lots of short fibres to a central core – like a very thin strip of velvet. Depending on the length of the pile, chenille can be quite tricky to handle, as the 'fluff' of the yarn can hide the stitch definition, making it difficult to place the stitches correctly. On the plus side, chenille has a lush, dense and velvety texture when worked up.

Classic This type of yarn is what you would normally regard as a knitting yarn – quite tightly twisted and fairly smooth. Available in all sorts of weights, from 3ply to super-chunky, these yarns can be made in any type of fibre, from silk to wool.

Crepe Crepe yarns are perfect for crocheting with – they are smooth and easy to handle. The crocheted stitches are clearly visible so are easy to place, and the resulting crocheted fabric is clean and crisp. These yarns can be made from any type of fibre, but they are most commonly found in easy-care synthetic fibres.

Fancy Modern technology means that yarn producers can combine different sorts of yarns within one yarn. These

One of the greatest joys of crochet is the glorious array of yarns that are available to explore.

fancy, or speciality, yarns can be easy or difficult to crochet with depending on the combination of yarns they are constructed from. The only way to find out whether you can crochet successfully with a fancy yarn is to experiment with it! Some will work; others won't.

Fluffy These are exactly what their name suggests – fluffy! These yarns can be made from any naturally fluffy fibre, such as mohair or angora, or they can be fluffy because the yarn has been brushed to give it a fluffy appearance. Either way, they can be tricky to use; the hook can catch the fluff of the yarn, not its core, and stitches can be missed or misplaced. If you persevere, such yarns can produce a beautifully light fabric with a soft haze of colour.

Perle Normally made of cotton, a perle yarn is the classic fine crochet yarn. Its name derives from the way the yarn is constructed: it is tightly twisted, giving the effect of a string of beads or pearls.

Ribbon As their name suggests, these yarns are simply ribbon! Generally made of lightweight synthetic fibres, they can also be made of cotton or silk, or combinations of fibres, and are quite easy and quick to crochet with.

Roving Sometimes referred to as lopi yarns, a roving yarn has almost no twist to it, with the fibres just laying neatly next to each other. Generally made of woolly fibres, these yarns can be tricky to crochet with. They have a tendency to split, and the hook can catch on the fibres of previous stitches, leaving a messy appearance to the work. If you can get the hang of working with them, these yarns produce a pleasingly chunky and robust texture.

Slub A slubbed yarn does not maintain a consistent thickness along its length. Instead, the yarn features stretches of thin fibre and then areas of thicker fibre, known as slubs. Slubbed yarns can be made from almost any fibre. They are often constructed from a combination of fibres – one fibre that is used to create the smooth core that gives the yarn its strength, and a second fibre that forms the slubby thread twisted around the core. These yarns produce an intriguing fabric with a lot of depth, but it can be difficult to pull a slub through one of the thinner areas.

Tape These yarns consist of a tube of very finely knitted yarn. Lurex yarns and many summer-weight cotton yarns have such a construction. The yarn's smooth texture makes it ideal for crochet. One drawback is that, unless the ends are well secured, the knitted tube itself can unravel.

Yarn weights

The thickness of a yarn is referred to as its 'weight'. Any type of yarn construction and any type of fibre, or fibre combination, can be made into any thickness of yarn. Originally, the names given to the weights of yarns related to the number of strands, or 'plys', used to make it. However, nowadays modern yarn construction has rather thrown this out of the window. Although a yarn may still be referred to as a '4ply' yarn, it may appear to be made of only two or three strands of twisted fibres.

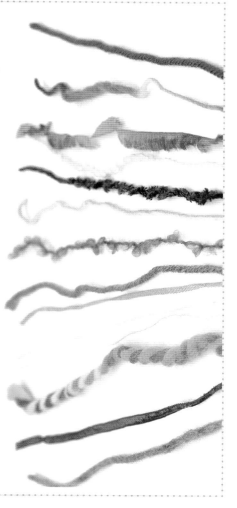

Crochet cotton These tightly twisted cotton yarns are more like a sewing thread than a crochet yarn. Traditionally used for the ultra-fine crochet of our grandmothers, their popularity has waned in recent years – but they are still widely available.

2ply and 3ply These are both very fine yarns, traditionally used for baby clothes and Shetland lace knitting.

4ply This fine yarn is possibly the most common thin yarn currently available, and it is one of the best weights for crochet. 4ply yarns are ideal for little tops, baby clothes and an assortment of household items.

Double knitting Often abbreviated to 'DK', this weight of yarn is possibly the most commonly used and best-known of all yarns. Suitable for almost any end use, it is another ideal yarn for crochet.

Aran Based on the weight of yarn used for traditional fishermen's sweaters (also known as aran sweaters), this weight of yarn is slightly thicker than a DK yarn. It is easy to crochet with and makes a good, firm fabric that is ideal for jackets and coats.

Chunky This weight of yarn, as its name suggests, is very thick – roughly two or three times as thick as a DK yarn. Although suitable for crochet, it can be a little tricky for a beginner to handle, but it works up very quickly and makes wonderfully warm coats and jackets.

Super-chunky and mega-chunky These are yarns that are even thicker than a chunky yarn. Although they work up very quickly, they can be tricky to use and often you may spend as long searching for the correct size hook as making the garment!

Fancy weights Apart from the basic yarn weights, there are many weights that fall between the standard weights. Shetland-weight yarn is a slightly thin DK weight, for example, whereas the once popular baby quickerknit is halfway between a DK and an aran weight. Many of the fancy fashion yarns available now come in their own idiosyncratic weights.

Yarn fibres

There is a wonderful array of yarns available for crochet, both natural and manmade or synthetic in origin. Natural yarns can be sourced from either plant fibres or animal fur, ranging hugely in texture, thickness, weight and elasticity, from the fluffy lightness of angora, to the sleek fluidity of silk, to the warmth and robustness of chunky sheep's wool. Natural yarns are not always hard-wearing and robust, and items made from them often need special care. Consequently, many manufacturers produce blends of natural and synthetic fibres to get the best of both worlds.

Alpaca, camel hair and other 'wools' Any animal that has fur can be shorn and the resulting fibres made into a yarn, but some are more commonly used than others. Alpaca, camel hair and llama are rather exotic yarns, but becoming increasingly easy to find. Alpaca, a llama-like animal, is native to the highlands of Peru, and has evolved a very dense fleece to keep it warm in those cold, harsh conditions. The resulting yarn is rather like sheep's wool in texture but is much warmer.

Angora Angora comes from rabbits – and we all know just how soft a rabbit's fur is! However, the fibres are quite short and an angora yarn will often shed these fibres both when you work with it and when it is worn. It is not particularly strong and is fairly expensive, so it is often combined with other fibres to make it more affordable and stronger – and also less prone to shedding.

Cashmere Cashmere is taken from the extremely soft fur of the cashmere goat. It makes the softest, lightest, cuddliest yarn that simply hugs you with warmth and luxury – in fact, this fibre makes the ultimate in luxury yarn! Regrettably, its price often reflects this, so manufacturers often combine it with other fibres to produce a more affordable yarn.

Cotton This plant-based fibre makes a yarn that lends itself perfectly to summer garments. However, cotton can be heavy and has no stretch or elasticity to it. As such, anything made from a pure cotton yarn may sag and grow once it is made. As with wool, there are many different finishes that can be applied to a cotton yarn, the most common being mercerization. Mercerized cotton has a glossy sheen that stays there wash after wash.

Linen, ramie and bamboo These plant-based fibres are lightweight and breathable and often best-suited to summer garments. Linen has a cool, dry texture with a lot of drape. Like cotton, it has little elasticity by itself and is often found in blends with other fibres to make it more resilient and easier to work with. Bamboo has a silk-like texture. It is promoted as an eco-friendly yarn, as bamboo is very fast-growing and needs no pesticides, unlike cotton. Ramie yarn comes from the nettle plant family, and the fibre has a lovely lustrous texture.

Manmade and synthetic fibres

The major difference between these fibres is that one starts from a natural product and 'man'makes it into a fibre, whereas the other is totally synthetic. Many manmade fibres, such as viscose and rayon, are derived from material such as wood pulp. On the other hand, synthetic fibres, such as acrylic and nylon, are often petro-chemical derivatives and basically consist of a very fine thread of a plastic-like substance. Names such as 'acrylic' and 'nylon' are generic names that relate to the type of fibre, but each manufacturer will give their fibre its own brand name, such as Lycra®. Manmade and synthetic fibres can be soft or coarse, economic or expensive, cool or warm, thick or thin – they can be virtually anything that the manufacturer chooses! These yarns are generally strong and hard-wearing, and are often combined with a natural fibre to create a more versatile yarn than the natural fibre alone could produce.

Mohair This yarn comes from the hair of the angora goat. It is very fluffy, but, as the mohair fibres are quite long, it is a very different fluff from an angora or wool fluff. Mohair yarns generally consist of a fine core of yarn with long fluffy fibres extending from the core. To show off the fibres to their best effect, mohair yarns are best worked very loosely – the central core creates a mesh and the loose fibres fill out the holes.

Silk As with silk fabrics, there are many different qualities of silk yarns. The smoother yarns have a wonderful sheen and lustre. However, one thing that they all have in common is that, as silk fibre takes dye very well, the colours will generally be clear and strong. This natural fibre can be delicate and needs to be looked after carefully. It has little elasticity so the finished item can sag.

Wool Wool is perhaps the classic yarn. There are many different types of wool and many different treatments that it can be given. Lambswool is the softest type and gets its name from the fact that it is the first sheared wool taken from a lamb. The fibres are particularly soft as one end of each fibre is not cut, but is the naturally soft, rounded end the lamb was born with. The quality of wool is also dictated by the breed of sheep it comes from: manufacturers now sell woollen yarns made from specific breeds of sheep, such as Herdwick and Jacob. Merino wool is often considered the Rolls-Royce of wools, as it is very smooth, sleek and soft, making it the perfect choice for a good yarn. It is also widely available and good value for money. Once the wool has been sheared from the sheep, it can be given all sorts of treatments to change its appearance and the way that it behaves as a yarn. Most untreated woollen yarns need to be washed very gently to stop the fibres matting together, or felting, and to stop the yarn shrinking.

Easy-care wool

In today's easy-care society, you will generally find that woollen yarns have been treated during their manufacture to stop them shrinking and to allow them to be machine-washed. There are now even felted wool yarns available! These have been especially treated to give a felted, or 'washed and well-worn', appearance that will stay exactly as it is without shrinking or felting further.

These four GLORIOUS GLAMOUR SCARVES are crocheted to the same pattern. However the different types of yarn used for the four variations (tweedy yarn, cashmere blend, silk and super kid mohair) show just how significantly your choice of texture and fibre for a yarn can affect the look of the finished item.

techniques

Basic stitches

Unlike when knitting, crochet only ever has one stitch in work at any time, making it far easier not to drop stitches! Each stitch is made by forming a loop of yarn and drawing this loop through existing loops. In this section, we look at the basics of holding the hook and the yarn, and introduce the most commonly used crochet stitches. When you are learning the basic stitches, it is a good idea to use a classic yarn – a DK wool yarn, for example. The yarn is smooth, so will be easy to handle, and you will be able to see each stitch clearly as you form it.

Holding the hook and the yarn

Before you can make any crochet stitches, you need to know how to hold the yarn and the hook.

The traditional way is to hold the hook in the right hand and the yarn in the left hand. However, many crocheters who also knit find it easier to hold the yarn in their right hand too, leaving just the work and the working loop to be held in their left hand. There is no right or wrong way; just find the way **you** feel most comfortable with!

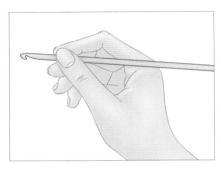

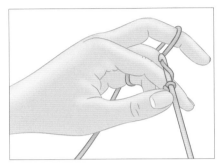

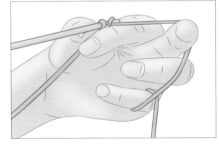

The traditional technique is to hold the hook as though it were a pen, gripping it between your thumb and first finger just near the actual hook section – the same way as you would hold a knitting needle.

The traditional method to work is by holding the yarn and the base of the working loop in your left hand. Start by gripping the base of the starting slipknot underneath the hook and between the thumb and first finger of your left hand. Leave the cut end of the yarn to dangle free and take the ball end over your fingers, wrapping it round your little finger.

To make each stitch, you either twist the hook clockwise around the yarn, or loop the yarn over the hook to wrap the yarn around the hook, ready for the next stitch. Extend your middle finger to regulate the flow of the yarn, taking care not to pull the yarn too tightly.

The starting loop or slipknot

Before you begin, you will need to make your first stitch. This will form the basis for all the following stitches.

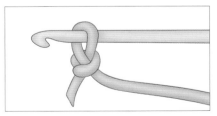

Make a loop near the cut end of the yarn and insert the crochet hook into the loop, picking up the end of the yarn leading to the ball.

Draw this new loop of yarn through the existing loop, and gently pull on the cut end to tighten this new loop around the hook. This is your first stitch.

Make this now!

This classic cardigan is given a new twist when decorated with pretty flowers and leaves. Simply made using a combination of double crochet and chain stitches, the clever denim yarn makes the cardigan both sporty and casual while remaining feminine. The flower and leaf decoration is applied afterwards, so you can add as many or as few pieces as you want.

The **FLOWER-TRIMMED CARDIGAN** is made in a DK-weight denim yarn (which will fade in colour just like real denim fabric when you launder it), while the flowers and leaves are made in 4ply cotton. The main body of the cardigan is made with a 4.00mm (G6) hook, while the border is made with a 3.50mm (E4) hook and the trimmings with a 2.50mm (C2) hook. See pages 291–293 for the pattern.

Chain

(abbreviation = ch)

Almost all crochet items start with a length of chain stitches, and they also often appear within stitch patterns. Wherever the chain is required, it is made in the same way.

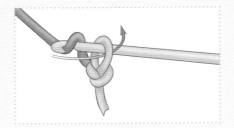

To make a chain stitch, take the yarn over the hook, wrapping it from the back, up over the hook towards the front, and then down and under the hook (every time the yarn is taken over the hook it should be done in this way). Now draw this new loop of yarn through the loop on the hook to complete the chain stitch.

Double crochet

(abbreviation = dc)

A double crochet stitch is one of the most commonly used and easiest crochet stitches to make.

To make a double crochet, start by inserting the hook into the work at the required point. Take the yarn over the hook and draw this new loop of yarn through the loop on the hook – there are now 2 loops on the hook.

Take the yarn over the hook again and draw this new loop through **both** the loops on the hook. This completes the double crochet stitch.

Treble

(abbreviation = tr)

This is the other most commonly used crochet stitch: while a double crochet stitch is a very short, compact stitch, a treble stitch is taller and will add more height to the work.

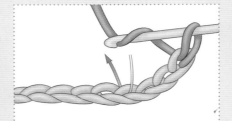

To make a treble, wrap the yarn around the hook **before** inserting it into the work.

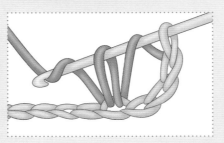

Wrap the yarn around the hook again and draw this new loop through both loops on the hook to complete the treble stitch.

Wrap the yarn around the hook again and draw this loop through the work – there are now 3 loops on the hook. Wrap the yarn around the hook once more and draw this new loop through just the first 2 loops on the hook – the original loop and this new loop.

Half treble

(abbreviation = htr)

A half treble stitch is a variation of a treble; its height is halfway between that of a double crochet and a treble stitch.

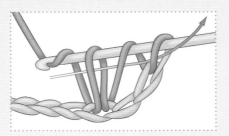

To make a half treble, start in exactly the way a treble is made until there are 3 loops on the hook. Wrap the yarn around the hook once more and draw this new loop through **all 3** loops on the hook to complete the half treble stitch.

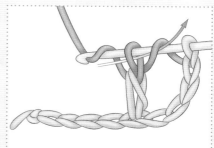

Double treble

(abbreviation = dtr)
Another variation of a treble is the double treble stitch. This gets its name from the fact that the yarn is wrapped twice around the hook before it is inserted into the work.

To make a double treble stitch, start by wrapping the yarn around the hook **twice** before inserting it into the work.

There are now 3 loops on the hook. Wrap the yarn around the hook again and draw this new loop through the first 2 loops on the hook, leaving just 2 loops on the hook.

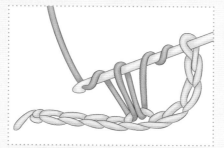

Wrap the yarn around the hook again and draw this new loop through the work. There are now 4 loops on the hook. Take the yarn around the hook once more and draw this new loop through just the **first 2** loops on the hook.

To complete the double treble stitch, wrap the yarn around the hook once more and draw this new loop through both the remaining loops on the hook.

Taller treble variations

Triple treble (abbreviation = ttr)
Quadruple treble (abbreviation = qtr)

A double treble is formed by wrapping the yarn around the hook twice before it is inserted into the work, and taller treble variations can be made by wrapping the yarn around the hook more times before inserting it into the work.

For a triple treble, wrap the yarn around the hook 3 times before inserting it. For a quadruple treble, wrap it round the hook 4 times.

However many times the yarn is wrapped round the hook, the stitch is completed in the same way: insert the hook into the work, wrap the yarn around the hook and draw the new loop through. Now complete the stitch by wrapping the yarn

around the hook and drawing the new loop through just the first 2 loops on the hook. Repeat this last process until there is only one loop left on the hook. The stitch is now completed.

Slip stitch

(abbreviation = ss)
This stitch adds virtually no height to the work and is generally used either to move the hook and working loop to a new point, or to join pieces.

To make a slip stitch, insert the hook into the work at the required point. Take the yarn over the hook and draw this new loop through **both** the work **and** the loop on the hook to complete the slip stitch.

Placing the crochet stitches

Although different effects can be created in crochet by working the different crochet stitches, you can also vary the fabric that each stitch forms by varying exactly where each stitch is placed in relation to the previous stitches. It is most common to work stitches into the top of stitches on the row below. However, it is also possible to work between existing stitches, or to work into chain spaces. We examine the various possibilities over the next few pages.

Working into the top of stitches

This is the most common position for the new stitches to be worked and, unless a pattern states otherwise, this is how all stitches should be placed.

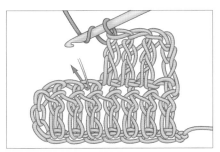

Across the top of crochet stitches there is a 'V' shape, formed by two bars of yarn. To work into the top of the existing stitches to make the new ones, insert the hook through the work by sliding it from front to back under this 'V'. Working stitches in this way encloses the whole of the 'V' in the new stitch.

Working into a foundation chain

The foundation chain is the name given to the string of chain stitches that will form the base, or foundation, for the rest of the crochet. Each chain stitch consists of 3 bars of yarn – 2 forming a 'V' and a third running across the back of the work.

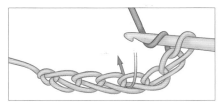

When working into a foundation chain – or any chain stitch – it is best to insert the hook through the middle of the stitch. Insert it

from above and from front to back between the 2 bars creating the 'V', keeping the hook in front of the third bar underneath the 'V'. Working stitches in this way encloses 2 of the 3 strands making up each chain stitch, leaving just the front bar of the 'V' free.

....

Working into one loop only

Working into just one of the two bars that form the 'V' of the previous stitches can create yet more effects.

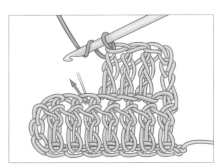

To work into the **back loop only** of the previous stitches, slide the hook through the work between the 2 bars forming the 'V', picking up just the back loop.

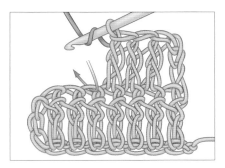

To work into the **front loop only** of the previous stitches, slide the hook through the work underneath just the front bar forming the 'V', bringing it up in front of the back loop.

Working in this way encloses just one bar of the existing stitch in the new one. If a row of stitches is worked in this way, the remaining 'free' bar of the 'V' will form a line across the work. This line of threads can be used to create a particular effect. It will also tend to make the work 'fold' along that line, making it a useful tool when working three-dimensional items.

....

Working between stitches

Sometimes the new stitches of the crochet are not placed on top of the previous stitches but worked between them. This creates a more lacy effect to what would otherwise be a very solid fabric. When working with fancy textured yarns, this can be a simple way to place the stitches as it is easy to see where to insert the hook.

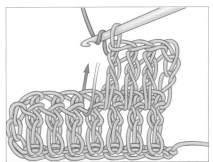

To work a new stitch between the previous stitches, simply insert the hook through the work, from front to back, between the stems of the 2 existing stitches. Although this method can be used with any type of stitch, it is much easier to work in this way when the existing stitches are tall stitches, such as trebles, where the stems of the stitches are quite long and obvious.

Working into chain spaces

Some fancy stitch patterns are made up of a combination of different types of stitches and little strings of chain stitches, known as chain spaces (abbreviated to 'ch sp').

To work a stitch into a chain space, simply insert the hook through the work through the hole below the string of chain stitches, inserting it from front to back. Working stitches into a chain space will enclose the whole of the chain stitches in the base of the new stitches.

Sometimes a design that is made up of lots of chain spaces will NOT have the next batch of stitches actually worked into the chain space, but into one of the chain stitches that makes up this chain space. This is likely to be the case for clusters, puffs and bobbles where the base of the stitch needs to be kept tight and narrow – to work into the chain space would allow the base of the stitches to fan out and would not create the desired effect. Ensure you read the pattern carefully and work the stitches above a chain space in the correct way.

Make this now!

This stunning throw is simply worked in blocks of glorious colours of fancy textured yarns. This type of yarn can be difficult to crochet with, as it is not that easy to see the tops of the existing stitches. However, this fabric is simply made up of trebles worked between the trebles of the previous rows.

RAINBOW RIBBON THROW is made in a selection of four vibrantly coloured yarns. Two of the yarns are 90% merino and 10% nylon; one is 50% wool and 50% cotton; and the fourth yarn is 50% cotton, 40% rayon and 10% nylon. The varieties of fibre create a throw with a wonderfully rich and diverse texture, and the yarns are hand-dyed so no two hanks are the same. These are chunky yarns that work up quickly on a 6.00mm (J10) hook. See pages 304–305 for pattern.

Combining stitch placements

Many crochet fabrics will not place all the stitches in exactly the same way, and it is often this variation in the way the stitches are placed that will create the different textures. It is therefore vitally important that you read the pattern and place the stitches exactly as stated in the pattern. If they are not placed correctly, you will have serious problems matching the required row **and** stitch tension for that particular design.

Although the widths of the stitches will probably remain the same, their heights will more than likely vary as different placements of stitches will alter their heights. A treble placed between stitches of a previous row will add less height than if it were worked into the top of a stitch. Similarly, if it is worked into just one of the 2 loops, more height may be created as the base stitch will 'stretch', adding to the treble's height. This variation in height may not be that apparent over one or two rows, but it will become far more obvious as more rows are worked, making it very difficult to achieve the correct row tension for a design.

Make this now!

This beautifully feminine, lacy scarf will add some glamour to your wardrobe. One version is shown here, but we offer four alternatives on page 273. The scarves are crocheted to the same pattern, but the different types of yarn used for the four variations show just how significantly choice of texture and fibre for a yarn can affect the look of the finished garment.

GLORIOUS GLAMOUR SCARF is shown here in a tweed yarn. This has a felted effect, and is made from merino wool, alpaca and viscose. The scarf was made with a 3.50mm (E4) hook for the DK-weight yarn. See page 273 for pattern.

Making crochet fabrics

Once you have learnt how to make the various crochet stitches and how they should be placed, you can start to make crochet fabrics. As crochet only ever has one stitch actually in work at any one time, it is easy to join the stitches together either in rows, to make a flat sheet of crochet, or to work the stitches in rounds, to make flat disks of crochets (like the traditional doily) or to create 'tubes' of crochet fabric – like the sleeve of a garment, for example. Crochet is a truly versatile craft!

Working in rows

Working in rows consists of piling lots of rows, or strings, of stitches on top of previous rows or strings of crochet.

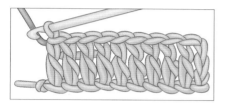

A flat piece of crochet will be formed by making a foundation chain and then working back along this chain. The stitches worked into the foundation chain form the first row.

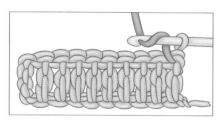

Once this first row is complete, the second row can be worked. But, as almost all crochet stitches are worked from the right towards the left, the fabric needs to be turned at the end of each row so that you can work back across the stitches just made to form the next row.

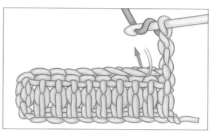

The working loop for any piece of crochet sits at the top of the stitches. Therefore, to start the next row of crochet you need to raise the hook and working loop up to the required point. This is done by working what is called a turning chain. The length of this turning chain will vary depending on the type of stitch being worked. Below is a guide to the length of the turning chain equivalent to the most commonly used crochet stitches.

stitch	length of turning chain
double crochet	1 ch
half treble	2 ch
treble	3 ch
double treble	4 ch

Sometimes the turning chain will be there to replace the first stitch of the new row, and sometimes it will simply be used to raise the hook to the right place. Most crochet patterns will tell you which is the case for this particular row.

If the turning chain counts as the first stitch of the new row, the first 'real' stitch of this row that you work will effectively be the second stitch. To ensure this stitch is placed correctly, you need to miss the stitch sitting at the base of the turning chain and work it into the next stitch.

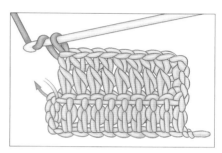

If the turning chain does count as the first stitch of a row, it is vitally important that you work into this 'stitch' at the end of the next row! If you do not work into the top of this length of chain, you will accidentally decrease a stitch and your crochet fabric will be spoilt.

Take care, as sometimes the length of chain at the beginning of a row will be there to replace more than just the first stitch of this new row – but this should be detailed in the pattern!

crochet craft

At the end of each row of a pattern, it will say 'turn' so you are ready to work the next row. To turn the work, you do exactly that – turn the work around so that the side that was away from you now faces you and the hook is now at the right-hand side of the work, not the left.

Fastening off

Once the last stitch of the last row or round of a piece of crochet has been completed, there will still be the one working loop, or stitch, on the hook. To complete the work, this stitch needs to be fastened off.

To fasten off the work, cut the yarn and simply draw this cut end of yarn through the loop on the hook. Pull gently on the yarn end to tighten the stitch so that it does not unravel.

Working in rounds

Due to the way a crochet fabric is formed, it can also be made in rounds to create flat disks or three-dimensional tubes. Working rounds of crochet is a quick way to make items as it can avoid the need to sew seams afterwards.

To start a piece, you will need to join the ends of the foundation chain to make it into a ring. This is generally done by making the required number of chain and then working a slip stitch into the first of these chain stitches. Take care not to twist the chain when joining the ends, as this could distort the work.

The first round of crochet can either be worked into the centre of this ring as though it were a chain space (as will generally be the case with flat disks of crochet), or into the chain stitches themselves as you would normally do with a foundation chain (as will generally be the case with tubes of crochet).

At the end of the first round of any crochet piece, the first and last stitches need to be joined together to complete the circle. This is usually done by working a slip stitch into the top of the first stitch – but consult your pattern to be sure, as this can vary for fancy stitch patterns.

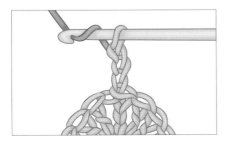

To make the second and every following round of crochet, the hook must, as when working in rows, be raised up to the height of the new stitches. So each new round of crochet will start with a turning chain, exactly as when working in rows.

crochet craft

If you are working into the centre of a ring, it is quite likely there will be more stitches to work than it would appear will fit in! As you work the stitches, gently ease them along the chain so that they all sit neatly next to each other.

To turn or not to turn

Crochet stitches look different on one side from how they appear on the other side. So, when working rounds of crochet, you can create more types of fabrics by choosing to either turn or not turn the work at the end of each round.

If the work is turned at the beginning of each new round of crochet, the resulting fabric will look exactly like one made using rows of crochet. Therefore, if an item combines sections made in rows **and** in rounds, this is the best way to work to ensure that all sections match. Generally, crochet fabrics made where the work is turned before beginning each new row or

Crochet worked in rows (*above*) can look identical to that worked in rounds (*below*).

round will look exactly the same on both sides of the fabric.

If the work is not turned at the beginning of each new round, the fabric created will be totally different on one side from on the other side – and totally different again to one made where the work has been turned! To make sure your crochet looks as it should, take care to read the pwattern and check whether you should turn the work or not at the end of each round.

From right side, not turning at ends of rounds.

From wrong side, not turning at ends of rounds.

Same stitch but turning after every round.

Make these now!

This hat, bag and belt set all use the same stitch pattern – but the hat and the bag have been worked in rounds, while the belt was worked just in rows. To make sure that the stitches look the same on all three pieces, the work was turned at the beginning of each round.

SEASIDE AND SHELLS SET is made in an ocean-blue 4ply mercerized cotton. The mercerization process helps the cotton to take the dye, so such yarns have a particularly strong depth of colour. All the pieces in the set are made to the same tension, using a 2.50mm (C2) hook. See pages 281–283 for pattern.

Tension

The size of crochet stitches is described as the 'tension' they are worked to. In a crochet pattern, tension is usually expressed as the number of stitches and rows that measure a certain amount – generally 10cm (4in). For example, the pattern might tell you that you need 10 stitches and 14 rows of double crochet to make a 10cm (4in) square. It is vitally important when crocheting any item that you achieve the exact tension stated. If your tension does not match that stated, your final item will not look like the guide picture and will not be the correct size.

Effects of incorrect tension

To ensure success, you **must** check your tension before you begin every project! If your tension is out, you will face several problems:
- The resulting crochet fabric will not feel the way it should.
- The tension of the crochet governs the size of the finished item; if the tension is incorrect, the item will not fit as it should.
- The tension will affect the amount of yarn required. If your tension is tight, you could have yarn left over; if your tension is loose, you may require additional yarn.

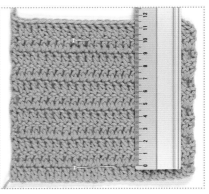

Making a tension swatch

Before starting to crochet any item, take time to check your tension by making a tension swatch.

1 To make a tension swatch, look at the pattern and find out what hook size you need to use and what stitch pattern the tension is measured over.

2 Once you have sorted out what stitch and hook to use, make the tension swatch. Although the tension will normally be given as a number of stitches and rows to 10cm (4in), it is best to make the tension swatch larger than this – ideally, your tension swatch should be about 12–15cm (5–6in) square.

3 Calculate the number of stitches you will need: for a tension swatch 15cm (6in) wide you will need one and a half times the number of stitches stated if the tension is measured over 10cm (4in).

4 Make your foundation chain the length required, adjusting the number of chain to fit in with any pattern repeat, and then work the stated stitch pattern until you have a square of crochet. Fasten off the work but do NOT press it.

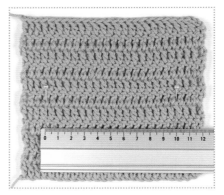

Measuring the tension

Once your tension swatch is complete, lay it flat and mark out, with pins, the number of stitches stated for the tension. Now measure the distance between these pins. If this measurement is the same as stated for the tension, you are crocheting to the correct tension.

If the distance between the pins is less than stated in the tension, your crochet is too tight. Change to a larger size (thicker) hook and make another swatch.

If the distance between the pins is larger than the tension states, your crochet is too loose. Change to a smaller size (thinner) hook and try again.

Continue making swatches until you achieve the correct number of stitches to match the tension.

Checking rows

Once you have made a swatch that has the correct number of stitches to match the tension, check you are achieving the correct number of rows. In the same way as before, mark out the number of rows stated and measure the distance between these pins. Generally, if the number of stitches is correct, the number of rows will be too – but you do need to check.

crochet craft

Occasionally you may find you cannot exactly match both the number of stitches and the number of rows. If this is the case, try working one row (or round) with one size hook and the next row (or round) with a size larger (or smaller) hook.

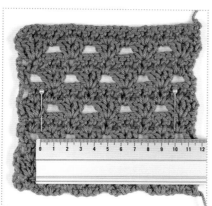 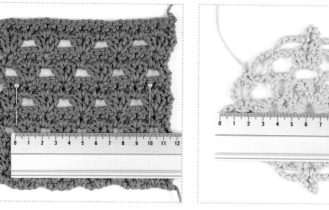 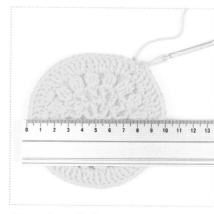

Fancy stitch pattern

When the item is made in a fancy stitch pattern, the tension will often be expressed as a number of pattern repeats, not stitches, to a measurement. If this is the case, make the tension swatch with at least 2 more pattern repeats than stated for the tension. Once the swatch is made, measure the tension as before, but now count the number of pattern repeats, not stitches or rows.

Motif tension

If an item is made up of lots of motifs, the tension section will often give you the size that one motif should be.

To check the tension, make one motif and check its size. If it matches that stated, then your tension is correct. If too big, start again with a smaller hook. If too small, make another with a larger size hook.

Circular disks

Flat items made in the round and large circular motifs often have their tension expressed as the size of the first few rounds. If so, work the stated number of rounds and then measure their diameter.

crochet craft

Crochet 'shrinks' the larger the piece you work, so the tension of a swatch may be different from that of a large piece. Always double-check your tension while working the large pieces to ensure they are the correct size.

Make these now!

These cute toy bunnies show just how much tension can affect the size of the finished item. Each bunny is worked to the same pattern – it is just the yarn and the hook size, and therefore the tension, that has changed.

MISS PINK is worked in an aran-weight yarn with a 3.5mm (E4) hook. MR GREY is in a classic DK-weight yarn with a 3.00mm (D3) hook. SPARKLES is in a glittery lurex 4ply with a 2.50mm (C2) hook. FLUFFY is in a very fine kid mohair yarn with a 1.75mm (5) hook. See pages 312–314 for pattern.

MR GREY

MISS PINK

SPARKLES

FLUFFY

Combination stitches

The basic crochet stitches can be combined to form groups of stitches that create different effects. They can add texture to a plain base, or simply add visual interest to the work.

The types and quantities of stitches used for these combinations will vary depending on the effect required – but the abbreviation used within the pattern may be the same as that used for a similar stitch group in another pattern. However, the abbreviations section of the pattern should clearly explain how each of these stitch groups should be made for this design.

Shells

The finished appearance of this stitch group is exactly as its name suggests – it looks like a shell. Shells look most effective when worked in the longer crochet stitches, such as trebles and double trebles. A shell does not add any extra surface interest to the crochet fabric but, if worked along an edge, will create a scalloped effect.

Shells are formed by working lots of the same type of stitch into one point. This point is usually a stitch, rather than a chain space, as the shell effect is created by all the stitches fanning out from one point.

To work a shell, simply work the required number of stitches into the same place.

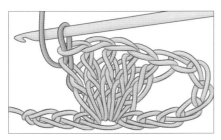

This sample shows a shell fabric with a shell edging added afterwards in a contrast colour. One row of the fabric has also been worked in the contrast colour to show how each shell 'sits' neatly on top of the previous row of shells.

Clusters

Clusters are basically the reverse of a shell. For a cluster, lots of stitches are worked into lots of points but all these stitches are joined at the top, creating a shell-like effect that fans out downwards, not upwards. Again, they are best worked using the longer crochet stitches.

To make a treble cluster, work each treble into the relevant point until just before it is completed – to the point where the last 'yarn over hook and draw through last 2 loops' is about to be made. Make all the necessary trebles that will form this cluster in this way – you will have the original loop on the hook plus one extra loop for each treble that has been nearly completed.

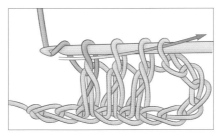

To close the top of the cluster, take the yarn over the hook and draw this new loop through all the loops on the hook. The finished cluster has one stitch at the top point.

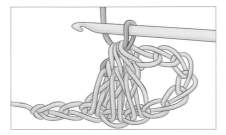

Bobbles

Bobbles are a combination of a shell and a cluster. They are worked in virtually the same way as a cluster, but all the stitches that form the bobble are worked into the same point, as for a shell.

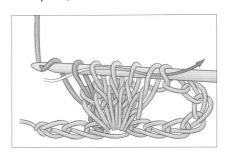

Bobble stitches will add texture to the surface of the work. As the stitches that make up the bobble are often longer than those of the surrounding crochet fabric, and many stitches are squeezed into one place, the group of stitches will stand proud of the work, thereby causing a small, protruding bobble.

Sometimes a bobble will be secured at the top by a chain stitch. This closes the top of the bobble, holding all the stitches securely together. Always check the abbreviation section of the pattern to find out whether this is the case for the bobble you are working.

Puff stitches

A puff stitch is basically a bobble worked using half treble stitches. Because of the way a half treble stitch is made, the resulting 'bobble' consists of lots of strands of yarn lying next to each other, rather than separate stitches.

To make a puff stitch, make each stitch to the point where the new loop of yarn has been drawn through the base position for the stitch. To accentuate the effect, the pattern will often specify that each new loop drawn through the base stitch should be pulled up taller than it would normally.

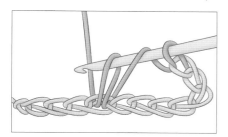

Once the required number of half-worked half treble stitches have been made, complete all the stitches by taking the yarn over the hook and pulling this new loop through all the loops on the hook.

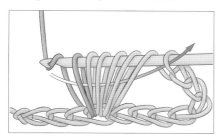

As with bobbles and popcorns, there may be a chain stitch worked at the end of each puff stitch to close the top. Check the abbreviation to see if this is the case.

Popcorns

These stitch combinations are similar to a shell but, because of the way the 'shell' is drawn together at the top, they create added surface texture.

To make a popcorn, work the first part of the stitch combination in the same way as if working a shell, by working a group of stitches all into one point. Now take the hook out of the working loop. Insert the hook through the top of the first stitch that makes up this group and then back into the working loop.

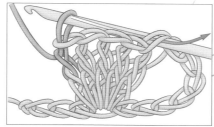

Take the yarn over the hook and pull this new loop through both the working loop and the first stitch of the group. This completes the popcorn.

A completed popcorn forms a tiny 'bell' of stitches that sits away from the surface of the work.

PICTURE-PERFECT CUSHION COVERS, below, in plum, soft green, gold and taupe, are worked in classic DK-weight yarn with a 3.50mm (E4) hook. See pages 306–309 for patterns.

Make these now!

These aran-effect cushion covers show exactly how much extra texture can be added to a simple double crochet fabric. The trellis effect is created by travelling lines of relief treble stitches; each diamond has a bobble sitting inside it. The flower heads of the panelled cushion covers are formed by popcorns; simple loops of chains create the leaves and stems. The textured border is again created by relief stitches, with added interest created by the bobbles that sit next to the zig-zag lines.

Relief stitches

Extra surface texture can be created by working what are called 'relief' stitches. These stitches do exactly what their name suggests: they add extra surface relief, or texture, to the work. They are sometimes also known as 'raised' stitches. You can use these to create fascinating patterns, including ones that look like basketweave and ones that look like ribbing. Almost any type of stitch can be worked as a relief stitch but, as there needs to be a 'stem' of a stitch to work around, they are generally only worked as treble stitches.

Working relief stitches

Relief stitches can be worked from either the front of the crochet or the back. The abbreviation normally used for a relief stitch is a combination of the type of basic stitch being worked, the fact that it is a relief stitch and the side from which the hook is inserted. For example, a relief front treble stitch is often abbreviated to 'rftr' – a combination of 'r' (meaning a relief stitch), 'f' (meaning it is worked from the front) and 'tr' (as it is a treble stitch that is worked).

The actual stitch being worked is made in exactly the same way as that type of stitch would normally be worked – it is just how the hook is inserted through the work that changes. Instead of the stitch being worked into another stitch or a space, it is worked around the stem of one of the previous stitches.

Working a relief front treble

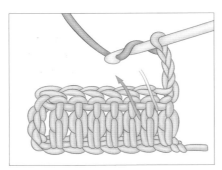

To make a relief front treble, start by taking the yarn around the hook as you would to start any treble stitch. Once the yarn is wrapped around the hook, insert the hook through the work, from the front, just to the right of the stem of the stitch this relief stitch is to be worked around. Bring the hook back through to the front of the work just to the left of the stem of this stitch. The hook is inserted from the front of the work, and from the right to the left under the stem of the stitch.

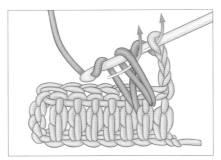

Take the yarn around the hook and draw this new loop through the work, behind the stem of the stitch. There are now 3 loops on the hook.

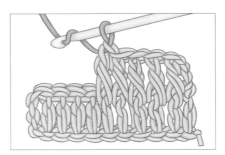

Complete the treble stitch in the usual way. A relief front treble leaves the whole of the top section of the stitch it is worked around visible on the back of the work.

Working a relief back treble

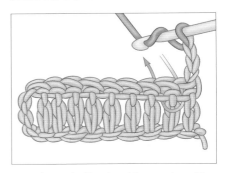

To make a relief back treble, start by taking the yarn around the hook as you would to start any treble stitch. Once the yarn is wrapped around the hook, insert the hook through the work, from the back, just to the right of the stem of the stitch this relief stitch is to be worked around. Return the hook to the back of the work just to the left of the stem of this stitch. The hook is inserted from the back of the work, and from the right to the left around the stem of the stitch.

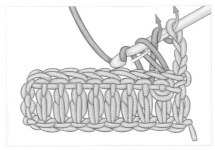

Take the yarn around the hook and draw this new loop through the work so that there are 3 loops on the hook. Complete the treble stitch in the usual way. A relief back treble leaves the whole of the top section of the stitch it is worked around visible on the front of the work.

Preparing to work relief stitches

As there needs to be a stem to any stitch that a relief stitch is worked around, it is really only successfully worked onto a base of stitches no shorter than half treble stitches. This allows there to be sufficient room and definition between the stitches to accurately place and work the relief stitch.

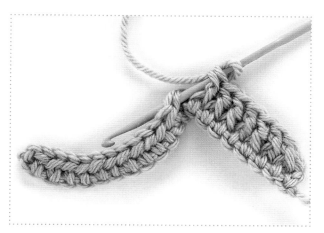

Generally, stitch patterns made up of relief treble stitches will start with a foundation row of simple half treble stitches. Once the stitches of the relief stitch pattern are worked, these base stitches become virtually invisible so do not detract from the finished effect.

Turning chains for relief stitch patterns

A relief stitch is not as tall as this type of stitch would normally be; some of the height of this new stitch is lost as its base is placed below the top of the previous row. It is therefore necessary to reduce the length of the turning chain required so that the edges of the crochet remain the same length as the body of the work.

Generally, the turning chain required in a relief stitch pattern will be one chain shorter than would normally be required for the type of stitch being worked. For example, normally a treble fabric would start with a turning chain of 3 ch (to count as the first treble), but when working a relief treble fabric the turning chain is reduced to 2 ch (to count as the first stitch).

crochet craft

When ending a row of relief stitches, take care that you work the last stitch around the turning chain at the beginning of the previous row so that the whole row remains the correct height. Although this stitch is a relief stitch, the effect created on this end stitch will not be as apparent as on the rest of the work.

Creating relief stitch patterns

Relief front and back stitches can be combined both with themselves and with all sorts of non-relief stitches to create a myriad of fancy stitch patterns.

Working a relief stitch leaves the whole of the top section of the previous stitch sitting on one side of the work so, to create a 'bar' of relief stitches sitting on one side of the work, the type of relief stitch must be alternated on every row. If the stitch is a relief **front** stitch on a right-side row, it needs to be worked as a relief **back** stitch on the following wrong-side row so that the top section of the stitch it is worked around always remains on the same side of the work.

If a relief stitch is worked on a base of non-relief stitches, it needs to be worked as a longer stitch than those around it. If the base fabric is a treble fabric, working a relief treble stitch will not add sufficient height to the work and you will notice that, once numerous rows have been worked, this insufficiently tall line of stitches will pull and pucker the work. To prevent this happening, you should always work the relief stitch one 'height' of stitch greater than those around it. On a half treble fabric, work relief trebles; on treble fabric, work relief double trebles.

Make this now!

The basketweave effect on this cute child's coat has been created using alternating blocks of relief front and back trebles. This stitch pattern is simple to work, and the fabric created is totally reversible, so it doesn't matter if the wrong side of the work shows. The resulting fabric has the feel of a woven fabric, and is cosy, warm and hard-wearing.

AUTUMN COLOUR COAT is made in a multi-coloured marled 100% wool yarn that creates a tweedy effect with a lovely depth and richness of colour. Although this is only a DK-weight yarn, worked on a 4.00mm (G6) hook, the relief stitches form a thick, dense fabric. See pages 269–271 for pattern.

Creating rib effects

Simple lines of relief stitches can be left sitting on the surface of the work by replacing a stitch with a relief stitch.

These bars of stitches can be placed close to each other, to create vertical textured stripes, or one can be worked on its own, to divide one section from another or to create a natural line along which the work will fold. Working a bar of relief stitches in this way leaves the fabric quite flat on the wrong side, with just the relief stitches sitting proud on the surface of the right side of the work.

A more 'true' rib effect can be created by alternating relief front and back stitches across a row – as you would if knitting a rib fabric. This creates a fabric that is textured on both sides.

Creating woven effects

Working alternating blocks of relief front and back stitches will push the top of the previous stitches from one side of the work to the other. This line created by the tops of the previous stitches will form horizontal bars across the work, while the relief stitches themselves form vertical lines up the work on the other side.

Alternating blocks of relief front and back stitches will create alternating vertical and horizontal bands of texture on the surface of the work to give a woven effect that is totally reversible. It will also create a much thicker fabric than would normally be formed as there are, effectively, two layers of stitches sitting on top of each other. This means a much warmer, thicker and firmer fabric can be created with quite a fine yarn – but it also means that you will use much more yarn than you would normally.

Picots

Picots are little loops of chain stitches that are generally used to add interest to an edging or within an open lacy pattern. Picots are often used to trim garments; for example, adding a pretty edge to the neckline and the hem. A picot looks different on one side to how it looks on the other side, so try out both ways to find the look you prefer. If needs be, change the side the last row will be worked on to achieve the effect you want.

How to make a picot

A picot will sit on top of another stitch – so start by working up to the point where the picot is to be made.

Make the required number of chain stitches for the picot. Usually picots consist of 3 ch – but check the abbreviations section to make sure this is correct for the design you are making.

To complete the picot, a stitch needs to be worked into the top of the last stitch worked before the little length of chain. To work this closing stitch, twist the hook back on itself and insert it down through the top of the last 'real' stitch worked. Picots can be closed with a slip stitch or a double crochet to create a tiny ring of chain stitches, and the effect created is slightly different. Completing a picot with a slip stitch keeps the ends of the chain tightly together, meaning it sits proud on the base stitch. Closing the picot with a double crochet increases the size of the tiny ring as the double crochet forms part of this ring. Check the pattern to ensure the correct closing stitch is worked.

Picots on edges

Picots can be used to create a pretty edging, either by working them at the same time as the foundation chain, or by adding them along the final row or round of the piece.

To add picots to a foundation-chain edge, simply replace the required chain stitch of the foundation chain with 1 ch and 1 picot. To ensure the edge remains the length it should be, it is best to close this type of picot with a slip stitch. When working back along the foundation ch, take care to work only into the foundation chain stitches and not those of the picot as well.

crochet craft

Take care when working into a picot that you actually insert the hook through the centre of the ring of chain stitches. If the picot consists of just 3 ch it can be quite tricky to find the centre.

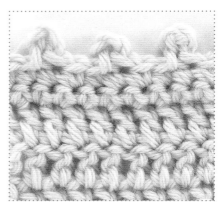

To add picots to any finished edge, simply work a picot at the required position. Working picots at regular intervals along an edge creates a classic edging that adds a pretty touch to an item – you will often find picots used to decorate the edges of baby clothes and lacy designs.

Working into a picot

As a picot is just a tiny loop of chain stitches, you work into the picot in the same way as when working into any chain space – simply insert the hook through the centre of the tiny loop and work the stitch so that the whole of the chain stitch is enclosed in the base of the new stitch.

Bullion stitches and clones knots

Crocheted bullion stitches look like bullion stitches (or large, long french knots) used in embroidery and are worked in a similar way. A clones knot is similar to both a picot and a bullion stitch – it starts with a length of chain and is formed by repeatedly wrapping the yarn around the hook. It is generally worked along a length of chain stitches, although it could be worked on any type of stitch.

Making a bullion stitch

To make a crocheted bullion stitch, start by wrapping the yarn around the hook as many times as specified in the pattern – usually anything between 7 and 10 times. Insert the hook into the work, take the yarn over the hook and draw this new loop through. Now take the yarn over the hook again and draw this new loop through **all**

the loops on the hook. This can be quite tricky; you may need to pick off each loop separately. Complete the bullion stitch by working one chain stitch to close it.

Working the chain stitch that closes the bullion stitch quite loosely will leave a wrapped bar of yarn in the work.

Working the chain stitch that closes the bullion stitch tightly will pull the ends of the wrapped bar together. This means that the resulting bullion stitch curls back on itself and forms a little looped knot on the work.

Making a clones knot

Start the clones knot in the same way as when making a picot, by making a short length of chain. *Wrap the yarn over the hook. Pass the hook under the length of chain, wrap the yarn around the hook again and bring the hook back up. Repeat from * as many times as required – usually 4 or 5 times, but your pattern should tell you exactly how many times. Now take the yarn over the hook again and draw this new loop through **all** the loops on the hook.

Carefully slide the wrapped thread towards the hook until the chain stitch at the start of the clones knot is visible, and complete the knot by working a slip stitch into this chain. The resulting knot forms a little ring of wrapped chain.

A clones knot adds an attractive loop of yarn to the edge of the crochet work.

Linked stitches

When you are making a fabric from tall crochet stitches, such as double trebles or one of the even taller stitches, you will notice that little vertical holes will appear between the stems of each stitch. If you wish to create a much more solid and densely packed fabric, it is possible to link the stitches together while they are being made. You can also use this method when you need to create vertical slits in a fabric, as explained below.

Making a linked stitch

A double treble stitch is started by wrapping the yarn around the hook twice before it is inserted into the work. When linking one double treble to the side of another double treble, these 'wrappings' are formed by drawing loops through the side of the previous stitch.

crochet craft

When working a series of linked stitches, try to make sure that you insert the hook through the side of each stitch in the same place. This will ensure that the look of the finished stitches is smooth and even. Also make sure you don't pull the yarn too tight as you make the 'wrappings', as this could cause the work to pucker and pull.

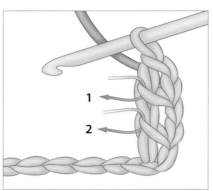

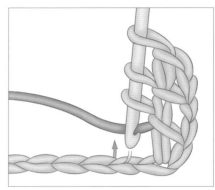

Start the linked stitch by inserting the hook through the side of the previous double treble near the top. Take the yarn over the hook and draw a loop through – this is your first wrap. Now insert the hook through the side of the same double treble again, but near the bottom. Take the yarn over the hook again and draw this loop through to create the second wrap of yarn around the hook.

Now that you have your original working loop on the hook and the 2 wraps of yarn around the hook, the hook can be inserted into the work at the required position and the double treble can be completed in the usual way.

Making holes for ribbon

Rows of linked and unlinked double or triple trebles can be used in place of several rows of double crochet where vertical slits are required that are longer than the height of one row of double crochet. This is particularly useful if a wide ribbon is to be threaded through, as the yarn does not need to be repeatedly cut and rejoined as each section is worked backwards and forwards in rows between the slits. Here, 3 rows of double crochet have been replaced with one row of linked and unlinked triple trebles to leave the slits required for a wide ribbon.

Making holes for ribbon

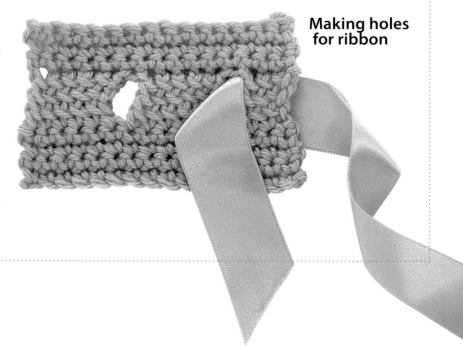

Crossed stitches

When you are working with tall stitches, such as trebles, it is possible to cross them over each other in order to create a variety of different effects. These crossed stitches can either be totally separate from each other, or the second stitch can enclose the first stitch. You can create some interesting stitch patterns using this technique – try it out and see for yourself.

Separate crossed stitches

When working 2 double trebles that cross each other, but remain totally separate, it is a good idea to separate the 2 double trebles with one stitch to accentuate the cross. The completed cross will then sit on 3 base stitches and consist of 3 stitches.

Start by working to the point where the cross is to fall. Miss the first 2 stitches across the base of the 3 stitches needed for the cross, and work a double treble into the next stitch. Work one chain stitch to separate the 2 crossed double trebles at the top.

Now work the second double treble that will complete the cross. Wrap the yarn around the hook twice, twist it back on itself and insert it into the first of the 2 missed stitches, passing it behind the previous double treble. Complete this double treble in the usual way to complete the cross. The stems of the 2 crossed double trebles remain totally separate, with one simply laying on top of the other.

Joined crossed stitches

To work 2 crossed stitches where the second stitch encloses the stem of the first stitch, it is really best to work with stitches no taller than a treble, as the stitches tend to cross near their base. With this type of crossed stitch, there is no real need to space them apart so the crossed stitches cover just 2 base stitches.

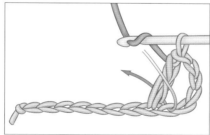

Start a pair of crossed trebles by missing one stitch at the base and working a treble into the next stitch. Then wrap the yarn around the hook and insert it into the missed stitch.

crochet craft

As crossed stitches and branched stitches (see page 190) don't add as much height to the work as their simple versions, you may need to reduce the length of the turning chain needed. For crossed or branched double trebles, a turning chain of 3 ch (to count as first treble) is probably enough. Remember to replace the last stitch of the row with a correspondingly shorter stitch.

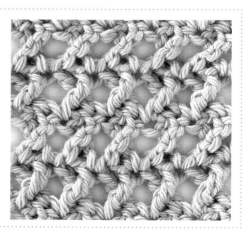

Draw the new loop through the work – the stem of the previous treble is now enclosed between the 2 loop strands of yarn at the front and 2 strands at the back. Take the yarn over the hook again and draw the new loop through the first 2 loops on the hook.

Complete the second treble by wrapping the yarn round the hook and pulling the new loop through both loops on the hook. The stem of the first treble is now firmly enclosed within the second treble.

Branched stitches

Crossed stitches either enclose or sit on top of each other, and a similar effect can be created with taller stitches by working a branched stitch. The effect that these create can be a simple 'X', a 'Y', or an upside-down 'Y' shape. As the branched stitches need to have a definite stem in order to show the branches distinctly, they are most effective when based on double treble or taller stitches.

Making an X

In order to make the 'X' quite apparent, these are best worked over at least 3 base stitches so that the top and bottom branches are clearly visible.

To make a branched X-shape of double trebles over 4 stitches, start by working half of the first double treble into the first base stitch. Wrap the yarn round the hook twice and insert the hook into the work.

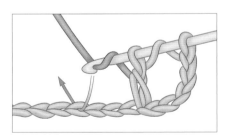

Wrap the yarn around the hook again and draw this new loop through, then wrap the yarn once more and draw this loop through the first 2 loops on the hook. There are now 3 loops on the hook. This completes the first lower branch of the X. Now start to work the other lower branch. Wrap the yarn around the hook again, miss 2 stitches and then insert the hook into the next (4th) stitch along.

Wrap the yarn around the hook and draw this new loop through the work. Take the yarn over the hook once more and draw this loop through the first 2 loops on the hook. There are now 4 loops on the hook. This completes the second lower branch of the X shape.

Now complete the first top branch of the X by repeating the (yarn over hook and draw through 2 loops) process until there is just one loop left on the hook. This completes the first upper branch of the X.

Before working the second upper branch, work 2 chain stitches to separate the upper branches. To make this last branch, wrap the yarn around the hook and insert it into the point where all 3 existing branches meet, picking up 2 strands of yarn.

Draw the new loop through the work and complete the stitch by repeating the (yarn over hook and draw through 2 loops) process until there is just one loop left on the hook. This completes the entire X.

Making an upside-down Y

An upside-down Y-shaped stitch needs to be worked over an odd number of stitches as there will be a branch only at the top.

To make the upside-down Y shape over 3 base stitches, start by working one chain. Now make the first 3 branches of an X shape, inserting the hook into the first and third stitches across the base. Complete the stitch by working one more chain stitch.

Fur stitch

A fur-like effect can be created in crochet by working lots of loops of yarn on a double crochet base. The fur, or loop, stitches leave a loop of yarn sitting on the back of the work, so they are usually worked on wrong-side rows.

Making a Y

As with an upside-down Y-shape, this needs to be worked over an odd number of stitches as there is only one branch at the base.

To make a double treble Y-shaped stitch over 5 base stitches, start by working a double treble into the third of the 5 base stitches. This will form the single lower branch and the first of the upper branches. Now work 3 chain stitches to separate the upper branches.

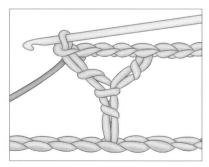

Complete the Y shape by working the third branch in the same way as for the final branch of an X-shaped stitch, inserting the hook through the work halfway down the existing double treble.

Making the fur stitch

As a fur stitch is a variation of double crochet, start with a base of double crochet stitches.

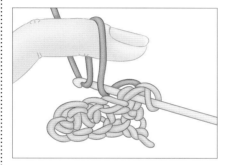

To make a fur stitch, insert the hook into the work. Wrap the yarn around the first finger of your left hand and draw this loop out to the required length – your pattern will tell you how long this should be. Pick up both of the strands of this loop with the crochet hook.

Draw both of these strands through the work. There are now 3 loops on the hook. Take the yarn over the hook again, as you would for any double crochet stitch.

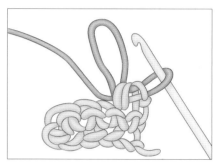

Draw this new loop of yarn through all 3 loops on the hook to complete the stitch, leaving the loop of yarn on the back of the work. If the fur stitches are worked correctly, the loops on the back of the work will be quite secure. However, you may wish to gently tug on them to neaten up both them and the stitch.

Alternating right-side rows of double crochet stitches and wrong-side rows of fur stitches creates a densely packed fur effect. As the loops of the fur stitches are well secured, it is possible to snip these loops to create a really furry and fluffy fabric that is surprisingly hard-wearing.

Solomon's knots

A Solomon's knot is simply an elongated chain stitch that is secured with a double crochet. Each knot is made up of the 3 strands that form the elongated chain stitch and the double crochet stitch that secures it. When working into the knot, it is usual to work into just the double crochet securing it, leaving the elongated chain stitch free. This stitch creates a very light, open and airy fabric perfect for summer-weight accessories.

Start by elongating the working loop to the required length (your pattern will tell you how long this should be).

Take the yarn over the hook as though to make another chain stitch.

Now draw this loop through the elongated loop on the hook, leaving this loop the 'normal' size. There are now 3 strands of yarn running from the stitch on the hook back to the stitch at the base of the knot: the 2 original strands forming the first elongated loop and another strand at the back.

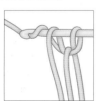

Insert the hook under this back strand of yarn and take the yarn over the hook again.

Draw this new loop through so that there are now 2 loops on the hook. Take the yarn over the hook again.

Draw this new loop through both of the loops that are on the hook to complete the Solomon's knot.

Make this now!

This lovely lacy wrap is made up of a simple mesh of Solomon's knots. The resulting fabric is gossamer-light and airy, making it perfect for cool summer evenings. And, as there are more holes than stitches, it's quick to make, too!

SOLOMON'S KNOT WRAP is worked in a drapy DK-weight pure silk yarn on a 4.00mm (G6) hook. This yarn has the wonderful lustre that is unique to silk. See page 277 for pattern.

Joining in new balls of yarn

Almost all crochet projects use more than one ball of yarn, so you are likely to need to join in a new ball of yarn at some stage. Ideally this should be done at the edges of the work. Simply complete one row with the old ball of yarn and start the new row with the new ball of yarn. Do NOT knot the yarn ends together as this knot could affect the texture of the finished work. Leave the two yarn ends free and darn them in once the work is completed. If the ends are left quite long, they can be used later to sew the seams.

Joining in new yarn

Sometimes it is not possible to join in new yarn at the edges of the work – especially with a circular piece of crochet as there are, quite simply, no edges!

If this is the case, simply change to the new ball of yarn at a point in the round where it will be most easy to darn the ends in, leaving both yarn ends hanging on the wrong side of the work. If a stitch pattern consists of lacy areas and solid areas, change to the new yarn within one of the solid areas as this will mean you have a solid area in which to darn in the ends.

If you are working in a solid stitch pattern (such as a simple double crochet fabric), it is possible to darn in the ends as the stitches are worked.

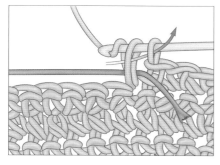

When you have sufficient yarn left to work only 6 or 7 more stitches using the existing ball of yarn, introduce the yarn from the new ball. Lay the new yarn across the top of the next stitches to be worked and work the last few stitches using the old ball of yarn, enclosing this new yarn in the stitches.

Once the new yarn end is well secured within the stitches, simply change to the yarn from the new ball. Lay the old yarn

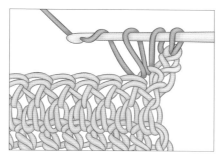

end across the top of the next set of stitches and work the next few stitches, enclosing the old yarn end in these stitches. Make sure both yarn ends come out of the stitches enclosing them on the wrong side of the work.

Once the next row or round has been completed, gently pull on the free yarn ends to secure the stitches where the old and new yarns meet, and cut off the two yarn ends. If worked correctly, the point where the two yarns meet should be virtually invisible on the right side of the work. The number of stitches you will need to work to safely and securely enclose the two yarn ends will depend on the type of yarn being used and how dense the crochet is but, as a general rule, enclosing the yarn ends in 5 or 6 stitches should be sufficient.

Rejoining yarn

Sometimes a pattern will require the work to be fastened off and the yarn rejoined at a different point along the top of a row or round.

To rejoin the yarn at a new point, insert the hook through the work at the required point. Wrap the yarn around the hook and draw this loop of yarn through the work.

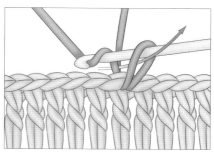

This loop becomes your new working loop. Make the required number of turning chain, remembering to use the yarn running to the ball, not the cut end, and continue across the row. Depending on the type of stitch being worked, the cut end can either be left free and darned in later or it can be laid across the top of the existing stitches and enclosed in the next few stitches.

crochet craft

When rejoining yarn, take care that you read the pattern to check exactly where the first new stitch needs to be placed. Depending on the stitch pattern being worked, the first 'real' stitch of this new section may also be worked into the stitch where you have rejoined the yarn. Working this first stitch in the wrong place will throw out of place the positioning of all future stitches.

Changing colour of yarn

Not all crochet items use just one colour of yarn, and care needs to be taken when joining in a new colour. The way in which crochet stitches are formed means that the last loop of one stitch actually sits on top of the next stitch, creating the 2 bars of yarn that form the 'V' across the top of this next stitch. It is therefore important to change to the new colour of yarn just before completing the last stitch in the old colour yarn.

How to change colours

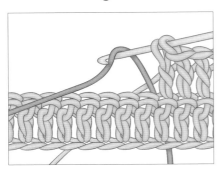

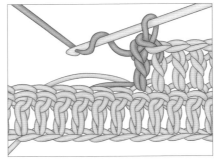

Work the last stitch using the old yarn colour up to the stage where the next 'step' to complete this stitch would be to wrap the yarn around the hook and draw this new loop through all the loops on the hook. For most types of stitch, this will be stopping at the point where there are only 2 loops on the hook. However, for some stitches, such as half trebles, there may be more loops on the hook. Let the old colour of yarn drop to the wrong side of the work and pick up the new colour of yarn, leaving the end of this new yarn on the wrong side of the work.

Now work the next stitches using the new colour of yarn. The two yarn ends left on the wrong side of the work can either be left free and darned in later, or they can be enclosed within the new stitches. As when joining in any new yarn, this will depend entirely on the type of stitch being worked, the thickness of the yarn and the types of yarn colours being used.

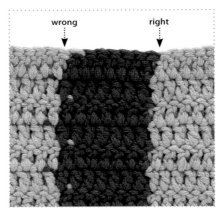

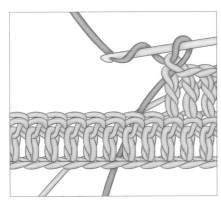

Wrap the new colour of yarn around the hook and complete the stitch using this yarn.

Changing the colour of yarn just before completing a stitch ensures that each complete stitch appears to be just one colour. Completing the last stitch in the old colour will create a broken-colour effect across the top of a row and can influence the positioning of any future stitches.

Working in stripes

When working in stripes, you will be changing yarn colour at the beginning of a new row or round.

Whether the turning chain at the beginning of the row or round counts as the first stitch of the new row, you should change to the new yarn to complete the last stitch of the previous row. Even if the turning chain does **NOT** count as a stitch, it will sit with the stitches of that row or round and should therefore be in the appropriate colour.

When working in rows of narrow stripes, the yarn not being used should be loosely carried up the side of the work from one stripe to the next. However, if the stripes are quite wide, it is best to cut the yarn once each stripe is completed and rejoin it for the next stripe. This avoids long strands of yarn 'floating' up the side of the work that may spoil the look of the finished item.

When working in rounds of narrow stripes, the yarn can still be loosely carried up the wrong side of the work from one stripe to the next. Make sure the yarn not being used is left free on the wrong side of the work at the end of each round so that the floats of yarn running between each stripe are not visible from the right side of the work.

If you are working in rows of stripes, try to make sure you work an even number of rows in each colour. This will mean that the yarn left for the next stripe will be at the right side of the work when you need to use it again. It also avoids the need to repeatedly cut and rejoin the yarn. Another way to avoid repeatedly rejoining yarn is

to work each first row of a stripe starting at the side of the work where that colour yarn has been left. However, this will mean that you will be working 2 rows in the same direction, so check that this will not affect the look of the work too much.

On the other hand, if you are working in rounds of stripes, each stripe can be made up of as many rows as you want. This is because the beginning and end point of every round is in the same place, regardless of whether you are turning the work or not before beginning each new round.

crochet craft

If you are stranding the yarn from one stripe to another, take great care not to pull the yarn too tight. If it is pulled too tight, this edge of your finished piece will be shorter than the other edge! The stranded yarn needs to be slightly longer than the edge it sits next to so that, in wear or use, this edge still has as much elasticity as the rest of the work.

Make these now!

Simple stripes of trebles are used to make this cute baby sweater and hat in fresh, cheerful colours. The sweater is worked in rows, while the hat has been worked in rounds. The stripes are fairly narrow, so it is quite possible to strand the yarn not being used up the side of the work from one stripe to the next.

SUNNY DAY STRIPES sweater and hat are worked in a 4ply-weight cotton yarn using a 2.50mm (C2) hook. This is a fine yarn, but the rows of trebles and simple construction make the sweater quick to make. See pages 261–263 for pattern.

Multi-coloured designs

It is possible to work designs in crochet that are similar to the Fair Isle or intarsia designs that appear in knitting. Instead of simple stripes, where each row or round is worked using just one colour, each row or round will have some stitches worked in one colour and other stitches worked in another colour. These designs can be as simple as patterns that feature single spots of a second colour, or they can be complicated multi-coloured designs, using several colours within one row or round.

Regardless of the quantity of stitches worked using each colour, the way the new colour is introduced will remain the same: it should be used to complete the last stage of the last stitch before the one to be worked in the new colour.

The crochet patterns for designs that feature rows or rounds worked in more than one colour can have this use of colour explained in two different ways: they are either written out within the pattern or shown on a chart.

Charted colourwork designs

If the colourwork design is fairly complicated, you will often find this is shown on a chart. This chart gives you a clear visual image of exactly what colours are used and where they sit in relation to the other stitches.

Charts for colourwork designs can be shown in two different ways: in colours that relate to those actually being used, or by using a different symbol for each different colour. Either way, the chart will consist of a grid of small squares. Each of the squares on this chart relates to one stitch on the crochet, with each row or round of the crochet being shown as a new row of squares. Within each square of the chart will be the colour or symbol that relates to the colour of yarn that should be used to work this stitch, and each chart will be accompanied by a key that explains exactly what colour of yarn you should use to work each stitch. When a chart is shown in colour, it is usually quite obvious what colour you will use and where, but if the chart features symbols you will need to refer to the key to find out what colour each symbol relates to.

Written instructions for colourwork designs

Where there are just a few stitches of each row, or round, worked in a different colour, you will often find that this is detailed within the instructions for the particular rows, or rounds, where this colour change occurs.

Along with details of exactly what crochet stitches should be worked and how these should be placed, you will find your pattern will tell you what colour of yarn to use for each set of stitches. Remember that the pattern will tell you to work, say, 2 trebles using a second colour, but you **must** change to this second colour to complete the stitch **before** these 2 trebles.

....

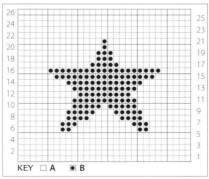

Pattern repeats

Sometimes a colourwork design will repeat a group of stitches using a set of colours. This is called a pattern repeat.

When the colourwork design is written out within the instructions, this colour pattern repeat will be expressed in exactly the same way as any stitch pattern repeat would be. An asterisk appears at the beginning of the pattern repeat and, once the whole pattern repeat has been explained, the pattern tells you to repeat the section from this asterisk across the rest of the row or round. The colourwork pattern repeat may also appear within a set of brackets, with details as to how many times you repeat this section.

On a charted colourwork design, the pattern repeat is indicated at the edge of the chart. This may be a set of stitches repeated across a row, or a set of rows that are repeated up the work, or both.

If it is a stitch repeat, repeat the indicated area as many times as possible (or as indicated) across the row, working the stitches at the beginnings and ends of the rows as shown on the chart.

If it is a row repeat, work the rows that form this repeat, then start again and work these rows once more. Continue in this

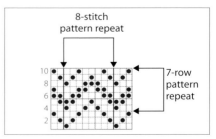

way, working all the rows that make up the pattern repeat again and again, until the work is completed.

Following a colourwork chart

Each square on the chart relates to one stitch of the crochet and the key tells you what colour to use.

To use a colourwork chart, work the first row by working across the first row of squares on the chart, changing colour as required. To work the next row, work the next row of squares on the chart. Generally, the first row of squares on a chart is a right-side row on the work; read the row of the chart from right to left. For the next row, you will work back across the crochet, so you need to work back across the chart, reading the next row of squares from left to right.

If you are working in rounds, you may find that every row of the chart should be followed in one direction. Or, if some sections are worked in rows and others in rounds, you may need to vary the way in

Shaping in a charted design

A colourwork chart shows you what colours to use for which stitches. It will not tell you to increase or decrease any stitches – there will just be more or fewer squares on the chart where any shaping occurs. If the design has shaping while the chart is being worked, this will be explained in the written section of the pattern. You must refer to both the written pattern and the chart while working a design such as this.

which you follow the chart accordingly. Your pattern should tell you exactly how to read the chart to achieve the effect desired for this design.

Carrying yarn across

A colourwork design that uses more than one colour in each row will require the colour of yarn not in use to be carried across the wrong side to the point where it is next needed.

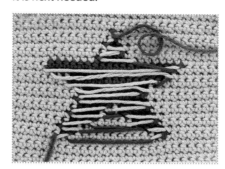

To move the yarn not in use to where it is next needed, simply strand the yarn loosely across the wrong side of the work. Make sure these strands, or floats, of yarn are not pulled too tightly as this can distort the finished work. Stranding the yarn across the back of the work will result in a fabric that has lots of floats of yarn at the back.

If the stitch pattern being worked is quite solid – such as a double crochet fabric – and the colours of yarn are fairly similar in tone, the yarn not being used can be laid across the top of the stitches and enclosed within these stitches as the next colour is used. Carrying the yarn between the different areas of colour in this way will result in a fabric that looks virtually the same from both sides, with no visible strands of yarn on either side.

Make this now!

This bag, based on an ancient Peruvian textile design, is worked in a combination of rounds and rows of simple double crochet. The colourwork design is quite complicated, with quite a few colours in use at any one time. To make it easy to see exactly what colours are used and where, the colourwork design for this bag is shown on a chart (see page 274).

PERUVIAN-STYLE BAG made in five shades of DK-weight mercerized cotton with a 4.00mm (G6) hook. See pages 274–276 for pattern.

Shaping in crochet

Very few crochet items are made up of just simple rectangles or tubes of crochet; at some point, you are going to need to know how to alter the number of stitches in each row or round – either by increasing or decreasing stitches – in order to shape the section as required. Note when increasing that the 'distortion' sometimes created by working lots of stitches into one base stitch is required to achieve the shape needed, such as when shaping a toy – so always work the increases as the pattern states!

Shaping a simple crochet fabric

If you are making a crochet item in a simple crochet fabric – such as rows or rounds of just double crochet or trebles – the shaping is easy to work.

● Simple increase

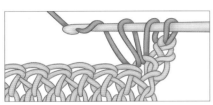

To increase one stitch in a row of basic stitches, simply work 2 stitches into the place where you would normally have worked just one stitch. Increasing a stitch in this way can appear anywhere within a row or round: on the first stitch, the end stitch, or at any point across the row or round. However, if you are increasing in this way at the beginning of a row or round, remember that the turning chain may, or may not, count as your first stitch. If it does count as the first stitch of the new row, you would normally miss the stitch at the base of this turning chain. To increase here, work the increasing stitch into the stitch at the base of the turning chain (the stitch usually missed). Similarly, if the turning chain does **NOT** count as a stitch, work 2 stitches into the place where you would normally have just worked the first stitch.

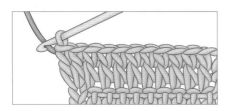

Increasing stitches in this manner retains the appearance of the crochet fabric and, depending on the height of the stitches being worked, this method can be used to increase up to a maximum of about 3 stitches at any one time. Attempting to work more than about 4 stitches into any one base stitch may end up distorting the work. A better effect may be achieved by spreading out the increases over several stitches, or by using another method to increase the stitches.

● Simple decrease

A simple decrease of one or two stitches at any point in a row can be worked in two ways.

It is possible to decrease just one stitch by simply missing a stitch of the base row or round. Although this will decrease the required stitch, it may also leave a tiny hole in the work. And, obviously, the more stitches decreased in this way and the taller the stitches are, the larger this 'hole' will be. Sometimes this will be the effect that is required for the item you are making, so check your pattern to ensure this is the correct method to use.

A better way to decrease one or two stitches at any point in a row or round is to work these stitches together, so that they join at the top. This method does not really affect the look of the fabric and will therefore be an ideal choice in most situations.

The abbreviation used to describe this type of decreasing stitch is a combination of the abbreviations used to create the stitch: it will feature the type of stitch to work, the number of stitches it is made up of, and the abbreviation 'tog' to show that it is a decrease. For example, working 3 treble stitches together to leave just one stitch will be abbreviated to 'tr3tog' – 'tr' to show you are working treble stitches, '3' to show you are working a total of 3 trebles, and 'tog' to indicate it is a decrease. The pattern will also tell you where to position each of these stitches.

The stage that completes every crochet stitch is to take the yarn over the hook and draw this new loop through the loops on the hook, leaving just one new working loop on the hook ready to start the next stitch.

With most stitches, there will be only 2 loops left on the hook before the last stage is worked. When working stitches together to make a decrease, each stitch is made up to this point. All the stitches are then completed in one action. At the base of the decrease there are 'legs' (the stems of the stitches) into each stitch of the base row or round, but at the top there is only one stitch.

To work 'tr3tog over next 3 sts', start by working the first treble into the first of these 3 base stitches. Stop just before the

stitch is completed, at the point when there are just 2 loops left on the hook – the original working loop and the loop just drawn through the wrappings.

Now work another treble up to exactly this point again, placing this treble into the second of the base 3 stitches. There are now 3 loops on the hook – the original working loop, the loop left from the previous partly worked treble, and the new loop from this partly worked treble.

Work the third treble of this decreasing stitch in exactly the same way as the second, working this stitch into the third base stitch. There are now 4 loops on the hook – the original working loop and one loop from each of the 3 trebles that have been partly worked.

To complete the tr3tog, take the yarn over the hook and draw this new loop through all the loops on the hook. The lower section of the tr3tog will consist of the lower sections, or 'legs', of 3 separate trebles, but the top section of the tr3tog will consists of just one stitch; thereby, 2 stitches have been decreased.

Make these now!

This cute little baby cardigan combines simple double crochet fabric with a fancy lacy stitch. It would be quite tricky to shape through a lacy stitch like this, so all the shaping appears within the simple double crochet sections, making this garment easy to crochet. The pretty co-ordinating shawl is made just in the lacy stitch. This is straightforward, as there's no shaping at all!

PRETTY IN PINK baby cardigan and shawl are both made in a soft pink shade of 4ply merino wool using a 2.50mm (C2) hook. See pages 166–168 for pattern.

Working stitches together in this way can be adapted to almost any type of stitch and used to decrease quite a few stitches at any one time. The number of stitches decreased is one fewer than those worked into on the row or round below, as there will be one stitch remaining after the decrease has been completed.

It is possible to decrease in this way to create a lacy effect by combining stitches worked together with stitches that are missed. This is particularly useful when shaping through

a lacy or mesh stitch pattern. In the red swatch (*left*), a tr2tog has been worked over 3 stitches of the previous row to retain the mesh effect. The first partly worked treble, or 'leg', has been worked into a treble of the previous row, the next chain stitch has been missed (thereby decreasing one stitch), and the second 'leg' of the tr2tog has then been worked into the following treble. Although only 2 stitches have been joined, creating

one stitch at the top, as these 2 stitches cover 3 stitches of the row below, a total of 2 stitches has been decreased.

When working stitches together in this way at the beginning of a row or round, where the turning chain counts as the first stitch, care needs to be taken to 'balance' the decreases worked at each end of the row or round, as in the yellow swatch (*left*). For example, if there are 2 trebles to be decreased at each end of the row by working 3 stitches together, the row needs to end with 'tr3tog over last 3 sts'. To balance this at the beginning of the row, work the turning chain that would normally count as the first stitch but do **NOT** include this in any stitch count (thereby decreasing one stitch). Complete the double decrease by working 'tr2tog over next 2 sts'. Take care when working back across this decrease row to remember whether or not the turning chains are to be counted as stitches or not!

Large increases and decreases

Increasing or decreasing just a few stitches creates a gentle slope at the edge of the crochet. But sometimes you may need to increase or decrease lots of stitches at one time to create a definite 'step' along the edge of the work – such as when shaping an armhole or a neckline. Obviously, these multiple increases or decreases cannot be worked in the same way as smaller shapings.

crochet craft

When working a multiple decrease, take care to check whether the turning chain at the beginning of the previous row counts as a stitch or not. If it does, you must remember to include this in the number of stitches to decrease; otherwise, the shaping will be wrong and any following rows will not work properly.

● *Multiple decreases – end of a row*
To decrease a lot of stitches at the end of a row is simple.

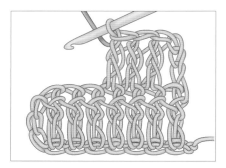

Work across the row until there are the number of stitches left at the end of the row that need to be decreased. Now simply turn the work, leaving these stitches unworked, and begin the new row in the usual way. The stitches left unworked at the end of the row are the decreased stitches and will form the 'step' shaping.

● *Multiple decreases – start of a row*
Decreasing lots of stitches at the beginning of a row can be achieved in one of two ways. The best method to use will be determined by the thickness of the yarn being used and the type of stitch pattern being worked.

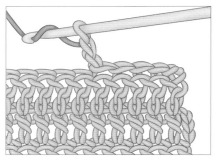

If the yarn is fairly thin and there are not very large quantities of stitches to decrease, start the new (decrease) row by simply slip-stitching across the last few stitches of the previous row until you reach the point at which this new row is to start. If there are 4 stitches to decrease, work one slip stitch into each of the first 4 stitches of the decrease row (the last 4 stitches of the previous row). Now work a slip stitch into the next stitch – this will be the base of the first stitch of the new row.

Work the turning chain at this point, in order to raise the working loop to the required height for this new row of stitches, and check your pattern instructions to find out whether this turning chain counts as the first stitch of the new row or not. If it does count, this last slip stitch and the turning chain form the first stitch of the new row and the next stitch of this row should be worked into the next stitch of the previous row.

If the turning chain does **NOT** count as your first stitch, then the first new stitch needs to be worked into the stitch at the base of the turning chain. This will be into the same stitch as used for the last slip stitch.

Working a slip stitch adds virtually no height to the work, so decreasing in this way will create a step effect. However, although no real height is added, slip stitches can add bulk to the work.

If you are using a very thick yarn or there is a large number of stitches to decrease, it is often better to break off and rejoin the yarn.

Make these now!

These casual sweaters are worked in a simple textured stitch pattern that combines trebles and double crochet stitches. Due to the nature of the textured stitch, the shaping is worked in a combination of ways so that the overall effect is even. Although the shaping may look complex, the garments remain surprisingly easy to make.

CASUAL COMFORT SWEATERS are made in a yarn that is 75% cotton and 25% microfibre; this has more 'give' than a pure cotton yarn and keeps its shape well. This yarn is slightly heavier than a DK-weight yarn, but is worked on a 4.00mm (G6) hook to create a sturdy, dense fabric. See pages 298–299 for pattern.

At the end of the last row before the decrease row, fasten off and cut the yarn. Turn the work and count across the top of the last row to the point where the new row is to start. If there are 6 stitches to be decreased, the first 6 stitches of the next row need to be left unworked. Rejoin the yarn to the next stitch and work the required turning chain. Working a multiple decrease in this way ensures that no additional bulk is formed by the slip stitches but creates exactly the same effect.

● *Multiple increases at the beginning of a row*
All crochet stitches need a base to be worked on and, when working a large step increase at the beginning of a row, a foundation chain needs to be made first. The new increased stitches of the next row will 'sit' on these chain stitches.

crochet craft

Take care to read the pattern correctly so that you work the correct number of chain – this will be a combination of foundation and turning chains. It is also important to work the first 'real' stitch of this row into the correct chain stitch. Exactly which chain this is will vary depending on whether the turning chain counts as a stitch or not.

Start the increase row by working one chain stitch for each stitch that is to be increased. This will form the foundation chain edge of the step increase. At the end of the foundation chain, work the required extra chain for the turning chain.

Now begin the new row by working the first set of stitches – the increased stitches – into the foundation chain. Once these increased stitches have been worked, continue across the rest of the row in the usual way.

Combinations of shaping
Depending on the type of stitch pattern being worked, the type of yarn being used and the shapes required, often a pattern will use a combination of all these different ways of increasing and decreasing to create the required effect. Make sure you follow the pattern accurately – the way the shaping is given in the pattern has been carefully worked out to create the best result possible.

Often you will find that a pattern explains exactly how to work the first increase or decrease, and then tells you to continue to work any further increases or decreases in this way. Again, take care to follow these instructions. If you alter the way the shaping is worked, you may find the end result is not as it should be!

● *Multiple increases at the end of a row*

In the same way as increased stitches at the beginning of a row need a foundation chain, so do those at the end of a row. But, as the yarn and the working loop are at the opposite end of the row, this foundation chain needs to be worked separately.

Before beginning the increase row, remove the hook from the working loop and slip this loop onto a safety pin. Do **NOT** fasten off or cut the yarn. Using a separate length of yarn, attach this new yarn to the top of the first stitch of the last row, at the opposite end to where the working loop is. Work the required number of chain for each stitch to be increased. Fasten off and cut off this length of yarn.

Return to the beginning of the increase row, slip the working loop (the one that was left on the safety pin) back onto the hook and work across the row until a stitch has been worked into the same stitch as where the yarn was attached for the little length of chain. Now work across the foundation chain for the increase stitches, working one stitch into each chain stitch.

Sometimes, to reduce the bulk, a pattern will start by telling you to make and set aside a short length of chain for a multiple increase that happens later. If this is the case, simply follow the pattern and, when required, pick up this little chain and work across it as specified in the pattern. Once the yarn end has been darned in, the effect created is identical to that achieved by attaching the yarn before making the chain. However, as the yarn is not as firmly attached, the 'join' between the increased and main stitches is not quite as secure and, particularly in the case of tall stitches, a hole can appear later.

Shaping through a fancy stitch pattern

If a stitch pattern is made of groups of stitches that create a lacy or textured pattern, your pattern will usually explain exactly how each row or round needs to be worked to achieve the required shape.

If this is the case, you may find that, rather than simply increasing or decreasing one or two stitches at a time, you will be adding or losing a part of a pattern repeat. This will allow the next few rows or rounds to be worked so that the overall effect remains constant. Take care to follow the pattern instructions carefully so that the stitches of any following rows or rounds are positioned correctly and the original stitch pattern is not distorted.

TECHNIQUES

203

Following a crochet pattern

A crochet pattern will give you all the information you need to make the item in the photograph. The different sections of the pattern will tell you various pieces of information that you need, and the order these are given in should be followed. Before you begin to make anything from a crochet pattern, read through the whole of the pattern so that you have an idea of exactly what you need to do to complete the project as required.

Measurements

If the pattern is in just one size (as in the case of a scarf or a throw) this section will tell you how big the finished item will be. If there is a choice of sizes for the item (as in the case of a sweater) this section tells you what those sizes are.

Generally you will find details of what size the item will fit; usually a bust or chest size. This measurement relates to the actual size of the **body** the garment is to fit and does **NOT** refer to the finished size of the garment. The actual size of the garment will be given below this, and the 'actual size' measurement will generally be bigger than the 'to fit' measurement. For a garment to be comfortable, it needs to be slightly bigger than your body and this additional size is called the 'ease'. This section will also tell you how long the garment will be, both in the body, measured from the shoulder to the lower edge, and in the sleeve.

crochet craft

If you are unsure what size to make, measure a garment in your wardrobe that you like the fit of. Compare the measurements of this garment with the actual measurements of the pattern and select the size to make accordingly. To help you follow the pattern more easily, you may find it useful to circle all the figures that relate to the size you are making before you start.

Materials

In this section, you will find details of what brand and type of yarn you need to buy, and exactly how much you should need. The patterns in this book also tell you what colour was used for the item in the photograph.

It is advisable to use the actual yarn stated in the pattern to ensure the item works up properly. Although many yarns are similar, they are not the same and, although the difference may not be apparent before you begin, there is no guarantee the pattern will work as it should in another yarn. You may need more or less yarn, or you might end up with something that is far too floppy or far too solid.

If the pattern is in more than one size, you will find the yarn quantities given as a string of figures in square brackets [ ]. These refer to the amounts needed for each size. The first figure (before the first bracket) is how much you need for the first size; the second figure (first one inside the bracket) is how much to buy for the second size, and so on. From now on, you will find that, throughout the pattern, the different figures needed for each size will be given in this way. Where only one figure, or set of figures, appears, this relates to all sizes.

The amount of yarn stated in this section is based on the amount used to make the item in the photograph and you may find you need a little more or a little less, especially if you decide to lengthen or shorten the item.

The Materials section will also tell you what else you need – such as buttons – and what size, or sizes, of crochet hook you are likely to need.

Tension

Here you will find details of what tension you need to achieve to make your item look the same as the one in the photograph. It is very important to check your tension (see pages 178–179).

Abbreviations

Throughout this book, certain standard abbreviations have been used, and these appear on page 238. This section will give you details of any abbreviation that does NOT appear within the standard list.

Making the crochet pieces

Most crochet items are made up of smaller sections that are joined together afterwards. Exactly how each of these sections should be joined will be explained separately.

It is important to make the different component pieces in the order given in the pattern. If not, you may find that you cannot work one piece, such as an edging, as one section this needs to be joined to has not been made yet. Also, one section will often refer you back to how another section has been made, or its length, so that first section needs to have been completed for the next section to work.

Repeating sections of pattern

Within a pattern, it is likely that one little set of instructions, or stitches, will need to be repeated across a row or round. If this is the case, the pattern will show this in one of two different ways.

First, the group of stitches to be repeated may appear inside a set of round brackets ( ). In this instance, the number of times these stitches should be repeated will be given after the closing bracket. Second, you may find that an asterisk (*) appears within a written row of instructions. This marks the beginning of the repeat and, if you follow along the written row, you will come to a phrase that says 'rep from * to…'. Do exactly as the pattern says: work across the row or round to the point where it states to start repeating a section, then go back to the * and repeat that section as many times as specified.

However the repeat is given, be aware that the number of times the section is repeated may vary depending on the size you are making. You may find instructions within round brackets (the repeating section) followed by figures in square brackets (the number of times these need to be repeated for each size).

When a repeating section is started by a *, you may often find the pattern states to end the last time this repeat is worked at **. Again, do exactly as the pattern states: repeat the section from the star across the row. It is likely there will not be sufficient stitches to work the whole of the repeat at the end of the row, so stop the last repeat at the ** point indicated. You may find there are a few stitches left at the end of the row, but your pattern should explain exactly how to work across these end stitches.

Make this now!

*This cosy rug is made in simple rows of double crochet and loop, or fur, stitches. The amount of yarn stated on this pattern is how much was used to make this particular rug. But the amount of yarn **you** need could vary quite dramatically! If you make the loops a little longer, or a little shorter, than stated on the pattern, you will need more, or less, yarn than stated. You'll find this explained in the 'special note' that accompanies the pattern.*

ROSE-RED HEART RUG was made in a robust 100% wool yarn. This is a chunky-weight yarn, substantial and hard-wearing enough to withstand being trodden on, worked on a 7.00mm (L11) hook. See pages 301–302 for pattern.

Crochet stitch diagrams

Although all crochet stitch patterns can be expressed in words, explaining exactly what stitch to make and how to place these stitches, it is also possible to show crochet stitch patterns in diagrammatic form. These diagrams give you a visual reference as to exactly how the different stitches sit in relation to each other within the work.

On a crochet stitch diagram, each type of stitch will be represented by a different symbol. Below is a list of the most commonly used symbols.

With each stitch diagram, there will generally be a key. This will tell you exactly what each symbol on this particular diagram means. You may well find that a symbol appears that is not one of the standard symbols – but the key will tell you what this symbol relates to. Refer back to the 'special abbreviation' section of the pattern to find out exactly how to work this stitch group.

Crochet stitch diagrams are there to help you place the stitches correctly and they need to be followed in conjunction with the written pattern. On the diagram, you will generally find just one or two pattern repeats given, and it is unlikely any shaping will be shown. This should all be explained within the written pattern.

●	ss (slip stitch)
○	ch (chain)
+	dc (double crochet)
T	htr (half treble)
⊤	tr (treble)
⊥	dtr (double treble)

Special notes

If there is something unusual about the particular pattern you are following you will find a 'special note' appears within the pattern.

This is there to help you understand the pattern and it is essential to read and follow this note!

Measuring the work

Some crochet patterns will tell you to work to a certain measurement, and tell you to stop after a particular pattern row.

When measuring the work, lay it flat on a firm surface to measure it, smoothing it out gently. Do **NOT** measure the work hanging down as the weight of the yarn could stretch the work and distort the measurement.

If the pattern says to stop after a particular row, make sure you do stop in the correct place. This could simply be after a wrong-side row, or it could be after a particular row of a stitch pattern. If you do not stop at the right point you will probably find the rest of the pattern will not work properly – you could end up with neck shaping at the armhole edge!

Completing the item

The last section of most crochet patterns is the 'making up' section. Here you will find out how to join the different pieces to form the final item.

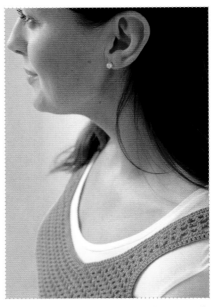

The making-up section is generally where you will find instructions for the decorative details and finishing touches for your item – such as this pretty neckline edging for a vibrant summer top.

It is also within this section where you will generally find out how to make any edgings, or extra decorative details, that need to be added to the item. **Take care to follow this section accurately.** If you have spent many hours making the main pieces, it is worth taking a little extra time here to ensure your item goes together correctly.

Not all items need to be 'made up' afterwards. If there is only one piece to make, you may find this section just tells you to press it – or even that this section is not there at all.

Aftercare

Once your item is complete, it is often a good idea to save a ball band and a little of the leftover yarn in case you need it at a later date.

Some people like to buy a spare button and store all these things together. Why not start a little catalogue of all the items you have made? Write down where the pattern came from and what size you made, and store all this information together. Should you ever decide to remake the same design at a later date, you will have a handy reference of exactly what you did and know where to find everything.

Filet crochet

Filet crochet is a style of crochet that consists of a mesh of stitches that form a grid of squares, with some of these squares left open and some filled in. These open and solid squares form a design, which can be geometric or floral. Filet crochet is a very traditional form of crochet that was traditionally worked in white using extremely fine crochet thread – often as fine as sewing thread! You can, however, achieve the effect using a thicker yarn and using any colour that appeals to you.

Basic filet

A basic filet mesh – the grid that forms the basis of any filet design – consists of rows of tall stitches that are separated by lengths of chain.

Although the stitches used and the size of the squares can vary, the most common type of filet mesh is one where each vertical side of each square is formed by a treble, and the top and bottom horizontal sides of each square are formed by 2 chain.

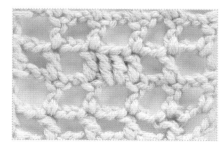

The filet crochet design that is placed on the mesh is made up by filling in some of the open squares of the grid (usually referred to as 'spaces') with stitches to form what is generally called a 'block'.

The stitches that fill in the block will be the same type of stitches that form the vertical sides of the square. These stitches can either be worked into the chain space at the base of the square, or they can be worked into the stitches across the base.

crochet craft

It doesn't really matter whether you work the filling stitches into the chain stitches or the chain space, so long as you are consistent and work them all the same way. Depending on the thickness of yarn being used, you may find it quicker and simpler to work into the chain space.

Make these now!

These lacily delicate pot pourri sachets are quickly and easily made in filet crochet. Although white is the traditional choice for filet crochet, we give it a new twist here by working a ruby-red heart, too.

POT POURRI SACHETS are worked in a fine 4ply mercerized cotton – this is about the thickest weight of yarn that works up well for a filet crochet mesh. The sachets were crocheted with a 2.50mm (C2) hook. See pages 300–301 for pattern.

● How to make a basic filet mesh

To make a basic filet mesh that consists of trebles forming the vertical sides and where each pair of trebles is separated by 2 chain stitches, start by making the foundation chain.

The length of the foundation chain is calculated as follows: you will need 3 chain for the base of each square of the grid. Now you need to work a turning chain to bring the working loop up to the point where the first actual treble will be placed. Work 3 extra chain (to count as the first vertical treble, or first side of the edge square) and 2 more (to run across the top of the first square).

Place the first 'real' stitch of the first row at the base of the other side of the edge square of this row. Count back as follows: you have 2 ch across the top, 3 ch down the side, and another 2 ch across the bottom – 7 ch in total. So the first treble should be worked into the 8th chain from the hook.

Now work across the foundation chain, making the top and side 'bars' of each consecutive square as follows: *2 ch (the top bar), miss 2 ch (the bottom bar), 1 tr into next ch (the next side bar). Repeat from * until the end of the foundation chain is reached. This forms the first row of completed open squares, or 'spaces'. Turn the work.

To work the next row of squares, make a turning chain of 3 ch (for the first vertical bar) and 2 more ch (for the first top bar). Work the vertical bar at the end of the first square by working a treble into the top of the corresponding treble below.

Continue across the row as follows: *2 ch, miss 2 ch, 1 tr into next tr, rep from * to end. Note that at the end of the row, the last treble will be worked into the top of the turning chain that counts as the first treble, not an actual treble stitch.

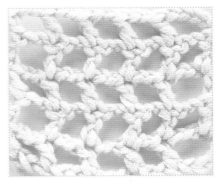

Repeating this last row will form the basic filet mesh of spaces, where each square is empty.

● To work a solid block

The design of a piece of filet crochet is formed by filling in some of the spaces of the mesh with a block of solid crochet.

To make a block, simply replace the 2 chain that would have run across the top of the space with 2 trebles. Instead of missing the 2 stitches at the base of the square, work these filling trebles into these stitches.

● Combining spaces and blocks

A filet crochet design will combine spaces and blocks to create the finished pattern. The way these squares are combined will vary, but the way each space and block is worked remains the same.

Regardless of what type of square sits below the new one, this new block will need a treble at each side and 2 stitches across its width. Whether these stitches are chain stitches or trebles will create the effect.

Lacy filet stitches

Most filet crochet designs will consist of just blocks and spaces. However, more interest can be given to the work through the introduction of lacets and bars.

● *Working a lacet*

A lacet is a variation of a double space and, as such, covers 2 of the squares below it.

When working 2 normal spaces, there would be a treble at each side and the centre 5 stitches would be '2 ch, miss 2 sts, 1 tr into next tr, 2 ch, miss 2 sts'. For a lacet, these centre 5 stitches are replaced with '3 ch, miss 2 sts, 1 dc into next tr, 3 ch, miss 2 sts'. These replacement stitches form a soft 'V' shape that creates a more lacy effect.

● *Working a bar*

If a lacet has been worked in the row below, it is not possible to work the 2 spaces above in the usual way: there is no centre treble into which to work the treble of the next row.

Instead of working 2 spaces above a lacet, you will normally find what is called a 'bar'. Here, the centre 5 sts are worked as '5 ch, miss (3 ch, 1 dc and 3 ch)'.

Above a bar, a pair of spaces or blocks is separated by working the dividing treble into the centre chain stitch of the 5 that run across the top of the bar.

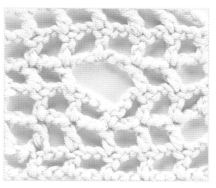

Although bars are generally found above lacets, they can appear elsewhere in the work. If a wider ribbon or cord is to be threaded through the work, a bar will make the perfect opening through which this can pass. If a bar does NOT sit above a lacet, but above 2 ordinary squares, the centre 5 stitches are worked as '5 ch, miss 5 sts'.

Filet charts

Because of the grid nature of filet crochet, the design is usually shown on a chart. Each section of the chart grid relates to a corresponding section of the crochet grid, with one square of the chart representing one square of the crochet.

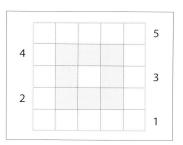

Filet charts show you where spaces and blocks should be placed to make up the design. Follow the chart, making the relevant spaces and blocks, by working across one row of squares, and then the next. You should follow the chart from right to left for right-side rows, and left to right for wrong-side rows.

Filet crochet shows up best when worked in a fine yarn. This means the squares that make up the mesh are smaller and therefore more detail can be given to the design. The thicker the yarn, the larger the squares and the less obvious the design becomes.

Any type of design can appear on filet crochet: a simple geometric design or an intricate and fancy realistic design. Whatever the design, it is created in silhouette by the use of the solid blocks and open spaces.

crochet craft

The chart will appear with a key explaining what the chart symbols represent. However, as you are basically working spaces and blocks it should be pretty obvious!

Joining pieces of crochet

Once the component pieces that will make up your crochet project have been completed, these will need to be joined together to make the final item. If you have spent many hours lovingly making the different sections, it is worth spending time and care at this stage – don't spoil your work now! There are many different ways in which the seams of crocheted sections can be joined. Some are better suited to certain types of crochet than others. The seams can be sewn, or they can be crocheted.

Sewing seams

If a seam is to be joined by sewing it, use a large blunt-pointed needle designed for sewing up knitted items. These are very similar to the needles that are used for tapestry and cross stitch and are widely available. Make sure you choose one that is large enough to easily thread with the yarn you are using.

Using a blunt-pointed needle for the seam means that the fibres forming the yarn are gently eased apart as the needle passes through. A sharp needle can pierce and break the fibres, weakening the yarn and creating unsightly little tufts of fibres along the seam line.

crochet craft

Ideally, the seams should be sewn with the yarn used to make the item. But sometimes this yarn will not be suitable to sew the seams with: it could be too fluffy, too thick, or too textured. If this is the case, sew the seams using a matching shade of a plain yarn instead. Rather than buying a whole ball just for the seams, use a tapestry or embroidery yarn that comes in a short skein.

● *Over-sewing a seam*

This type of seam is probably the best seam to use to join most types of crochet. It adds no bulk to the work and is virtually invisible if worked correctly.

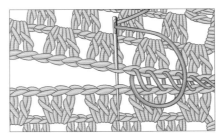

To over-sew a seam, lay the two edges to be joined next to each other. Stitch the seam by carefully over-sewing along the edges, picking up one strand of yarn from each edge and gently pulling the edges together as you sew.

If you are joining the tops of rows to each other, work one seam stitch for every one crochet stitch along the edges. When joining row-end edges, make the size of these seaming stitches the same as those across the crochet rows.

● *Flat seam*

This type of seam creates a similar effect to an over-sewn seam, as it draws the two edges together as it is worked, leaving the stitching virtually invisible. However, as you are stitching through the centre of the edge, this type of seam is really only suitable to use when the crochet fabric is fairly thick and solid.

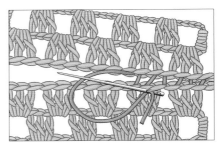

To make a flat seam, lay the two edges to be joined next to each other. Stitch the seam by taking one stitch through one edge, then another stitch through the other edge, creating a ladder-like effect, and gently pulling the edges together as you sew.

Try to keep the stitches small and even, and try not to pull the seaming yarn too tight. This could make the seam pucker and the yarn could snap, causing the seam to come undone.

Make this now!

This cosy wrap cardigan has the whole of its weight supported by the shoulder seams – so these need to be strong! Back-stitching them will give them the strength they need. The back and fronts are worked in one piece to reduce the number of seams that need to be sewn later. But there are sleeve seams to sew, and sleeves to insert into armholes. In order to keep these seams as flat as possible, these have been over-sewn.

LAZY STRIPE WRAP JACKET is made from a unique yarn composed of 70% wool and 30% soybean protein fibre in a standard DK weight. The main body of the jacket is worked using a 4.00mm (G6) hook; the cuff edgings and body edgings are crocheted with a 3.50mm (E4) hook. See pages 296–297 for pattern.

● *Back stitching a seam*

Sewing a seam in this way creates a strong and hard-wearing seam, making it the ideal choice for shoulder seams on large or heavy garments. However, its construction can create bulk on the inside of the work.

To back stitch a seam, hold the two edges to be joined with their right sides together.

 Working as close as possible to the edges, work a line of back stitch along the edges to be joined, taking each stitch through both layers of crochet.

Sometimes an edge along which shaping has been worked will not be totally straight and smooth, as the increases and decreases can cause tiny steps along the edge. If you are joining edges like this, back stitch is the perfect choice as it allows you to straighten off the edge while sewing the seam.

crochet craft

If you leave a long end at the beginning of each section of crochet, this end can be used to sew the seam with. This saves joining in lots of lengths of yarn later and saves time as there are fewer ends to darn in.

Crocheting seams

Joining edges with a line of crochet forms a strong and flexible seam. This type of seam is not as invisible as one that is sewn, but it is often much quicker to do.

If a seam is to be joined with a line of crochet, use the same size crochet hook as was used to make the sections being joined. If more than one size of hook was used when making the crochet sections, choose the hook used for the majority of the work when joining the seams. This will ensure the stitches used for the seam are worked at the same tension as the rest of the item.

● *Slip stitching a seam*

Joining the seam with a line of slip stitches creates a tight and strong seam, pulling the edges together quite closely.

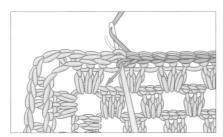

Hold the two edges that are to be joined with their right sides together. Attach the yarn at one end of the seam and make the seam by working a row of slip stitches, inserting the hook through the edges of both pieces to be seamed. Pick up just one strand of yarn from each edge and try not to work the slip stitches too tightly, as this could pucker the seam and distort the item. The seaming stitches should be the same size as those within the work, so the hook should be inserted through the edge at regular intervals to match the size of the main stitches.

crochet craft

If crocheting a seam across the tops of rows, pick up the two closest bars of yarn that make up the little 'V' at the top of each stitch. This will make the seam less visible on the right side of the work.

Once the seam has been completed, fasten off securely. When the two sections are opened out, the resulting seam will be virtually flat. Here, half the seam has been worked in a contrasting colour to show just how visible the slip stitching is. However, when worked in the same yarn, it is not nearly as noticeable.

● *Double crocheting a seam*

This forms a strong and very flexible seam that will have the same amount of stretch, or 'give', as the rest of the work.

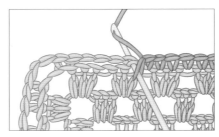

Joining a seam with a row of double crochet is made in exactly the same way as when joining it with a line of slip stitches – except, obviously, you will be working double crochets through the edges, not slip stitches.

A seam joined with a line of double crochet can appear quite bulky, as the double crochet stitches that form the seam create a slight ridge across the work. As the stitches are a little looser, they can show more on the right side of the work.

Often when a seam is joined with a line of double crochet, the two sections to be joined are held with their wrong sides together so that the seam, and the ridge it creates, shows on the outside, with the seam becoming part of the final design. If a seam is being joined in this way across the top of rows, it is best to insert the hook

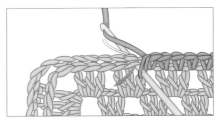

through the two layers under both of the strands that form the 'V'. This ensures both strands are enclosed within the seam.

Working a seam in this way, in a toning or contrasting colour, can be particularly effective. If you decide to do this, take care to work each stitch neatly and evenly spaced along the edge.

If the crocheted seam is to show on the right side of the work, replacing a simple line of double crochet with a row of crab stitch will create a clever corded effect where the sections meet. See page 225 for how to work crab stitch.

● *Flat slip-stitched seam*

A flat seam can be created when joining two edges with crochet by laying the two edges next to each other so that they overlap very slightly.

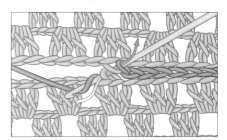

Join the edges by working a row of slip stitches along the seam, inserting the hook from above, picking up one strand from each edge.

A seam joined in this way will appear to have a line of back stitch on one side and a line of chain stitch on the other side.

● *Joining edges with chain bars*

A very pretty effect can be created by joining two edges with little bars of chain stitches. This is particularly useful if the sections being joined are lacy, as this will echo the main body of the work. This method is often used to join lacy motifs.

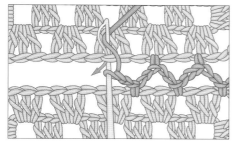

Start by laying the two edges to be joined next to each other and attaching the yarn at one end of the seam on one piece of the crochet. Work a stitch – either a double crochet or a slip stitch – into the point where the yarn has been attached, and then work a few chain stitches. Now work another stitch into the other edge a little way along the edge. Continue in this way, working into each edge alternately and spacing out the stitches worked into the edges with little bars of chain stitches, so that an even line of zig-zagging chains joins the two edges together.

Make this now!

The simple motifs that create this cosy shrug are joined with rows of double crochet. This makes it much quicker to join all the seams and ensures they are as flexible as the rest of the work. Joining the seams with the same colour as used around the edges of the motifs, with their right sides together, makes the seams virtually invisible. However to achieve a more pronounced motif edging, why not break the rules and make a feature of the seams, as shown here?

MULTI-COLOURED MOTIF SHRUG is made in five shades of DK-weight pure wool yarn. The main body of the garment is worked with a 4.00mm (G6) hook, while the edgings are crocheted with a 3.50mm (E4) hook. See pages 294–295 for pattern.

Making crochet motifs

One of the most frequently used elements of crochet is the crocheted motif. These can be lacy or solid, textured or smooth, round or square. In fact, they can be made up of any type of stitch or combination of stitches and appear in any shape at all! Regardless of the final shape of a motif and the type of stitch used to make it, motifs are almost always made in rounds, not rows. The motif will begin at the centre with stitches worked in rounds around this centre point to create the final shape. If the motif is not a simple circle, the height and type of stitches used will be varied to create the corners.

Motif centres

As with any circular piece of crochet, a motif will generally start with a length of chain stitches where the ends are joined with a slip stitch. It is this centre ring that the stitches of the first round are usually worked into.

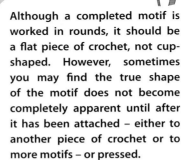

The starting chain ring of a motif will generally consist of far fewer stitches than those made in the course of the first round. These extra stitches are needed to ensure the motif lays flat and often a small circular hole will be left at the centre of the completed motif.

Sometimes a hole is not wanted at the centre of a motif; there are two ways this hole can be avoided.

Replace the chain ring at the beginning of a motif with one single chain stitch. Work the required number of turning chain needed to raise the hook to the correct height for the stitches of the first round, and then work all the stitches of this round into the first chain stitch, closing the round as specified in the pattern.

Once the first round has been completed, gently pull on the free end of yarn to tighten and close up the first chain stitch, thereby closing the hole. Take care to securely fasten off this end, or it may work loose and the unwanted hole may reappear.

crochet craft

Although a completed motif is worked in rounds, it should be a flat piece of crochet, not cup-shaped. However, sometimes you may find the true shape of the motif does not become completely apparent until after it has been attached – either to another piece of crochet or to more motifs – or pressed.

If the stitches of the first round are simple double crochet stitches, another way to remove the centre hole is by starting with just a simple loop of yarn and working into this loop.

Form the free end of the yarn into a simple loop and insert the hook through the centre of this loop. Take the yarn over the hook and draw this new loop through.

Take the yarn over the hook again and draw this loop through the loop on the hook.

Once more, wrap the yarn around the hook and draw this new loop through the loop on the hook. This completes the first stitch of the first round.

Now make the remaining number of double crochet stitches that are required for the first round, working each stitch into this loop as though it were a chain space and enclosing both strands forming the loop in the stitches.

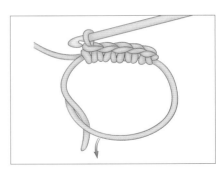

Once the required number of stitches have been made, gently pull on the free end to close up the slip loop at the centre, and join the ends of the round as specified in the pattern instructions.

crochet craft

Instead of making a simple single loop of yarn at the centre of a motif, try wrapping the yarn around a few times. This will create a chunkier ring of stitches at the centre. However, you will still be able to pull up the free end to close the hole.

Make these now!

In order to make these mitts and hat stay cosy and warm, without any 'holes', the stitches at the centres of the motifs here have all been worked into the one chain stitch – but there's no reason why you couldn't work them into a slip loop if you wanted. These motifs are square, but they are worked in rounds. Once the round of stitches that form the contrast circle has been worked, tall and short stitches have been combined on the following round to make the square shape.

CIRCLES AND STRIPES SET is made in a DK-weight tweed yarn that is 50% merino wool, 25% alpaca and 25% viscose/rayon. The contrasting flecks of colour in the tweed give the yarn real depth of colour. Both the hat and the mittens are worked with a 3.00mm (D3) hook. See pages 278–280 for pattern.

Making motifs

Throughout this book (and in many other crochet patterns), you will find the pattern gives you instructions on how to make one basic motif. There will then generally be a paragraph that explains exactly what your motif should look like, with details of what shape it should be and what sort of stitches there are around its outer edge.

Start by making your first motif and then check that your motif matches the description given in the instructions. This allows you to check you have made the motif correctly, and will help you understand how the motifs go together later. Once your first motif is completed, now is the time to check you are working to the correct tension, too.

Joining motifs

The instructions for items that are made up of lots of motifs will tell you how to join them together to form the required shape, or shapes, needed for the completed item. Sometimes this will be a simple strip of motifs, a rectangle or a loop, and sometimes it may be a more complicated shape. You may be joining the motifs as they are made, or you may be joining them all together later. Take time to read through your pattern before you begin so that you understand fully, before you start, exactly when and how the motifs go together.

crochet craft

Although a slip stitch or double crochet stitch are the most commonly used joining stitches, motifs can be joined by working almost any type of stitch; check your pattern to ensure you work the correct type of stitch. If the item you are making is comprised of lots of joined motifs, working the wrong type of joining stitch could completely alter the finished size of the item.

• *When to join motifs*

If the motifs are to be joined together by seams once they have all been completed, you can make all the motifs you need and then join them in the way your pattern specifies afterwards.

Often motifs are joined to each other while the last round is being worked. Joining motifs in this way creates a very secure join, and often these joins become part of and add to the final design. If motifs are to be joined in this way, your pattern will usually explain this in the paragraph that details the shape and structure of your

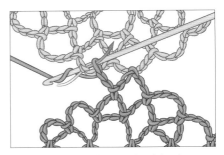

basic motif. Motifs joined while they are being made will usually have chain loops along their edges. These are where they are most likely to be joined to each other.

When motifs are joined at their chain loops, the centre chain stitch of the second, or following, motif is replaced with a stitch worked into the corresponding chain loop of the original motif. Hold the completed motif against the motif being made so that their wrong sides are together, and work the appropriate type of stitch into the corresponding chain loop.

crochet craft

Take time to read the 'tension' section of your chosen pattern before you make the first motif. Sometimes, especially if the motifs are large, you will need to measure the size of the motif before it is completed.

Joining motifs...

• *To form a strip*

Often when a design requires just a simple strip of motifs to be made, you will be told to join the motifs to form a strip of a specific number of motifs.

Start by making the first full motif and fastening off. Now start the second motif, stopping at the beginning of the round where the joins are to be worked. Following the pattern instructions, join this motif to the first one along the relevant edge. Continue in this way, joining each motif to the previous motif as you go along. Take time to check that you are joining them correctly as you make them. Square motifs that are to be joined to form a strip need to be joined along opposite sides of the square, and it can be very easy to accidentally start joining a motif to the previous one in the wrong place.

• *To form a loop*

A simple strip of motifs are often joined together at their ends to create a loop of motifs – as is the case with the hat featured on page 215.

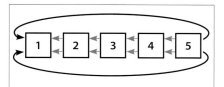

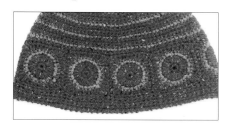

To join the motifs into a loop, start by joining the motifs into a strip, leaving the final motif unworked. While making this last motif, join it to both the appropriate edge of the previous motif and to the appropriate edge of the first motif to form the required loop.

• *To form a rectangle*

Motifs are often joined together in rows to form rectangles and squares that create the main fabric of an item – as is the case with the bedspread on page 219.

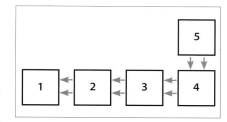

To form the final shape, start by making the first strip of the required number of motifs. Make the first motif of the second row, or strip, joining this motif to one end motif of the existing strip – but joining it along the side of the strip, not at the end.

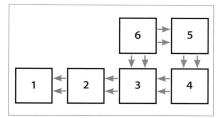

Make the second motif of the second strip, joining it to both the first motif of this strip and the second motif of the first strip. This motif will be joined to other motifs along two adjacent sides. Continue in this way, joining motifs to both the strip being worked and the previous strip, until the required shape is formed.

• *Following a diagram*

Often the way in which the motifs are joined will be shown by a diagram. This can be because the shape required is quite a complicated shape; because the motifs do not simply sit in rows; or because they are worked in different colours.

To make a design where the motifs are joined following a diagram, simply join them together as shown by the diagram. Sometimes you may find that the diagram and written instructions detail extra 'edges' to be joined together to complete the final three-dimensional shape. Read through the pattern before you start to join the motifs so that you are sure which extra edges need to be joined.

Part motifs

Sometimes a design will feature part motifs. These are motifs that are similar to a section of the full basic motif, and will appear in designs where the final desired shape cannot be achieved using only full motifs.

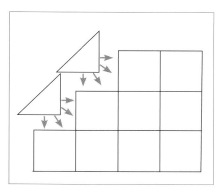

One of the most common places for part motifs to appear is along the edges of a V-neck design made using square motifs: a part (triangular) motif will be needed along the neck edge to obtain the correct shape. If a design requires full and part motifs to be made, start by making and joining all the full motifs. Once these are complete, the part motifs can be made and attached to form the correct shape.

crochet craft

A part motif can be comprised of any part of the full motif: it can be a half or a quarter of a square motif, or it can be a wedge of a circular motif. However, because it is not a full motif, it will usually be worked in rows, rather than rounds. If this is the case, make sure you check the full motif pattern and turn the work where required after the relevant rounds so that the fabric formed by the part motif matches that of the main full motifs.

Layered motifs

Pretty three-dimensional flower effects can be created on motifs by working layers of stitches forming petals that sit neatly on each other. This effect is created by working behind the stitches of the previous round to form the stitches of the new round, leaving those already worked sitting free on the surface.

• *Working into the separate loops*

Unless otherwise stated, the new stitches of a round are usually worked by inserting the hook under both of the bars of yarn that form the 'V' sitting on top of the previous stitches. However, if only one of these strands is worked into, the other strand remains free, allowing a second round to be worked independent of the previous round.

Start by making the centre of the motif up to the point where the first layer of petals is to sit. Now work the round that will form these petals, inserting the hook under the front loop only of the stitches of the previous round.

Now work the next round, inserting the hook through the back loops of the stitches left free in the previous round. This will leave the stitches of the previous petal round sitting on the surface of the work.

• *Multi-layered motifs*

Repeat this effect to create layers of petals sitting on top of each other like a real flower. Here, a double crochet circle was turned into a flower by working rounds of petals into the front loops of every other round. To increase the flower effect, the size of the stitches that form the petals increases as the bands of petals move outwards. The first-layer petals are half trebles; the outer-layer ones triple trebles.

• *Working around the stems of stitches*

One way to form a layered effect is to work the round after the petal round by working the stitches of this new round around the stems of the stitches used for the previous round. This is particularly effective if the base round of the petal round consists of chain spaces and fairly tall stitches. The action of pulling out these stems of these stitches causes the petals to fold upwards and adds to the three-dimensional effect they create.

Start by making the centre of the motif (below left) up to the point where the first layer of petals has been completed. Layered motifs made in this way will generally place the petal stitches into the chain space between the taller stitches of the previous round.

Now work the next round, working the stitches around the stems of the stitches of the base round used for the petals and taking care to keep the petals at the front of the work.

Filling motifs

If the motifs being joined are very lacy, the gaps between them can be too large to leave as they are on the finished item. In these situations, filling motifs are used to fill in these spaces.

Obviously, before the filling motifs can be worked, the surrounding full motifs need to be made and joined. Following the pattern instructions, and any diagram, now fill in each relevant hole between motifs with the filling motif. You will often find filling motifs used to complete a fabric made of circular motifs; these filling motifs can add greatly to the look of the finished work.

Make this now!

This stunning heirloom-style bedspread is made of motifs with simple three-dimensional flowers at their centres. Although time-consuming to complete, due to the bedspread's size and the nature of the yarn used, the individual motifs are easy to make – and the final effect is undoubtedly worth the effort. You could make some motifs in a pastel-coloured yarn to create a contrasting cushion cover.

HEIRLOOM BEDSPREAD is made in pure white 4ply cotton to create a vintage look. All the work is done with a 2.50mm (C2) hook. See pages 310–311 for pattern.

Pressing crochet items

Crochet forms a neat fabric that often does not require any pressing at all – to do so would damage the surface texture of the stitches. However, often you will need to press something to even up the stitches, smooth out the fabric and neaten the seamed areas. Whatever reason there is for pressing an item, care needs to be taken with how this is done. The way the item is pressed will depend on the type and composition of the yarn that has been used, and the type of stitches that have been worked.

Pressing

Before you begin to press any item, look at the ball band of the yarn that has been used and follow the directions given there. Although pure wool or cotton yarns can be pressed with a damp cloth and a fairly hot iron, synthetic yarns will be ruined if treated the same way.

● *When to press*

Often it is a good idea to press the crochet sections before they are seamed together. Not only can this make the seaming process easier, as the edges are flat, but it can also allow you to get into areas that would be impossible to reach once the seams are joined – such as the sleeve tops of children's clothes. Once the item has been seamed together, the actual seam lines can be pressed if required.

● *How to press*

To press a piece of crochet, lay it flat on a soft but firm surface. A table covered with a towel and a clean sheet is ideal. Ensure the **wrong** side of the crochet is uppermost (to avoid any chance of damaging the right side of the work) and gently smooth each piece out to the correct shape and size, referring

back to the pattern if necessary. Cover the crochet with a clean pressing cloth (check the ball band to find out whether this should be a dry or a damp cloth) and heat the iron to the correct temperature for the yarn used.

Remember – pressing is very different from ironing! When you iron, you slide the iron backwards and forwards over the fabric. To do this to a piece of crochet could stretch or distort it, possibly causing permanent damage. A pressing action is one where the iron is gently lowered and raised onto different areas of the work. Do NOT push down on the iron; simply let it gently rest on the pressing cloth for a

crochet craft

Regardless of the type of yarn being used, you are safe to use a damp cloth when blocking a piece of crochet, as there is no heat involved at all. It is the steam generated by a hot iron used in conjunction with a damp cloth that damages synthetic fibres.

crochet craft

If a crochet item combines more than one type of yarn, it must be pressed according to the needs of the most delicate yarn within the work. If you don't do this, this area of the work may be irrevocably damaged.

second or two. Depending on the texture of the work, you may not even need the iron to touch the fabric. Pure wool items can be very effectively pressed by holding the iron just above a damp cloth, as the heat of the iron will push the steam through the crochet and do all the pressing for you.

Once the crochet has been pressed, you should leave it to cool and, if relevant, dry naturally **before** removing it from the pressing surface.

Pressing versus blocking

The way in which an item is 'pressed' will vary depending on the character of the crochet. If the surface is quite smooth, without masses of textured stitches, it can be pressed. However, if it is heavily textured, placing an iron on this texture will squash and damage it. For heavily textured items, blocking

Items with a smooth surface, such as this motif shrug, should stand up well to pressing, but check the details on the ball band to see if any special care needs to be taken. This shrug was made from pure wool yarn, so, to press it effectively, you could cover it with a damp cloth and hold an iron just over the cloth.

Blocking

If a crochet item has been made using a synthetic yarn, or if it is very heavily textured, blocking it is a much better option than pressing.

To block out an item, start with the same soft but firm surface as if you were pressing it. Lay the crochet section flat on this surface, but with the right side uppermost. If necessary, pin the crochet to the pressing surface around its outer edge, easing it into the correct shape and placing the pins 5 to 10cm (2 to 4in) apart. Cover the crochet with a damp cloth and leave everything to dry naturally. Once totally dry, remove the cloth and any pins and you can complete the item if necessary.

Make this now!

This pretty baby blanket is worked in a yarn that combines pure merino wool with pure cotton so, in theory, it could be pressed with a warm iron over a damp cloth. However, if this were done too fiercely, it could damage the delicate surface texture. To ensure this doesn't happen, press this type of stitch by holding the iron just above a damp cloth and allowing the iron to just push the steam it generates through the work.

THREE-COLOUR BABY BLANKET is made using three shades of a yarn that is 50% merino wool and 50% cotton. The yarn is quite a fine DK weight and is worked using a 3.00mm (D3) hook. See pages 303–304 for pattern.

Borders and edgings

Crochet fabrics can have a tendency to be a little wavy along their edges, so you will often find that a border is added to these edges in order to neaten them and to help the item 'hold' its intended shape. In addition, decorative borders and edgings can be worked to add a little extra detail and interest to a crocheted item. Borders and edgings can also have a practical purpose, for example, to add a buttonband and button loops to a cardigan, or to add ties to hold a garment closed.

To work a border along an edge

Start by attaching the yarn at one end of the edge. Make the required turning chain for the type of stitch to be worked, and then work along the edge, inserting the hook through the edge of the work.

If you are working along the top of a row, insert the hook through the existing stitches in exactly the same way as if making any new row of stitches.

If working along a foundation-chain edge, work each border stitch into the remaining free loops of the foundation chain.

When working along row-end edges, the actual placement of the border stitches will vary greatly depending on the stitch pattern that has been worked within the main section. Experiment to see how best to place the new stitches – work a few stitches and see how they sit on the work. If you are not happy, undo them and try again.

How many stitches to work

Unfortunately, there is no golden rule as to exactly how many stitches you should work along any type of edge – although there are some guidelines.

If you are working with a simple plain crochet fabric, such as a double crochet fabric, working one border stitch for every stitch of the main section should generally create a good border. Along row-end edges, the number of stitches that you will need to work will vary depending on the height of the stitches making up the fabric. Working one double crochet of the border for each row of double crochet on the main fabric works well, as does working two border stitches for every row of trebles.

The only way to ensure the border sits well and does its job properly is to work a small section to check the number of stitches you are making is right. The stitches of a border are usually there to hold the edge in slightly and, as just a few rows of crochet have a tendency to stretch easily, you may find it best to work fewer stitches than you think you will need. Once the border is complete, any tightness can simply be released by very gently easing the edge out to the correct length.

A border that is worked correctly should be slightly shorter than the edge that it sits

along, not longer. If, as you are working the border, it appears to be starting to form a frilly edge, you are most likely working too many stitches. You will either need to start again completely, or change to a smaller size of hook and work the stitches of the border more tightly.

- ● *Contrast colour borders*

If you are working a border using a contrast colour, it is often a good idea to work the initial row or round with the colour used for the main body of the item. The first row or round of the border can tend to be a little uneven, especially where you are working into row-end edges.

If the contrast colour is introduced for the second row or round of a border, you will find that the line where the two colours meet is much more even and neat than if the whole of the border had been worked in the contrast colour.

- ● *Working borders in rows or rounds*

If a border is being added once the sections have been joined, it is usually easiest to work it in rounds, rather than rows. However, if there are a few borders to be made and some are to be worked in rows and some in rounds, remember to turn at the end of each round so that the resulting fabric of this border matches that of the borders worked in rows.

Shaping borders

Often a border will fall along a shaped edge, such as around an armhole or a curved neck or hemline. A border should lay flat unless the pattern specifies otherwise. To ensure your border does lay flat around these shaped edges, it may be necessary to increase or decrease a few stitches along the curved edges so that the edge is the correct length.

● **Working a border around a corner**

When a border runs around a corner of a piece of crochet, extra stitches will need to be either made or lost at the actual corner point.

To turn an external corner, such as at the base of a front opening edge, work extra stitches into the actual corner point. If the border is worked in double crochet, work 3 double crochet into the corner point, instead of just one. On the next row or round, you need to work 3 stitches into the corner stitch. The number of extra stitches you need to make to turn the corner will vary depending on the height of the stitches being worked. However, you will always need to work an odd number so that there is a central stitch into which the corner stitches can be worked on the following row or round.

To turn an internal corner, such as one at the base of a V-shaped neckline, stitches need to be decreased at either side of the corner. After the first row or round has been worked, decrease the same number of stitches either side of the actual corner point. Again, the number of stitches to decrease depends on the height of the stitches being worked and the angle of the corner. A border worked in double crochet around a square corner will probably sit nicely if one stitch is decreased at each side of the corner.

Make this now!

This mesh top has neat and narrow double crochet borders around all the edges. Around the lower edge (which is straight) there are the same number of stitches in both rounds of the border. However, both the armhole and neck edges are curved.

As the borders consist of just 2 rounds, they can be shaped either by missing the occasional stitch while working the second round, or by working the first round a little too tightly by spacing the stitches a little too far apart. Once the second round has been added, the edge can be gently eased out to the correct shape.

SUMMER SKY MESH TOP is made from a crisp 4ply mercerized cotton in a vibrant turquoise. The top is worked with a 2.50mm (C2) hook. See pages 286–287 for pattern.

Making buttonholes in borders

You will often find that any buttonholes needed for a garment are made while working the borders. These buttonholes can either be parallel to the border rows or rounds, or placed at right angles.

● *Buttonholes placed along a row or round*

To make a buttonhole that sits along a row or round, work along the row to the point where the buttonhole is to be placed. To form the actual buttonhole opening, replace the next few stitches with the equivalent number of chain instead. Miss the required number of stitches in the row, and then complete the row.

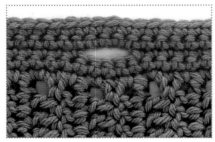

When working back across the stitches, work as many stitches as have been missed into the chain space that forms the buttonhole opening. You can either work these stitches into the chain space, or into the actual chain stitches.

● *Buttonholes placed at right angles*

Buttonholes placed at right angles to the border stitches are best worked in a border worked in rows. If the border is worked in rounds, it will be necessary to turn the work after each round to ensure all the border stitches and rows look the same.

To make this type of buttonhole, work across the row to the point where the buttonhole is to be placed (*above right*). Stop and turn the work, and work back across the stitches. Repeat these short rows until the buttonhole is the required size.

Rejoin the yarn to the last full row at the required point after the first buttonhole placement and work across to where the next buttonhole will be (*above*). Again, turn and now work backwards and forwards in rows on the stitches that sit between the buttonholes.

Continue in this way, working the sections between the buttonholes in separate batches of rows, until all the buttonholes have been completed. Now work one complete row, working across each set of stitches between the buttonholes in turn, and complete the border.

Making button loops

Often a crochet item is fastened with a button loop rather than a buttonhole. Button loops are easy to make while you are working the last row or round of the border.

To make a simple chain button loop, work the border up to the point in the last row or round where the button loop is to fall. Now replace the next few stitches with a length of chain. Miss the next few stitches and complete the row or round. Unlike when making a buttonhole, the number of chain stitches used for a button loop will usually be greater than the number of stitches of the row that are missed, so that the little chain loop will extend slightly from the finished edge. Adjust the number of chain you make so that the button loop snugly fits around the button.

To make a more solid button loop, work the last row or round up to the point where the button loop is to finish, not start. Now turn the work and make the required number of chain for the loop. Miss the required number of stitches for the loop and work a slip stitch into each of the next 2 stitches. Turn the work again and work the same number of double crochet into the chain loop as there were chain stitches, adding one or two extra so the loop forms a neat curve. Now complete the border by working into the remaining stitches of the previous row or round.

Adding ties to a border

Simple ties that are used to fasten the item can be made while working the last row or round of a border. Attaching a tie in this way makes it very secure, as it becomes an integral part of the crochet, and reduces the number of yarn ends to be darned in.

To place a tie within the last row or round of a border, work along the row to the point where the tie is required. Now make the length of chain that will form the base of the tie.

Work a double crochet into the second chain from the hook, and then work back along the length of chain, working one double crochet into each chain.

When all the chain stitches have been worked into, simply complete the row or round, leaving the tie extending free at the edge of the border.

Crab stitch

Crab stitch is a variation of simple double crochet, and is also known as corded or reversed double crochet. It creates a neat edge that looks virtually the same on either side, with tiny knotted bobbles sitting along the edge.

Almost every row or round of crochet is worked starting at the right of the work and progressing along the row or round towards the left. To work a row or round of crab stitch, you simply work double crochet stitches in the opposite direction, starting at the left and working towards the right.

Because you are working back on yourself, and you can find yourself getting a bit tangled up, it can take a while to get the hang of crab stitch. But the effect it creates is well worth the effort of practising until you get it right. It is one of the stitches many people have problems mastering – even experienced crocheters. But it's like learning to ride a bike – you struggle for ages then it suddenly works and there's no looking back!

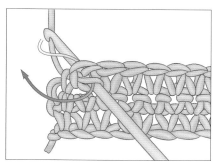

As crab stitch is worked from left to right, instead of right to left, there is no need to turn the work before starting the crab stitch. Make the required one turning chain and then twist the hook forwards and downwards to insert it, from front to back, through the top of the first stitch to be worked into – keep the yarn at the back

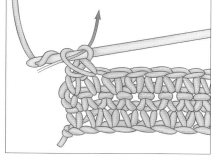

of the work. Take the yarn under the hook at the back of the work and draw this new loop through, so that there are 2 loops on the hook.

Take the yarn around the hook in the usual way and draw this new loop through both the loops on the hook. This completes the first stitch.

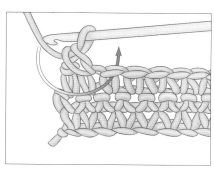

Again, keeping the yarn at the back of the work, twist the hook towards you and downwards and insert it through the next stitch to the right of the one that you just made. Take the yarn under the hook at the back of the work and draw this new loop through the work so that there are, once more, 2 loops left on the hook. Complete the double crochet stitch in the usual fashion, by wrapping the yarn around the hook and drawing this new loop through both loops on the hook. Continue in this way along the row.

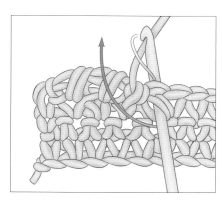

crochet craft

Crochet edgings

Crochet is a great medium to use to make any sort of edging. This could be a simple border to neaten a garment or it could be a fancy lacy edging used to decorate any number of items.

Crocheted edgings can be created either by working directly into an edge, or they can be worked separately and attached afterwards. Edgings can be made in either direction – you can work a few rows on lots of stitches, or you can work lots of rows on a few stitches.

● ***Working an edging into an edge***

If an edging is worked directly onto the item, it effectively becomes a fancy border and would be worked accordingly.

● ***Attaching a separate edging***

If the edging is made independently of the item and needs to be attached afterwards, the way the edging is seamed onto the item will depend on the effect to be created. Why not try different types of seams (see pages 210–213) to find out which looks best?

Make these now!

This cute baby set has contrast-colour frilly edgings added after the main sections have been completed. Here, the edging stitches have been worked into those of the foundation-chain edge of the main sections so you have a clear guideline as to how many stitches to make. There's no reason why you couldn't adapt this set to suit a baby boy. Simply replace the frilly edging with a simple border of double crochet or crab stitch!

PRECIOUS PASTELS BABY SET is worked using a DK-weight 100% merino wool for both the main part of the garments and the frilly trimmings. The work is done using a 3.50mm (E4) hook. See pages 263–265 for pattern.

● *Working a crochet edging into the edge of a ready-made item*

Often crochet edgings are used to decorate a ready-made item, such as a towel, a pillowcase or a shop-bought sweater. Although often it is best to seam these edgings in place, it is possible to attach them in the same way as if they were being worked into a piece of crochet.

Whether or not you can work the crochet edging directly onto the item depends on whether you can easily get the crochet hook you intend to use through the edge of the item without damaging it. Obviously, in the case of a shop-bought sweater, this should not be too difficult. However, it may be tricky on a woven fabric, especially if it is tightly woven. Before you start, try to push the crochet hook through the fabric somewhere where it will not be visible should any damage be caused – such as within a seam. If the hook goes through fairly easily, you will be able to work the edging. If it is a bit tight, try working the first row or round of the edging using a smaller hook and changing to the correct hook for the following rows or rounds. If the hook passes through quite easily but, once through, a small hole is left in the fabric, don't worry too much – careful pressing or laundering should make the fibres close up again to hide this.

Working a crocheted edge onto a woven fabric.

Hand-sewing an edging into place.

crochet craft

Take care to gently ease the hook through the fabric so that the fibres are pushed apart, not broken. If the fibres break, small holes will appear along the edge, spoiling the final look of the item.

When working an edging onto a woven fabric, there will not be any guidelines as to how often you should place the stitches. If you need to, mark points along the edge before you start; these can either be even sections, between which you will work a certain number of stitches, or they could be the evenly spaced points at which you will pass the hook through the fabric. If you are concerned about pushing the hook through the fabric too often, replace a complete row or round of double crochet into the edge with a combination of double crochet and chain. On the following row or round, work into these chains to give you the correct number of stitches.

● *Hand-sewing an edging in place*

If a crochet edging is to be attached to a fabric item by hand-sewing it in place, the type of thread that you use to attach it will depend on the type of fabric it is being attached to. If you are attaching a fine crochet edging to a shop-bought knitted item, you may find it possible to attach the edging using the same yarn as was used to make the edging.

If the yarn used for the edging is thicker than that used for the item it is being attached to, it is best to sew it in place using a sewing thread. To attach the edging, hold the edge of the item and the edge of the edging that is to be attached so that their right sides are together. Sew the edging in place by taking tiny over-sewing stitches through both edges, making a back stitch every now and then to secure the thread.

Once the seam has been sewn, fold the edging out away from the item and press the seam carefully. If worked correctly, the stitches that join the two pieces should be virtually invisible. In the example above, the two sections have been sewn together with a contrast-colour thread so that you can see exactly how much the stitches are likely to show. If you are attaching a contrast-colour edging, attach it using a thread that matches the colour of the item, not the edging. The bulk of the edging is likely to swallow up the stitches and the seam will be far less visible.

● *Machine-stitching an edging in place*

If you are going to attach an edging to a very long edge, you may decide to attach it by machine-stitching it in place. Although you may think this will save time, it often doesn't. The crochet will move as you sew and you may well end up with a messy seam that you need to unpick and re-sew. And every time you unpick the stitching, you run the risk of damaging both the edging and the item. It is far better to stitch the edging in place by hand.

Getting the length of the edging right

If an edging is not being worked directly into the main body of the item, it can be tricky to know how long it needs to be. Crocheted edgings have a tendency to 'pull up' once they are attached and when they are laundered. If the edging is too short, your item will be spoilt by the edge it is attached to becoming puckered. To avoid this, your edging needs to start off slightly longer than the edge it will be attached to – adding about 10% to its length should be sufficient. In other words, if the edge is 60cm (24in) long, make your edging about 65–67cm (26–27in) long, depending on the pattern repeat of the edging. When attaching the edging, distribute this slight fullness evenly along the edge, pinning the edging in place at even intervals before sewing it on.

Decorative details

Crochet can be used to create all sorts of little extra embellishments and details, and is ideal for making three-dimensional shapes that give your projects a fabulous finish. Create balls, spirals and leaf-shapes for pretty details and accessories, and cords of various widths and textures for both practical and decorative ties. You can decorate not only crochet projects but also ready-made items. Consider adding a detailed crochet embellishment to a simple knitted bag, or giving a sewn accessory a touch of crocheted interest.

Leaves

Leaf shapes are simple to make in crochet, and they can easily be varied in size to suit their end use.

Start by making a length of chain the length the finished leaf is to be, plus one extra ch. Work a dc into the 2nd ch from hook, and then work along the rest of the ch making sts that gradually get taller then shorter, ending with a dc into the end ch. The finished width of the leaf will be twice the height of these sts used for the first side.

Now work 1 or 2 ch and another dc into this last ch to form the tip of the leaf. Turn the work around and work back along the original length of ch, making sts the same height as used along the first side, ending with a dc into the same ch as used for the first dc of the first side. Fasten off.

If the leaf is to have a stalk, add this stalk length to the starting ch and work along these extra ch in dc before beginning the first side of the leaf. When working back for the second side of the leaf, end this side by working a ss into the ch where the leaf joins its stalk.

Balls

Crochet can be worked to make balls that can be used to form buttons or decorative details.

To make a crochet ball, start by making 2 ch. Now work 6 dc into 2nd ch from hook and join this first round with a ss into the first dc. Turn the work, make 1 ch (as the turning ch) and then work 2 dc into each of the 6 dc of the previous round, closing this round by working a ss into the first dc. Turn the work again, make 1 turning ch and then work 1 dc into each dc of the previous round, closing the round with a ss into the first dc. This completes the lower half of the ball.

Turn the work again, make the turning ch, and then work dc2tog into each pair of dc of the previous round to start to shape in the top half of the ball. Close this round with a ss into the first dc2tog and fasten off, leaving a long end. Tuck the starting yarn end inside the ball and then insert a little toy filling so that it forms a neat, well-rounded ball shape. Thread the yarn end onto a needle and run a line of gathering stitches around the top of the last round. Pull the end up tight and fasten off securely. This completes the ball.

Crochet balls can be made to any size simply by working more or fewer rounds and stitches until the required size is achieved.

Make this now!

Add some crochet leaves to a simple crochet rose to make it more realistic. This rose can be used as a corsage and pinned onto a sweater or a hat. Alternatively, you could make lots of corsages to adorn an evening bag.

THE CORSAGE is made in a luxurious yarn mixture of kid mohair and silk; the red yarn has a touch of lurex in it for an extra glamorous sparkle. The piece is made with a 2.50mm (C2) hook. See page 272 for pattern.

Spirals

Spiralling coils of crochet can be used to form tendrils to decorate an appliquéd floral design, to create a fancy fringe or even on their own to make a narrow boa-style scarf.

To make a simple treble spiral: make a ch the length the finished spiral needs to be plus 3 extra (turning) ch, work 3 tr into the 4th ch from hook, then 3 tr into each ch to end. Fasten off.

As the stitches are worked they will form themselves into a spiral. You can vary the amount of twist in the spiral by increasing or decreasing the number of stitches worked into each chain. The more stitches are worked into each chain, the more the spiral will twist.

crochet craft

To make a much wider, frilly spiral, work a second row of stitches into the first row. Once the base row is complete, turn the work, make the required number of turning chain and then work back along the previous row, working 1–3 sts into each st.

Cords

Crochet can be used to make cords that will work as ties and drawstrings, or to create decorative details.

Make a very simple crochet cord by simply working a length of chain stitches. This is the most basic type of cord, but it can have a tendency to curl up on itself.

A slightly thicker cord can be made in exactly the same way but by using two or more strands of the yarn. If there are lots of colours used for the item the cord is to be attached to, use strands of different colours to create a multi-coloured cord.

Double crochet cord

It is possible to make a thin cord that lays flat without twisting, forming a fine tape-like strip.

Start by making 2 ch and work 1 dc into the 2nd ch from hook. *Insert the hook into this dc, from front to back, under the strand of yarn that runs up the left side of this dc. Take the yarn over the hook and draw through a new loop. Take the yarn over the hook again and draw this new loop through both loops on the hook to finish this new dc. Repeat from * until the cord is the required length, then fasten off.

Tubular cord

Spiralling tubes of double crochet can make firm, chunky cords that are ideal to use for bag handles or where a thick, strong cord is required.

Begin the tubular cord by making the required number of ch (4 or 5 should be sufficient) and join these with a ss to form a ring. Now work 1 ch (as a turning ch) and then work 1 dc into each ch forming the ring. At the end of this round do NOT join the last st to the first st with a ss but simply carry on round and round the ring, making a spiralling tube of 1 dc worked into each dc of the previous round. Once the tube is the required length, complete it by working a ss into the next dc and fastening off.

CORD   SLIGHTLY THICKER CORD   DOUBLE CROCHET CORD   TUBULAR CORD

Using tubular cords

Tubular cords can be made in almost any size, so they are ideal to use as handles for bags. Try threading a purchased piping cord, or several strands of thick yarn, through the centre to stop the crochet stretching and to make sure it stays nice and round in use.

Working with beads

Adding beads to a crochet item can be done either by sewing them in place once the crochet is complete, or by actually working them into the crochet. This second option is the better choice as it means they are firmly secured in position and unlikely to work free and come off. Be aware that if the crochet is quite loose, beads may slip through the work. If this happens, simply ease them back through the crochet so they appear on the correct side.

Threading the beads onto the yarn

If the beads are to be worked into the crochet, they need to be threaded onto the yarn before you begin.

The hole of the beads is often too small to thread straight onto the yarn. Instead, thread the beads onto the yarn by threading a fine needle – one that will pass through the bead – with a length of strong sewing thread. Knot the ends of the sewing thread to form a loop. Check that this knotted length of thread will pass through the centres of the beads.

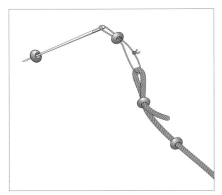

Pass the cut end of the yarn through the loop of the sewing thread. Now slip a bead onto the needle and gently slide it along the thread, and then onto the yarn. Do this slowly so that the thread does not snap and the yarn end remains within the thread loop. Continue in this way until the required number of beads are on the yarn. They will sit on the yarn, ready to be used as and when required. Until they are required, simply slide them along the yarn, away from where you are working.

Working the beads into the crochet

Although beads can be placed virtually anywhere within a piece of crochet, they are most commonly placed on double crochet and chain stitches.

To place a bead on a chain stitch, work up to the point where the beaded chain stitch appears. Now slide one of the beads up the yarn so that it sits next to the hook. Take the yarn over the hook in the usual way, ensuring the bead sits between the hook and the last stitch worked, and draw the new loop through. The bead is securely caught inside the chain stitch.

To place a bead on a double crochet stitch, work up to the point where the beaded double crochet stitch falls. Slide the bead up next to the hook and work the double crochet in the usual way. The bead is trapped between the 2 stitches.

A bead can be caught in any type of stitch in this way. However, as the beads sit on the back of the work, they are best placed on wrong-side rows or rounds.

crochet craft

If you are using a lot of beads within a design, repeatedly sliding all these along the yarn until they are needed can damage the yarn. It is a good idea to thread on some of the beads, use these up and then break the yarn to re-thread it with more beads. If the beads only appear on certain rows or rounds, use one ball of yarn for the unbeaded rows, picking up the yarn from the ball threaded with the beads for the rows where they are needed.

Working with sequins

It is very easy to place sequins within a crochet item – just treat them exactly as though they were beads.

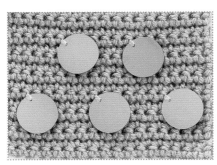

The best type of sequin to use with crochet has its hole placed near one edge. These sequins sit more smoothly on the final crochet fabric.

Make this now!

Antique-effect silver beads decorate the lacy borders of this summer top. As the beads feature only on the borders, there is no need to thread them on to the yarn until you are ready to make these sections. Here, each bead is caught inside a chain stitch.

BEAD-EDGED BEAUTY is made in 4ply cotton. The main body of the garment is worked with a 2.50mm (C2) hook, while the neck edging is crocheted with a 2.00mm (B1) hook. See pages 288–290 for pattern.

● *Sewing sequins in place*

If your sequins have their hole at the centre, it is best to attach them afterwards by sewing them in place, using a matching colour of sewing thread. There are lots of ways to do this.

If you want the sequin to sit flat against the crochet, attach it by making a few straight stitches radiating out from the centre hole. Bring the needle and thread through to the right side of the work where the sequin is to be placed, and thread the sequin onto the thread. Take the needle back through the fabric at the edge of the sequin. Work another 1 or 2 stitches in this way, positioning the stitches evenly around the edge of the sequin.

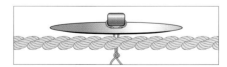

You could also attach the sequin using a tiny bead. Bring the needle and thread through the work where you want to place the sequin. Thread the sequin onto the thread, then thread on the tiny bead. Take the needle and thread back through the work by passing it back through the centre of the sequin. This will leave the sequin securely attached to the work, with the bead sitting at its centre.

crochet craft

Sequins can twist out of position as they are worked into the crochet. If this happens, simply smooth the sequins back into place afterwards.

Embroidery on crochet

A good way to embellish crochet is to work embroidery on its surface. You will probably find it most effective if the embroidery is worked with a yarn or thread of the same sort of thickness as that used for the crochet. Due to the nature of crochet fabric, it can be tricky to place the embroidery stitches. If you are working on a fabric made up of tall stitches, the holes between the stems of the stitches influence where each stitch can be placed. It is therefore best to work embroidery on a more solid stitch pattern.

Chain stitch

Lines of chain stitch are great for adding design details such as simple lines or swirling curls and spirals.

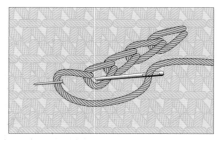

To embroider a line of chain stitch, start by bringing the needle through the fabric at one end of the chain stitch line. Take a stitch through the fabric, inserting the needle at the point where it just came up, and bring it back up further along the line. Loop the thread under the point of the needle and gently pull the needle through the work. Don't pull too tightly, as the resulting chain stitch should be left nice and fat on the surface. Continue along the line in this way. When the last stitch has been made, take the needle back through the work just near where it last came out, securing the last loop in place.

Chain stitch uses up a lot of thread and, when embroidering it, you can find yourself repeatedly joining in new lengths of thread. One way to avoid this is by crocheting a line of chain stitches through the work instead.

To crochet a line of chain stitch, start with the yarn at the back of the work. Insert the hook through the work at the end of the line of stitching and draw through a loop of yarn. Keeping this loop on the hook, insert the hook back through the work a little further along the line and bring a new loop of yarn through both the work and the loop on the hook. Continue in this way until you reach the other end of the line.

Cut off the yarn at the back of the work and complete the last stitch by pulling the cut end through the final loop. Thread the end onto a needle and complete the last stitch in the same way as if the line had been embroidered.

crochet craft

Whatever type of embroidery you work, use a blunt-pointed needle for it. This ensures that the yarn forming the crochet fabric is not damaged, as this type of needle gently pushes apart the fibres, rather than splitting and breaking them.

crochet craft

However you work a line of chain stitch, work the stitches evenly and at the same tension. On the right side you will have a neat, full, rounded stitch and on the other side there will appear to be a line of back stitch.

Blanket stitch

This stitch creates a neat decoration along the edge of a fabric.

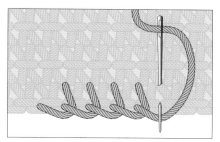

To embroider a line of blanket stitch, start by bringing the thread through the fabric near its edge. Over-sew along the edge, but catch the loop of the previous stitch in the next stitch so that the thread runs from where it comes through, out to the edge of the fabric, where it is caught by the next stitch, and then along the edge of the fabric.

It is possible to create the effect of an embroidered blanket stitch with a row of crochet worked over the edge. Simply work a row of double crochet enclosing the edge: insert the hook through the work a fair distance in from the edge and space the stitches quite widely apart. On one side, you will appear to have blanket stitch, with lots of V-shapes appearing on the other side.

Lazy daisy stitch

A lazy daisy stitch is just one chain stitch worked on its own.

Lazy daisy stitches look like petals or leaves and are an easy way to add floral designs to your work. Make a simple flower by working a group of lazy daisy stitches radiating out from one central point, and try adding a few leaves around the edges. Decorate the centre of your flower by attaching a few beads or sequins or by making a french knot.

Bullion knots

Similar to their crochet counterparts (see page 187), embroidered bullion knots are made up of a wrapped length of thread.

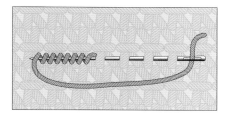

Make a bullion knot in the same way as a french knot, but wrap the thread around the needle a lot more times and make the stitch holding it in place longer.

French knots

French knots can be used to add tiny highlights of colour and texture to the work. However, due to the holey nature of many crochet fabrics, extra care needs to be taken to ensure they sit on the surface, without disappearing down inside the crochet stitches.

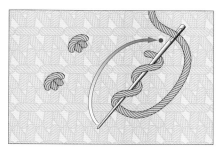

To make a french knot, bring the needle and thread through the work at the required point. Wrap the thread around the needle point 3 or 4 times and, holding this coil of thread in place, take the needle back through the fabric just next to where it came out.

crochet craft

To ensure that the french knot stays on the right side of the crochet, make sure there is sufficient fabric underneath the knot to hold it in place.

Tartan effects

It is possible to create a woven tartan effect in crochet by weaving lengths of chain in and out of a simple crochet mesh. By working the crochet mesh in stripes and using different colours for the lengths of the chains, the check effect created gives the appearance of a tartan fabric. The resulting fabric is surprisingly solid and hard-wearing.

Designing your tartan

You will need to plan your tartan before starting to make it.

Start by deciding on the stripes for the mesh. It is best to use the same colour for both the foundation chain and the first row. Once you are happy with the mesh stripes, make the chains in the same stripe sequence. This will ensure your tartan is even. However, as the 'squares' of the mesh will not be true squares, your design will be slightly elongated.

Making the mesh base

The base through which the chains are woven is a simple treble and chain mesh.

Start by making the foundation chain. This needs to be an even number of stitches plus 4 extra (for the turning chain). Begin the first row by working a treble into the 6th chain from the hook. Continue the row by repeating (1 ch, miss 1 ch, 1 tr into next ch) until the end of the row is reached.

Now turn the work and work back as follows: 4 ch (to count as 1 tr and 1 ch), miss (tr at end of last row and 1 ch), 1 tr into next tr, *1 ch, miss 1 ch, 1 tr into next tr, rep from

* to end, working last tr into top of turning ch at beg of previous row, turn.

Continue to build up rows of the mesh in this way, working in stripes as required. Once the required number of rows are completed, fasten off.

Making the weaving chains

To complete the 'tartan', chains are made that are woven in and out of the base mesh.

Using the same size hook as that used to make the base mesh, make a length of chain. The chains are going to be woven up and down the rows of the mesh, not across them – so this is the length you need. However, as some of the length of the chain will be taken up by weaving it in and out of the mesh, these chains need to be slightly longer than the base mesh; adding about 8 to 10% to their length should be sufficient.

If you are not sure you have made the chain lengths quite long enough, fasten off loosely and leave a long end. That way, if they are a little too short, you can undo the fastening off and work a little more chain to get to the correct length.

In the same way as the various rows of the base mesh have been worked in different colours, your lengths of chain also need to be made in different colours.

Make these now!

This cosy muffler scarf and bag are made of woven crochet tartan. The resulting fabric is both warm and hard-wearing – making it ideal for both the scarf and the bag.

TARTAN-STYLE SET is made using three colours of a cosy aran-weight cashmere-blend yarn (57% extra-fine merino, 33% microfibre and 10% cashmere). Both the scarf and the bag are made using a 4.50mm (7) hook. See pages 284–285 for pattern.

Weaving the finished fabric

Once the mesh base and all the chain lengths have been made, you are ready to start weaving the finished tartan fabric.

Start by attaching the end of one length of chain to the foundation-chain edge of the mesh – attach it to one of the 'free' chain stitches, not one that has a treble worked into it. Now carefully thread the chain through the mesh by taking it over the first chain bar and then under the chain bar of the row above.

Continue in this way, taking the chain alternately over and under the chain bars of the mesh, until you reach the final row. Check the fabric lays flat and that the chain is not too loose or too tight and, if necessary, adjust its length. Once you are happy that it fits correctly, fasten off and attach this end of the chain to the chain bar of the last row.

Now attach another length of chain to the next chain bar of the foundation chain of the mesh and weave this in and out of the mesh in the same way – except, for this length, take the chain over the chain bars of the rows where the previous chain length passed under, and vice versa.

Continue in this way until all the chain spaces of the mesh have been filled with woven lengths of chain. Your tartan fabric is now complete.

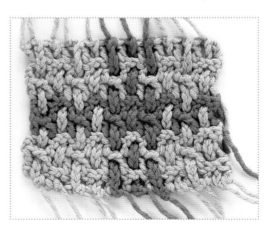

Fringes, tassels and pompons

Fringes, tassles and pompons make great decorative finishes. A fringe is formed by hooking and knotting lengths of yarn through the edges of a piece of crochet. The resulting fringe forms a neat and attractive finish along the edge. Tassels are a good decorative detail to add to the tops of hats or hoods, or to the corners of cushions or throws. Pompons are little fluffy balls of yarn that are often used to decorate scarves and hats.

Making a simple fringe

Start by cutting lots of lengths of yarn. These need to be just over twice the finished length of the fringe. A good way to ensure all the lengths are the same is to wind the yarn around something rigid, like a small book. Once you have sufficient wrappings, cut through the loops to create the strands that will make the fringe.

The knots that form the fringe can be made up of any number of strands of yarn. However, as the strands are folded in half as they are knotted, each strand of yarn will result in two strands in each finished knot.

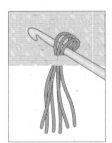

Fold the group of strands of yarn in half, insert a crochet hook through the edge of the work and loop the fold of the fringe strands over the hook.

Carefully pull the folded strands through the work, pulling the loop out so it is quite large.

Now pick up all the free ends of the strands with the hook, and gently pull these through the loop you have just pulled through the fabric.

Remove the hook and then gently tighten the knot by pulling on the cut ends of the strands.

Continue to knot lengths of yarn through the edge until you are happy with the effect you have created. The knots can be made up of just one or two strands of yarn and positioned close to each other, or they can consist of lots of strands and be positioned quite far apart. However thick or thin, or close or distant you place the knots, make sure they are even. Space them out evenly along the edge and ensure that each knot contains the same number of strands, cutting more strands if required.

Once the fringe is complete, the cut ends will probably be a little uneven. You can leave them like this, or you can cut them all off straight. If you decide to trim them even, be careful; it's easy to cut the fringe crookedly and for it to slowly become shorter and shorter as you attempt to form a straight line!

crochet craft

Make sure all the knots are placed the same distance below the previous row of knots. You may find it helpful to slip something like a ruler between each row of knots so that this helps you keep the distances correct.

Making a fancy knotted fringe

Fancy effects can be created with a fringe by dividing the strands that form each original knot and knotting these strands together with strands from the next knot.

If you decide to make a fancy knotted fringe, start by making a simple fringe but leaving the ends very long.

Starting at one end, divide the strands of the first knot into two even groups. Divide the strands of the second (next) knot into two equal groups too. Knot together half the strands of the first group with half the strands of the second group, positioning this knot the required distance below the original knots. Continue along the fringe, knotting together half the strands of each original knot with half the strands from the next original knot, until you reach the other edge of the work. At each end there will be a group of unknotted strands left over from each new end-knot.

To work another row of knots, repeat this process of dividing each group of strands and knotting it with strands from the next knot. On this row of knots, use the strands

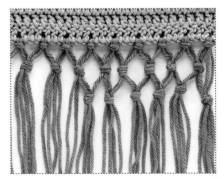

left free at each end on the previous row of knots in the end-knots. Once you are happy with the effect, trim the ends level.

Tassels

Make tassels using the same yarn as used for the item, or choose a contrasting colour or texture to add interest.

To make a simple tassel, wind some yarn round a rigid item roughly the length you want your tassel to be. Wrap the yarn around until you have as many strands as you need. At one folded end, pass a doubled length of yarn under all the strands. Pull this up tight so all the strands are held together securely, and knot the ends together firmly. Leave the ends of these strands quite long.

Very carefully cut through all the strands at the other folded end and remove whatever they were wrapped around. Take care at this point, as the strands are not securely held together.

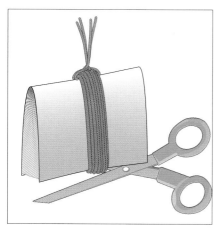

Take another length of yarn and wrap this tightly round all the strands near the folded end. Wrap this length of yarn around all the strands as tightly as you can. Fasten off this length of yarn and darn in the ends.

Pompons

It is possible to buy devices to help you make a pompon, but all you really need is some firm card.

On firm card, draw a circle that is about one and a half to two times the size you want your finished pompon to be. Now draw another circle inside this first circle. The distance between the two circles should be just over half the diameter of your completed pompon. Cut out this ring of card, then cut out a second ring exactly the same size.

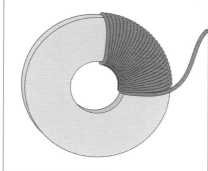

Place the two rings of card together and wrap lengths of yarn around them, passing it through the centre hole, so that there is no card left visible. Carry on wrapping yarn round and round the rings until the centre hole is filled up.

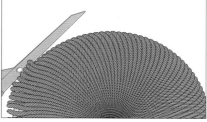

Carefully slip the point of a pair of scissors between the strands of yarn and the two card rings, and cut through all the strands of yarn around the outer edge of the rings.

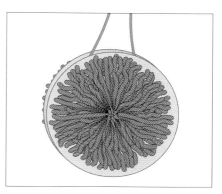

Slip another length of yarn between the two card rings and tie all the pompon strands together around the middle. Pull the strands together tightly and knot the ends together securely. Leave the ends of this length of yarn quite long for now – it can be used to attach the pompon to the work later.

Very carefully cut through the card rings and remove them. Fluff up the pompon to make a little round ball and, if necessary, trim any ends so that it is even all over.

crochet craft

Pompons don't have to be made using just one colour of yarn. For a multi-coloured pompon, wind the yarn around the rings using several different coloured strands at the same time. This creates a speckled finish to the pompon. Winding one colour around the rings and then the next colour will create a pompon that appears to be striped. Experiment with different ways of wrapping the different colours to see what sorts of fancy effects you can create.

stitch library

We have given a name for each stitch shown in this stitch library for ease of identification. You may recognize some of these stitches and know them by a different name. This is because there is no overall consensus on what stitches 'should' be called, but don't worry: the main point is learning how to create the stitch.

Abbreviations

Crochet patterns use abbreviations as shorthand to describe each stitch, and each type of stitch is abbreviated to a few letters. Many of these abbreviations are the same whatever crochet pattern you follow. Below you will find a list of all the standard abbreviations that are used throughout this book. Some of these abbreviations relate to the actual stitches being worked (such as a treble), and some relate to the way you are working (such as continuing in a certain way).

0	no sts, times or rows to be worked for this size	inc	increas(e)(ing)
		mm	millimetres
alt	alternate	patt	pattern
beg	beginning	rem	remain(ing)
ch	chain	rep	repeat
cm	centimetres	RS	right side
cont	continue	sp(s)	space(s)
dc	double crochet	ss	slip stitch
dec	decreas(e)(ing)	st(s)	stitch(es)
dtr	double treble	tr	treble
foll	following	ttr	triple treble
htr	half treble	WS	wrong side
in	inches		

Special abbreviations

Some crochet patterns use a special group or combination of crochet stitches to create a particular effect. This group of stitches will be given a name within the pattern, and this name will often be abbreviated as well. You will find the special abbreviation detailed with the pattern it relates to, along with instructions for how this stitch or group of stitches should be worked. Before you begin, take time to read this special abbreviation so you fully understand what stitches to work and how to place them for the design you are making. This is particularly important, as sometimes a special abbreviation on one pattern will appear to be the same as on another pattern, but the actual stitches needed will vary.
For example, a group of treble stitches is often called a 'cluster'. On one pattern, this cluster may consist of 3 trebles and on another pattern it may consist of 6 trebles – but both patterns will list 'cluster' in the special abbreviations section. Working the wrong type of cluster will mean the crochet fabric will not turn out as it should.

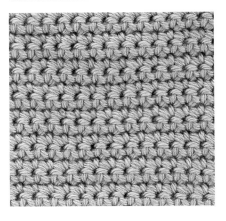

1: Double crochet
Multiple of any number of sts.
Start with any number of ch, plus 1 extra.

Foundation row 1 dc into 2nd ch from hook, 1 dc into each ch to end, turn.
Cont in patt as follows:
Row 1 1 ch (does NOT count as st), 1 dc into each dc to end, turn.
This row forms patt.

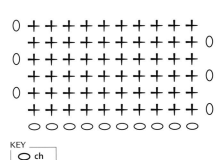

KEY
- ◯ ch
- ✛ dc

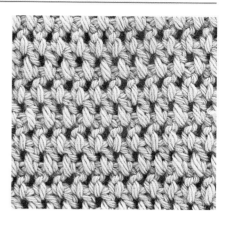

2: Half treble

Multiple of any number of sts.
Start with any number of ch, plus 1 extra.

Foundation row 1 htr into 3rd ch from hook, 1 htr into each ch to end, turn.
Cont in patt as follows:
Row 1 2 ch (counts as first htr), miss htr at base of 2 ch, 1 htr into each htr to end, working last htr into top of 2 ch at beg of previous row, turn.
This row forms patt.

3: Treble

Multiple of any number of sts.
Start with any number of ch, plus 2 extra.

Foundation row 1 tr into 4th ch from hook, 1 tr into each ch to end, turn.
Cont in patt as follows:
Row 1 3 ch (counts as first tr), miss tr at base of 3 ch, 1 tr into each tr to end, working last tr into top of 3 ch at beg of previous row, turn.
This row forms patt.

4: Offset treble

Multiple of any number of sts.
Start with any number of ch, plus 2 extra.

Foundation row 1 tr into 4th ch from hook, 1 tr into each ch to end, turn.
Cont in patt as follows:
Row 1 3 ch (counts as first tr), miss tr at base of 3 ch, *1 tr between tr just missed and next tr, miss 1 tr, rep from * to end, working last tr between first tr of previous row and 3 ch at beg of previous row, turn.
This row forms patt.

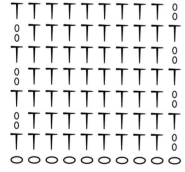

KEY

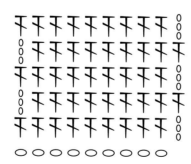

KEY

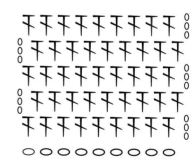

KEY

Textured stitches

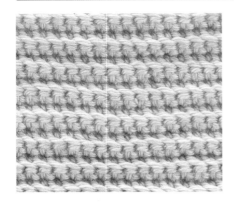

5: Ridged double crochet

Multiple of any number of sts.
Start with any number of ch, plus
1 extra.

Foundation row 1 dc into 2nd ch from
hook, 1 dc into each ch to end, turn.
Cont in patt as follows:

Row 1 1 ch (does NOT count as st), working
into back loops only of sts of previous
row: 1 dc into each dc to end, turn.
This row forms patt.

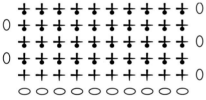

KEY
- **O** ch
- **+** dc
- **+** dc into back loop only

6: Mock rib

Multiple of 2 sts plus 1.
Start with an odd number of ch, plus
1 extra.

Special abbreviations

rftr work treble in the usual way but
working around stem of st of
previous row, inserting hook around
stem from front to back and from
right to left.

rbtr work treble in the usual way but
working around stem of st of
previous row, inserting hook around
stem from back to front and from
right to left.

Foundation row 1 htr into 3rd ch from
hook, 1 htr into each ch to end, turn.
Cont in patt as follows:

Row 1 2 ch (counts as first st), miss st at
base of 2 ch, *1 rftr around stem of next
st, 1 rbtr around stem of next st, rep from
* to last st, 1 rftr around 2 ch at beg of
previous row, turn.

Row 2 2 ch (counts as first st), miss st at
base of 2 ch, *1 rbtr around stem of next
st, 1 rftr around stem of next st, rep from
* to last st, 1 rbtr around 2 ch at beg of
previous row, turn.
These 2 rows form patt.

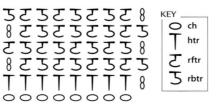

KEY
- **O** ch
- **T** htr
- **rftr**
- **rbtr**

7: Tweed stitch

Multiple of 2 sts plus 1.
Start with an odd number of ch, plus
1 extra.

Foundation row 1 dc into 2nd ch from
hook, *1 ch, miss 1 ch, 1 dc into next ch,
rep from * to end, turn.
Cont in patt as follows:

Row 1 1 ch (does NOT count as st), 1 dc
into first dc, *1 dc into next ch sp, 1 ch,
miss 1 dc, rep from * to last 2 sts, 1 dc into
last ch sp, 1 dc into last dc, turn.

Row 2 1 ch (does NOT count as st), 1 dc
into first dc, *1 ch, miss 1 dc, 1 dc into
next ch sp, rep from * to end, working
dc at end of last rep into dc at beg of
previous row, turn.
These 2 rows form patt.

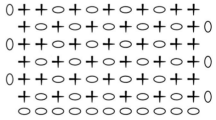

KEY
- **O** ch
- **+** dc

240

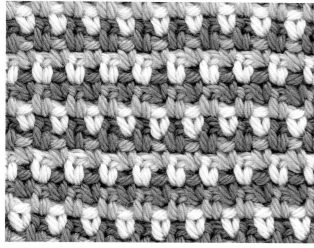

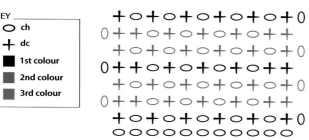

KEY

- ○ ch
- + dc
- ■ 1st colour
- ■ 2nd colour
- ■ 3rd colour

8: Multi-coloured tweed stitch

Multiple of 2 sts plus 1.
Worked in 3 colours.
Start with an odd number of ch, plus 1 extra.

Foundation row Using 1st colour, 1 dc into 2nd ch from hook, *1 ch, miss 1 ch, 1 dc into next ch, rep from * to end, turn.

Cont in patt as follows:

Row 1 Using 2nd colour, 1 ch (does NOT count as st), 1 dc into first dc, *1 dc into next ch sp, 1 ch, miss 1 dc, rep from * to last 2 sts, 1 dc into last ch sp, 1 dc into last dc, turn.

Row 2 Using 3rd colour, 1 ch (does NOT count as st), 1 dc into first dc, *1 ch, miss 1 dc, 1 dc into next ch sp, rep from * to end, working dc at end of last rep into dc at beg of previous row, turn.

Row 3 Using 1st colour, as row 1.

Row 4 Using 2nd colour, as row 2.

Row 5 Using 3rd colour, as row 1.

Row 6 Using 1st colour, as row 2.

These 6 rows form patt.

9: Griddle stitch

Multiple of 2 sts plus 1.
Start with an odd number of ch, plus 1 extra.

Foundation row (RS) 1 dc into 2nd ch from hook, 1 dc into each ch to end, turn.

Cont in patt as follows:

Row 1 1 ch (does NOT count as st), 1 dc into first dc, *1 tr into next dc, 1 dc into next dc, rep from * to end, turn.

Row 2 1 ch (does NOT count as st), 1 dc into each st to end, turn.

Row 3 1 ch (does NOT count as st), 1 dc into each of first 2 dc, *1 tr into next dc, 1 dc into next dc, rep from * to last dc, 1 dc into last dc, turn.

Row 4 As row 2.

These 4 rows form patt.

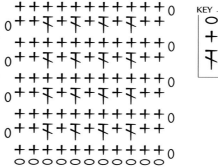

KEY

- ○ ch
- + dc
- ⊤ tr

Chevron and wave stitches

10: Treble chevron stitch

Multiple of 8 sts plus 1.
Start with a multiple of 8 ch, plus 4 extra.
Special abbreviation, *see* box below.

Foundation row 1 tr into 4th ch from hook, *1 tr into each of next 2 ch, tr2tog over next 3 ch, working first 'leg' into next ch, missing 1 ch and working second 'leg' into next ch, 1 tr into each of next 2 ch**, (1 tr, 1 ch and 1 tr) into next ch, rep from * to end, ending last rep at **, 2 tr into last ch, turn.

Cont in patt as follows:

Row 1 3 ch (counts as first tr), 1 tr into tr at base of 3 ch, *1 tr into each of next 2 tr, tr2tog over next 3 sts, working first 'leg' into next tr, missing tr2tog and working second 'leg' into next tr, 1 tr into each of next 2 tr**, (1 tr, 1 ch and 1 tr) into next ch sp, rep from * to end, ending last rep at **, 2 tr into top of 3 ch at beg of previous row, turn.

This row forms patt.

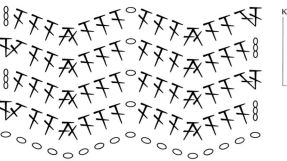

KEY

⬭	ch
Ŧ	tr
𝕏	tr2tog

11: Wave stitch

Multiple of 12 sts.
Start with a multiple of 12 ch, plus 2 extra.
Special abbreviation, *see* box right.

Foundation row 1 tr into 4th ch from hook, tr2tog over next 2 ch, *2 tr into each of next 4 ch**, (tr2tog over next 2 ch) 4 times, rep from * to end, ending last rep at **, (tr2tog over next 2 ch) twice, turn.

Cont in patt as follows:

Row 1 3 ch (does NOT count as st), miss tr2tog at base of 3 ch, 1 tr into next tr2tog, tr2tog over next 2 tr, *2 tr into

Special abbreviation

tr2tog *yarn over hook and insert hook as indicated, yarn over hook and draw loop through, yarn over hook and draw through 2 loops, rep from * once more, yarn over hook and draw through all 3 loops on hook.

each of next 4 tr**, (tr2tog over next 2 sts) 4 times, rep from * to end, ending last rep at **, (tr2tog over next 2 sts) twice, turn, leaving 3 ch at beg of previous row unworked.

This row forms patt.

KEY

⬭	ch
Ŧ	tr
𝕏	tr2tog

12: Double crochet chevron stripes

Multiple of 9 sts plus 1.
Worked in 2 colours.
Start with a multiple of 9 ch, plus 1 extra.

Foundation row (RS) Using 1st colour, 2 dc into 2nd ch from hook, *1 dc into each of next 3 ch, miss 2 ch, 1 dc into each of next 3 ch**, 3 dc into next ch, rep from * to end, ending last rep at **, 2 dc into last ch, turn.

Cont in patt as follows:

Row 1 Using 1st colour, 1 ch (does NOT count as st), 2 dc into first dc, *1 dc into each of next 3 dc, miss 2 dc, 1 dc into each of next 3 dc**, 3 dc into next dc, rep from * to end, ending last rep at **, 2 dc into last dc, turn.
Rows 2 and 3 Using 2nd colour, as row 1.
Row 4 As row 1.
These 4 rows form patt.

13: Wavy stripes

Multiple of 8 sts plus 4.
Worked in 2 colours.
Start with a multiple of 8 ch, plus 5 extra.

Foundation row (RS) Using 1st colour, 1 dc into 2nd ch from hook, 1 dc into each of next 3 ch, *1 tr into each of next 4 ch, 1 dc into each of next 4 ch, rep from * to end, turn.
Cont in patt as follows:
Row 1 Using 2nd colour, 1 ch (does NOT count as st), 1 dc into each st to end, turn.
Row 2 As row 1.
Row 3 Using 1st colour, 3 ch (counts as first tr), miss dc at base of 3 ch, 1 tr into each of next 3 dc, *1 dc into each of next 4 dc, 1 tr into each of next 4 dc, rep from * to end, turn.
Row 4 Using 1st colour, 3 ch (counts as first tr), miss tr at base of 3 ch, 1 tr into each of next 3 tr, *1 dc into each of next 4 dc, 1 tr into each of next 4 tr, rep from * to end, working tr at end of last rep into top of 3 ch at beg of previous row, turn.
Rows 5 and 6 As row 1.
Row 7 Using 1st colour, 1 ch (does NOT count as st), 1 dc into each of first 4 dc, *1 tr into each of next 4 dc, 1 dc into each of next 4 dc, rep from * to end, turn.

Row 8 Using 1st colour, 1 ch (does NOT count as st), 1 dc into each of first 4 dc, *1 tr into each of next 4 tr, 1 dc into each of next 4 dc, rep from * to end, turn.

These 8 rows form patt.

Note: So that finished work is an even height throughout, end after a 3rd or 7th patt row.

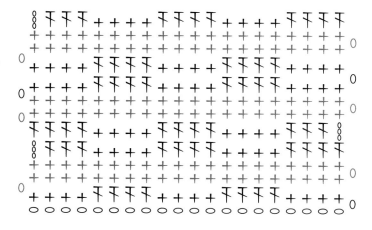

Chevron and wave stitches

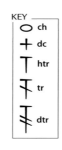

14: Alternating waves
Multiple of 6 sts plus 1.
Worked in 2 colours.
Start with a multiple of 6 ch, plus 2 extra.

Foundation row (RS) Using 1st colour, 1 dc into 2nd ch from hook, *1 htr into next ch, 1 tr into next ch, 1 dtr into next ch, 1 tr into next ch, 1 htr into next ch, 1 dc into next ch, rep from * to end, turn.

Cont in patt as follows:

Row 1 Using 2nd colour, 4 ch (counts as first dtr), miss dc at base of 4 ch, *1 tr into next htr, 1 htr into next tr, 1 dc into next dtr, 1 htr into next tr, 1 tr into next htr, 1 dtr into next dc, rep from * to end, turn.

Row 2 Using 2nd colour, 4 ch (counts as first dtr), miss dtr at base of 4 ch, *1 tr into next tr, 1 htr into next htr, 1 dc into next dc, 1 htr into next htr, 1 tr into next tr, 1 dtr into next dtr, rep from * to end, working dtr at end of last rep into top of 4 ch at beg of previous row, turn.

Row 3 Using 1st colour, 1 ch (does NOT count as st), 1 dc into dtr at base of 1 ch, *1 htr into next tr, 1 tr into next htr, 1 dtr into next dc, 1 tr into next htr, 1 htr into next tr, 1 dc into next dtr, rep from * to end, working dc at end of last rep into top of 4 ch at beg of previous row, turn.

Row 4 Using 1st colour, 1 ch (does NOT count as st), 1 dc into first dc, *1 htr into next htr, 1 tr into next tr, 1 dtr into next dtr, 1 tr into next tr, 1 htr into next htr, 1 dc into next dc, rep from * to end, turn.

These 4 rows form patt.

Note: *So that finished work is an even height throughout, end after a 1st or 3rd patt row.*

KEY

○	ch
+	dc
T	htr
干	tr
丰	dtr

244

15: Spiked lozenge stitch

Multiple of 4 sts plus 2.
Worked in 2 colours.
Start with a multiple of 4 ch, plus 3 extra.

Foundation row (RS) Using 1st colour, 1 dc into 2nd ch from hook, 1 dc into each ch to end, turn.

Cont in patt as follows:

Row 1 Using 1st colour, 1 ch (does NOT count as st), 1 dc into each dc to end, turn.

Rows 2 and 3 As row 1.

Row 4 Using 2nd colour, 1 ch (does NOT count as st), 1 dc into first dc, *1 dc into next dc, 1 dc into corresponding dc one row below next dc, 1 dc into corresponding dc 2 rows below next dc, 1 dc into corresponding dc 3 rows below next dc, rep from * to last dc, 1 dc into last dc, turn.

Rows 5 to 7 Using 2nd colour, as row 1.

Row 8 Using 1st colour, 1 ch (does NOT count as st), 1 dc into first dc, *1 dc into next dc, 1 dc into corresponding dc one row below next dc, 1 dc into corresponding dc 2 rows below next dc, 1 dc into corresponding dc 3 rows below next dc, rep from * to last dc, 1 dc into last dc, turn.

These 8 rows form patt.

Note: *To keep continuity of fabric, end after a 4th or 8th patt row.*

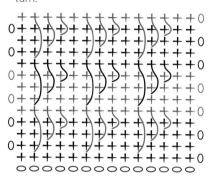

KEY

○ ch	⊤ dc into corresp. dc 2 rows below next dc
+ dc	
⊥ dc into corresp. dc 1 row below next dc	⊤ dc into corresp. dc 3 rows below next dc

16: Spiked chevron stitch

Multiple of 6 sts plus 1.
Worked in 2 colours.
Start with a multiple of 6 ch, plus 2 extra.

Foundation row (RS) Using 1st colour, 1 dc into 2nd ch from hook, 1 dc into each ch to end, turn.

Cont in patt as follows:

Row 1 Using 1st colour, 1 ch (does NOT count as st), 1 dc into each dc to end, turn.

Rows 2 and 3 As row 1.

Row 4 Using 2nd colour, 1 ch (does NOT count as st), 1 dc into first dc, *1 dc into corresponding dc one row below next dc, 1 dc into corresponding dc 2 rows below next dc, 1 dc into corresponding dc 3 rows below next dc, 1 dc into corresponding dc 2 rows below next dc, 1 dc into corresponding dc one row below next dc, 1 dc into next dc, rep from * to end, turn.

Rows 5 to 7 Using 2nd colour, as row 1.

Row 8 Using 1st colour, 1 ch (does NOT count as st), 1 dc into first dc, *1 dc into corresponding dc one row below next dc, 1 dc into corresponding dc 2 rows below next dc, 1 dc into corresponding dc 3 rows below next dc, 1 dc into corresponding dc 2 rows below next dc, 1 dc into corresponding dc one row below next dc, 1 dc into next dc, rep from * to end, turn.

These 8 rows form patt.

Note: *To keep continuity of fabric, end after a 4th or 8th patt row.*

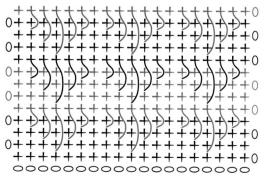

KEY

○ ch	⊤ dc into corresp. dc 2 rows below next dc
+ dc	
⊥ dc into corresp. dc 1 row below next dc	⊤ dc into corresp. dc 3 rows below next dc

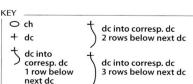

Lacy stitches

17: Shell stitch

Multiple of 6 sts plus 1.
Start with a multiple of 6 ch, plus 2 extra.

Foundation row 1 dc into 2nd ch from hook, *miss 2 ch, 5 tr into next ch, miss 2 ch, 1 dc into next ch, rep from * to end, turn.

Cont in patt as follows:

Row 1 3 ch (counts as first tr), 2 tr into dc at base of 3 ch, *miss 2 tr, 1 dc into next tr, miss 2 tr**, 5 tr into next dc, rep from * to end, ending last rep at **, 3 tr into last dc, turn.

Row 2 1 ch (does NOT count as st), 1 dc into first tr, *miss 2 tr, 5 tr into next dc, miss 2 tr, 1 dc into next tr, rep from * to end, working dc at end of last rep into top of 3 ch at beg of previous row, turn.

These 2 rows form patt.

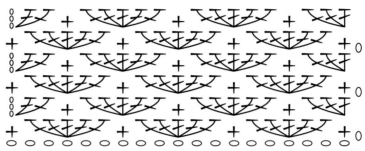

KEY	
⬭	ch
+	dc
⊤	tr

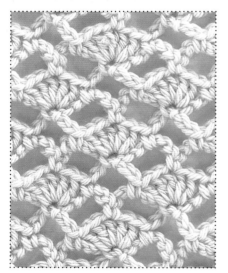

18: Shell mesh

Multiple of 12 sts plus 7.
Start with a multiple of 8 ch, plus 6 extra.

Foundation row (RS) 1 dc into 2nd ch from hook, *5 ch, miss 3 ch, 1 dc into next ch, rep from * to end, turn.

Next row 5 ch (counts as first tr and 2 ch), 1 dc into first ch sp, *5 ch, 1 dc into next ch sp, rep from * until dc has been worked in last ch sp, 2 ch, 1 tr into dc at beg of previous row, turn.

Cont in patt as follows:

Row 1 1 ch (does NOT count as st), 1 dc into first tr, miss first 2-ch sp, *5 ch**, 1 dc into next ch sp, 5 tr into next dc, 1 dc into next ch sp, rep from * to end, ending last rep at **, 1 dc into 3rd of 5 ch at beg of previous row, turn.

Row 2 5 ch (counts as first tr and 2 ch), 1 dc into first ch sp, *5 ch, miss (1 dc and 2 tr), 1 dc into next tr, 5 ch, miss (2 tr and 1 dc), 1 dc into next ch sp, rep from * until dc has been worked in last ch sp, 2 ch, 1 tr into dc at beg of previous row, turn.

Row 3 1 ch (does NOT count as st), 1 dc into first tr, miss first 2-ch sp, *5 tr into next dc**, 1 dc into next ch sp, 5 ch, 1 dc into next ch sp, rep from * to end, ending last rep at **, 1 dc into 3rd of 5 ch at beg of previous row, turn.

Row 4 5 ch (counts as first tr and 2 ch), miss (1 dc and 2 tr), 1 dc into next tr, *5 ch, miss (2 tr and 1 dc), 1 dc into next ch sp, 5 ch, miss (1 dc and 2 tr), 1 dc into next tr, rep from * until dc has been worked in centre tr of last 5-tr group, 2 ch, 1 tr into dc at beg of previous row, turn.

These 4 rows form patt.

Note: *To straighten off upper edge, end after a 2nd or 4th patt row and work finishing row as follows:*

Finishing row 1 ch (does NOT count as st), 1 dc into first tr, miss first 2-ch sp, *3 ch, 1 dc into next ch sp, rep from * to end, working dc at end of last rep into 3rd of 5 ch at beg of previous row.

KEY	
⬭	ch
+	dc
⊤	tr

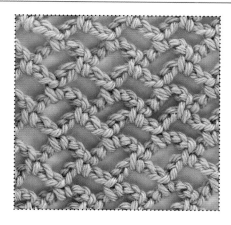

19: Diamond mesh
Multiple of 6 sts plus 1.
Start with a multiple of 4 ch, plus 2 extra.

Foundation row 1 dc into 2nd ch from hook, *5 ch, miss 3 ch, 1 dc into next ch, rep from * to end, turn.
Cont in patt as follows:
Row 1 5 ch (counts as first tr and 2 ch), 1 dc into first ch sp, *5 ch, 1 dc into next ch sp, rep from * until dc has been worked in last ch sp, 2 ch, 1 tr into dc at beg of previous row, turn.
Row 2 1 ch (does NOT count as st), 1 dc into first tr, miss first 2-ch sp, *5 ch, 1 dc into next ch sp, rep from * to end, working dc at end of last rep into 3rd of 5 ch at beg of previous row, turn.
These 2 rows form patt.

Note: *To straighten off upper edge, end after a 1st patt row and work finishing row as follows:*
Finishing row 1 ch (does NOT count as st), 1 dc into first tr, miss first 2-ch sp, *3 ch, 1 dc into next ch sp, rep from * to end, working dc at end of last rep into 3rd of 5 ch at beg of previous row.

20: Mesh stitch
Multiple of 2 sts plus 1.
Start with an odd number of ch, plus 3 extra.

Foundation row 1 tr into 6th ch from hook, *1 ch, miss 1 ch, 1 tr into next ch, rep from * to end, turn.
Cont in patt as follows:
Row 1 4 ch (counts as first tr and 1 ch), miss (1 tr and 1 ch) at end of previous row, 1 tr into next tr, *1 ch, miss 1 ch, 1 tr into next tr, rep from * to end, working tr at end of last rep into 3rd of 4 ch at beg of previous row, turn.
This row forms patt.

21: V stitch
Multiple of 3 sts plus 2.
Start with a multiple of 3 ch, plus 4 extra.

Foundation row (1 tr, 1 ch and 1 tr) into 5th ch from hook, *miss 2 ch, (1 tr, 1 ch and 1 tr) into next ch, rep from * to last 2 ch, miss 1 ch, 1 tr into last ch, turn.
Cont in patt as follows:
Row 1 3 ch (counts as first tr), miss 2 tr at end of previous row, *(1 tr, 1 ch and 1 tr) into next ch sp**, miss 2 tr, rep from * to end, ending last rep at **, miss 1 tr, 1 tr into top of 3 ch at beg of previous row, turn.
This row forms patt.

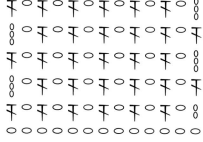

KEY
○ ch
𝖳 tr

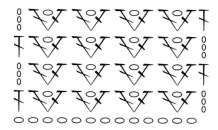

KEY
○ ch
𝖳 tr

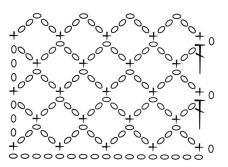

KEY
○ ch
+ dc
𝖳 tr

Lacy stitches

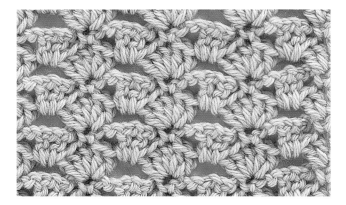

KEY
○ ch
✛ dc
Ŧ tr

22: Alternating shell and V stitch
Multiple of 6 sts plus 1.
Start with a multiple of 5 ch, plus 3 extra.

Foundation row (RS) 2 tr into 3rd ch from hook, *1 ch, miss 4 ch**, 5 tr into next ch, rep from * to end, ending last rep at **, 3 tr into last ch, turn.

Cont in patt as follows:

Row 1 1 ch (does NOT count as st), 1 dc into last tr, *2 ch, miss 2 tr, (1 tr, 1 ch and 1 tr) into next ch sp, 2 ch, miss 2 tr, 1 dc into next tr, rep from * to end, working dc at end of last rep into top of 3 ch at beg of previous row, turn.

Row 2 3 ch (counts as first tr), 2 tr into dc at base of 3 ch, *1 ch, miss (2 ch, 1 tr, 1 ch, 1 tr and 2 ch)**, 5 tr into next dc, rep from * to end, ending last rep at **, 3 tr into last dc, turn.

These 2 rows form patt.

Note: *To straighten off upper edge, end after a 2nd patt row and work finishing row as follows:*

Finishing row 1 ch (does NOT count as st), 1 dc into last tr, *2 ch, miss 2 tr, 1 tr into next ch sp, 2 ch, miss 2 tr, 1 dc into next tr, rep from * to end, working dc at end of last rep into top of 3 ch at beg of previous row.

23: Boxed flowers
Multiple of 10 sts plus 1.
Start with a multiple of 10 ch, plus 2 extra.

Foundation row (WS) 1 dc into 2nd ch from hook, *3 ch, miss 3 ch, 1 dc into next ch, 3 ch, miss 1 ch, 1 dc into next ch, 3 ch, miss 3 ch, 1 dc into next ch, rep from * to end, turn.

Next row 1 ch (does NOT count as st), 1 dc into first dc, *1 ch, miss (3 ch and 1 dc), tr2tog into next ch sp, (3 ch, tr2tog into same ch sp as last tr2tog) 4 times, 1 ch, miss (1 dc and 3 ch), 1 dc into next dc, rep from * to end, turn.

Cont in patt as follows:

Row 1 7 ch (counts as first dtr and 3 ch), miss (1 dc, 1 ch, tr2tog, 3 ch and tr2tog), *1 dc into next ch sp, 3 ch, 1 dc into next ch sp, 3 ch, miss (tr2tog, 3 ch, tr2tog and 1 ch), 1 dtr into next dc**, 3 ch, miss (1 ch, tr2tog, 3 ch and tr2tog), rep from * to end, ending last rep at **, 3 tr into last dc, turn.

Row 2 1 ch (does NOT count as st), 1 dc into first dtr, *1 ch, miss (3 ch and 1 dc), tr2tog into next ch sp, (3 ch, tr2tog into same ch sp as last tr2tog) 4 times, 1 ch, miss (1 dc and 3 ch), 1 dc into next dtr, rep from * to end, working dc at end of last rep into 4th of 7 ch at beg of previous row, turn.

These 2 rows form patt.

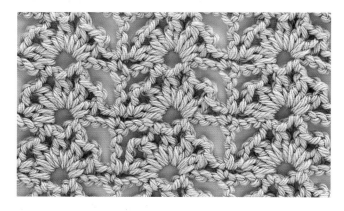

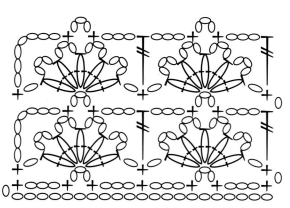

KEY
○ ch
✛ dc
⟁ tr2tog
Ŧ dtr

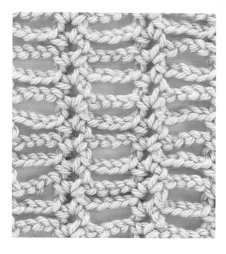

24: Mini ladder stitch

Multiple of 5 sts plus 1.
Start with a multiple of 5 ch, plus 6 extra.

Foundation row (1 dc, 3 ch and 1 dc) into 11th ch from hook, *4 ch, miss 4 ch, (1 dc, 3 ch and 1 dc) into next ch, rep from * to last 5 ch, 4 ch, miss 4 ch, 1 htr into last ch, turn.
Cont in patt as follows:

Row 1 6 ch (counts as first htr and 4 ch), miss (1 htr, 4 ch and 1 dc), *(1 dc, 3 ch and 1 dc) into next ch sp, 4 ch**, miss (1 dc, 4 ch and 1 dc), rep from * to end, ending last rep at **, 1 htr into 2nd of 6 ch at beg of previous row, turn.
This row forms patt.

Note: *To straighten off upper edge, work finishing row as follows:*

Finishing row 6 ch (counts as first htr and 4 ch), miss (1 htr, 4 ch and 1 dc), *1 dc into next ch sp, 4 ch**, miss (1 dc, 4 ch and 1 dc), rep from * to end, ending last rep at **, 1 htr into 2nd of 6 ch at beg of previous row.

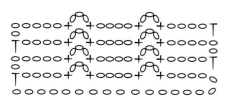

KEY
O ch
+ dc
T htr

25: Slanting diamonds

Multiple of 4 sts.
Start with a multiple of 4 ch, plus 5 extra.

Foundation row 3 tr into 5th ch from hook, *miss 3 ch, (1 dc, 3 ch and 3 tr) into next ch, rep from * to last 4 ch, miss 3 ch, 1 dc into last ch, turn.
Cont in patt as follows:

Row 1 4 ch, 3 tr into 4th ch from hook, *miss (1 dc and 3 tr)**, (1 dc, 3 ch and 3 tr) into next ch sp, rep from * to end, ending last rep at **, 1 dc into last ch sp, turn.
This row forms patt.

KEY
O ch
+ dc
T tr

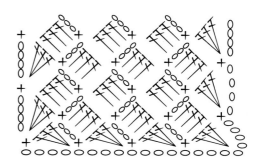

26: Bamboo stitch

Multiple of 4 sts plus 2.
Start with a multiple of 4 ch, plus 3 extra.

Foundation row (2 dtr, 1 ch and 1 tr) into 4th ch from hook, *miss 3 ch, (2 dtr, 1 ch and 1 tr) into next ch, rep from * to last 3 ch, miss 2 ch, 1 dtr into last ch, turn.
Cont in patt as follows:

Row 1 3 ch, miss (1 dtr and 1 tr), *(2 dtr, 1 ch and 1 tr) into next ch sp**, miss (2 dtr and 1 tr), rep from * to end, ending last rep at **, miss 2 dtr, 1 dtr into top of 3 ch at beg of previous row, turn.
This row forms patt.

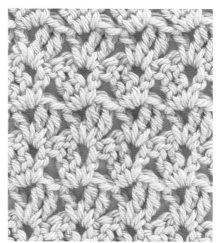

KEY
O ch
T tr
F dtr

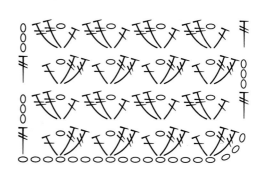

Edgings

27: Shell edging

Multiple of 4 sts plus 1.
Start with a multiple of 4 ch, plus 2 extra.

Row 1 (WS) 1 dc into 2nd ch from hook, 1 dc into each ch to end, turn.

Row 2 1 ch (does NOT count as st), 1 dc into first dc, *miss 1 dc, 5 tr into next dc, miss 1 dc, 1 dc into next dc, rep from * to end.

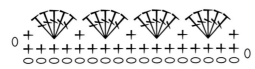

KEY
- ◯ ch
- + dc
- ⊤ tr

28: Scallop edging

Multiple of 4 sts plus 1.
Start with a multiple of 4 ch, plus 4 extra.

Row 1 (RS) 1 tr into 6th ch from hook, *1 ch, miss 1 ch, 1 tr into next ch, rep from * to end, turn.

Row 2 1 ch (does NOT count as st), 1 dc into first tr, *5 ch, miss (1 ch, 1 tr and 1 ch), 1 dc into next tr, rep from * to end, turn.

Row 3 (2 dc, 1 htr, 1 tr, 1 htr and 2 dc) into each ch sp to end, ss to dc at beg of previous row.

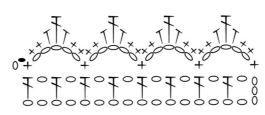

KEY
- ◯ ch
- + dc
- ⊤ htr
- ⊤ tr
- ● ss

29: Diamond edging

Multiple of 6 sts plus 3.
Start with a multiple of 6 ch, plus 4 extra.

Row 1 (RS) 1 dc into 2nd ch from hook, 1 dc into each ch to end, turn.

Row 2 4 ch (counts as first tr and 1 ch), miss first 4 dc, *(1 dtr, 3 tr and 1 dtr) into next dc, 1 ch**, miss 5 dc, rep from * to end, ending last rep at **, miss 3 dc, 1 tr into last dc, turn.

Row 3 6 ch (counts as first tr and 3 ch), miss tr at end of previous row, *1 cluster**, 5 ch, rep from * to end, ending last rep at **, 3 ch, 1 tr into 3rd of 4 ch at beg of previous row, turn.

Row 4 1 ch (does NOT count as st), 1 dc into tr at base of 1 ch, 1 dc into each ch and cluster to end, working last dc into 3rd of 6 ch at beg of previous row.

Special abbreviations

cluster (yoh) twice and insert hook into next ch sp (note: next time a cluster is worked, place this 'leg' of cluster into same ch sp as used for last 'leg' of previous cluster), yoh and draw loop through, (yoh and draw through 2 loops) twice, miss 1 dtr, *yoh and insert hook into next tr, yoh and draw loop through, yoh and draw through 2 loops, rep from * twice more, miss 1 dtr, (yoh) twice and insert hook into next ch sp, yoh and draw loop through, (yoh and draw through 2 loops) twice, yoh and draw through all 6 loops on hook.

yoh yarn over hook.

KEY
- ◯ ch
- + dc
- ⊤ tr
- ⊤ dtr
- ⋀ cluster

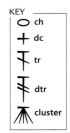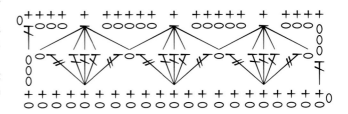

30: Ric rac edging
Multiple of 10 sts.
Start with a multiple of 10 ch, plus 2 extra.

Row 1 (RS) Miss first 3 ch, tr3tog over next 3 ch, *4 tr into each of next 2 ch**, (tr4tog over next 4 ch) twice, rep from * to end, ending last repeat at **.

Special abbreviations

tr3tog *yoh and insert hook into next ch, yoh and draw loop through, yoh and draw through 2 loops, rep from * twice more, yoh and draw through all 4 loops on hook.

tr4tog *yoh and insert hook into next ch, yoh and draw loop through, yoh and draw through 2 loops, rep from * 3 more times, yoh and draw through all 5 loops on hook.

yoh yarn over hook.

KEY
- ○ ch
- ⊤ tr
- ⋔ tr4tog
- ⋏ tr3tog

31: Trefoil edging
Multiple of 5 sts.
Start with a multiple of 5 ch, plus 1 extra.

Row 1 (WS) 1 dc into 2nd ch from hook, 1 dc into each ch to end, turn.
Row 2 3 ch (counts as first tr), miss dc at base of 3 ch, 1 tr into each dc to end, turn.
Row 3 1 ch (does NOT count as st), 1 dc into each of first 2 tr, *(1 dc, 4 ch, 1 dc, 6 ch, 1 dc, 4 ch and 1 dc) into next tr**, 1 dc into each of next 4 tr, rep from * to end, ending last rep at **, 1 dc into each of last 2 dc.

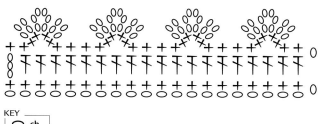

KEY
- ○ ch
- + dc
- ⊤ tr

32: Butterfly edging
Worked lengthwise, to length required.
Make 4 ch.

Foundation row (2 tr, 2 ch and 3 tr) into 4th ch from hook, turn.
Cont in patt as follows:
Row 1 8 ch, (1 ss, 5 ch and 1 ss) into 6th ch from hook, 2 ch, miss 3 tr, (3 tr, 2 ch and 3 tr) into next ch sp, turn.
Row 2 Ss across top of first 3 tr and into first ch sp, 3 ch, (2 tr, 2 ch and 3 tr) into same ch sp, turn.
These 2 rows form patt.

Work to required length, ending after a 1st patt row.

KEY
- ○ ch
- ⊤ tr
- ● ss

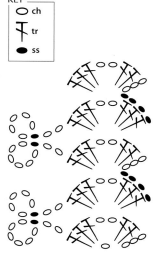

33: Granny square
Make 4 ch and join with a ss to form a ring.

Round 1 (RS) 3 ch (counts as first tr), 2 tr into ring, (2 ch, 3 tr into ring) 3 times, 1 htr into top of 3 ch at beg of round.

Round 2 3 ch (counts as first tr), (2 tr, 2 ch and 3 tr) into first ch sp, *2 ch, miss 3 tr, (3 tr, 2 ch and 3 tr) into next ch sp, rep from * twice more, miss 3 tr, 1 htr into top of 3 ch at beg of round.

Round 3 3 ch (counts as first tr), 2 tr into first ch sp, *2 ch, miss 3 tr, (3 tr, 2 ch and 3 tr) into next ch sp**, 2 ch, miss 3 tr, 3 tr into next ch sp, rep from * to end, ending last rep at **, miss 3 tr, 1 htr into top of 3 ch at beg of round.

Round 4 3 ch (counts as first tr), 2 tr into first ch sp, 2 ch, miss 3 tr, 3 tr into next ch sp, *2 ch, miss 3 tr, (3 tr, 2 ch and 3 tr) into next ch sp**, (2 ch, miss 3 tr, 3 tr into next ch sp) twice, rep from * to end, ending last rep at **, miss 3 tr, 1 htr into top of 3 ch at beg of round.
Fasten off.

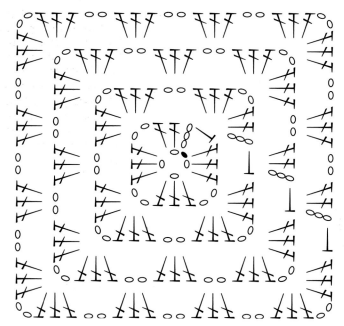

KEY

⃝	ch
⬤	ss
⊤	htr
⊤	tr

34: Lacy flower motif
Make 6 ch and join with a ss to form a ring.

Round 1 (RS) 3 ch (does NOT count as st), tr2tog into ring, (3 ch, tr3tog into ring) 7 times, 1 ch, 1 htr into top of tr2tog at beg of round.

Round 2 1 ch (does NOT count as st), 1 dc into ch sp partly formed by htr at end of previous round, (5 ch, 1 dc into next ch sp) 7 times, 2 ch, 1 tr into top of dc at beg of round.

Round 3 1 ch (does NOT count as st), 1 dc into ch sp partly formed by tr at end of previous round, *5 ch, (tr3tog, 3 ch and tr3tog) into next ch sp**, 5 ch, 1 dc into next ch sp, rep from * to end, ending last rep at **, 2 ch, 1 tr into top of dc at beg of round.

Round 4 1 ch (does NOT count as st), 1 dc into ch sp partly formed by tr at end of previous round, *5 ch, 1 dc into next ch sp, 5 ch, (1 dc, 5 ch and 1 dc) into next ch sp, 5 ch, 1 dc into next ch sp, rep from * to end, replacing dc at end of last rep with ss to first dc.

Fasten off.

KEY

⬭	ch
⬬	ss
+	dc
T	htr
⊤	tr
⋔	tr2tog
⋔	tr3tog

Special abbreviations

tr2tog *yoh and insert hook into ch sp, yoh and draw loop through, yoh and draw through 2 loops, rep from * once more, yoh and draw through all 3 loops on hook.

tr3tog *yoh and insert hook into ch sp, yoh and draw loop through, yoh and draw through 2 loops, rep from * twice more, yoh and draw through all 4 loops on hook.

yoh yarn over hook.

Special abbreviations

tr2tog *yoh and insert hook into ch sp, yoh and draw loop through, yoh and draw through 2 loops, rep from * once more, yoh and draw through all 3 loops on hook.

tr3tog *yoh and insert hook into ch sp, yoh and draw loop through, yoh and draw through 2 loops, rep from * twice more, yoh and draw through all 4 loops on hook.

yoh yarn over hook.

STITCH LIBRARY

Motifs

35: Popcorn motif

Make 6 ch and join with a ss to form a ring.

Round 1 (RS) 1 ch (does NOT count as st), 12 dc into ring, ss to first dc.

Round 2 5 ch (counts as first tr and 2 ch), miss dc at base of 5 ch, (1 tr into next dc, 2 ch) 11 times, 1 ss into 3rd of 5 ch at beg of round.

Round 3 Ss into 1st ch sp, 3 ch, 4 tr into first ch sp, remove hook from working loop and insert hook through top of 3 ch at beg of round, pick up working loop and draw loop through, 1 ch, (3 ch, 1 popcorn into next ch sp) 11 times, 3 ch, 1 ss into top of 'popcorn' at beg of round.

Round 4 Ss into first ch sp, 3 ch (counts as first tr), 3 tr into same ch sp, (1 ch, 4 tr into next ch sp) 11 times, 1 dc into top of 3 ch at beg of round.

Round 5 Ss into 'ch sp' formed by dc at end of previous round, 4 ch (counts as 1 tr and 1 ch), 1 tr into same 'ch sp', *2 ch, (3 tr, 3 ch and 3 tr) into next ch sp, 2 ch**, (1 tr, 1 ch and 1 tr) into next ch sp, rep from * to end, ending last rep at **, ss to 3rd of 4 ch at beg of round.

Fasten off.

Special abbreviation

popcorn 5 tr into next ch sp, remove hook from working loop and insert hook through top of first of these 5 tr, pick up working loop and draw loop through top of first tr, 1 ch.

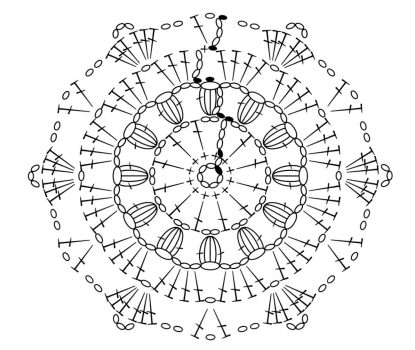

KEY

O	ch
+	dc
●	ss
⊤	tr
	popcorn

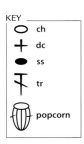

36: Popcorn triangle

Make 6 ch and join with a ss to form a ring.

Round 1 (RS) 6 ch (counts as 1 tr and 3 ch), (1 tr into ring, 3 ch) 10 times, 1 tr into ring, 1 ch, 1 htr into 3rd of 6 ch at beg of round.

Round 2 3 ch (counts as first tr), 4 tr into top of htr at end of previous round, remove hook from working loop and insert hook through top of 3 ch at beg of round, pick up working loop and draw loop through, 1 ch, *5 ch, 1 dc into next ch sp, 5 ch, miss (1 tr and 1 ch)**, 1 popcorn into next ch, rep from * to end, ending last rep at **, 1 ss into top of 'popcorn' at beg of round.

Round 3 1 ch (does NOT count as st), 1 dc into st at base of 1 ch, *3 ch, 1 tr into next dc, 3 ch, ss to top of tr just worked, 3 ch, (4 dtr, 4 ch, ss to 3rd ch from hook, 1 ch and 4 dtr) into next popcorn, 3 ch, 1 tr into next dc, 3 ch, ss to top of tr just worked, 3 ch, 1 dc into next popcorn, rep from * to end, replacing dc at end of last rep with ss to first dc.

Fasten off.

Special abbreviation

popcorn 5 tr into next ch sp, remove hook from working loop and insert hook through top of first of these 5 tr, pick up working loop and draw loop through top of first tr, 1 ch.

KEY

⬭	ch
⬬	ss
⊤	tr
⊤	htr
+	dc
🮲	popcorn
⊤	dtr

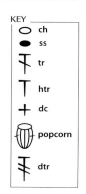

projects

Band of bunnies

These cuddly bunnies show just how much the weight of a yarn and the tension you work to can affect the outcome of the overall project. The toys are worked in simple double crochet stitch, with the bunnies' facial features worked in embroidery afterwards.

PROJECT NOTES

MEASUREMENTS
(All measurements include ears)
Miss Pink is 30cm (11¾in) tall
Mr Grey is 26cm (10¼in) tall
Sparkles is 21cm (8¼in) tall
Fluffy is 16cm (6¼in) tall

YARN
Miss Pink: 1 x 50g (1¾oz) ball of aran-weight merino, angora, nylon and metallic fibre in soft pink

Mr Grey: 1 x 50g (1¾oz) ball of DK-weight 50% merino, 50% cotton mix yarn in soft grey

Sparkles: 1 x 50g (1¾oz) ball of 4ply viscose and metallized polyester yarn in rainbow blues and pinks

Fluffy: 1 x 25g (⅞oz) ball of 4ply super kid mohair and silk yarn in cream

HOOKS
Miss Pink: 3.50mm (E4) hook
Mr Grey: 3.00mm (D3) hook
Sparkles: 2.50mm (C2) hook
Fluffy: 1.75mm (5) hook

NOTIONS
ALL BUNNIES:
Washable toy filling
Oddments of embroidery thread for nose and mouth
2 beads for eyes
Length of ribbon

SPECIAL ABBREVIATIONS
dc2tog (insert hook as indicated, yarn over hook and draw loop through) twice, yarn over hook and draw through all 3 loops.

TENSION

Miss Pink: 20 sts and 20 rows to 10cm (4in) measured over double crochet fabric on 3.50mm (E4) hook, or the size required to achieve stated tension.

Mr Grey: 24 sts and 24 rows to 10cm (4in) measured over double crochet fabric on 3.00mm (D3) hook, or the size required to achieve stated tension.

Sparkles: 27 sts and 30 rows to 10cm (4in) measured over double crochet fabric on 2.50mm (C2) hook, or the size required to achieve stated tension.

Fluffy: 35 sts and 33 rows to 10cm (4in) measured over double crochet fabric on 1.75mm (5) hook, or the size required to achieve stated tension.

THE PATTERN

ARMS (make 2)
With appropriate size hook, make 3 ch.

Round 1 (RS) 2 dc into 2nd ch from hook, 4 dc into next ch, then working back along other side of foundation ch work 2 dc into next ch (this is same ch as used for first 2 dc), ss to first dc, turn. 8 sts.

Round 2 1 ch (does NOT count as st), 2 dc into first dc, 1 dc into each of next 2 dc, 2 dc into each of next 2 dc, 1 dc into each of next 2 dc, 2 dc into last dc, ss to first dc, turn. 12 sts.

Round 3 1 ch (does NOT count as st), 1 dc into each st to end, ss to first dc, turn.

Round 4 1 ch (does NOT count as st), 2 dc into first dc, 1 dc into each of next 3 dc, [dc2tog over next 2 dc] twice, 1 dc into each of next 3 dc, 2 dc into last dc, ss to first dc, turn.

Round 5 As round 3.

Round 6 1 ch (does NOT count as st), 1 dc into each of first 4 dc, [dc2tog over next 2 dc] twice, 1 dc into each of last 4 dc, ss to first dc, turn. 10 sts.

Rounds 7 to 14 As round 3.
Fasten off.
Insert toy filling into arms.

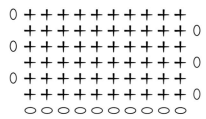

KEY
O ch
+ dc

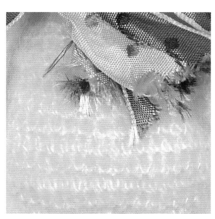

Here the fluffy yarn obscures the stitch pattern.

The double crochet pattern is clearer here.

LEGS (make 2)

Work as given for arms to end of round 2. 12 sts.

Round 3 1 ch (does NOT count as st), 2 dc into first dc, 1 dc into each of next 4 dc, 2 dc into each of next 2 dc, 1 dc into each of next 4 dc, 2 dc into last dc, ss to first dc, turn. 16 sts.

Round 4 1 ch (does NOT count as st), 2 dc into first dc, 1 dc into each of next 14 dc, 2 dc into last dc, ss to first dc, turn. 18 sts.

Round 5 1 ch (does NOT count as st), 1 dc into each st to end, ss to first dc, turn.

Round 6 As round 5.

Round 7 1 ch (does NOT count as st), 1 dc into each of first 7 dc, [dc2tog over next 2 dc] twice, 1 dc into each of last 7 dc, ss to first dc, turn. 16 sts.

Round 8 1 ch (does NOT count as st), 1 dc into each of first 6 dc, [dc2tog over next 2 dc] twice, 1 dc into each of last 6 dc, ss to first dc, turn. 14 sts.

Round 9 1 ch (does NOT count as st), 1 dc into each of first 5 dc, [dc2tog over next 2 dc] twice, 1 dc into each of last 5 dc, ss to first dc, turn. 12 sts.

Rounds 10 to 13 As round 5.

Round 14 1 ch (does NOT count as st), 1 dc into each of first 5 dc, 2 dc into each of next 2 dc, 1 dc into each of last 5 dc, ss to first dc, turn. 14 sts.

Rounds 15 to 16 As round 5.

Fasten off.

Insert toy filling into legs.

BODY AND HEAD

With RS facing, rejoin yarn to top of last round of one leg by working a ss into 13th dc of last round and then work around top of both legs as follows:

Round 1 (RS) 1 ch (does NOT count as st), 1 dc into st where yarn was rejoined, 1 dc into each of next 13 dc of this leg, starting on 3rd dc of round 16 of other leg, 1 dc into each of the 14 dc of this leg, then ss to first dc, turn. 28 sts.

Round 2 1 ch (does NOT count as st), 1 dc into each of first 6 dc, 2 dc into each of next 2 dc, 1 dc into each of next 5 dc, 2 dc into each of next 2 dc, 1 dc into each of next 5 dc, 2 dc into each of next 2 dc, 1 dc into each of last 6 dc, ss to first dc, turn. 34 sts.

Round 3 1 ch (does NOT count as st), 1 dc into each of first 7 dc, [2 dc into each of next 2 dc, 1 dc into each of next 7 dc] 3 times, ss to first dc, turn. 40 sts.

Round 4 1 ch (does NOT count as st), 1 dc into each of first 8 dc, 2 dc into each of next 2 dc, 1 dc into each of next 20 dc, 2 dc into each of next 2 dc, 1 dc into each of last 8 dc, ss to first dc, turn. 44 sts.

Round 5 1 ch (does NOT count as st), 1 dc into each dc to end, ss to first dc, turn.

Rounds 6 and 7 As round 5.

Round 8 1 ch (does NOT count as st), 1 dc into each of first 20 dc, [dc2tog over next 2 dc] twice, 1 dc into each of last 20 dc, ss to first dc, turn. 42 sts.

Round 9 As round 5.

Round 10 1 ch (does NOT count as st), 1 dc into each of first 8 dc, [dc2tog over next 2 dc] twice, 1 dc into each of next 18 dc, [dc2tog over next 2 dc] twice, 1 dc into each of last 8 dc, ss to first dc, turn. 38 sts.

Round 11 1 ch (does NOT count as st), 1 dc into each of first 17 dc, [dc2tog over next 2 dc] twice, 1 dc into each of last 17 dc, ss to first dc, turn. 36 sts.

Round 12 1 ch (does NOT count as st), 1 dc into each of first 7 dc, [dc2tog over next 2 dc] twice, 1 dc into each of next 14 dc, [dc2tog over next 2 dc] twice, 1 dc into each of last 7 dc, ss to first dc, turn. 32 sts.

Round 13 As round 5.

Round 14 1 ch (does NOT count as st), 1 dc into each of first 6 dc, [dc2tog over next 2 dc] twice, 1 dc into each of next 12 dc, [dc2tog over next 2 dc] twice, 1 dc into each of last 6 dc, ss to first dc, turn. 28 sts.

Round 15 As round 5.

Round 16 1 ch (does NOT count as st), 1 dc into each of first 5 dc, [dc2tog over next 2 dc] twice, 1 dc into each of next 10 dc, [dc2tog over next 2 dc] twice, 1 dc into each of last 5 dc, ss to first dc, turn. 24 sts.

Round 17 1 ch (does NOT count as st), 1 dc into each of first 4 dc, [dc2tog over next 2 dc] twice, 1 dc into each of next 8 dc, [dc2tog over next 2 dc] twice, 1 dc into each of last 4 dc, ss to first dc, turn. 20 sts.

MR GREY

MISS PINK

SPARKLES

FLUFFY

Round 18 1 ch (does NOT count as st), 1 dc into each of first 3 dc, [dc2tog over next 2 dc] twice, 1 dc into each of next 6 dc, [dc2tog over next 2 dc] twice, 1 dc into each of last 3 dc, ss to first dc, turn. 16 sts.
Insert toy filling into body.

● *Join arms*

Round 19 1 ch (does NOT count as st), [dc2tog over next 2 sts] twice, now starting on 8th dc of 14th round of one arm, [dc2tog over next 2 dc] 5 times around top of this arm, now working into body again: [dc2tog over next 2 sts] twice, now starting on 3rd dc of 14th round of other arm, [dc2tog over next 2 dc] 5 times around top of this arm, now working into body again: [dc2tog over next 2 sts] twice, ss to first dc2tog, turn. 18 sts.

Round 20 As round 5.
Insert a little more toy filling into neck.

● *Shape head*

Round 1 (RS) 1 ch (does NOT count as st), 2 dc into first dc, 1 dc into each of next 2 dc, [2 dc into each of next 2 dc, 1 dc into each of next 3 dc] twice, 2 dc into each of next 2 dc, 1 dc into each of next 2 dc, 2 dc into last dc, ss to first dc, turn. 26 sts.

Round 2 1 ch (does NOT count as st), 2 dc into first dc, 1 dc into each of next 4 dc, [2 dc into each of next 2 dc, 1 dc into each of next 5 dc] twice, 2 dc into each of next 2 dc, 1 dc into each of next 4 dc, 2 dc into last dc, ss to first dc, turn. 34 sts.

Round 3 1 ch (does NOT count as st), 1 dc into each of first 7 dc, [2 dc into each of next 2 dc, 1 dc into each of next 7 dc] 3 times, ss to first dc, turn. 40 sts.

Round 4 1 ch (does NOT count as st), 2 dc into first dc, 1 dc into each of next 18 dc, 2 dc into each of next 2 dc, 1 dc into each of next 18 dc, 2 dc into last dc, ss to first dc, turn. 44 sts.

Round 5 1 ch (does NOT count as st), 1 dc into each dc to end, ss to first dc, turn.

Round 6 1 ch (does NOT count as st), 1 dc into each of first 20 dc, [dc2tog over next 2 sts] twice, 1 dc into each of last 20 dc, ss to first dc, turn. 42 sts.

Round 7 1 ch (does NOT count as st), 1 dc into each of first 19 dc, [dc2tog over next 2 sts] twice, 1 dc into each of last 19 dc, ss to first dc, turn. 40 sts.

Round 8 1 ch (does NOT count as st), 1 dc into each of first 18 dc, [dc2tog over next 2 sts] twice, 1 dc into each of last 18 dc, ss to first dc, turn. 38 sts.

Round 9 1 ch (does NOT count as st), dc2tog over first 2 sts, 1 dc into each of next 5 dc, *[dc2tog over next 2 sts] twice, 1 dc into each of next 6 dc, rep from * once more, [dc2tog over next 2 sts] twice, 1 dc into each of next 5 dc, dc2tog over last 2 sts, ss to first dc, turn. 30 sts.

Round 10 1 ch (does NOT count as st), 1 dc into each of first 5 dc, *[dc2tog over next 2 sts] twice, 1 dc into each of next 4 dc, rep from * once more, [dc2tog over next 2 sts] twice, 1 dc into each of last 5 dc, ss to first dc, turn. 24 sts.

Round 11 1 ch (does NOT count as st), dc2tog over first 2 sts, *1 dc into each of next 2 dc, [dc2tog over next 2 sts] twice, rep from * twice more, 1 dc into each of next 2 dc, dc2tog over last 2 sts, ss to first dc, turn. 16 sts.

Insert toy filling into head.

Round 12 1 ch (does NOT count as st), [dc2tog over next 2 sts] 8 times, ss to first dc, turn. 8 sts.

Round 13 1 ch (does NOT count as st), [dc2tog over next 2 sts] 4 times, ss to first dc, turn. 4 sts.

Fasten off.

EARS (make 2)

With appropriate size hook, make 2 ch.

Round 1 (RS) 4 dc into 2nd ch from hook, ss to first dc, turn. 4 sts.

Round 2 1 ch (does NOT count as st), 1 dc into each dc to end, ss to first dc, turn.

Round 3 1 ch (does NOT count as st), 2 dc into each dc to end, ss to first dc, turn. 8 sts.

Round 4 As round 2.

Round 5 1 ch (does NOT count as st), 2 dc into first dc, 1 dc into each of next 2 dc, 2 dc into each of next 2 dc, 1 dc into each of next 2 dc, 2 dc into last dc, ss to first dc, turn. 12 sts.

Round 6 As round 2.

Round 7 1 ch (does NOT count as st), 2 dc into first dc, 1 dc into each of next 4 dc, 2 dc into each of next 2 dc, 1 dc into each of next 4 dc, 2 dc into last dc, ss to first dc, turn. 16 sts.

Rounds 8 to 12 As round 2.

Round 13 1 ch (does NOT count as st), dc2tog over first 2 dc, 1 dc into each of next 4 dc, [dc2tog over next 2 dc] twice, 1 dc into each of next 4 dc, dc2tog over last 2 dc, ss to first dc2tog, turn. 12 sts.

Rounds 14 to 16 As round 2.
Fasten off.

FINISHING

Using photograph (left) as a guide, embroider satin-stitch nose and back-stitch mouth under nose.
Attach beads to form eyes.
Tie ribbon in a bow around neck.

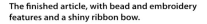

The finished article, with bead and embroidery features and a shiny ribbon bow.

Sunny day stripes

The cheerful colours of this baby sweater and hat are worked in simple rows and rounds of treble crochet. The yarn not being used is simply carried up the edge of the work, which means that there are very few yarn ends for you to darn in when making up.

PROJECT NOTES

MEASUREMENTS
To fit age approximately: 0–3 [3–6: 6–12: 12–18] months

BODY

21 [26:29:34]cm
8¼ [10¼:11½:13¼] in

SLEEVE

13 [14:19:22]cm
(5in [5½:7½:8½]in)

SWEATER:
To fit chest: 41cm (16in) [46cm (18in): 51cm (20in): 56cm (22in)]
Actual size: 45cm (17¾in) [50cm (19½in): 55cm (21½in): 60cm (23½in)]
Full length: 21cm (8¼in) [26cm (10¼in): 29cm (11½in): 34cm (13¼in)]
Sleeve seam: 13cm (5in) [14cm (5½in): 19cm (7½in): 22cm (8½in)]

HAT:
Width around head: 33cm (13in) [35cm (13¾in): 38cm (15in): 40cm (15¾in)]

YARN
All 4ply 100% cotton
SWEATER:
A 2 [2: 2: 3] x 50g (1¾oz) balls in turquoise
B 2 [2: 2: 3] x 50g (1¾oz) balls in lemon yellow

HAT:
A 1 x 50g (1¾oz) ball in turquoise
B 1 x 50g (1¾oz) ball in lemon yellow

HOOK
2.50mm (C2) hook

SPECIAL ABBREVIATIONS
tr2tog *yarn over hook and insert hook as indicated, yarn over hook and draw loop through, yarn over hook and draw through 2 loops, rep from * once more, yarn over hook and draw through all 3 loops on hook.

TENSION
24 sts and 12½ rows to 10cm (4in) measured over treble fabric on 2.50mm (C2) hook, or the size required to achieve stated tension.

THE PATTERN

SWEATER: BACK

With 2.50mm (C2) hook and yarn A, make 55 [61: 67: 73] ch.

Foundation row (RS) 1 dc into 2nd ch from hook, 1 dc into each ch to end, turn. 54 [60: 66: 72] sts.

Next row 1 ch (does NOT count as st), 1 dc into each dc to end, turn.

Rep last row twice more, ending after a WS row.

Join in yarn B and cont in tr fabric as follows:

Next row (RS) 3 ch (counts as first tr), miss st at base of 3 ch, 1 tr into each st to end, turn.

This row forms tr fabric. (*Note: on following rows, last tr will be worked into top of 3 ch at beg of previous row.*)

Cont in tr fabric in stripes as follows:

Using B, work 1 row.
Using A, work 2 rows.
Last 4 rows form striped tr fabric.
Cont in striped tr fabric for a further 8 [12: 14: 18] rows, ending after 2 rows using A [A: B: B] and a WS row.

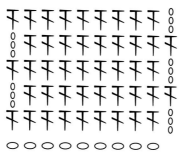

KEY
○ ch
⊤ tr

• *Shape armholes*
Keeping stripes correct, cont as follows:

Next row (RS) Ss across and into 4th st, 3 ch (counts as first tr), miss tr at base of 3 ch (3 sts decreased), 1 tr into each tr to last 3 sts and turn, leaving rem 3 sts unworked (3 sts decreased). 48 [54: 60: 66] sts.

Next row 3 ch (counts as first tr), miss tr at end of previous row, tr2tog over next 2 sts (1 st decreased), 1 tr into each tr to last 3 sts, tr2tog over next 2 sts (1 st decreased), 1 tr into top of 3 ch at beg of previous row, turn.

Working all decreases as set by last row, dec 1 st at each end of next 4 [4: 5: 6] rows. 38 [44: 48: 52] sts.**

Work 4 [6: 7: 8] rows, ending after 2 rows using B [A: A: B] and a WS row.

- *Shape back neck*

Next row Patt 7 sts and turn, leaving rem sts unworked.

Dec 1 st at neck edge of next row.

Place marker at armhole edge of last row – this denotes shoulder point.

Dec 1 st at neck edge of next 4 rows. 2 sts.

Fasten off.

Return to last complete row worked, miss centre 24 [30: 34: 38] sts, rejoin appropriate yarn to next st, 3 ch (counts as first st), patt to end, turn. 7 sts.

Complete to match first side, reversing shaping.

SWEATER: FRONT

Work as given for back to **.

Work 0 [2: 3: 4] rows, ending after 2 rows using B [A: A: B] and a WS row.

- *Shape front neck*

Next row Patt 11 sts and turn, leaving rem sts unworked.

Dec 1 st at neck edge of next 5 rows.

Place marker at armhole edge of last row – this denotes shoulder point.

Dec 1 st at neck edge of next 4 rows. 2 sts. Fasten off.

Return to last complete row worked, miss centre 16 [22: 26: 30] sts, rejoin appropriate yarn to next st, 3 ch (counts as first st), patt to end, turn. 11 sts.

Complete to match first side, reversing shaping.

SWEATER: SLEEVES

With 2.50mm (C2) hook and B [A: A: A], make 30 [32: 34: 36] ch.

Foundation row (RS) 1 dc into 2nd ch from hook, 1 dc into each ch to end, turn. 29 [31: 33: 35] sts.

Next row 1 ch (does NOT count as st), 1 dc into each dc to end, turn.

Rep last row twice more, ending after a WS row.

Join in A [B: B: B] and cont as follows:

Next row (RS) Using A [B: B: B], 3 ch (counts as first tr), miss st at base of 3 ch, 2 tr into next tr (1 st increased), 1 tr into each st to last 2 sts, 2 tr into next tr (1 st increased), 1 tr into last st, turn.

This row sets striped tr fabric as given for back and starts sleeve shaping.

Working all increases as set by last row and keeping striped tr fabric correct, inc 1 st at each end of 2nd [next: next: next] and foll 0 [3: 1: 3] rows, then on foll 4 [4: 8: 9] alt rows. 41 [49: 55: 63] sts.

Cont in striped tr fabric for a further 3 rows, ending after 2 rows using A [A: B: B] and a WS row.

- *Shape top*

Working all shaping in same way as for back armhole, dec 3 sts at each end of next row. 35 [43: 49: 57] sts.

Dec 1 st at each end of next 7 [7: 9: 9] rows, ending after 2 rows using A and a WS row. 21 [29: 31: 39] sts.

Fasten off.

MAKING UP

- *Neck edgings*

With RS facing, 2.50mm (C2) hook and A [B: B: A], rejoin yarn at fasten-off point of right back neck edge, 1 ch (does NOT count as st), work 1 row of dc down right back neck slope, across centre sts, then up left back neck slope to left back fasten-off point, turn.

Next row (WS) 1 ch (does NOT count as st),

The neck edging is added after the main pieces of the sweater have been made.

2 dc into first dc, 1 dc into each dc to last dc, 2 dc into last dc, turn.

Rep last row twice more.

Fasten off.

Work edging along front neck edge in same way.

Lay the back piece over the front so that markers denoting shoulder points match (to create envelope neck) and sew together at armhole edges.

Join side seams. Join sleeve seams. Insert sleeves into armholes, enclosing ends of neck edgings in seams.

HAT

With 2.50mm (C2) hook and A, make 78 [84: 90: 96] ch and join with a ss to form a ring.

Foundation round (RS) 1 ch (does NOT count as st), 1 dc into each ch to end, ss to first dc, turn. 78 [84: 90: 96] sts.

Next round 1 ch (does NOT count as st), 1 dc into each dc to end, ss to first dc, turn.

Rep last round twice more, ending after a WS round.

Join in B and cont in tr fabric as follows:

Next round (RS) 3 ch (counts as first tr), miss st at base of 3 ch, 1 tr into each st to end, ss to top of 3 ch at beg of round, turn.

This round forms tr fabric.

Cont in tr fabric in stripes as follows:

Using B, work 1 round.

Using A, work 2 rounds.

Last 4 rounds form striped tr fabric.

Cont in striped tr fabric for a further 7 rounds, ending after 1 round using A and a RS round.

Keeping stripes correct, shape hat as follows:

Round 1 (WS) 3 ch (counts as first tr), miss st at base of 3 ch, 1 tr into each of next 10 [11: 12: 13] tr, (tr2tog over next 2 tr, 1 tr into each of next 11 [12: 13: 14] tr) 5 times, tr2tog over last 2 tr, ss to top of 3 ch at beg of round, turn. 72 [78: 84: 90] sts.

Round 2 and every foll alt round 3 ch

(counts as first tr), miss st at base of 3 ch, 1 tr into each st to end, ss to top of 3 ch at beg of round, turn.

Round 3 3 ch (counts as first tr), miss st at base of 3 ch, 1 tr into each of next 9 [10: 11: 12] tr, (tr2tog over next 2 tr, 1 tr into each of next 10 [11: 12: 13] tr) 5 times, tr2tog over last 2 tr, ss to top of 3 ch at beg of round, turn. 66 [72: 78: 84] sts.

Round 5 3 ch (counts as first tr), miss st at base of 3 ch, 1 tr into each of next 8 [9: 10: 11] tr, (tr2tog over next 2 tr, 1 tr into each of next 9 [10: 11: 12] tr) 5 times, tr2tog over last 2 tr, ss to top of 3 ch at beg of round, turn. 60 [66: 72: 78] sts.

Round 7 3 ch (counts as first tr), miss st at base of 3 ch, 1 tr into each of next 7 [8: 9: 10] tr, (tr2tog over next 2 tr, 1 tr into each of next 8 [9: 10: 11] tr) 5 times, tr2tog over last 2 tr, ss to top of 3 ch at beg of round, turn. 54 [60: 66: 72] sts.

Round 9 3 ch (counts as first tr), miss st at base of 3 ch, 1 tr into each of next 6 [7: 8: 9] tr, (tr2tog over next 2 tr, 1 tr into each of next 7 [8: 9: 10] tr) 5 times, tr2tog over last 2 tr, ss to top of 3 ch at beg of round, turn. 48 [54: 60: 66] sts.

Round 11 3 ch (counts as first tr), miss st at base of 3 ch, 1 tr into each of next 5 [6: 7: 8] tr, (tr2tog over next 2 tr, 1 tr into each of next 6 [7: 8: 9] tr) 5 times, tr2tog over last 2 tr, ss to top of 3 ch at beg of round, turn. 42 [48: 54: 60] sts.

Round 13 3 ch (counts as first tr), miss st at base of 3 ch, 1 tr into each of next 4 [5: 6: 7] tr, (tr2tog over next 2 tr, 1 tr into each of next 5 [6: 7: 8] tr) 5 times, tr2tog over last 2 tr, ss to top of 3 ch at beg of round, turn. 36 [42: 48: 54] sts.

Cont in this way, dec 6 sts on every foll alt round, until the foll round has been worked:

Next round (RS) 3 ch (counts as first tr), miss st at base of 3 ch, (tr2tog over next 2 tr, 1 tr into next tr) 5 times, tr2tog over last 2 tr, ss to top of 3 ch at beg of round, turn. 12 sts.

Next round As round 2.

Next round 3 ch (does NOT count as st), miss st at base of 3 ch, (tr2tog over next 2 tr) 5 times, 1 tr into last tr, ss to top of first tr2tog at beg of round, turn. 6 sts.

Next round As round 2.

Fasten off.

Using B, make a 10cm (4in) tassel and attach to top of hat.

Precious pastels baby set

This set of matching baby hat, bootees and mittens is worked in variegated yarn with trimmings worked in a matching plain yarn. Toning ribbons create a pretty finishing touch.

PROJECT NOTES

MEASUREMENTS
One size, to fit a newborn baby
BOOTEES:
Length of foot 9cm (3½in)
MITTENS:
Width around hand 10cm (4in)
HAT:
Width around head 32cm (12½in)

YARN
All DK-weight 100% merino wool
M 2 x 50g (1¾oz) balls in variegated pinks
C 1 x 50g (1¾oz) ball in pale pink

HOOK
3.50mm (E4) hook

NOTIONS
2.4m (95in) of 7mm (¼in)-wide ribbon

SPECIAL ABBREVIATIONS
dc2tog (insert hook as indicated, yoh and draw loop through) twice, yoh and draw through all 3 loops
yoh yarn over hook.

TENSION
20 sts and 24 rows to 10cm (4in) measured over pattern on 3.50mm (E4) hook, or the size required to achieve stated tension.

THE PATTERN

BOOTEES

With 3.50mm (E4) hook and yarn M, make 24 ch and join with a ss to form a ring.

Round 1 (RS) 1 ch (does NOT count as st), 1 dc into each ch to end, ss to first dc, turn. 24 sts.

Round 2 1 ch (does NOT count as st), 1 dc into first dc, (1 ch, miss 1 dc, 1 dc into each of next 2 dc) 7 times, 1 ch, miss 1 dc, 1 dc into last dc, ss to first dc, turn.

Round 3 1 ch (does NOT count as st), 1 dc into first dc, (1 dc into next ch sp, 1 dc into

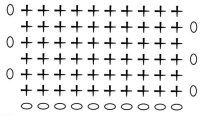

KEY
○ ch
+ dc

each of next 2 dc) 7 times, 1 dc into next ch sp, 1 dc into last dc, ss to first dc, turn.

Round 4 1 ch (does NOT count as st), 1 dc into each dc to end, ss to first dc, turn.

● *Shape instep*
Slip working loop onto a safety pin.

With RS facing and separate length of yarn M, miss first 9 dc of next round, rejoin yarn to next dc, 1 ch (does NOT count as st), 1 dc into dc where yarn was rejoined, 1 dc into each of next 5 dc, turn.

Work on this set of 6 sts only for instep.

Next row 1 ch (does NOT count as st), 1 dc into each dc to end, turn.

Rep last row 5 times more.

Next row (WS) 1 ch (does NOT count as st), dc2tog over first 2 dc, 1 dc into each of next 2 dc, dc2tog over last 2 dc. 4 sts.

Fasten off.

Return to working loop left on safety pin, slip this loop back onto hook and cont as follows:

Round 5 (RS) 1 ch (does NOT count as st), 1 dc into each of first dc, 1 dc into each of next 8 row-ends of instep, 1 dc into each of 4 sts across end of instep, 1 dc into each of next 8 row-ends of other side of instep, 1 dc into each of last 9 dc, ss to first dc, turn. 38 sts.

Rounds 6 to 10 As round 4.

● *Shape sole*

Round 11 (RS) 1 ch (does NOT count as st), 1 dc into first dc, dc2tog over next 2 dc, 1 dc into each of next 11 dc, dc2tog over next 2 dc, 1 dc into each of next 6 dc, dc2tog over next 2 dc, 1 dc into each of next 11 dc, dc2tog over next 2 dc, 1 dc into last dc, ss to first dc, turn. 34 sts.

Round 12 1 ch (does NOT count as st), 1 dc into each of first 2 sts, dc2tog over next 2 sts, 1 dc into each of next 10 sts, dc2tog over next 2 sts, 1 dc into each of next 2 sts, dc2tog over next 2 sts, 1 dc into each of next 10 sts, dc2tog over next 2 sts, 1 dc into each of last 2 sts, ss to first dc, turn. 30 sts.

Round 13 1 ch (does NOT count as st), dc2tog over first 2 sts, 1 dc into each of next 9 sts, dc2tog over next 2 sts, 1 dc into each of next 4 sts, dc2tog over next 2 sts, 1 dc into each of next 9 sts, dc2tog over last 2 sts, ss to first dc2tog, turn. 26 sts.

Round 14 1 ch (does NOT count as st), 1 dc into first st, dc2tog over next 2 sts, 1 dc into each of next 8 sts, (dc2tog over next 2 sts)

twice, 1 dc into each of next 8 sts, dc2tog over next 2 sts, 1 dc into last st, ss to first dc, turn. 22 sts.

Round 15 1 ch (does NOT count as st), dc2tog over first 2 sts, 1 dc into each of next 7 sts, (dc2tog over next 2 sts) twice, 1 dc into each of next 7 sts, dc2tog over last 2 sts, ss to first dc2tog, turn. 18 sts.

Fold bootee flat with RS facing and join sole seam by working a row of dc through sts of both layers.

Fasten off.

MAKING UP

● *Edging*

With RS facing and C, attach yarn to beg of foundation ch edge, 1 ch (does NOT count as st), 1 dc into each foundation ch around top of bootee, ss to first dc.

Round 1 (RS) 4 ch, 1 ss into same place as ss closing last round, *4 ch, (1 ss, 4 ch and 1 ss) into next dc, rep from * to end, 2 ch, 1 htr into same place as ss at beg of round.

Round 2 1 ch (does NOT count as st), 1 ss into ch sp partly formed by ss at end of previous round, *4 ch, 1 ss into next ch sp, rep from * to end, working last ss into ss at beg of round.

Fasten off.

Cut two 45cm (17¾in) lengths of ribbon and thread each length through holes of round 2 as in photograph. Tie ends in a bow on front of bootees.

MITTENS

With 3.50mm (E4) hook and M, make 20 ch and join with a ss to form a ring.

Round 1 (RS) 1 ch (does NOT count as st), 1 dc into each ch to end, ss to first dc, turn. 20 sts.

Round 2 1 ch (does NOT count as st), 1 dc into first dc, (1 ch, miss 1 dc, 1 dc into next dc, 1 ch, miss 1 dc, 1 dc into each of next 2 dc) 3 times, 1 ch, miss 1 dc, 1 dc into next dc, 1 ch, miss 1 dc, 1 dc into last dc, ss to first dc, turn.

Round 3 1 ch (does NOT count as st), 1 dc into first dc, (1 dc into next ch sp, 1 dc into next dc, 1 dc into next ch sp, 1 dc into each of next 2 dc) 3 times, 1 dc into next ch sp, 1 dc into next dc, 1 dc into next ch sp, 1 dc into last dc, ss to first dc, turn.

Round 4 1 ch (does NOT count as st), 1 dc into each dc to end, ss to first dc, turn.

Rounds 5 to 14 As round 4.

Shape top

Round 15 (RS) 1 ch (does NOT count as st), dc2tog over first 2 dc, 1 dc into each of next 6 dc, (dc2tog over next 2 dc) twice, 1 dc into each of next 6 dc, dc2tog over last 2 dc, ss to first dc2tog, turn. 16 sts.

Round 16 As round 4.

Round 17 1 ch (does NOT count as st), dc2tog over first 2 dc, 1 dc into each of next 4 dc, (dc2tog over next 2 dc) twice, 1 dc into each of next 4 dc, dc2tog over last 2 dc, ss to first dc2tog, turn. 12 sts.

Round 18 1 ch (does NOT count as st), dc2tog over first 2 sts, 1 dc into each of next 2 dc, (dc2tog over next 2 sts) twice, 1 dc into each of next 2 dc, dc2tog over last 2 sts, ss to first dc2tog, turn.

Fold mitten flat with RS facing and join top seam by working a row of dc through sts of both layers.

Fasten off.

MAKING UP

● Edging

With RS facing and yarn C, attach yarn to beg of foundation ch edge, 1 ch (does NOT count as st), 1 dc into each foundation ch around lower edge of mitten, ss to first dc.

Work rounds 1 and 2 of edging as given for bootees.

Fasten off.

Cut two 40cm (15¾in) lengths of ribbon and thread each length through holes of round 2 as in photograph. Tie ends in a bow on back of mittens.

HAT

With 3.50mm (E4) hook and yarn M, make 64 ch and join with a ss to form a ring.

Round 1 (RS) 1 ch (does NOT count as st), 1 dc into each ch to end, ss to first dc, turn. 64 sts.

Round 2 1 ch (does NOT count as st), 1 dc into first dc, (1 ch, miss 1 dc, 1 dc into next dc) twice, (1 ch, miss 1 dc, 1 dc into each of next 2 dc, 1 ch, miss 1 dc, 1 dc into next dc) 11 times, 1 ch, miss 1 dc, 1 dc into next dc, 1 ch, miss 1 dc, 1 dc into last dc, ss to first dc, turn.

Round 3 1 ch (does NOT count as st), 1 dc into first dc, (1 dc into next ch sp, 1 dc into next dc) twice, (1 dc into next ch sp, 1 dc into each of next 2 dc, 1 dc into next ch sp, 1 dc into next dc) 11 times, 1 dc into next ch sp, 1 dc into next dc, 1 dc into next ch sp, 1 dc into last dc, ss to first dc, turn.

Round 4 1 ch (does NOT count as st), 1 dc into each dc to end, ss to first dc, turn.

Rounds 5 to 18 As round 4.

Round 19 1 ch (does NOT count as st), (1 dc into each of next 6 dc, dc2tog over next 2 dc) 8 times, ss to first dc, turn. 56 sts.

Rounds 20 to 22 As round 4.

Round 23 1 ch (does NOT count as st), (1 dc into each of next 5 dc, dc2tog over next 2 dc) 8 times, ss to first dc, turn. 48 sts.

Round 24 As round 4.

Round 25 1 ch (does NOT count as st), (1 dc into each of next 4 dc, dc2tog over next 2 dc) 8 times, ss to first dc, turn. 40 sts.

Round 26 As round 4.

Round 27 1 ch (does NOT count as st), (1 dc into each of next 3 dc, dc2tog over next 2 dc) 8 times, ss to first dc, turn. 32 sts.

Round 28 As round 4.

Round 29 1 ch (does NOT count as st), (1 dc into each of next 2 dc, dc2tog over next 2 dc) 8 times, ss to first dc, turn. 24 sts.

Round 30 As round 4.

Round 31 1 ch (does NOT count as st), (1 dc into next dc, dc2tog over next 2 dc) 8 times, ss to first dc, turn. 16 sts.

Round 32 1 ch (does NOT count as st), (dc2tog over next 2 sts) 8 times, ss to first dc, turn. 8 sts.

Round 33 1 ch (does NOT count as st), (dc2tog over next 2 sts) 4 times, ss to first dc, turn. 4 sts.

Fasten off.

MAKING UP

● Edging

With RS facing and yarn C, attach yarn to beg of foundation ch edge, 1 ch (does NOT count as st), 1 dc into each foundation ch around lower edge of hat, ss to first dc.

Work rounds 1 and 2 of edging as given for bootees.

Fasten off.

Cut 70cm (27½in) length of ribbon and thread through holes of round 2 as in photograph. Tie ends in a bow at front of hat.

Pretty in pink cardigan and shawl

This fetching baby cardigan combines two stitches to great effect. The upper part is worked in a tightly defined double crochet fabric, while the lower half is worked in a pretty lace stitch for a more flouncy look. This lace stitch is also used for a matching shawl made in the same soft pink yarn.

PROJECT NOTES

MEASUREMENTS
CARDIGAN:
To fit age approximately: 0–3 [3–6: 6–12 months]
To fit chest: 41cm (16in) [46cm (18in): 51cm (20in)]
Actual size, at underarm: 46cm (18in) [51cm (20in): 56cm (22in)]
Full length: 23cm (9in) [27cm (10½in): 31cm (12¼in)]
Sleeve seam: 12cm (4¾in) [15cm (6in): 19cm (7½in)]

SHAWL:
Actual size:
90 x 90cm (35½ x 35½in)

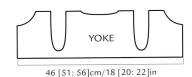

YOKE

46 [51: 56]cm/18 [20: 22]in

SLEEVE

12 [15: 19]cm 4¾ [6: 7½]in

YARN
All 4ply 100% merino wool

CARDIGAN:
3 [4: 4] x 50g (1¾oz) balls in soft pink
SHAWL:
11 x 50g (1¾oz) balls in soft pink

HOOK
2.50mm (C2) hook

NOTIONS
3 small buttons

TENSION
24 sts and 28 rows to 10cm (4in) measured over double crochet fabric on 2.50mm (C2) hook, or the size required to achieve stated tension.

THE PATTERN

CARDIGAN: YOKE
(Worked in one piece to armholes.)
With 2.50mm (C2) hook, make 112 [124: 136] ch.
Foundation row (RS) 1 dc into 2nd ch from hook, 1 dc into each ch to end, turn. 111 [123: 135] sts.
Cont in dc fabric as follows:
Row 1 1 ch (does NOT count as st), 1 dc into each dc to end, turn.
This row forms dc fabric.
Row 2 (RS) 1 ch (does NOT count as st), 1 dc into each of first 2 dc, 1 ch, miss 1 dc (to make a buttonhole – work 1 dc into this ch sp on next row), 1 dc into each dc to end, turn.
Cont in dc fabric for a further 1 row, ending after a WS row.

● **Shape right front**
Next row (RS) 1 ch (does NOT count as st), 1 dc into each of first 27 [29: 32] dc and turn, leaving rem sts unworked.

Work on this set of 27 [29: 32] sts only for right front.
Next row 1 ch (does NOT count as st), dc2tog over first 2 sts (1 st decreased), 1 dc into each dc to end, turn.

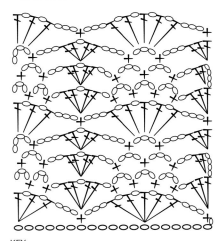

KEY
○ ch
+ dc
⊤ tr

Next row 1 ch (does NOT count as st), 1 dc into each dc to last 2 sts, dc2tog over last 2 sts (1 st decreased), turn.

1st and 2nd sizes only:
Working all decreases as set by last 2 rows, dec 1 st at armhole edge of next and foll 2 alt rows and at same time make a 2nd buttonhole in 3rd [5th] of these rows by replacing last 3 sts of this row with (1 ch, miss 1 dc, 1 dc into each of last 2 dc).

3rd size only:
Working all decreases as set by last 2 rows, dec 1 st at armhole edge of next and foll 3 alt rows and at same time make a 2nd buttonhole in 6th of these rows by replacing first 3 sts of this row with (1 dc into each of first 2 dc, 1 ch, miss 1 dc).

All sizes:
22 [24: 26] sts.
Work 7 [11: 11] rows, making a 3rd buttonhole in 5th [9th: 9th] of these rows by replacing first 3 sts of this row with (1 dc into each of first 2 dc, 1 ch, miss 1 dc) and ending after a RS row.

Shape neck

Next row (WS) 1 ch (does NOT count as st), 1 dc into each of first 16 [17: 19] dc and turn, leaving rem 6 [7: 7] sts unworked.

Dec 1 st at neck edge of next 6 rows, then on foll 1 [1: 2] alt rows. 9 [10: 11] sts.

Work 2 rows, ending after a WS row.

Fasten off.

Shape back

Return to last complete row worked before dividing for right front, miss next 4 [6: 6] dc, rejoin yarn to next dc, 1 ch (does NOT count as st), 1 dc into same dc as where yarn was rejoined, 1 dc into each of next 48 [52: 58] dc and turn, leaving rem sts unworked.

Work on these 49 [53: 59] sts only for back.

Dec 1 st at each end of next 3 rows, then on foll 2 [2: 3] alt rows. 39 [43: 47] sts.

Work 15 [19: 21] rows, ending after a RS row.

Shape back neck

Next row (WS) 1 ch (does NOT count as st), 1 dc into each of first 11 [12: 13] dc and turn, leaving rem sts unworked.

Dec 1 st at neck edge of next 2 rows, ending after a WS row. 9 [10: 11] sts.

Fasten off.

Return to last complete row worked before shaping back neck, miss next 17 [19: 21] dc, rejoin yarn to next dc, 1 ch (does NOT count as st), 1 dc into same dc as where yarn was rejoined, 1 dc into each of dc to end, turn. 11 [12: 13] sts.

Dec 1 st at neck edge of next 2 rows, ending after a WS row. 9 [10: 11] sts.

Fasten off.

Shape left front

Return to last complete row worked before dividing for back and right front, miss next 4 [6: 6] dc, rejoin yarn to next dc, 1 ch (does NOT count as st), 1 dc into same dc as where yarn was rejoined, 1 dc into each dc to end, turn.

Work on this set of 27 [29: 32] sts only for left front.

Dec 1 st at armhole edge of next 3 rows, then on foll 2 [2: 3] alt rows. 22 [24: 26] sts.

Work 7 [11: 11] rows, ending after a RS row.

Shape neck

Next row (WS) Ss along and into 7th [8th: 8th] dc, 1 ch (does NOT count as st), 1 dc

into same dc as last ss, 1 dc into each dc to end, turn. 16 [17: 19] sts.

Dec 1 st at neck edge of next 6 rows, then on foll 1 [1: 2] alt rows. 9 [10: 11] sts.

Work 2 rows, ending after a WS row.

Fasten off.

CARDIGAN: SLEEVES

With 2.50mm (C2) hook, make 30 [34: 38] ch.

Work foundation row as given for yoke. 29 [33: 37] sts.

Cont in dc fabric as follows:

Work 1 row, ending after a WS row.

Row 3 (RS) 1 ch (does NOT count as st), 2 dc into first dc (1 st increased), 1 dc into

each dc to last dc, 2 dc into last dc (1 st increased), turn.

Working all increases as set by last row, inc 1 st at each end of every foll 6th [6th: 7th] row until there are 39 [45: 51] sts.

Work 7 [9: 9] rows, ending after a WS row.

Shape top

Next row (RS) Ss across and into 3rd [4th: 4th] dc, 1 ch (does NOT count as st), 1 dc into same dc as last ss, 1 dc into each dc to last 2 [3: 3] dc and turn, leaving rem 2 [3: 3] sts unworked. 35 [39: 45] sts.

Dec 1 st at each end of next 12 [14: 16] rows. 11 [11: 13] sts.

Fasten off.

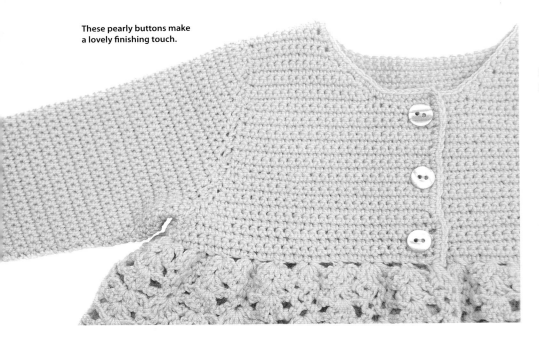

These pearly buttons make a lovely finishing touch.

MAKING UP

Join shoulder seams. Join sleeve seams. Matching centre of top of last row of sleeve to shoulder seam and sleeve seam to centre of sts left unworked at underarm, insert sleeves into armholes.

CARDIGAN: SKIRT

With RS facing and 2.50mm (C2) hook, rejoin yarn at base of left front opening edge, 4 ch (counts as first tr and 1 ch), working into base of each st of first row of bodice, cont as follows: (1 tr, 1 ch and 1 tr) into st at base of 4 ch, *3 ch, miss 2 sts, 1 dc into next st, 3 ch, miss 2 sts, 1 tr into next st, (1 ch, 1 tr into same place as last tr) 4 times*, rep from * to * 7 [8: 9] times more, 3 ch, miss 2 sts, 1 dc into next st, 3 ch, miss 3 [2: 3] sts, 1 tr into next st, (1 ch, 1 tr into same place as last tr) 4 times, 3 ch, miss 3 [2: 3] sts, 1 dc into next st, 3 ch, miss 2 sts, 1 tr into next st, (1 ch, 1 tr into same place as last tr) 4 times, rep from * to * 7 [8: 9] times more, 3 ch, miss 2 sts, 1 dc into next st, 3 ch, miss 2 sts, 1 tr into last st, (1 ch, 1 tr into same place as last tr) twice, turn. 18 [20: 22] patt reps.

Now cont in lace patt as follows:

Row 1 (WS) 3 ch, miss tr at end of previous row, 1 dc into next ch sp, 3 ch, *1 dc into next ch sp, 1 ch, miss (1 tr and 3 ch), (2 tr, 1 ch and 2 tr) into next dc, 1 ch, miss (3 ch and 1 tr)**, (1 dc into next ch sp, 3 ch) 3 times, rep from * to end, ending last rep at **, 1 dc into next ch sp, 3 ch, 1 dc into next ch sp, 1 ch, 1 htr into 3rd of 4 ch at beg of previous row, turn.

Row 2 1 ch (does NOT count as st), 1 dc into htr at end of previous row, 3 ch, miss 1 dc, *1 dc into next ch sp, 2 ch, miss (1 dc, 1 tr and 2 tr), (2 tr, 1 ch and 2 tr) into next ch sp, 2 ch, miss (2 tr, 1 ch and 1 dc)**, (1 dc into next ch sp, 3 ch) twice, rep from * to end, ending last rep at **, 1 dc into next ch sp, 3 ch, 1 dc into last ch sp, turn.

Row 3 4 ch, miss dc at base of 4 ch, *1 dc into next ch sp, 3 ch, miss (1 dc, 2 ch and 2 tr), (2 tr, 1 ch and 2 tr) into next ch sp, 3 ch, miss (2 tr, 2 ch and 1 dc), 1 dc into next ch sp**, 3 ch, rep from * to end, ending last rep at **, 2 ch, 1 htr into dc at beg of previous row, turn.

Row 4 4 ch (counts as first tr and 1 ch), (1 tr, 1 ch and 1 tr) into first ch sp, *3 ch, miss (1 dc, 3 ch and 2 tr), 1 dc into next ch sp, 3 ch, miss (2 tr, 3 ch and 1 dc), 1 tr into next ch sp**, (1 ch, 1 tr into same ch sp as last tr) 4 times, rep from * to end, ending last rep at **, (1 ch, 1 tr into same ch sp as last tr) twice, turn.

These 4 rows form patt.

Work in patt for a further 16 [20: 24] rows.

Fasten off.

Sew on buttons.

SHAWL

With 2.50mm (C2) hook, make 256 ch.

Foundation row (RS) (1 tr, 1 ch and 1 tr) into 4th ch from hook, *3 ch, miss 5 ch, 1 dc into next ch, 3 ch, miss 5 ch, 1 tr into next ch**, (1 ch, 1 tr into same ch as last tr) 4 times,

rep from * to end, ending last rep at **, (1 ch, 1 tr into same ch as last tr) twice, turn. 21 patt reps.

Now cont in lace patt as follows:

Row 1 (WS) 3 ch, miss tr at end of previous row, 1 dc into next ch sp, 3 ch, *1 dc into next ch sp, 1 ch, miss (1 tr and 3 ch), (2 tr, 1 ch and 2 tr) into next dc, 1 ch, miss (3 ch and 1 tr)**, (1 dc into next ch sp, 3 ch) 3 times, rep from * to end, ending last rep at **, 1 dc into next ch sp, 3 ch, 1 dc into next ch sp, 1 ch, 1 htr into 3rd of 4 ch at beg of previous row, turn.

Row 2 1 ch (does NOT count as st), 1 dc into htr at end of previous row, 3 ch, miss 1 dc, *1 dc into next ch sp, 2 ch, miss (1 dc, 1 tr and 2 tr), (2 tr, 1 ch and 2 tr) into next ch sp, 2 ch, miss (2 tr, 1 ch and 1 dc)**, (1 dc into next ch sp, 3 ch) twice, rep from * to end, ending last rep at **, 1 dc into next ch sp, 3 ch, 1 dc into last ch sp, turn.

Row 3 4 ch, miss dc at base of 4 ch, *1 dc into next ch sp, 3 ch, miss (1 dc, 2 ch and 2 tr), (2 tr, 1 ch and 2 tr) into next ch sp, 3 ch, miss (2 tr, 2 ch and 1 dc), 1 dc into next ch sp**, 3 ch, rep from * to end, ending last rep at **, 2 ch, 1 htr into dc at beg of previous row, turn.

Row 4 4 ch (counts as first tr and 1 ch), (1 tr, 1 ch and 1 tr) into first ch sp, *3 ch, miss (1 dc, 3 ch and 2 tr), 1 dc into next ch sp, 3 ch, miss (2 tr, 3 ch and 1 dc), 1 tr into next ch sp**, (1 ch, 1 tr into same ch sp as last tr) 4 times, rep from * to end, ending last rep at **, (1 ch, 1 tr into same ch sp as last tr) twice, turn.

These 4 rows form patt.

Work in patt for a further 144 rows.

Fasten off.

This beautiful lacy fabric is simple to make from double crochet and treble stitches.

Autumn colour coat

This duffle coat is made from a warm, earthy yarn with a wonderful depth of colour that looks like autumn leaves. This textured stitch creates a basketweave effect that makes a robust and cosy fabric, perfect for keeping your little one warm on chilly autumn days – particularly with the addition of the snug hood. See pages 182–185 for more information on relief stitches.

PROJECT NOTES

MEASUREMENTS
To fit age, approx: 1–2 [2–3: 4–5: 5–6] years

To fit chest: 51cm (20in) [56cm (22in): 61cm (24in): 66cm (26in)]

Actual size: 60cm (23½in) [68cm (26¾in): 76cm (30in): 84cm (33in)]

Full length: 49cm (19¼in) [55cm (21½in): 61cm (24in): 67cm (26¼in)]

Sleeve seam: 26cm (10¼in) [30cm (11¾in): 34cm (13¼in): 38cm (15in)]

YARN
14 [15: 16: 17] x 50g (1¾oz) balls of DK-weight 100% wool in variegated reds and browns

HOOK
4.00mm (G6) hook

NOTIONS
4 buttons

SPECIAL ABBREVIATIONS
rbtr work treble in the usual way but working around stem of st of previous row, inserting hook around stem from back to front and from right to left.

rftr work treble in the usual way but

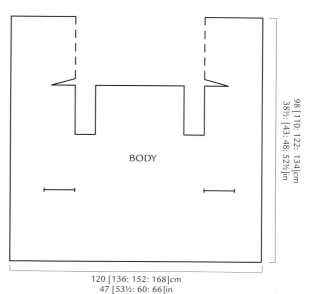

BODY

120 [136: 152: 168]cm
47 [53½: 60: 66]in

98 [110: 122: 134]cm
38½ [43: 48: 52½]in

working around stem of st of previous row, inserting hook around stem from front to back and from right to left.

TENSION
20 sts and 12½ rows to 10cm (4in) measured over pattern on 4.00mm (G6) hook, or the size required to achieve stated tension.

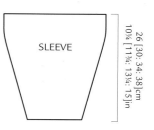

SLEEVE

26 [30: 34: 38]cm
10¼ [11¾: 13¼: 15]in

THE PATTERN

POCKET LININGS (make 2)
With 4.00mm (G6) hook, make 21 ch.

Foundation row (WS) 1 htr into 3rd ch from hook, 1 htr into each ch to end, turn. 20 sts.

Cont in patt as follows:

Row 1 (RS) 2 ch (counts as first st), miss st at base of 2 ch, 1 rbtr around stem of each of next 3 sts, *1 rftr around stem of each of next 4 sts, 1 rbtr around stem of each of next 4 sts, rep from * to end, working last

rbtr around stem of 2 ch at beg of previous row, turn.

Row 2 2 ch (counts as first st), miss st at base of 2 ch, 1 rftr around stem of each of next 3 sts, *1 rbtr around stem of each of next 4 sts, 1 rftr around stem of each of next 4 sts, rep from * to end, working last rftr around stem of 2 ch at beg of previous row, turn.

Row 3 As row 2.

Row 4 As row 1.

These 4 rows form patt.

Cont in patt for a further 6 rows, ending after 2nd patt row and a WS row.

Fasten off.

KEY
O ch
T htr
ꓴ rbtr
ꓵ rftr

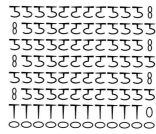

BODY

(Worked in one piece to armholes.)

With 4.00mm (G6) hook, make 133 [149: 165: 181] ch.

Foundation row (WS) 1 htr into 3rd ch from hook, 1 htr into each ch to end, turn. 132 [148: 164: 180] sts.

Cont in patt as follows:

Row 1 (RS) 2 ch (counts as first st), miss st at base of 2 ch, 1 rftr around stem of each of next 3 sts, *1 rbtr around stem of each of next 4 sts, 1 rftr around stem of each of next 4 sts, rep from * to end, working last rftr around stem of 2 ch at beg of previous row, turn.

Row 2 2 ch (counts as first st), miss st at base of 2 ch, 1 rbtr around stem of each of next 3 sts, *1 rftr around stem of each of next 4 sts, 1 rbtr around stem of each of next 4 sts, rep from * to end, working last rbtr around stem of 2 ch at beg of previous row, turn.

Row 3 As row 2.

Row 4 As row 1.

These 4 rows form patt.

Cont in patt until work measures approx 21cm (8¼in) [23cm (9in): 27cm (10½in): 29cm (11½in)] ending after 4th patt row and a WS row.

● *Place pockets*

Next row (RS) Patt 12 [12: 20: 20] sts, miss next 20 sts and, in their place, patt across 20 sts of first pocket lining, patt to last 32 [32: 40: 40] sts, miss next 20 sts and, in their place, patt across 20 sts of second pocket lining, patt to end, turn.

Cont straight until work measures 34cm (13¼in) [39cm (15¼in): 44cm (17¼in): 49cm (19¼in)] ending after a WS row.

● *Divide for armholes*

Next row (RS) Patt 28 [32: 36: 40] sts and turn, leaving rem sts unworked.

Work on this set of sts only for right front.

Cont straight until work measures 14cm (5½in) [15cm (6in): 16cm (6¼in): 17cm (6½in)] from dividing row, ending after a WS row.

The main bulk of the coat is crocheted in one piece, but the snuggly hood is attached afterwards.

Slip working loop onto a safety pin and set aside this ball of yarn – it will be used for the hood.

Place marker 10 [13: 16: 19] sts in from armhole edge to denote neck point of shoulder seam.

● *Shape back*

Return to last complete row worked, miss 16 sts (for underarm), rejoin yarn to next st, 2 ch (counts as first st), miss st at base of 2 ch, patt 43 [51: 59: 67] sts and turn.

Work on this set of 44 [52: 60: 68] sts only for back.

Cont straight until work measures 14cm (5½in) [15cm (6in): 16cm (6¼in): 17cm (6½in)] from dividing row, ending after a WS row.

Fasten off, placing markers either side of centre 24 [26: 28: 30] sts to denote back neck.

● *Shape left front*

Return to last complete row worked, miss 16 sts (for underarm), rejoin yarn to next st, 2 ch (counts as first st), miss st at base of 2 ch, patt to end, turn.

Work on this set of 28 [32: 36: 40] sts only for left front.

Cont straight until work measures 14cm (5½in) [15cm (6in): 16cm (6¼in): 17cm (6½in)] from dividing row, ending after a WS row.

Fasten off, placing marker 10 [13: 16: 19] sts in from armhole edge to denote neck point of shoulder seam.

SLEEVES

With 4.00mm (G6) hook, make 33 [35: 37: 39] ch.

Work foundation row as given for body. 32 [34: 36: 38] sts.

Cont in patt as follows:

Row 1 (RS) 2 ch (counts as first st), miss st at base of 2 ch, 1 rftr around stem of each of next 1 [2: 3: 4] sts, *1 rbtr around stem of each of next 4 sts, 1 rftr around stem of each of next 4 sts, rep from * to last 6 [7: 8: 1] sts, 1 rbtr around stem of each of next 4 [4: 4: 1] sts, 1 rftr around stem of each of next 2 [3: 4: 0] sts, working last st around stem of 2 ch at beg of previous row, turn.

This row sets position of patt as given for body.

Keeping patt correct, cont as follows:

Work 1 row.

Next row 2 ch (counts as first st), work appropriate st (to keep patt correct) around stem of st at base of 2 ch (1 st increased), patt to last st, working 2 sts around stem of 2 ch at beg of previous row, working appropriate sts to keep patt correct (1 st increased), turn.

Working all increases as set by last row, inc 1 st at each end of 2nd and foll 8 [7: 4: 3] alt rows, then on every foll 3rd row until there are 56 [60: 64: 68] sts, taking inc sts into patt.

Cont straight until sleeve measures 29cm (11½in) [33cm (13in): 37cm (14½in): 41cm (16in)] ending after a WS row.

Fasten off, placing markers along row-end edges 4cm (1½in) down from top of last row.

MAKING UP

Join shoulder seams: there will be 18 [19: 20: 21] sts free at neck edge of each front and 24 [26: 28: 30] sts across back neck.

● *Hood*

With RS facing and 4.00mm (G6) hook, slip working loop left on safety pin at neck edge of right front back onto hook and, using ball of yarn set to one side with right front, cont as follows:

2 ch (counts as first st), miss st at base of 2 ch, patt next 13 [14: 17: 18] sts of right front, keeping patt correct as set by last set of sts work across rem sts of right front, then back neck, then left front as follows:

(work appropriate 2 sts around stem of next st, patt 1 [2: 1: 2] sts) 7 [5: 7: 5] times, work appropriate 2 sts around stem of next st, patt 2 sts, work appropriate 2 sts around stem of next st, (patt 1 [2: 1: 2] sts, work appropriate 2 sts around stem of next st) 7 [5: 7: 5] times, patt to end, turn. 76 [76: 84: 84] sts.

Cont in patt until hood measures 20cm (7¾in) [21cm (8¼in): 22cm (8½in): 23cm (9in)] from pick-up row, ending after a WS row.

Fold hood in half with RS together and join top seam by working a row of dc across top of last row of patt, working each st through both layers.

Fasten off.

Join sleeve seams below markers. Insert sleeves into armholes, matching sleeve markers to centre of sts missed at underarm and centre of last row of sleeve to shoulder seam.

This basketweave effect is simple to create. Choose your buttons carefully to match the yarn.

● *Edging*

With RS facing and 4.00mm (G6) hook, rejoin yarn to foundation ch edge of body, 1 ch (does NOT count as st), work 1 round of dc evenly around entire hem, front opening and hood edges, working 3 dc into each hem corner point and ending with ss to first dc, do NOT turn.

Now work 1 round of crab st (dc worked from left to right, instead of right to left), ending with ss to first dc.

Fasten off.

Work edging around lower edges of sleeves in same way, rejoining yarn at base of sleeve seams.

Work edging across top of pocket openings in same way.

Sew pocket linings in place on inside. Attach buttons 6 sts in from front opening edge (left front for a girl, or right front for a boy), placing lowest button 20cm (7¾in) up from lower edge, top button 10cm (4in) below hood pick-up row, and rem 2 buttons evenly spaced between. Fasten coat by pushing buttons through fabric along other front opening edge.

Corsage

A corsage is a lovely accessory easily created in crochet fabric. This corsage has been made in realistic colours, with a scarlet-red yarn for a rose-like flower, but you could make it in more fanciful colours to coordinate it with a favourite outfit.

PROJECT NOTES

MEASUREMENTS
Actual size, across flower:
9cm (3½in)

YARN
A 1 x 25g (⅞oz) ball of 4ply super kid mohair and silk yarn in leaf green

B 1 x 25g (⅞oz) ball of 4ply super kid mohair, silk, polyester and nylon yarn in scarlet

HOOK
2.50mm (C2) crochet hook

NOTIONS
Brooch back
TENSION
One completed leaf measures 5cm (2in) long and 2.5cm (1in) wide, at widest point, on 2.50mm (C2) hook, or the size required to achieve stated tension.

THE PATTERN

LEAVES (make 3)
With 2.50mm (C2) hook and A, make 13 ch.
Round 1 (RS) 1 dc into 2nd ch from hook, *1 htr into next ch, 1 tr into next ch, 1 dtr into each of next 6 ch, 1 tr into next ch, 1 htr into next ch*, 4 dc into last ch, working back along other side of foundation ch, rep from * to * once more, 1 dc into next ch (this is same ch as used for first dc).
Fasten off.

FLOWER
● *Petal strip*
With 2.50mm (C2) hook and B, make 87 ch.
Row 1 (RS) 1 dc into 2nd ch from hook, 1 dc into each ch to end, turn. 86 sts.
Row 2 1 ch (does NOT count as st), 1 dc into each dc to end, turn.

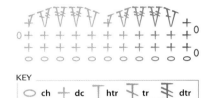

KEY

◯ ch	✛ dc	⊤ htr	Ŧ tr	₮ dtr

Row 3 1 ch (does NOT count as st), 1 dc into first dc, *(1 htr and 1 tr) into next dc, 2 dtr into each of next 2 dc, (1 dtr and 1 tr) into next dc, (1 htr and 1 dc) into next dc, rep from * to end, turn. 171 sts, 17 petals.
Row 4 1 ch (does NOT count as st), miss dc at base of 1 ch, *1 dc into next st, 2 tr into each of next 7 sts, 1 dc into next st, 1 ss into next st, rep from * to end.
Fasten off.

● *Flower centre*
With 2.50mm (C2) hook and B, make 2 ch.
Round 1 5 dc into 2nd ch from hook, ss to first dc.
Now join foundation ch edge of petal strip to flower centre as follows:
1 ch (does NOT count as st), 1 dc into first dc of next round of flower centre inserting hook through first foundation ch of petal strip at same time (to attach petal strip to flower centre), 1 dc into same dc of flower centre inserting hook through next foundation ch of petal strip at same time, *1 dc into next dc of flower centre inserting hook through next foundation ch of petal strip at same time, 1 dc into same dc of flower centre inserting hook through next foundation ch of petal strip at same time, rep from * 41 times more, working around sts of flower centre in a spiral, ss to next dc of flower centre.
Fasten off.

MAKING UP
Do NOT press. Using photograph as a guide, attach leaves to back of flower.
Attach brooch back to back of flower centre.

Glorious glamour scarves

These elegant, feminine scarves demonstrate how one stitch can be transformed depending on the yarn that is used. The stitch texture stands out clearly in the glossy silk yarn and the cashmere-mix, but looks more sturdy and robust in the tweed yarn, while the mohair yarn gives the stitch a wispy, gauzy effect.

PROJECT NOTES

MEASUREMENTS
Actual size 19 x 180cm (7½ x 70¾in)

YARN
CLASSIC VERSION:
4 x 50g (1¾oz) balls of DK-weight merino, microfibre and cashmere mix yarn in lilac

EVENING VERSION:
2 x 25g (⅞oz) balls of 4ply kid mohair yarn in heather
SILK VERSION:
4 x 50g (1¾oz) balls of DK-weight silk yarn in lilac
TWEEDY VERSION:
3 x 50g (1¾oz) balls of DK-weight merino, alpaca, and viscose mix yarn in purple

HOOK
3.50mm (E4) hook

TENSION
19 sts and 13 rows to 10cm (4in) measured over pattern on 3.50mm (E4) hook, or the size required to achieve stated tension.

THE PATTERN

SCARF

With 3.50mm (E4) hook, make 41 ch.
Foundation row (WS) (1 tr, 2 ch and 1 tr) into 8th ch from hook, *3 ch, miss 4 ch, (1 tr, 2 ch and 1 tr) into next ch, rep from * to last 3 ch, 2 ch, miss 2 ch, 1 tr into last ch, turn.
Cont in patt as follows:
Row 1 4 ch (counts as first dtr), miss (tr at base of 4 ch, 2 ch and next tr), *5 dtr into next ch sp**, miss (1 tr, 3 ch and 1 tr), rep from * to end, ending last rep at **, miss (1 tr and 2 ch), 1 dtr into next ch, turn. 37 sts, 7 patt reps.
Row 2 5 ch (counts as first tr and 2 ch), miss last 3 dtr of previous row, *(1 tr, 2 ch and 1

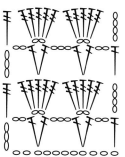

KEY
- ○ ch
- 十 tr
- ╪ dtr

tr) into next dtr**, 3 ch, miss 4 dtr, rep from * to end, ending last rep at **, 2 ch, miss 2 dtr, 1 tr into top of 4 ch at beg of previous row, turn.
These 2 rows form patt.

Cont in patt until scarf measures 180cm (70¾in), ending after a 2nd patt row.
Fasten off.

MAKING UP

Press carefully, following the instructions on the ball band.

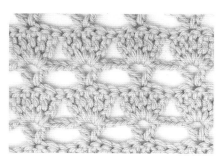

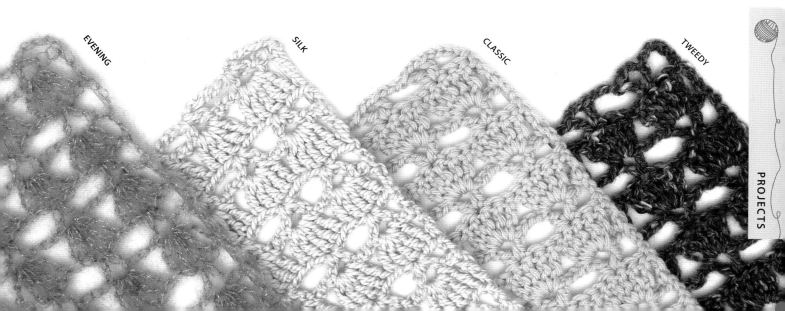

EVENING   SILK   CLASSIC   TWEEDY

Peruvian-style bag

This stunning bag, which was inspired by traditional Peruvian designs, is worked in simple double crochet, but derives its impact from the strong geometric design and the bold colour changes. See page 197 for more information on working from a chart.

PROJECT NOTES

MEASUREMENTS
Width at widest point 26cm (10¼in)
Depth to opening edge 27cm (10¼in)

YARN
All DK 100% mercerized cotton
A 2 x 50g (1¾oz) balls in dark brown
B 1 x 50g (1¾oz) ball in soft orange
C 1 x 50g (1¾oz) ball in olive

D 1 x 50g (1¾oz) ball in rose
E 2 x 50g (1¾oz) balls in dark purple

HOOK
4.00mm (G6) hook

NOTIONS
Piece of lining fabric 70 x 75cm (27½ x 29½in)

TENSION
20 sts and 20 rows to 10cm (4in) measured over pattern on 4.00mm (G6) hook, or the size required to achieve stated tension.

THE PATTERN

BAG

With 4.00mm (G6) hook and A, make 30 ch.
Changing yarns as required, cont as follows:

Round 1 (RS) Using B, 2 dc into 2nd ch from hook, 1 dc into next ch, (using A 1 dc into each of next 2 ch, using B 1 dc into each of next 2 ch) twice, (using A 1 dc into each of next 2 ch, using C 1 dc into each of next 2 ch) 4 times, using A 1 dc into each of next 2 ch, using B 4 dc into last ch, now working back along other side of foundation ch: using A 1 dc into each of next 2 ch, (using C 1 dc into each of next 2 ch, using A 1 dc into each of next 2 ch) 4 times, (using B 1 dc into each of next 2 ch, using A 1 dc into each of next 2 ch) twice, using B 1 dc into next ch, 2 dc into next ch (this is same ch as used for 2 dc at beg of round), ss to first dc, turn. 62 sts.

This round sets position of chart: on all rounds read chart from right to left for first half of

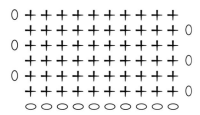

KEY
⟨O⟩ ch
+ dc

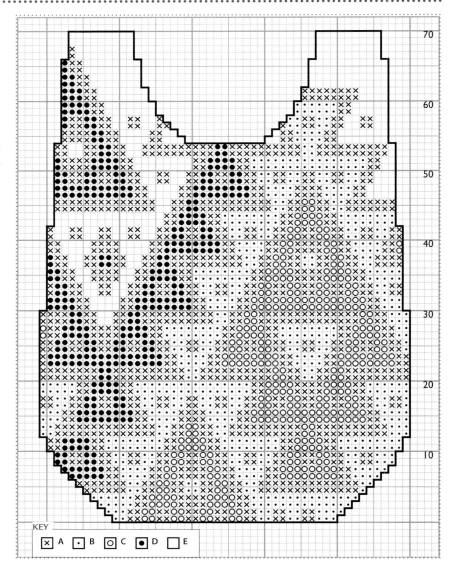

KEY
⊠ A   ⊡ B   ⊙ C   ⊛ D   ☐ E

sts, then read chart from left to right for second half of sts (to reverse design on other side of bag).

Keeping chart correct as now set and remembering to turn at end of each round, shape bag as follows:

Round 2 1 ch (does NOT count as st), 2 dc into first dc, 1 dc into each of next 29 dc, 2 dc into each of next 2 dc, 1 dc into each of next 29 dc, 2 dc into last dc, ss to first dc, turn. 66 sts.

Round 3 1 ch (does NOT count as st), 2 dc into first dc, 1 dc into each of next 31 dc, 2 dc into each of next 2 dc, 1 dc into each of next 31 dc, 2 dc into last dc, ss to first dc, turn. 70 sts.

Round 4 1 ch (does NOT count as st), 2 dc into first dc, 1 dc into each of next 33 dc, 2 dc into each of next 2 dc, 1 dc into each of next 33 dc, 2 dc into last dc, ss to first dc, turn. 74 sts.

Round 5 1 ch (does NOT count as st), 2 dc into first dc, 1 dc into each of next 35 dc, 2 dc into each of next 2 dc, 1 dc into each of next 35 dc, 2 dc into last dc, ss to first dc, turn. 78 sts.

Round 6 1 ch (does NOT count as st), 2 dc into first dc, 1 dc into each of next 37 dc, 2 dc into each of next 2 dc, 1 dc into each of next 37 dc, 2 dc into last dc, ss to first dc, turn. 82 sts.

Round 7 1 ch (does NOT count as st), 2 dc into first dc, 1 dc into each of next 39 dc, 2 dc into each of next 2 dc, 1 dc into each of next 39 dc, 2 dc into last dc, ss to first dc, turn. 86 sts.

Round 8 1 ch (does NOT count as st), 2 dc into first dc, 1 dc into each of next 41 dc, 2 dc into each of next 2 dc, 1 dc into each of next 41 dc, 2 dc into last dc, ss to first dc, turn. 90 sts.

Round 9 1 ch (does NOT count as st), 2 dc into first dc, 1 dc into each of next 43 dc, 2 dc into each of next 2 dc, 1 dc into each of next 43 dc, 2 dc into last dc, ss to first dc, turn. 94 sts.

The dark brown areas serve to make the vivid colours and bold shapes stand out even more.

Round 10 1 ch (does NOT count as st), 1 dc into each dc to end, ss to first dc, turn.

Round 11 1 ch (does NOT count as st), 2 dc into first dc, 1 dc into each of next 45 dc, 2 dc into each of next 2 dc, 1 dc into each of next 45 dc, 2 dc into last dc, ss to first dc, turn. 98 sts.

Round 12 As round 10.

Round 13 1 ch (does NOT count as st), 2 dc into first dc, 1 dc into each of next 47 dc, 2 dc into each of next 2 dc, 1 dc into each of next 47 dc, 2 dc into last dc, ss to first dc, turn. 102 sts.

Rounds 14 to 30 As round 10.

Round 31 1 ch (does NOT count as st), dc2tog over first 2 dc, 1 dc into each of next 47 dc, (dc2tog over next 2 dc) twice, 1 dc into each of next 47 dc, dc2tog over last 2 dc, ss to first dc, turn. 98 sts.

Rounds 32 to 42 As round 10.

Round 43 1 ch (does NOT count as st), dc2tog over first 2 dc, 1 dc into each of next 45 dc, (dc2tog over next 2 dc) twice, 1 dc into each of next 45 dc, dc2tog over last 2 dc, ss to first dc, turn. 94 sts.

Rounds 44 to 46 As round 10.

● *Divide for sides*

Now working in rows, not rounds, divide for each side of bag as follows:

Row 47 (RS) 1 ch (does NOT count as st), 1 dc into each of next 47 dc and turn, leaving rem sts unworked.

Keeping chart correct as now set (by now reading WS rows in opposite direction to RS rows), work on this set of 47 sts only for first side of bag.

***Row 48** 1 ch (does NOT count as st), 1 dc into each dc to end, turn.

Rows 49 to 54 As row 48.

● *Divide for straps*

Row 55 (RS) 1 ch (does NOT count as st), dc2tog over first 2 dc, 1 dc into each of next 15 dc, dc2tog over next 2 dc and turn, leaving rem sts unworked. 17 sts.

**Row 56 1 ch (does NOT count as st), dc2tog over first 2 dc, 1 dc into each dc to end, turn. 16 sts.

Row 57 1 ch (does NOT count as st), 1 dc into each dc to last 2 sts, dc2tog over last 2 sts, turn. 15 sts.

Rows 58 and 59 As rows 56 and 57. 13 sts.

Row 60 As row 48.

Row 61 As row 57. 12 sts.

Row 62 As row 48.

Row 63 As row 57. 11 sts.

Rows 64 to 66 As row 48.

Row 67 1 ch (does NOT count as st), dc2tog over first 2 dc, 1 dc into each dc to last 2 sts, dc2tog over last 2 sts, turn. 9 sts.

Rows 68 to 70 As row 48.

This completes all 70 rows of chart.

Break off all contrasts and cont using E only.

Rep row 48 until strap measures 45cm (17¾in) from last complete round worked.**

Fasten off.

Return to last complete row worked before shaping first strap, miss next 9 dc, rejoin yarn to next dc, 1 ch (does NOT count as st), dc2tog over dc where yarn was rejoined and next dc, 1 dc into each dc to last 2 dc, dc2tog over last 2 dc, turn. 17 sts.

Complete second strap by working as given for first strap from ** to **.

Join ends of straps by holding them with RS together and working 1 row of dc through sts of last row of both sets of sts.

Fasten off.***

Return to last complete round worked before shaping first side, rejoin yarn to next dc, 1 ch (does NOT count as st), 1 dc into each of next 47 dc, turn.

Keeping chart correct as now set (by now reading WS rows in opposite direction to RS rows), work on this set of 47 sts only for second side of bag.

Work as given for first side of bag from *** to ***.

MAKING UP

Press carefully following the instructions on the ball band.

● *Edging*

With RS facing, using 4.00mm (G6) hook and E, attach yarn to one strap seam, 1 ch (does NOT count as st), work 1 round of dc evenly around opening edge, ending with ss to first dc.

Fasten off.

Work edging around all other strap and opening edges in same way.

Cut 2 pieces of lining fabric same size as crochet piece, adding seam allowance along all edges. Join seams to form same shape as crochet bag. Slip lining inside bag, fold under raw edges and slip stitch folded edge of lining in place around strap and opening edges.

Solomon's knot wrap

This beautiful, airy wrap is a truly special garment that is constructed in a pure silk yarn and a subtle, classy colour that will complement all the outfits in your wardrobe. See page 192 for more information on making Solomon's knots.

See page 192 for more information on making Solomon's knots.

PROJECT NOTES

MEASUREMENTS
Actual size 77 x 183cm (30¼ x 72in)

YARN
4 x 50g (1¾oz) balls of DK-weight 100% silk yarn in peach

HOOK
4.00mm (G6) hook

SPECIAL ABBREVIATIONS
LSK longer Solomon's knot worked as follows: lengthen loop on hook to approx 3.5cm (1½in), yoh and draw loop through, 1 dc under back loop of ch.

SSK shorter Solomon's knot worked as follows: lengthen loop on hook to approx 2.5cm (1in), yoh and draw loop through, 1 dc under back loop of ch.

yoh yarn over hook

TENSION
3 patt reps to 12½cm (5in) and 6 rows to 14cm (5½in) measured over pattern on 4.00mm (G6) hook, or the size required to achieve stated tension.

THE PATTERN

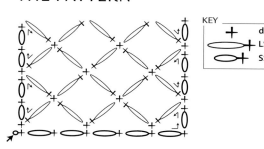

KEY

+ dc
⬯+ LSK
⬭+ SSK

WRAP
With 4.00mm (G6) hook, make 2 ch, 38 SSK, 1 LSK, turn.

Foundation row (RS) 1 dc into dc between 3rd and 4th set of loops, *2 LSK, miss 2 sets of loops, 1 dc into next dc, rep from * to end, working last dc into ch at beg of foundation ch, turn. 18½ patt reps.

Cont in patt as follows:

Row 1 2 SSK, 1 LSK, miss dc at end of previous row, 1 dc into next dc, *2 LSK, miss 2 sets of loops, 1 dc into next dc, rep from * to end, turn.

This row forms patt.

Cont in patt until wrap measures approx 183cm (72in).

Next row 2 SSK, miss dc at end of previous row, 1 dc into next dc, *2 SSK, miss 2 sets of loops, 1 dc into next dc, rep from * to end, turn.

Fasten off.

MAKING UP
Do NOT press.

Solomon's knots make a very open fabric.

Circles and stripes set

One of the things that makes crochet so versatile is that circular motifs can be combined with linear work. Combine this with colour changes, and you have the opportunity to create some stunning patterns. Here we use simple motifs and bold colour contrasts for a cosy hat-and-mitten set.

THE PATTERN

BASIC MOTIF

With 3.00mm (D3) hook and yarn A, make 2 ch.

Round 1 (RS) 7 dc into 2nd ch from hook, ss to first dc. 7 sts.

Round 2 3 ch (counts as first tr), 2 tr into dc at base of 3 ch, 3 tr into each dc to end, ss to top of 3 ch at beg of round. 21 sts.
Join in yarn B.

Round 3 Using B, 1 ch (does NOT count as st), *1 dc into each of next 2 sts, 2 dc into next st, rep from * 6 times, ss to first dc. 28 sts.
Break off B and cont using A only.

Round 4 4 ch (counts as first dtr), 1 tr into st at base of 4 ch, *1 htr into each of next 2 dc, 1 dc into next dc, 1 htr into each of next 2 dc, (1 tr and 1 dtr) into next dc**, (1 dtr and 1 tr) into next dc, rep from * to end, ending last rep at **, ss to top of 4 ch at beg of round. 36 sts.
Fasten off.

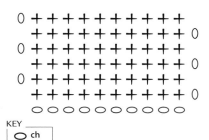

Basic motif is a square, with 9 sts along each side. Corner points fall between the 2 dtr. Using A, join motifs by holding them RS together and working a row of dc along sides to be joined, working each dc through sts of both motifs.

HAT

● Motif band

Make and join 9 basic motifs to form a loop.

● Main section

With RS facing, 3.00mm (D3) hook and A, attach yarn to one join between motifs around upper edge of motif band and cont as follows:

Round 1 (RS) 1 ch (does NOT count as st), *1 dc into motif joining seam, 1 dc into each of next 9 sts along side of motif, rep from * to end, ss to first dc, turn. 90 sts.

Round 2 Using A, 1 ch (does NOT count as st), 1 dc into each dc to end, ss to first dc, turn. Join in B.

Round 3 Using B, 1 ch (does NOT count as st), 1 dc into each dc to end, ss to first dc, turn.

Rounds 4 to 6 As round 2.

Round 7 As round 3.

Rounds 8 and 9 As round 2.

Round 10 Using A, 1 ch (does NOT count as st), *1 dc into each of next 8 dc, dc2tog over next 2 dc, rep from * to end, ss to first dc, turn. 81 sts.

Round 11 As round 3.

Rounds 12 and 13 As round 2.

Round 14 Using A, 1 ch (does NOT count as st), *1 dc into each of next 7 dc, dc2tog over next 2 dc, rep from * to end, ss to first dc, turn. 72 sts.

Round 15 As round 3.

Rounds 16 and 17 As round 2.

Round 18 Using A, 1 ch (does NOT count as st), *1 dc into each of next 6 dc, dc2tog over next 2 dc, rep from * to end, ss to first dc, turn. 63 sts.

Round 19 As round 3.

Round 20 As round 2.

Round 21 Using A, 1 ch (does NOT count as st), *dc2tog over next 2 dc, 1 dc into each of next 5 dc, rep from * to end, ss to first dc, turn. 54 sts.

Round 22 As round 2.

Round 23 Using B, 1 ch (does NOT count as st), *dc2tog over next 2 dc, 1 dc into each

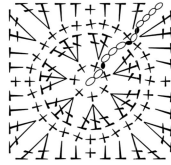

of next 4 dc, rep from * to end, ss to first dc, turn. 45 sts.

Break off B and cont using A only.

Round 24 As round 2.

Round 25 1 ch (does NOT count as st), *dc2tog over next 2 dc, 1 dc into each of next 3 dc, rep from * to end, ss to first dc, turn. 36 sts.

Round 26 1 ch (does NOT count as st), *1 dc into each of next 2 dc, dc2tog over next 2 dc, rep from * to end, ss to first dc, turn. 27 sts.

Round 27 1 ch (does NOT count as st), *dc2tog over next 2 dc, 1 dc into next dc, rep from * to end, ss to first dc, turn. 18 sts.

Round 28 1 ch (does NOT count as st), *dc2tog over next 2 dc, rep from * to end, ss to first dc, turn. 9 sts.

Round 29 1 ch (does NOT count as st), *dc2tog over next 2 dc, 1 dc into next dc, rep from * to end, do NOT turn. 6 sts.

Round 30 1 dc into each of next 6 dc, do NOT turn.

Rounds 31 to 34 As round 30.

Round 35 (dc2tog over next 2 dc) 3 times. 3 sts.

Fasten off.

● *Lower border*

With RS facing, 3.00mm (D3) hook and A, attach yarn to one join between motifs around lower edge of motif band and cont as follows:

Round 1 (RS) 1 ch (does NOT count as st), *1 dc into joining seam, 1 dc into each of next 9 sts along side of motif, rep from * to end, ss to first dc, turn. 90 sts.

Round 2 1 ch (does NOT count as st), 1 dc into each dc to end, ss to first dc, turn.

Rounds 3 to 5 As round 2 but do NOT turn at end of last round.

Now work 1 round of crab st (dc worked from left to right, instead of right to left) around entire lower edge of hat.

Fasten off.

MAKING UP

Press carefully following the instructions on the ball band.

RIGHT MITTEN

Using 3.00mm (D3) hook and A, make 38 ch and join with a ss to make a ring.

Round 1 (RS) 1 ch (does NOT count as st), 1 dc into each ch to end, ss to first dc, turn. 38 sts.

The thin gold stripes make a lively contrast.

Round 2 Using A, 1 ch (does NOT count as st), 1 dc into each dc to end, ss to first dc, turn.

Rounds 3 and 4 As round 2.

Join in B.

Round 5 Using B, 1 ch (does NOT count as st), 1 dc into each dc to end, ss to first dc, turn.

Rounds 6 to 8 As round 2.

Rounds 9 to 16 As rounds 5 to 8, twice.

Break off B and cont using A only.

● *Shape thumb gusset*

Round 17 1 ch (does NOT count as st), 1 dc into each of first 23 dc, 3 dc into next dc, 1 dc into each of last 14 dc, ss to first dc. 40 sts.

Break off yarn.

● *Shape motif opening*

With WS facing, miss first 35 dc of next round, attach yarn to next dc, 1 ch (does NOT count as st), 1 dc into dc at base of 1 ch, 1 dc into each of first 4 dc of last round, then 1 dc into each of last 25 dc of last round, turn. 30 sts.

Now working in rows, not rounds, cont as follows:

Row 19 1 ch (does NOT count as st), 1 dc into each dc to end, turn.

Row 20 1 ch (does NOT count as st), 1 dc into

each of first 19 dc, 2 dc into next dc, 1 dc into next dc, 2 dc into next dc, 1 dc into each of last 8 dc, turn. 32 sts.

Rows 21 and 22 As row 19.

Row 23 1 ch (does NOT count as st), 1 dc into each of first 8 dc, 2 dc into next dc, 1 dc into each of next 3 dc, 2 dc into next dc, 1 dc into each of last 19 dc, turn. 34 sts.

Rows 24 and 25 As row 19.

Row 26 1 ch (does NOT count as st), 1 dc into each of first 19 dc, 2 dc into next dc, 1 dc into each of next 5 dc, 2 dc into next dc, 1 dc into each of last 8 dc, turn. 36 sts.

Rows 27 and 28 As row 19.

Row 29 1 ch (does NOT count as st), 1 dc into each of first 8 dc, 2 dc into next dc, 1 dc into each of next 7 dc, 2 dc into next dc, 1 dc into each of last 19 dc, turn. 38 sts.

Row 30 As row 19.

Break yarn.

● *Shape thumb*

With RS facing, miss first 8 dc of next row, attach yarn to next dc, 1 ch (does NOT count as st), 1 dc into dc at base of 1 ch, 1 dc into each of next 9 dc, 2 dc into next dc, ss to first dc of this row, turn. 12 sts.

***Now working in rounds, not rows, cont as follows:

Next round 1 ch (does NOT count as st), 1 dc into each dc to end, ss to first dc, turn.

Rep last round 11 times more.

Next round 1 ch (does NOT count as st), (dc2tog over first 2 dc, 1 dc into next dc) 4 times, ss to first dc2tog, turn. 8 sts.

Work 1 round.

Next round 1 ch (does NOT count as st), (dc2tog over next 2 dc) 4 times, ss to first dc2tog. 4 sts.

Fasten off.

Run gathering thread around top of last round. Pull up tight and fasten off securely.***

● *Shape hand*

With RS facing, return to last row worked before shaping thumb, attach yarn to 5th dc at beg of last row, 1 ch (does NOT count as st), 1 dc into dc at base of 1 ch, 1 dc into each of first 4 dc of last row, 10 ch, 1 dc into each of last 8 dc of last row, 1 dc into base of thumb, 1 dc into each of next 14 dc, ss to first dc, turn. 38 sts.

****Next round** 1 ch (does NOT count as st),

1 dc into each dc and ch to end, ss to first dc, turn.

Next round 1 ch (does NOT count as st), 1 dc into each dc to end, ss to first dc, turn.

Rep last round 17 times more, ending after a WS round.

● *Shape top*

Next round (RS) 1 ch (does NOT count as st), dc2tog over first 2 dc, 1 dc into each of next 15 dc, (dc2tog over next 2 dc) twice, 1 dc into each of next 15 dc, dc2tog over last 2

dc, ss to first dc2tog, turn. 34 sts.
Work 1 round.

Next round 1 ch (does NOT count as st), dc2tog over first 2 dc, 1 dc into each of next 13 dc, (dc2tog over next 2 dc) twice, 1 dc into each of next 13 dc, dc2tog over last 2 dc, ss to first dc2tog, turn. 30 sts.
Work 1 round.

Next round 1 ch (does NOT count as st), dc2tog over first 2 dc, 1 dc into each of next 11 dc, (dc2tog over next 2 dc) twice, 1 dc into each of next 11 dc, dc2tog over last 2

dc, ss to first dc2tog, turn. 26 sts.

Next round 1 ch (does NOT count as st), dc2tog over first 2 sts, 1 dc into each of next 10 dc, (dc2tog over next 2 sts) twice, 1 dc into each of next 10 dc, dc2tog over last 2 sts, ss to first dc2tog, turn. 22 sts.

Next round 1 ch (does NOT count as st), dc2tog over first 2 sts, 1 dc into each of next 9 dc, (dc2tog over next 2 sts) twice, 1 dc into each of next 9 dc, dc2tog over last 2 sts, ss to first dc2tog, turn. 18 sts.

Next round 1 ch (does NOT count as st), dc2tog over first 2 sts, 1 dc into each of next 8 dc, (dc2tog over next 2 sts) twice, 1 dc into each of next 8 dc, dc2tog over last 2 sts, ss to first dc2tog, turn. 14 sts.

Fold mitten inside out, then fold flat. Join top seam by working a row of dc across top of last round, working each dc through sts of both layers to close top of mitten.

LEFT MITTEN

Work as given for right mitten to start of thumb gusset shaping.

● *Shape thumb gusset*

Round 17 1 ch (does NOT count as st), 1 dc into each of first 14 dc, 3 dc into next dc, 1 dc into each of last 23 dc, ss to first dc. 40 sts.
Break off yarn.

● *Shape motif opening*

With WS facing, miss first 15 dc of next round, attach yarn to next dc, 1 ch (does NOT count as st), 1 dc into dc at base of 1 ch, 1 dc into each of first 24 dc of last round, then 1 dc into each of last 5 dc of last round, turn. 30 sts.

Now working in rows, not rounds, cont as follows:

Row 19 1 ch (does NOT count as st), 1 dc into each dc to end, turn.

Row 20 1 ch (does NOT count as st), 1 dc into each of first 8 dc, 2 dc into next dc, 1 dc into next dc, 2 dc into next dc, 1 dc into each of last 19 dc, turn. 32 sts.

Rows 21 and 22 As row 19.

Row 23 1 ch (does NOT count as st), 1 dc into

The double crochet fabric is dense and sturdy, making the hat and mittens cosy and warm.

each of first 19 dc, 2 dc into next dc, 1 dc into each of next 3 dc, 2 dc into next dc, 1 dc into each of last 8 dc, turn. 34 sts.

Rows 24 and 25 As row 19.

Row 26 1 ch (does NOT count as st), 1 dc into each of first 8 dc, 2 dc into next dc, 1 dc into each of next 5 dc, 2 dc into next dc, 1 dc into each of last 19 dc, turn. 36 sts.

Rows 27 and 28 As row 19.

Row 29 1 ch (does NOT count as st), 1 dc into each of first 19 dc, 2 dc into next dc, 1 dc into each of next 7 dc, 2 dc into next dc, 1 dc into each of last 8 dc, turn. 38 sts.

Row 30 As row 19.

Break yarn.

● *Shape thumb*

With RS facing, miss first 19 dc of next row, attach yarn to next dc, 1 ch (does NOT count as st), 1 dc into dc at base of 1 ch, 1 dc into each of next 9 dc, 2 dc into next dc, ss to first dc of this row, turn. 12 sts.

Work as given for thumb of right mitten from *** to ***.

● *Shape hand*

With RS facing, return to last row worked before shaping thumb, attach yarn to 6th dc from end of last row, 1 ch (does NOT count as st), 1 dc into dc at base of 1 ch, 1 dc into each of next 13 dc of last row, 1 dc into base of thumb, 1 dc into each of first 8 dc of last row, 10 ch, 1 dc into each of last 5 dc of last row, ss to first dc, turn. 38 sts.

Complete as given for right mitten from ****.

MAKING UP

Press carefully, following instructions on ball band.

MOTIF

Make one basic motif for each mitten and sew into 'hole' on back of hand.

LOWER EDGING

With RS facing, attach yarn at base of mitten and work 1 round of crab st (dc worked from left to right, instead of right to left) around foundation ch edge, ending with ss to first dc.

Fasten off.

Seaside and shells set

This accessories set of matching hat, belt and bag is made in a mercerized cotton yarn, which, despite the light weight of the yarn and its fineness, is surprisingly hard-wearing. The shade of this yarn is reminiscent of the colour of the ocean, so the fronds of the belt and the straps of the bag were trimmed with shells to continue the seaside theme. You could change the colour theme – lilacs or purples would work well – and use pretty beads to trim the work.

PROJECT NOTES

MEASUREMENTS
BELT: Actual size, excluding fringe: 12 x 163cm (4¾ x 64in)
HAT: Width around head 39cm (15¼in)
BAG: Actual size 24 x 27cm (9½ x 10½in)

YARN
4ply 100% mercerized cotton in ocean blue: 4 x 50g (1¾oz) balls for belt, 2 x 50g (1¾oz) balls for hat, and 3 x 50g (1¾oz) balls for bag

HOOK
2.50mm (C2) hook

NOTIONS
14 beads for belt, 4 for bag

SPECIAL ABBREVIATIONS
beaded ch slide bead up so that it sits on RS of work next to st just worked, yoh and draw loop through leaving bead caught in st.
tr2tog *yoh and insert hook as indicated, yoh and draw loop through, yoh and draw through 2 loops, rep from * once more, yoh and draw through all 3 loops on hook.
yoh yarn over hook.

TENSION
28 sts and 12 rows to 10cm (4in) measured over pattern on 2.50mm (C2) hook, or the size required to achieve stated tension.

THE PATTERN

BELT

With 2.50mm (C2) hook, make 34 ch.

Foundation row (RS) 1 tr into 4th ch from hook, 1 tr into each ch to end, turn. 32 sts.

Next row 3 ch (counts as 1 tr), miss st at base of 3 ch, 1 tr into each tr to end, working last tr into top of 3 ch at beg of previous row, turn.

Rep last row once more.

Cont in patt as follows:

Row 1 (WS) 3 ch (counts as 1 tr), miss st at base of 3 ch, 1 tr into each of next 5 tr, (2 ch, miss 2 tr, 1 tr into next tr) 3 times, 1 tr into each of next 3 tr, (2 ch, miss 2 tr, 1 tr into next tr) 3 times, 1 tr into each of last 5 sts, working last tr into top of 3 ch at beg of previous row, turn.

Row 2 3 ch (counts as 1 tr), miss st at base of

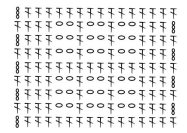

KEY

O ch   T tr

3 ch, 1 tr into each of next 5 tr, (2 ch, miss 2 ch, 1 tr into next tr) 3 times, 1 tr into each of next 3 tr, (2 ch, miss 2 ch, 1 tr into next tr) 3 times, 1 tr into each of last 5 sts, working last tr into top of 3 ch at beg of previous row, turn.

Row 3 As row 2.

Row 4 3 ch (counts as 1 tr), miss st at base of 3 ch, 1 tr into each of next 5 tr, (2 tr into

next ch sp, 1 tr into next tr) 3 times, 1 tr into each of next 3 tr, (2 tr into next ch sp, 1 tr into next tr) 3 times, 1 tr into each of last 5 sts, working last tr into top of 3 ch at beg of previous row, turn.

Rows 5 to 8 As rows 1 to 4.

Row 9 3 ch (counts as 1 tr), miss st at base of 3 ch, 1 tr into each tr to end, working last tr into top of 3 ch at beg of previous row, turn.

Row 10 As row 9.

These 10 rows form patt.

Cont in patt until belt measures 162cm (63¾in), ending after 10th patt row.

Fasten off.

MAKING UP
● *Edging*

Thread 14 beads onto yarn.

With RS facing, rejoin yarn at one end of foundation ch edge and work one row of crab st (dc worked from left to right, instead of right to left) up entire row-end edge to top of last row, turn, work across 32 sts of last row as follows: *1 dc into first dc, 45 ch, 1 beaded ch, miss beaded ch, 1 dc into each of next 45 ch, 1 dc into each of next 5 dc of last row, 42 ch, 1 beaded ch, miss beaded ch, 1 dc into each of next 42 ch, 1 dc into each of next 5 dc of last row, 39 ch, 1 beaded ch, miss beaded ch, 1 dc into each of next 39 ch, 1 dc into each of next 5 dc of last row, 50 ch, 1 beaded ch, miss beaded ch, 1 dc into each of next 50 ch, 1 dc into each of next 5 dc of last row, 44 ch, 1 beaded ch, miss beaded ch, 1 dc into each of next 44 ch, 1 dc into each of next 5 dc of last row, 36 ch, 1 beaded ch, miss beaded ch, 1 dc into each of next 36 ch, 1 dc into each of next 5 dc of last row, 48 ch, 1 beaded ch, miss beaded ch, 1 dc into each of next 48 ch, 1 dc into last dc of last row*, turn, work one row of crab st (dc worked from left to right, instead of right to left) down entire row-end edge to foundation ch edge, turn, work across foundation ch edge as for top of last row by working from * to *, ss to first dc.

Fasten off.

Press carefully following instructions on ball band.

All three pieces in this set are constructed from a treble and mesh stitch combination.

HAT

With 2.50mm (C2) hook, make 108 ch loosely and join with a ss to form a ring. (Check now that ch will stretch to fit on head.)

Round 1 (RS) 3 ch (counts as first tr), miss st at base of 3 ch, 1 tr into each ch to end, ss to top of 3 ch at beg of round, turn. 108 sts.

Round 2 3 ch (counts as 1 tr), miss st at base of 3 ch, 1 tr into each tr to end, ss to top of 3 ch at beg of round, turn.

Round 3 As round 2.

Round 4 5 ch (counts as 1 tr and 2 ch), miss st at base of 3 ch and next 2 tr, *1 tr into each of next 4 tr**, (2 ch, miss 2 tr, 1 tr into next tr) twice, 2 ch, miss 2 tr, rep from * to end, ending last rep at **, 2 ch, miss 2 tr, 1 tr into next tr, 2 ch, miss 2 tr, ss to 3rd of 5 ch at beg of round, turn.

Round 5 5 ch (counts as 1 tr and 2 ch), miss st at base of 3 ch and next 2 ch, 1 tr into next tr, *2 ch, miss 2 ch, 1 tr into each of next 4 tr**, (2 ch, miss 2 ch, 1 tr into next tr) twice, rep from * to end, ending last rep at **, 2 ch, miss 2 ch, ss to 3rd of 5 ch at beg of round, turn.

Round 6 5 ch (counts as 1 tr and 2 ch), miss st at base of 3 ch and next 2 ch, *1 tr into each of next 4 tr**, (2 ch, miss 2 ch, 1 tr into next tr) twice, 2 ch, miss 2 ch, rep from * to end, ending last rep at **, 2 ch, miss 2 ch, 1 tr into next tr, 2 ch, miss 2 ch, ss to 3rd of 5 ch at beg of round, turn.

Round 7 3 ch (counts as 1 tr), miss st at base of 3 ch, 2 tr into next ch sp, 1 tr into next tr, *2 tr into next ch sp, 1 tr into each of next 4 tr**, (2 tr into next ch sp, 1 tr into next tr) twice, rep from * to end, ending last rep at **, 2 tr into next ch sp, ss to top of 3 ch at beg of round, turn.

Rounds 8 to 11 As rounds 4 to 7.

Rounds 12 and 13 As round 2.

Round 14 3 ch (counts as 1 tr), miss st at base of 3 ch, 1 tr into each of next 6 tr, *tr2tog over next 2 tr**, 1 tr into each of next 7 tr, rep from * to end, ending last rep at **, ss to top of 3 ch at beg of round, turn. 96 sts.

Round 15 As round 2.

Round 16 3 ch (counts as 1 tr), miss st at base of 3 ch, 1 tr into each of next 5 tr, *tr2tog over next 2 tr**, 1 tr into each of next 6 tr, rep from * to end, ending last rep at **, ss to top of 3 ch at beg of round, turn. 84 sts.

Round 17 As round 2.

Round 18 3 ch (counts as 1 tr), miss st at base of 3 ch, 1 tr into each of next 4 tr, *tr2tog over next 2 tr**, 1 tr into each of next 5 tr, rep from * to end, ending last rep at **, ss to top of 3 ch at beg of round, turn. 72 sts.

Round 19 As round 2.

Round 20 3 ch (counts as 1 tr), miss st at base of 3 ch, 1 tr into each of next 3 tr, *tr2tog over next 2 tr**, 1 tr into each of next 4 tr, rep from * to end, ending last rep at **, ss to top of 3 ch at beg of round, turn. 60 sts.

Round 21 As round 2.

Round 22 3 ch (counts as 1 tr), miss st at base of 3 ch, 1 tr into each of next 2 tr, *tr2tog over next 2 tr**, 1 tr into each of next 3 tr, rep from * to end, ending last rep at **, ss to top of 3 ch at beg of round, turn. 48 sts.

Round 23 3 ch (counts as 1 tr), miss st at base of 3 ch, 1 tr into next tr, *tr2tog over next 2 tr**, 1 tr into each of next 2 tr, rep from * to end, ending last rep at **, ss to top of 3 ch at beg of round, turn. 36 sts.

Round 24 3 ch (counts as 1 tr), miss st at base of 3 ch, *tr2tog over next 2 tr**, 1 tr into next tr, rep from * to end, ending last rep at **, ss to top of 3 ch at beg of round, turn. 24 sts.

Round 25 3 ch (does NOT count as st), miss st at base of 3 ch, 1 tr into next tr, (tr2tog over next 2 tr) 11 times, ss to tr at beg of round, turn. 12 sts.

Round 26 1 ch (does NOT count as st), (dc2tog over next 2 tr) 6 times, ss to dc2tog at beg of round, turn. 6 sts.

Round 27 1 ch (does NOT count as st), (dc2tog over next 2 sts) twice, ss to dc2tog at beg of round. 3 sts.

Fasten off.

MAKING UP

● Edging

With RS facing, rejoin yarn to foundation ch edge and work 1 round of crab st (dc worked from left to right, instead of right to left) around entire foundation ch edge, ending with ss to first dc.

Fasten off.

Press following instructions on ball band.

BAG

With 2.50mm (C2) hook, make 132 ch and join with a ss to form a ring.

Round 1 (RS) 3 ch (counts as first tr), miss st at base of 3 ch, 1 tr into each ch to end, ss to top of 3 ch at beg of round, turn. 132 sts.

Round 2 3 ch (counts as 1 tr), miss st at base of 3 ch, 1 tr into each tr to end, ss to top of 3 ch at beg of round, turn.

Round 3 3 ch (counts as 1 tr), miss st at base of 3 ch, 1 tr into next tr, *2 ch, miss 2 tr**, 1 tr into each of next 2 tr, rep from * to end, ending last rep at **, ss to top of 3 ch at beg of round, turn.

Round 4 3 ch (counts as 1 tr), miss st at base of 3 ch, 1 tr into each tr and 2 tr into each ch sp to end, ss to top of 3 ch at beg of round, turn.

Rounds 5 to 7 As round 2.

Now work rounds 4 to 11 as given for hat.

Round 16 As round 2.

Rep last round until bag measures 27cm (10½in).

Fasten off.

MAKING UP

● Edging

With RS facing, rejoin yarn to foundation ch edge and work 1 round of crab st (dc worked from left to right, instead of right to left) around entire foundation ch edge, ending with ss to first dc.

Fasten off.

Fold bag flat and join top of last row to form base seam, ensuring patt is evenly placed across bag.

● Ties (make 2)

Thread a bead onto yarn.

With 2.50mm (C2) hook, make a ch 130cm (51in) long, 1 beaded ch, miss beaded ch, 1 dc into each ch to end.

Cut yarn leaving a long end and slip working loop onto a safety pin.

Starting at one fold of bag, thread tie through holes of round 3, ending at same folded edge.

Slip working loop back onto hook and thread a bead onto yarn, 1 beaded ch, ss to first ch.

Fasten off.

Knot ends of tie and attach knot to base corner of bag.

Make a second tie in the same way, threading tie through 3rd round from other folded edge.

Press following the instructions on the ball band.

Tartan-style set

Creating a tartan-style effect is surprisingly simple in crochet; this bag and scarf are created from a mesh crochet fabric with lengths of chain woven through it (see pages 234–235 for more information). The three strongly contrasting colours create a bold look, while the cashmere-mix yarn is lusciously soft but robust.

PROJECT NOTES

MEASUREMENTS
SCARF:
Actual size, excluding fringe 19 x 137cm (7½ x 54in)
BAG:
Actual size 28 x 28cm (11 x 11in)

YARN
All aran-weight merino, microfibre and cashmere mix yarn
MC 6 x 50g (1¾oz) balls in grey
A 2 x 50g (1¾oz) balls in red
B 2 x 50g (1¾oz) balls in green

HOOK
4.50mm (7) crochet hook

NOTIONS
FOR BAG:
48cm of 38mm-wide (19in of 1½in-wide) petersham ribbon
Piece of firm card approx 13 x 35cm (5 x 13¾in)

SPECIAL ABBREVIATIONS
dc2tog (insert hook as indicated, yarn over hook and draw loop through)

twice, yarn over hook and draw through all 3 loops.

TENSION
14½ sts and 16 rows to 10cm (4in) measured over double crochet fabric, 17 sts and 7 rows to 10cm (4in) measured over mesh fabric, both on 4.50mm (7) hook, or the size required to achieve stated tension.

THE PATTERN

SCARF

With 4.50mm (7) hook and MC, make 36 ch.
Foundation row (RS) 1 tr into 6th ch from hook, *1 ch, miss 1 ch, 1 tr into next ch, rep from * to end, turn. 33 sts, 16 ch sps.

Cont in patt as follows:
Row 1 (WS) 4 ch (counts as 1 tr and 1 ch), miss tr at base of 4 ch and next ch, 1 tr into next tr, *1 ch, miss 1 ch, 1 tr into next tr, rep from * to end, working last tr at end of last rep into 3rd of 4 ch at beg of previous row, turn.
This row forms mesh fabric.
Rep last row 3 times more.
Joining in and breaking off colours as required, cont in mesh fabric in stripes as follows:
Using B, work 2 rows.
Using MC, work 3 rows.
Using A, work 4 rows.
Using MC, work 3 rows.
Using B, work 2 rows.
Using MC, work 10 rows.
Rep last 24 rows twice more, then first 19 of these rows again, ending after 5 rows using MC. (96 rows worked in total.)
Fasten off.

MAKING UP
● **Weaving chains**
Using 4.50mm (7) hook and MC, attach yarn to foundation ch at base of one edge ch sp, make a ch approx 140cm (55in) long and fasten off.

KEY
○ ch ⊤ tr

Weave ch in and out of mesh fabric, taking ch over 1st row, under 2nd row, and so on.
Attach other end of ch to top of last row, adjusting length of ch as required so that fabric lays flat.
Using 4.50mm (7) hook and B, attach yarn to foundation ch at base of next ch sp, make a ch approx 140cm (55in) long and fasten off.
Weave ch in and out of mesh fabric, taking ch under 1st row, over 2nd row, and so on.
Attach other end of ch to top of last row.
Cont in this way, making and weaving chains in and out of mesh, making chains as follows: fill next ch sp with ch using B, next 3 ch sps with ch using MC, next 4 ch sps with ch using A, next 3 ch sps with ch using

MC, next 2 ch sps with ch using B, and last ch sp with ch using MC.

● **Fringe**

Cut 24 lengths of each of MC, A and B, each 26cm (10¼in) long. Using one strand of each colour, knot groups of 3 of these lengths across ends of scarf, positioning 12 knots evenly spaced across each end.

BAG

With 4.50mm (7) hook and MC, make 25 ch.

Round 1 (RS) 2 dc into 2nd ch from hook, 1 dc into each of next 22 ch, 4 dc into last ch, working back along other side of foundation ch: 1 dc into each of next 22 ch, 2 dc into last ch (this is same ch as used for 2 dc at beg of round, ss to first dc, turn. 52 sts.

Round 2 1 ch (does NOT count as st), 2 dc into each of first 2 dc, 1 dc into each of next 22 dc, 2 dc into each of next 4 dc, 1 dc into each of next 22 dc, 2 dc into each of last 2 dc, ss to first dc, turn. 60 sts.

Round 3 1 ch (does NOT count as st), 1 dc into each dc to end, ss to first dc, turn.

Round 4 1 ch (does NOT count as st), *(1 dc into next dc, 2 dc into next dc) twice, 1 dc into each of next 22 dc, (2 dc into next dc, 1 dc into next dc) twice, rep from * once more, ss to first dc, turn. 68 sts.

Round 5 1 ch (does NOT count as st), *1 dc into each of next 3 dc, 2 dc into next dc, 1 dc into each of next 26 dc, 2 dc into next dc, 1 dc into each of next 3 dc, rep from * once more, ss to first dc, turn. 72 sts.

Round 6 1 ch (does NOT count as st), *1 dc into each of next 2 dc, 2 dc into next dc, 1 dc into each of next 3 dc, 2 dc into next dc, 1 dc into each of next 22 dc, 2 dc into next dc, 1 dc into each of next 3 dc, 2 dc into next dc, 1 dc into each of next 2 dc, rep from * once more, ss to first dc, turn. 80 sts.

Round 7 As round 3.

Round 8 1 ch (does NOT count as st), *1 dc into each of next 4 dc, 2 dc into next dc, 1 dc into each of next 3 dc, 2 dc into next dc, 1 dc into each of next 22 dc, 2 dc into next dc, 1 dc into each of next 3 dc, 2 dc into next dc, 1 dc into each of next 4 dc, rep from * once more, ss to first dc, turn. 88 sts.

Round 9 1 ch (does NOT count as st), working into back loops only of sts of previous round: (1 dc into each of next 5 dc, 2 dc into next dc, 1 dc into each of next 5 dc) 8 times, ss to first dc, turn. 96 sts.

This completes base.

Trace outline of base onto firm card and set to one side.

● **Shape sides**

Now cont in mesh fabric for sides as follows:

Round 1 4 ch (counts as 1 tr and 1 ch), miss st at base of 4 ch and next st, *1 tr into next dc, 1 ch, miss 1 dc, rep from * to end, ss to 3rd of 4 ch at beg of round, turn. 48 ch sps.

Round 2 4 ch (counts as 1 tr and 1 ch), miss st at base of 4 ch and next ch, *1 tr into next tr, 1 ch, miss 1 dc, rep from * to end, ss to 3rd of 4 ch at beg of round, turn.

Last round forms mesh fabric.

Rep last row 3 times more.

Joining in and breaking off colours as required, cont in mesh fabric in stripes as follows:

Using B, work 2 rounds.

Using MC, work 3 rounds.

Using A, work 4 rounds.

Using MC, work 3 rounds.

Using B, work 2 rounds.

Using MC, work 2 rounds.

This completes mesh sides of bag.

● **Shape upper band**

Break off contrasts and cont using MC only.

Next round 1 ch (does NOT count as st), (1 dc into next st, dc2tog over next 2 sts) 32 times, ss to first dc, turn. 64 sts.

Next round 1 ch (does NOT count as st), 1 dc into each st to end, ss to first dc, turn.

Rep last round 12 times more.

Fasten off.

MAKING UP

● **Weaving chains**

Mark centre tr on one side of bag.

Using 4.50mm (7) hook and A, attach yarn to dc at base of one ch sp next to this centre tr, make a ch approx 26cm (10¼in) long and fasten off.

Weave ch in and out of mesh fabric, taking ch over 1st round, under 2nd round, and so on.

Attach other end of ch to top of last round of mesh (first round of top band), adjusting length of ch as required so that fabric stays flat.

Using 4.50mm (7) hook and A, attach yarn to dc at base of next ch sp (working away from centre marked tr), make a ch approx 26cm (10¼in) long and fasten off.

Weave ch in and out of mesh fabric, taking ch under 1st round, over 2nd round, and so on.

Attach other end of ch to top of last round of mesh (first round of top band), adjusting length of ch as required so that fabric stays flat.

Cont in this way, making and weaving chains in and out of mesh, working around bag and making chains as follows: fill next 3 ch sps with ch using MC, next 2 ch sps with ch using B, next 10 ch sps with ch using MC, next 2 ch sps with ch using B, next 3 ch sps with ch using MC, next 4 ch sps with ch using A, next 3 ch sps with ch using MC, next 2 ch sps with ch using B, next 10 ch sps with ch using MC, next 2 ch sps with ch using B, next 3 ch sps with ch using MC, and last ch sps with ch using A.

Join ends of petersham ribbon to form a loop of 44cm (17¼in). Fold top band in half to inside and slip stitch in place, enclosing loop of petersham ribbon inside.

● **Handle**

With 4.50mm (7) hook and MC, make 6 ch and join with a ss to form a ring.

Round 1 (RS) 1 ch (does NOT count as st), 1 dc into each dc to end. 6 sts.

Round 2 1 dc into each dc to end.

Rep last round until handle measures 48cm (18¾in), ending last round by working a ss into next dc.

Fasten off.

Using photograph as a guide, sew ends of handle to inside of top band.

Cut out base shape from firm card and slip inside bag.

Summer sky mesh top

This simple vest top, made from a crisp cotton yarn in a simple mesh stitch with an edging of double crochet around the neckline and shoulder straps, is the perfect garment for a gloriously sunny day. The vivid turquoise recalls the deep blue of a cloudless summer sky.

PROJECT NOTES

MEASUREMENTS

To fit bust: 81cm (32in) [86cm (34in): 91cm (36in): 97cm (38in): 102cm (40in): 107cm (42in)]

Actual size: 86cm (33¾in) [90cm (35½in): 96cm (37¾in): 100cm (39¼in): 106cm (41¾in): 110cm (43¼in)]

Full length: 52cm (20½in) [53cm (20¾in): 54cm (21¼in): 55cm (21½in): 56cm (22in): 57cm (22½in)]

YARN

4 [5: 5: 6: 6: 7] x 50g (1¾oz) of 4ply 100% mercerized cotton in turquoise

HOOK

2.50mm (C2) hook

SPECIAL ABBREVIATIONS

tr2tog *yoh and insert hook as indicated, yoh and draw loop through, yoh and draw through 2 loops, rep from * once more, yoh and draw through all 3 loops on hook.

yoh yarn over hook.

TENSION

28 sts and 12 rows to 10cm (4in) measured over pattern on 2.50mm (C2) hook, or the size required to achieve stated tension.

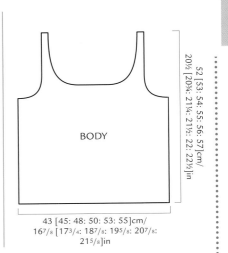

BODY

52 [53: 54: 55: 56: 57]cm/ 20½ [20¾: 21¼: 21½: 22: 22½]in

43 [45: 48: 50: 53: 55]cm/ 16⅞ [17¾: 18⅞: 19⅝: 20⅞: 21⅝]in

THE PATTERN

BODY

(Worked in one piece to armholes.)

With 2.50mm (C2) hook, make 240 [252: 268: 280: 296: 308] ch and join with a ss to form a ring.

Foundation round (RS) 4 ch (counts as first tr and 1 ch), miss first 2 ch, *1 tr into next ch, 1 ch, miss 1 ch, rep from * to end, ss to 3rd of 4th ch at beg of round, turn. 240 [252: 268: 280: 296: 308] sts.

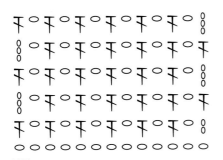

KEY

○ ch
￢ tr

Cont in patt as follows:

Round 1 (WS) 4 ch (counts as 1 tr and 1 ch), miss st at base of 4 ch and 1 ch, *1 tr into next tr, 1 ch, miss 1 ch, rep from * to end, ss to 3rd of 4th ch at beg of round, turn.

This round forms patt.

Cont in patt until body measures 31cm (12¼in) [32cm (12½in): 32cm (12½in): 33cm (13in): 33cm (13in): 34cm (13¼in)].

Fasten off.

● Divide for front and back (both alike)

Now working in rows, not rounds, cont as follows:

With appropriate side of work facing (by remembering to turn at end of last round), miss first 8 [8: 10: 10: 12: 12] sts of next round, rejoin yarn to next tr, 3 ch (does NOT count as st), miss tr at base of 3 ch and 1 ch, 1 tr into next tr, (1 ch, miss 1 ch, 1 tr into next tr) 49 [52: 54: 57: 59: 62] times, 1 ch, miss 1 ch, tr2tog over next 3 sts, working first 'leg' into next tr, missing 1 ch, and working 2nd 'leg' into next tr, turn.

Work on this set of 101 [107: 111: 117: 121: 127] sts only for first side.

***Next row** 3 ch (does NOT count as st), miss tr2tog at base of 3 ch and next ch, 1 tr into next tr (2 sts decreased), *1 ch, miss 1 ch, 1 tr into next tr, rep from * until tr has been worked into tr before last 2 ch sps, 1 ch, miss 1 ch, tr2tog over next 3 sts, working first 'leg' into next tr, missing 1 ch, and working 2nd 'leg' into next tr (2 sts decreased), turn (leaving 3 ch at beg of previous row unworked).

Working all decreases as set by last row, dec 2 sts at each end of next 4 rows. 81 [87: 91: 97: 101: 107] sts.

● Shape neck

Next row 3 ch (does NOT count as st), miss tr2tog at base of 3 ch and next ch, 1 tr into next tr (2 sts decreased), (1 ch, miss 1 ch, 1 tr into next tr) 9 [10: 11: 12: 13: 14] times, 1 ch, miss 1 ch, tr2tog over next 3 sts, working first 'leg' into next tr, missing 1 ch, and working 2nd 'leg' into next tr (2 sts decreased), turn, leaving rem sts unworked.

Work on this set of 21 [23: 25: 27: 29: 31] sts only for first shoulder strap.

**Working all decreases as set, dec 2 sts at neck edge of next 6 rows and at same time dec 2 sts at armhole edge of next 2 [3: 3: 4: 4: 5] rows. 5 [5: 7: 7: 9: 9] sts.

Note: When working a row-end edge without shaping, start rows with '4 ch (counts as first tr and 1 ch), miss st at base of 4 ch and next ch, 1 tr into next tr', and end rows with '1 ch, miss 1 ch, 1 tr into 3rd of 4 ch at beg of previous row, turn'.

Cont straight until armhole measures 20cm (7¾in) [20cm (7¾in): 21cm (8¼in): 21cm (8¼in) 22cm (8½in): 22cm (8½in)].

Fasten off.

With appropriate side of work facing, return to last complete row worked before shaping neck, miss next 31 [33: 33: 35: 35: 37] sts, rejoin yarn to next tr, 3 ch (does NOT count as st), miss tr at base of 3 ch and next ch, 1 tr into next tr (2 sts decreased), (1 ch, miss 1 ch, 1 tr into next tr) 9 [10: 11: 12: 13: 14] times, 1 ch, miss 1 ch, tr2tog over next 3 sts, working first 'leg' into next tr, missing 1 ch, and working 2nd 'leg' into next tr (2 sts decreased), turn, leaving rem sts unworked.

Work on this set of 21 [23: 25: 27: 29: 31] sts only for second shoulder strap by working as given for first shoulder strap from **.

With appropriate side of work facing, return to last complete round worked before dividing for front and back, miss next 15 [15: 19: 19: 23: 23] sts, rejoin yarn to next tr, 3 ch (does NOT count as st), miss tr at base of 3 ch and next ch, 1 tr into next tr, (1 ch, miss 1 ch, 1 tr into next tr) 49 [52: 54: 57: 59: 62] times, 1 ch, miss 1 ch, tr2tog over next 3 sts, working first 'leg' into next tr, missing 1 ch, and working 2nd 'leg' into next tr, turn, leaving rem sts unworked (there should be 15 [15: 19: 19: 23: 23] sts unworked between last st used here and first st used for first section).

Work on this set of 101 [107: 111: 117: 121: 127] sts only for second side by working as given for first side from ***.

MAKING UP

Join shoulder seams.

● *Neck edging*

With RS facing and 2.50mm (C2) hook, rejoin yarn at neck edge of left shoulder seam, 1 ch (does NOT count as st), work in dc evenly around entire neck edge, ending with ss to first dc, turn.

Next round 1 ch (does NOT count as st), 1 dc into each dc to end, missing dc as required to ensure edging lays flat and ending with ss to first dc, turn.

The neckline and shoulder strap edgings are worked in double crochet to stabilize the mesh stitch and provide a neat finishing.

Fasten off.

Work edging around armhole edges and lower edge in same way.

Bead-edged beauty

This pretty, lightweight lacy top worked in a fresh-looking crisp cotton yarn is just the garment for a hot summer's day. The sleeves are edged with silvery beads for an extra touch of glamour. See pages 230–231 for more information on working with beads.

PROJECT NOTES

MEASUREMENTS

To fit bust: 81cm (32in) [86cm (34in): 91cm (36in): 97cm (38in): 102cm (40in): 107cm (42in)]

Actual size: 87cm (34¼in) [93cm (36½in): 99cm (39in): 105cm (41¼in): 112cm (44in): 118cm (46½in)]

Full length: 53cm (20¾in) [53cm (20¾in): 55cm (21½in): 59cm (23¼in): 62cm (24½in): 62cm (24½in)]

Sleeve seam: 9cm (3½in) [9cm (3½in): 9cm (3½in): 9cm (3½in): 9cm (3½in): 9cm (3½in)]

YARN

6 [6: 6: 7: 8: 8] x 50g (1¾oz) of 4ply 100% cotton in cream

HOOKS

2.00mm (B1) and 2.50mm (C2) hooks

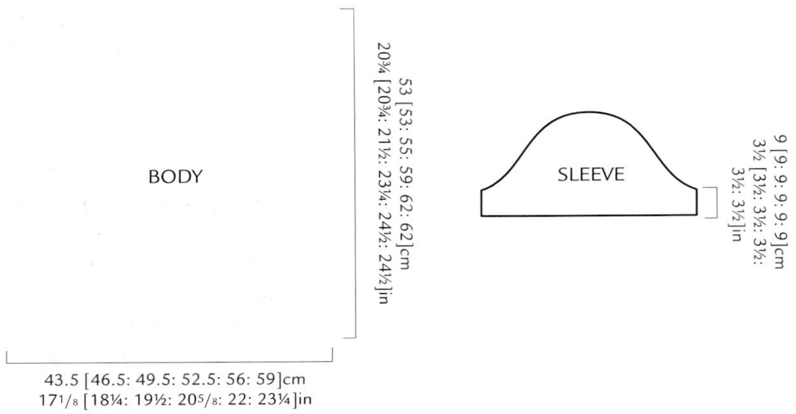

NOTIONS

288 [300: 330: 342: 372: 384] beads

SPECIAL ABBREVIATIONS

beaded ch slide bead up so that it sits on RS of work next to st just worked, yoh and draw loop through leaving bead caught in st

dtr2tog *(yoh) twice and insert hook as indicated, yoh and draw loop through, (yoh and draw through 2 loops) twice, rep from * once more, yoh and draw through all 3 loops on hook

tr2tog *yoh and insert hook as indicated, yoh and draw loop through, yoh and draw through 2 loops, rep from * once more, yoh and draw through all 3 loops on hook

yoh yarn over hook.

TENSION

26 sts and 13½ rows to 10cm (4in) measured over pattern on 2.50mm (C2) hook, or the size required to achieve stated tension.

BODY

53 [53: 55: 59: 62: 62]cm
20¾ [20¾: 21½: 23¼: 24½: 24½]in

43.5 [46.5: 49.5: 52.5: 56: 59]cm
17⅛ [18¼: 19½: 20⅝: 22: 23¼]in

SLEEVE

9 [9: 9: 9: 9: 9]cm
3½ [3½: 3½: 3½: 3½: 3½]in

THE PATTERN

BACK

With 2.50mm (C2) hook, make 114 [122: 130: 138: 146: 154] ch.

Foundation row (WS) 1 dc into 2nd ch from hook, 1 dc into each ch to end, turn. 113 [121: 129: 137: 145: 153] sts.

Cont in patt as follows:

Row 1 (RS) 4 ch (counts as 1 tr and 1 ch), miss first 2 dc, 1 tr into next dc, *1 ch, miss 1 dc, 1 tr into next dc, rep from * to end, turn.

Row 2 1 ch (does NOT count as st), 1 dc into tr at base of 1 ch, *1 dc into next ch sp, 1 dc into next tr, rep from * to end, working dc at end of last rep into 3rd of 4 ch at beg of previous row, turn.

Row 3 3 ch (does NOT count as st), miss first 2 dc, 1 dtr into next dc, *3 ch**, dtr2tog working first 'leg' into same dc as already worked into, missing 3 dc and working

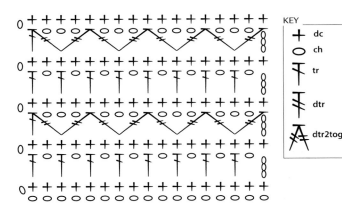

KEY

+ dc
○ ch
⊤ tr
⊥ dtr
⅄ dtr2tog

second 'leg' into next dc, rep from * to end, ending last rep at **, (yoh) twice, insert hook into same dc as already worked into, yoh and draw loop through, (yoh and draw through 2 loops) twice, yoh, miss 1 dc, insert hook into last dc, yoh and draw loop through, yoh and draw through 2 loops, yoh and draw through all 3 loops on hook, turn.

Row 4 1 ch (does NOT count as st), 1 dc into st at base of 1 ch, *3 dc into next ch sp, 1 dc into next dtr2tog, rep from * to end, working dc at end of last rep into top of dtr at beg of previous row, turn.

These 4 rows form patt.

Cont in patt for a further 36 [36: 36: 40: 40: 40] rows, ending after a 4th patt row and a WS row.

● **Shape armholes**

Next row Ss across and into 5th st, 3 ch (does NOT count as st), miss 1 dc, 1 tr into next dc (6 sts decreased), patt to last 8 sts, 1 ch, miss 1 dc, tr2tog working first 'leg' into next dc, missing 1 dc and working second 'leg'

into next dc and turn, leaving rem 6 sts unworked (6 sts decreased). 101 [109: 117: 125: 133: 141] sts.

Next row 1 ch (does NOT count as st), 1 dc into tr2tog at base of 1 ch, patt until dc has been worked into tr at beg of previous and turn, leaving 3 ch at beg of previous row unworked.

Next row 4 ch (does NOT count as st), miss first 4 dc, 1 dtr into next dc (2 sts decreased), 3 ch, patt until second 'leg' of last dtr2tog has been worked into dc at beg of previous row and turn (2 sts decreased). 97 [105: 113: 121: 129: 137] sts.

Next row 1 ch (does NOT count as st), 1 dc into dtr2tog at base of 1 ch, patt until dc has been worked into dtr at beg of previous and turn, leaving 4 ch at beg of previous row unworked.

Next row 3 ch (does NOT count as st), miss first 2 dc, 1 tr into next dc (2 sts decreased), patt to last 4 sts, 1 ch, miss 1 dc, tr2tog working first 'leg' into next dc, missing 1 dc and working second 'leg' into last dc, turn (2 sts decreased). 93 [101: 109: 117: 125: 133] sts.

Rep last 4 rows 0 [1: 1: 2: 2: 3] times more, then first 3 of these rows again. 89 [89: 97: 97: 105: 105] sts.***

Cont in patt for a further 12 [8: 12: 8: 12: 8] rows, ending after a 4th patt row and a WS row.

● **Shape back neck**

Next row (RS) Patt 21 [21: 25: 25: 29: 29] sts, 1 ch, miss 1 dc, tr2tog working first 'leg' into next dc, missing 1 dc and working second 'leg' into last dc and turn, leaving rem sts unworked. 23 [23: 27: 27: 31: 31] sts.

Working shaping in same way as for armhole shaping, work 3 rows, dec 2 sts at neck edge of 2nd of these rows. 21 [21: 25: 25: 29: 29] sts.

Fasten off.

With RS facing, return to last complete row worked, miss centre 39 dc, rejoin yarn to next dc, 3 ch (does NOT count as st), miss 1 dc, 1 tr into next dc, patt to end, turn. 23 [23: 27: 27: 31: 31] sts.

Working shaping in same way as for armhole shaping, work 3 rows, dec 2 sts at neck edge of 2nd of these rows. 21 [21: 25: 25: 29: 29] sts.

Fasten off.

FRONT

Work as for back to ***.

Cont in patt for a further 4 [0: 4: 0: 4: 0] rows, ending after a 4th patt row and a WS row.

● Shape back neck

Next row (RS) Patt 25 [25: 29: 29: 33: 33] sts, 1 ch, miss 1 dc, tr2tog working first 'leg' into next dc, missing 1 dc and working second 'leg' into last dc and turn, leaving rem sts unworked. 27 [27: 31: 31: 35: 35] sts.

Working shaping in same way as for armhole shaping, work 7 rows, dec 2 sts at neck edge of 2nd and foll 2 alt rows. 21 [21: 25: 25: 29: 29] sts.

Work 4 rows, ending after a 4th patt row and a WS row.

Fasten off.

With RS facing, return to last complete row worked, miss centre 31 dc, rejoin yarn to next dc, 3 ch (does NOT count as st), miss 1 dc, 1 tr into next dc, patt to end, turn. 27 [27: 31: 31: 35: 35] sts.

Complete second side to match first, reversing shaping.

SLEEVES

With 2.50mm (C2) hook, make 82 [82: 94: 94: 106: 106] ch.

Work foundation row as for back. 81 [81: 93: 93: 105: 105] sts.

Cont in patt as for back as follows:

Work 4 rows, ending after a 4th patt row and a WS row.

● Shape top

Working all shaping in same way as for back armhole, dec 6 sts at each end of next row. 69 [69: 81: 81: 93: 93] sts.

Dec 2 sts at each end of 2nd and foll 6 [6: 7: 7: 8: 8] alt rows. 41 [41: 49: 49: 57: 57] sts.

Work 1 row, ending after a WS row.

Fasten off.

MAKING UP

Join shoulder seams.

● Neck edging

With RS facing and 2.00mm (B1) hook, rejoin yarn at neck edge of left shoulder seam, 1

ch (does NOT count as st), work in dc evenly around entire neck edge, ending with ss to first dc, turn.

Next round 1 ch (does NOT count as st), 1 dc into each dc to end, missing dc as required to ensure Edging lays flat and ending with ss to first dc, turn.

Rep last round twice more. Fasten off.

Join side seams.

● Hem edging

Thread 168 [180: 192: 204: 216: 228] beads onto yarn.

With RS facing and 2.00mm (B1) hook, rejoin yarn at base of left side seam, 1 ch (does NOT count as st), work in dc evenly around entire foundation ch edge, working 1 dc into each foundation ch, missing 1 foundation ch at base of each side seam and ending with ss to first dc, turn. 224 [240: 256: 272: 288: 304] sts.

****Next round** 1 ch (does NOT count as st), 1 dc into each dc to end, ending with ss to first dc, turn.

Next round 1 ch (does NOT count as st), 1 dc into first dc, *5 ch, miss 3 dc, 1 dc into next

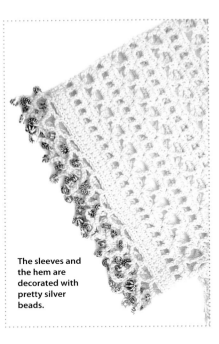

The sleeves and the hem are decorated with pretty silver beads.

dc, rep from * to last 3 sts, 2 ch, 1 tr into first dc.

Next round 1 ch (does NOT count as st), (1 dc, 1 beaded ch and 1 dc) into ch sp partly formed by tr at end of last round, *7 ch, (1 dc, 1 beaded ch and 1 dc) into next ch sp, rep from * until last full ch sp has been worked into, 3 ch, 1 dtr into first dc.

Next round 1 ch (does NOT count as st), (1 dc, 1 beaded ch and 1 dc) into ch sp partly formed by dtr at end of last round, *4 ch, 1 beaded ch, 4 ch**, (1 dc, 1 beaded ch and 1 dc) into next ch sp, rep from * to end, ending last rep at **, ss to first dc.

Fasten off.

Join sleeve seams.

● Sleeve edgings (both alike)

Thread 60 [60: 69: 69: 78: 78] beads onto yarn.

With RS facing and 2.00mm (B1) hook, rejoin yarn at base of sleeve seam, 1 ch (does NOT count as st), work in dc evenly around foundation ch edge, working 1 dc into each foundation ch, missing 1 foundation ch at base of sleeve seam and ending with ss to first dc, turn. 80 [80: 92: 92: 104: 104] sts.

Complete as given for hem edging from ****.

Insert sleeves into armholes.

Flower-trimmed cardigan

This project shows you just how much you can do with a simple stitch. The body of this versatile cardigan is constructed from simple double crochet and chain in a sturdy denim yarn, while the flowers and leaves add a colourful contrast and detail. Play around with the colours for the embellishments – you could always make them in the same colour as the cardigan if you prefer, or go for a really stunning colour combination.

PROJECT NOTES

MEASUREMENTS

To fit bust: 81cm (32in) [86cm (34in): 91cm (36in): 97cm (38in): 102cm (40in): 107cm (42in)]

Actual size: 86cm (33¾in) [91cm (35¾in): 97cm (38in): 102cm (40in): 107cm (42in): 112cm (44in)]

Full length: 58cm (22¾in) [59cm (23¼in): 60cm (23½in): 61cm (24in): 62cm (24½in): 63cm (24¾in)]

Sleeve seam: 43cm (17in) [43cm (17in): 44cm (17¼in): 44cm (17¼in): 44cm (17¼in): 45cm (17¾in)]

YARN

CARDIGAN:

MC 18 [19: 19: 20: 21: 21] x 50g (1¾oz) balls of DK-weight denim yarn

LEAVES AND FLOWERS:

All 4ply 100% cotton

A 1 x 50g (1¾oz) ball in yellow
B 1 x 50g (1¾oz) ball in maroon
C 1 x 50g (1¾oz) ball in dark red
D 1 x 50g (1¾oz) ball in lime green
E 1 x 50g (1¾oz) ball in leaf green

HOOKS

2.50mm (C2), 3.50mm (E4) and 4.00mm (G6) hooks

NOTIONS

7 buttons

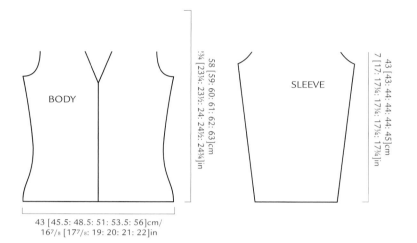

BODY

43 [45.5: 48.5: 51: 53.5: 56]cm/ 16⅞ [17⅞: 19: 20: 21: 22]in

58 [59: 60: 61: 62: 63]cm 22¾ [23¼: 23½: 24: 24½: 24¾]in

SLEEVE

43 [43: 44: 44: 44: 45]cm 17 [17: 17¼: 17¼: 17¼: 17¾]in

SPECIAL ABBREVIATIONS

dtr3tog *(yarn over hook) twice, insert hook as indicated, yarn over hook and draw loop through, (yarn over hook and draw through 2 loops) twice, rep from * twice more, yarn over hook and draw through all 4 loops on hook.

rfdc relief front double crochet: work a dc in the usual way but working around stem of st, inserting hook from front to back and from right to left.

TENSION

Before washing: 21 sts and 18 rows to 10cm (4in) measured over pattern on 4.00mm (G6) hook, or the size required to achieve stated tension.

After washing: 23 sts and 22 rows to 10cm (4in) measured over pattern on 4.00mm (G6) hook, or the size required to achieve stated tension.

NOTE: The yarn used for this project will shrink when washed for the first time. Allowances have been made for this shrinkage.

THE PATTERN

BACK

With 4.00mm (G6) hook and MC, make 100 [106: 112: 118: 124: 130] ch.

Foundation row (RS) 1 dc into 2nd ch from hook, *1 ch, miss 1 ch, 1 dc into next ch, rep from * to end, turn. 99 [105: 111: 117: 123: 129] sts.

Cont in patt as follows:

Row 1 1 ch (does NOT count as st), 1 dc into first dc, *1 dc into next ch sp, 1 ch, miss 1 dc, rep from * to last 2 sts, 1 dc into next ch sp, 1 dc into last dc, turn.

Row 2 1 ch (does NOT count as st), 1 dc into first dc, *1 ch, miss 1 dc, 1 dc into next ch sp, rep from * to last 2 sts, 1 ch, miss 1 dc, 1 dc into last dc, turn.

These 2 rows form patt.

Cont in patt for a further 3 rows, ending after a WS row.

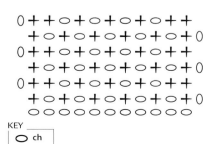

KEY

◯ ch
✚ dc

Next row (RS) 1 ch (does NOT count as st), dc2tog over first 2 sts (1 st decreased), patt to last 2 sts, dc2tog over last 2 sts (1 st decreased), turn.

Working all decreases as set by last row and keeping patt correct, dec 1 st at each end of 4th and every foll 4th row until 83 [89: 95: 101: 107: 113] sts rem.

Work 9 rows, ending after a WS row.

Next row (RS) 1 ch (does NOT count as st), 2 dc into first dc (1 st increased), patt to last st, 2 dc into last st (1 st increased), turn.

Working all increases as set by last row, inc 1 st at each end of 4th and every foll 4th row until there are 99 [105: 111: 117: 123: 129] sts, taking inc sts into patt.

Cont straight until back measures 46.5cm (18¼in) [47.5cm (18¾in): 47.5cm (18¾in): 49cm (19¼in): 49cm (19¼in): 50cm (19½in)] ending after a WS row.

● *Shape armholes*

Next row (RS) Ss across and into 5th [6th: 6th: 7th: 7th: 8th] st, 1 ch (does NOT count as st), 1 dc into same st as last ss (4 [5: 5: 6: 6: 7] sts decreased), patt to last 5 [6: 6: 7: 7: 8] sts, 1 dc into next st and turn, leaving rem 4 [5: 5: 6: 6: 7] sts unworked (4 [5: 5: 6: 6: 7] sts decreased). 91 [95: 101: 105: 111: 115] sts.

Working all armhole decs in same way as side seam decs, dec 1 st at each end of next 3 [3: 5: 5: 7: 7] rows, then on foll 4 [5: 5: 6: 6: 7] alt rows. 77 [79: 81: 83: 85: 87] sts.

Cont straight until armhole measures 24.5cm (9½in) [24.5cm (9½in): 25.5cm (10in): 25.5cm (10in): 27cm (10½in): 27 cm (10½in)] ending after a WS row.

● *Shape shoulders*

Fasten off.

Place markers either side of centre 39 [41: 41: 43: 43: 43] sts to denote back neck.

LEFT FRONT

With 4.00mm (G6) hook and MC, make 50 [53: 56: 59: 62: 65] ch.

81, 91 and 102cm sizes:

Work foundation row as given for back. 49 [55: 61] sts.

Work in patt as given for back for 5 rows, ending after a WS row.

86, 97 and 107cm sizes:

Foundation row (RS) 1 dc into 2nd ch from hook, *1 ch, miss 1 ch, 1 dc into next ch, rep from * to last ch, 1 dc into last ch, turn. [52: 58: 64] sts.

Cont in patt as follows:

Row 1 1 ch (does NOT count as st), 1 dc into first dc, *1 ch, miss 1 dc, 1 dc into next ch sp, rep from * to last st, 1 dc into last dc, turn.

Row 2 As 1st row.

These 2 rows form patt.

Cont in patt for a further 3 rows, ending after a WS row.

All sizes:

Working all shaping as given for back, dec 1 st at beg of next and every foll 4th row until 41 [44: 47: 50: 53: 56] sts rem.

Work 9 rows, ending after a WS row.

Inc 1 st at beg of next and every foll 4th row until there are 49 [52: 55: 58: 61: 64] sts, taking inc sts into patt.

Cont straight until 4 rows fewer have been worked than on back to start of armhole shaping, ending after a WS row.

● *Shape front slope*

Dec 1 st at end of next and foll alt row. 47 [50: 53: 56: 59: 62] sts.

Work 1 row, ending after a WS row.

● *Shape armhole*

Dec 4 [5: 5: 6: 6: 7] sts at beg and 1 st at end of next row. 42 [44: 47: 49: 52: 54] sts.

Dec 1 st at armhole edge of next 3 [3: 5: 5: 7: 7] rows, then on foll 4 [5: 5: 6: 6: 7] alt rows and at same time dec 1 st at front slope edge on 2nd and every foll alt row. 30 sts.

Dec 1 st at front slope edge only on next and foll 7 [8: 6: 7: 5: 4] alt rows, then on every foll 4th row until 19 [19: 20: 20: 21: 22] sts rem.

Cont straight until left front matches back to shoulder, ending after a WS row.

● *Shape shoulder*

Fasten off.

RIGHT FRONT

With 4.00mm (G6) hook and MC, make 50 [53: 56: 59: 62: 65] ch.

81, 91 and 102cm sizes:

Work foundation row as given for back. 49 [55: 61] sts.

Work in patt as given for back for 5 rows, ending after a WS row.

86, 97 and 107cm sizes:

Foundation row (RS) 1 dc into 2nd ch from hook, 1 dc into next ch, *1 ch, miss 1 ch, 1 dc into next ch, rep from * to end, turn. [52: 58: 64] sts.

Cont in patt as follows:

Row 1 1 ch (does NOT count as st), 1 dc into first dc, *1 ch, miss 1 dc, 1 dc into next ch sp, rep from * to last st, 1 dc into last dc, turn.

Row 2 As row 1.

These 2 rows form patt.

Cont in patt for a further 3 rows, ending after a WS row.

All sizes:

Working all shaping as given for back, dec 1 st at end of next and every foll 4th row until 41 [44: 47: 50: 53: 56] sts rem.

Complete to match left front, reversing shapings.

SLEEVES (make 2)

With 4.00mm (G6) hook and MC, make 54 [54: 56: 58: 58: 60] ch.

Work foundation row as given for back. 53 [53: 55: 57: 57: 59] sts.

Work in patt as given for back for 5 rows, ending after a WS row.

Working all increases as set by back, inc 1 st at each end of next and every foll 6th row to 57 [65: 65: 67: 75: 75] sts, then on every foll 8th row until there are 75 [77: 79: 81: 83: 85] sts, taking inc sts into patt.

Cont straight until sleeve measures 52.5cm (20½in) [52.5cm (20½in): 54cm (21¼in): 54cm (21¼in): 54cm (21¼in): 55cm (21½in)] ending after a WS row.

● *Shape top*

Working all shaping as set by back armholes, dec 4 [5: 5: 6: 6: 7] sts at each end of next row. 67 [67: 69: 69: 71: 71] sts.

Dec 1 st at each end of next 10 rows, then on every foll alt row to 39 sts, then on foll 9 rows, ending after a WS row. 21 sts.

Fasten off.

MAKING UP

Join shoulder seams. Join sleeve seams. Insert sleeves into armholes. Hot machine-wash and tumble-dry cardigan. (Note: garment needs to be washed and shrunk before border is worked, otherwise border will be too long and frilly.) When dry, mark positions for 7 buttonholes along right front opening edge – lowest buttonhole 1.5cm (½in) up from lower edge, top buttonhole just below start of front slope shaping, and rem 5 buttonholes evenly spaced between.

● *Front border*

With RS facing and 3.50mm (E4) hook, rejoin MC at base of right front opening edge, 1 ch (does NOT count as st), work 1 row of dc evenly up right front opening edge, right front slope, across back neck, down left front slope, then down left front opening edge, turn.

Next row 1 ch (does NOT count as st), 1 dc into each dc to end, making buttonholes to correspond with positions marked by replacing (1 dc into each of next 2 dc) with (2 ch, miss 2 dc), turn.

Next row 1 ch (does NOT count as st), 1 dc into each dc to end, working 2 dc into each buttonhole ch sp.

Fasten off.

Hot machine-wash and tumble-dry cardigan again (to shrink border to correct size). Sew on buttons.

SIX-PETAL FLOWERS (make 4)

With 2.50mm (C2) hook and A, make 4 ch and join with a ss to form a ring.

Round 1 5 ch (counts as 1 tr and 2 ch), (1 tr into ring, 2 ch) 5 times, ss to 3rd of 5 ch at beg of round.

Break off A and join in B.

Round 2 4 ch, miss st at base of 4 ch, *dtr3tog into next ch sp, 4 ch, 1 rfdc around stem of next tr**, 4 ch, rep from * to end, ending last rep at **, ss to next ch.

Fasten off.

Make another flower in exactly this way.

Now make another 2 flowers in exactly this way, but using C in place of B.

DOUBLE-LAYER FLOWER

With 2.50mm (C2) hook and A, make 2 ch.

Round 1 5 dc into 2nd ch from hook, ss to first dc. 5 sts.

Round 2 1 ch (does NOT count as st), working into front loops only of sts of previous round: 1 dc into first dc, (3 ch, 1 dc into next dc) 4 times, 3 ch, ss to first dc.

Break off A and join in B.

Round 3 1 ch (does NOT count as st), working into back loops only of sts of round 1: 2 dc into each dc to end, ss to first dc. 10 sts.

Round 4 2 ch (counts as first htr), 1 htr into dc at base of 2 ch, 2 htr into each dc to end, ss to top of 2 ch at beg of round. 20 sts.

Round 5 Working into front loops only of sts of previous round: 3 ch, 1 dtr into st at base of 3 ch, *2 dtr into each of next 2 htr, (1 dtr, 3 ch and 1 ss) into next htr**, (1 ss, 3 ch and 1 dtr) into next htr, rep from * to end, ending last rep at **, ss to st at base of 3 ch at beg of round. 5 petals.

Fasten off.

Round 6 Working into back loops only of sts of round 4: rejoin C to 1 htr at centre of one petal of previous round, 3 ch, 1 ttr into st at base of 3 ch, *2 ttr into each of next 2 htr, (1 ttr, 3 ch and 1 ss) into next htr**, (1 ss, 3 ch and 1 ttr) into next htr, rep from * to end, ending last rep at **, ss to st at base of 3 ch at beg of round.

Fasten off.

FIVE-PETAL FLOWERS (make 2)

With 2.50mm (C2) hook and A, make 6 ch and join with a ss to form a ring.

Round 1 3 ch (count as first tr), 19 tr into ring, ss to top of 3 ch at beg of round.

Break off A and join in B.

Round 2 1 ch (does NOT count as st), 1 dc into st at base of 1 ch, *1 ch, 1 tr into next tr, 2 tr into next tr, 1 tr into next tr, 1 ch, 1 dc into next tr, rep from * to end, replacing dc at end of last rep with ss to first dc. 5 petals.

Fasten off.

Make another flower in exactly this way, but using C in place of B.

LEAVES (make 6)

With 2.50mm (C2) hook and D, make 9 ch.

Row 1 (RS) 1 dc into 2nd ch from hook, 1 dc into each of next 6 ch, 3 dc into last ch, working back along other side of ch: 1 dc into each of next 6 ch, turn.

Working into back loops only of sts of previous row, cont as follows:

Row 2 1 ch (does NOT count as st), 1 dc into each of first 7 dc, 3 dc into next dc, 1 dc into each of next 6 dc, turn.

Rows 3 and 4 As row 2.

Row 5 1 ch (does NOT count as st), 1 dc into each of first 7 dc, 1 ss into next dc.

Fasten off.

Make another 2 leaves in exactly this way.

Now make another 3 leaves in exactly this way, but using E in place of D.

Using photograph above as a guide, arrange flowers and leaves onto front of cardigan and sew in place.

Multi-coloured motif shrug

This simple but boldly colourful shrug works a stylish twist on the traditional 'granny square'; here, the squares are joined together with rows of double crochet to form the garment. This pattern could easily be adapted to create vibrant cushion covers or a colourfully cosy throw. See pages 114–119 for more information on crochet motifs.

PROJECT NOTES

MEASUREMENTS
One size, to fit bust 81–102cm (32–40in)
Width at opening edge 180cm (71in)
Length, laid flat 32cm (12½in)

YARN
All DK-weight 100% wool
A 3 x 50g (1¾oz) balls in purple-red
B 2 x 50g (1¾oz) balls in raspberry
C 2 x 50g (1¾oz) balls in grey-blue
D 2 x 50g (1¾oz) balls in yellow
E 2 x 50g (1¾oz) balls in green

HOOKS
3.50mm (E4) and 4.00mm (G6) hooks

TENSION
Basic motif measures 10cm (4in) square on 4.00mm (G6) hook, or the size required to achieve stated tension.

SHRUG

32cm (12½in)

180cm (71in)

THE PATTERN

BASIC MOTIF

With 4.00mm (G6) hook and first colour, make 4 ch and join with a ss to form a ring.

Round 1 3 ch (counts as first tr), 2 tr into ring, (2 ch, 3 tr into ring) 3 times, 2 ch, ss to top of 3 ch at beg of round.
Break off first colour.

Round 2 Join in 2nd colour to 1-ch sp, 3 ch (counts as first tr), 2 tr into same ch sp, *1 ch, (3 tr, 2 ch and 3 tr) into next ch sp, rep from * twice more, 1 ch, 3 tr into same ch sp as used at beg of round, 2 ch, ss to top of 3 ch at beg of round.
Break off 2nd colour.

Round 3 Join in 3rd colour to one corner 2-ch sp, 3 ch (counts as first tr), 2 tr into same ch sp, *1 ch, 3 tr into next ch sp, 1 ch, (3 tr, 2 ch and 3 tr) into next corner ch sp, rep from * twice more, 1 ch, 3 tr into next ch sp, 1 ch, 3 tr into same ch sp as used at beg of round, 2 ch, ss to top of 3 ch at beg of round.
Break off 3rd colour.

Round 4 Join in A to one corner 2-ch sp, 3 ch (counts as first tr), 2 tr into same ch sp, *(1 ch, 3 tr into next ch sp) twice, 1 ch, (3 tr, 2 ch and 3 tr) into next corner ch sp, rep

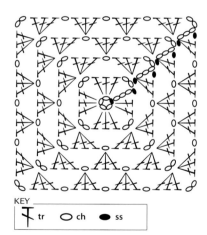

This is the basic four-round motif.

from * twice more, (1 ch, 3 tr into next ch sp) twice, 1 ch, 3 tr into same ch sp as used at beg of round, 2 ch, ss to top of 3 ch at beg of round.
Fasten off.

Completed basic motif is a square. In each corner there is a 2-ch sp between 2 blocks of 3 tr, and along each side there are a further 2 blocks of 3 tr, separated by a 1-ch sp. (17 sts along each side.)

MOTIF COLOURWAYS

Motifs are worked in 12 different colourways, but all motifs are made using yarn A for round 4. Use yarns for each colourway of motifs as shown in chart below.

SHRUG

Make 63 basic motifs: 6 motifs in each of colourways 1 to 3, and 5 motifs in each of colourways 4 to 12.

Following diagram (*above right*), join motifs to form one large rectangle 9 motifs wide and 7 motifs long. Numbers on diagram relate to colourways of motif. Using yarn A, join motifs by holding them RS together and

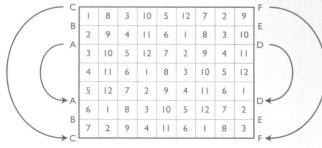

COLOURWAY	1	2	3	4	5	6	7	8	9	10	11	12
1ST COLOUR	B	C	D	E	B	C	D	E	B	C	D	E
2ND COLOUR	C	E	B	C	D	E	C	D	E	D	E	B
3RD COLOUR	D	E	C	D	E	D	E	B	C	E	B	C

working a row of dc along sides to be joined, working each dc through sts of both motifs. Once rectangle is complete, join side seams by joining side motifs as indicated on diagram: join A to A, B to B and so on. Completed joined section will form a bag shape that is 9 motifs wide and 3½ motifs deep. Openings left at the base corners of the bag shape form the armhole openings.

BODY OPENING EDGING

With RS facing, 3.50mm (E4) hook and yarn A, rejoin yarn with a ss into joined corner point indicated by C on diagram, 1 ch (does NOT count as st), work 1 round of dc around entire opening edge, ending with ss to first dc, turn.

Next round 1 ch (does NOT count as st), 1 dc into each dc to end, ss to first dc, turn.

Rep last round twice more.

Fasten off.

ARMHOLE EDGINGS

With RS facing, 3.50mm (E4) hook and yarn A, rejoin yarn with a ss into joined corner point indicated by A (or D) on diagram, 1 ch (does NOT count as st), work 1 round of dc around armhole opening edge, ending with ss to first dc, turn.

Next round 1 ch (does NOT count as st), 1 dc into each dc to end, ss to first dc, turn.

Rep last round twice more.

Fasten off.

MAKING UP

Press following the instructions on the ball band.

The 'sleeves' of this shrug are constructed from a few cunning folds and joins. The edgings are finished off with a band of double crochet.

Lazy stripe wrap jacket

The joy of using variegated yarn is that you can produce striping effects without the need for fiddly yarn changing. Here, the lovely muted tones of the yarn mean the colour changes of this wrap jacket merge subtly into one another. You could use a more vivid palette to produce bolder colour changes.

PROJECT NOTES

MEASUREMENTS
To fit bust: 81–86cm (32–34in) [91–97cm (36–38in): 102–107cm (40–42in)]
Actual size: 108cm (42½in) [117cm (46in): 126cm (49½in)]
Full length: 66cm (26in) [68cm (26¾in): 70cm (27½in)]
Sleeve seam: 43cm (17in) [44cm (17¼in): 45cm (17¾in)]

YARN
18 [20: 22] x 50g (1¾oz) balls of DK-weight wool and soybean protein fibre mix yarn in variegated greys and earth tones

HOOKS
3.50mm (E4) and 4.00mm (G6) hooks

SPECIAL ABBREVIATIONS
rftr relief front treble: work a tr in the usual way but working around stem of st, inserting hook from front to back

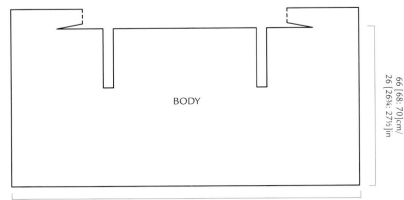

BODY

108 [117: 126]cm/42½ [46: 49½]in

66 [68: 70]cm/ 26 [26¾: 27½]in

and from right to left.

TENSION
20 sts and 15 rows to 10cm (4in) measured over pattern on 4.00mm (G6) hook, or the size required to achieve stated tension.

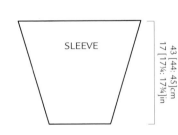

SLEEVE

43 [44: 45]cm 17 [17¼: 17¾]in

THE PATTERN

BODY

(Worked in one piece to armholes.)

With 4.00mm (G6) hook, make 255 [276: 297] ch.

Foundation row (WS) 1 dc into 2nd ch from hook, 1 dc into each ch to end, turn. 254 [275: 296] sts.

Next row 3 ch (counts as first tr), miss dc at base of 3 ch, *miss next 2 dc, 1 tr into next dc, 1 ch, 1 tr into first of 2 missed dc, rep from * to last dc, 1 tr into last dc, turn.

Cont in patt as follows:

Row 1 (WS) 1 ch (does NOT count as st), 1 dc into each tr and ch sp to end, work last dc into top of 3 ch at beg of last row, turn.

Row 2 3 ch (counts as first tr), miss dc at base of 3 ch, *miss next 2 dc, 1 tr into next dc, 1

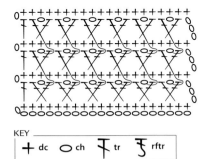

KEY

+ dc   ○ ch   ⊤ tr   ⊥ rftr

ch, 1 rftr loosely around stem of tr directly below first missed dc, rep from * to last dc, 1 tr into last dc, turn. 84 [91: 98] patt reps.

These 2 rows form patt.

Cont in patt until body measures 39cm (15¼in) [40cm (15¾in): 41cm (16in)] ending after a WS row.

The soft colours shift and change subtly.

● *Shape right front*

Next row (RS) Patt 67 [73: 79] sts, 1 tr into next dc and turn, leaving rem sts unworked.

Work on this set of 68 [74: 80] sts (22 [24: 26] patt reps) only for right front.

Cont straight in patt until armhole measures 23cm (9in) [24cm (9½in): 25cm (9¾in)] from

dividing row, ending after a WS row.
Fasten off.

Place marker 11 [12: 13] patt reps (34 [37: 40] sts) in from armhole edge to denote neck point.

● Shape back

Return to last complete row worked before dividing for right front, miss next 10 dc, rejoin yarn to next dc, 3 ch (counts as first tr), patt 102 [111: 120] sts, 1 tr into next dc and turn, leaving rem sts unworked.

Work on this set of 104 [113: 122] sts (34 [37: 40] patt reps) only for back.

Cont straight in patt until armhole measures 23cm (9in) [24cm (9½in): 25cm (9¾in)] from dividing row, ending after a WS row.

Fasten off.

Place markers 11 [12: 13] patt reps (34 [37: 40] sts) in from armhole edges to denote back neck. (There should be 12 [13: 14] patt reps between markers.)

● Shape left front

Return to last complete row worked before dividing for back and right front, miss next 10 dc, rejoin yarn to next dc, 3 ch (counts as first tr), patt to end, turn.

Work on this set of 68 [74: 80] sts (22 [24: 26] patt reps) only for left front.

Cont straight in patt until armhole measures 23cm (9in) [24cm (9½in): 25cm (9¾in)] from dividing row, ending after a WS row.

Fasten off.

Place marker 11 [12: 13] patt reps (34 [37: 40] sts) in from armhole edge to denote neck point.

SLEEVES (make 2)

With 4.00mm (G6) hook, make 51 [51: 57] ch.

Work foundation row and next row as given for body. 50 [50: 56] sts.

Now work in patt as given for body for 2 rows, ending with WS facing for next row. 16 [16: 18] patt reps.

Cont in patt, shaping sides as follows:

Row 5 (WS) 1 ch (does NOT count as st), 2 dc into first tr (1 st increased), 1 dc into each tr and ch sp to last st, 2 dc into top of 3 ch at beg of previous row (1 st increased), turn.

Row 6 3 ch (counts as first tr), 1 tr into dc at base of 3 ch (1 st increased), 1 tr into next dc, patt to last 2 sts, 1 tr into next dc, 2 tr into last dc (1 st increased), turn.

Row 7 1 ch (does NOT count as st), 2 dc into first tr (1 st increased), 1 dc into each tr and ch sp to last st, 2 dc into top of 3 ch at beg of previous row (1 st increased), turn.

Row 8 3 ch (counts as first tr), miss dc at base of 3 ch, 1 tr into each of next 3 dc, patt to last 4 sts, 1 tr into each of next 3 dc, 1 tr into last dc, turn. 56 [56: 62] sts, 18 [18: 20] patt reps.

Work 4 rows.

Rep last 8 rows 5 [6: 6] times more, then first 4 of these rows (the inc rows) again. 30 [32: 34] patt reps.

Cont straight until sleeve measures 41cm (16in) [42cm (16½in): 43cm (17in)] ending after a WS row.

Fasten off.

MAKING UP

Join shoulder seams. Join sleeve seams, leaving sleeve seam open for 2 rows at upper edge. Matching centre of top of last row of sleeve to shoulder seam and row-end edges of last 2 rows of sleeve to sts left unworked at underarm, insert sleeves into armholes.

● Collar

With RS facing and 4.00mm (G6) hook, rejoin yarn at top of right front opening edge, 3 ch (counts as first tr), patt next 33 [36: 39] sts of right front, patt 36 [39: 42] sts of back neck, then patt 34 [37: 40] sts of left front, turn. 104 [113: 122] sts, 34 [37: 40] patt reps.

Work in patt for a further 9 rows, ending after a WS row.

Fasten off.

● Cuff edgings (both alike)

With RS facing and 3.50mm (E4) hook, rejoin yarn at base of sleeve seam, 1 ch (does NOT count as st), work 1 round of dc evenly around entire lower edge of sleeve, ss to first dc, turn.

Next round 1 ch (does NOT count as st), 1 dc into each dc to end, ss to first dc, turn.

Rep last round 7 times more, ending after a RS round but do NOT turn at end of last round.

Now work 1 round of crab st (dc worked from left to right, instead of right to left), ending with ss to first dc.

Fasten off.

● Body edging

With RS facing and 3.50mm (E4) hook, rejoin yarn to lower edge directly below base of one armhole, 1 ch (does NOT count as st),

The edging is worked in neat double crochet.

work 1 round of dc evenly around entire lower, front opening and collar edges, working 3 dc into each corner point and ending with ss to first dc, turn.

Next round 1 ch (does NOT count as st), 1 dc into each dc to end, working 3 dc into each corner point and ending with ss to first dc, turn.

Rep last round 7 times more, ending after a RS round but do NOT turn at end of last round.

Now work 1 round of crab st (dc worked from left to right, instead of right to left), ending with ss to first dc.

Fasten off.

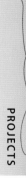

Casual comfort sweaters

The stitch used for this project creates a thick, dense fabric that will keep you warm. The yarn is a mixture of cotton and microfibre, which creates a robust, hard-wearing fabric that will keep its shape better than a pure cotton garment. Here, we've included instructions for both child- and adult-sized sweaters.

PROJECT NOTES

MEASUREMENTS
To fit chest/bust: 56–61cm (22–24in) [66–71cm (26–28in): 76–81cm (30–32in): 86–91cm (34–36in): 97–102cm (38–40in): 107–112cm (42–44in)]

Actual size: 69cm (27in) [80cm (31½in): 91cm (35¾in): 102cm (40in): 113cm (44½in): 124cm (49in)]

Full length: 38cm (15in) [46cm (18in): 54cm (21¼in): 58cm (22¾in): 62cm (24½in): 66cm (26in)]

Sleeve seam: 30cm (11¾in) [38cm (15in): 46cm (18in): 47cm (18½in): 48cm (19in): 49cm (19¼in)]

YARN
6 [8: 9: 11: 13: 14] x 50g (1¾oz) balls of aran-weight 75% cotton, 25% microfibre yarn in either khaki or coral

HOOK
4.00mm (G6) hook

TENSION
18 sts and 15 rows to 10cm (4in) measured over pattern on 4.00mm (G6) hook, or the size required to achieve stated tension.

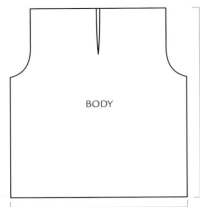

BODY

34.5 [40: 45.5: 51: 56.5: 62]cm
13½ [15¾: 17⅞: 20: 22¼: 24½]in

38 [46: 54: 58: 62: 66]cm
15 [18: 21¼: 22¾: 24½: 26]in

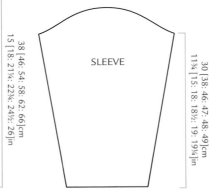

SLEEVE

30 [38: 46: 47: 48: 49]cm
11¾ [15: 18: 18½: 19: 19¼]in

THE PATTERN

BACK

With 4.00mm (G6) hook, make 63 [73: 83: 93: 103: 113] ch.

Foundation row (RS) 1 dc into 2nd ch from hook, *1 tr into next ch, 1 dc into next ch, rep from * to last ch, 1 tr into last ch, turn. 62 [72: 82: 92: 102: 112] sts.

Cont in patt as follows:

Row 1 1 ch (does NOT count as st), 1 dc into first tr, *1 tr into next dc, 1 dc into next tr, rep from * to last dc, 1 tr into last dc, turn. This row forms patt.

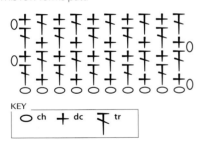

KEY
O ch   + dc   ⊤ tr

Cont in patt until back measures 23cm (9in) [29cm (11½in): 35cm (13¾in): 37cm (14½in): 39cm (15¼in): 41cm (16in)] ending after a WS row.

● Shape armholes

Next row Ss across and into 3rd st, 1 ch (does NOT count as st), 1 dc into same place as last ss (2 sts decreased), patt to last 2 sts and turn, leaving rem 2 sts unworked (2 sts decreased). 58 [68: 78: 88: 98: 108] sts.

Next row Ss across and into 2nd st, 3 ch (count as first tr), miss st at base of 3 ch (1 st decreased), patt to last st and turn, leaving rem st unworked (1 st decreased).

Next row Ss across and into 2nd st, 1 ch (does NOT count as st), 1 dc into tr at base of 1 ch (1 st decreased), patt to last st and turn, leaving rem st unworked (1 st decreased).

Working all shaping as set by last 2 rows, dec 1 st at each end of next 3 [4: 5: 6: 7: 8] rows. 48 [56: 64: 72: 80: 88] sts.**

Cont in patt until armhole measures 15cm

This stitch creates a dense, robust fabric.

(6in) [17cm (6½in): 19cm (7½in): 21cm (8¼in): 23cm (9in): 25cm (9¾in)] ending after a WS row.

(Note: For 1st, 3rd and 5th sizes, rows now start with 3 ch to count as first tr and end with 1 dc worked into top of 3 ch at beg of previous row.)

Shape shoulders

Fasten off, placing markers either side of centre 24 [26: 28: 30: 32: 34] sts to denote back neck.

FRONT

Work as for back to **.

Cont in patt until armhole measures 5cm (2in) [7cm (2¾in): 7cm (2¾in): 9cm (3½in): 10cm (4in): 12cm (4¾in)] ending after a WS row.

(Note: For 1st, 3rd and 5th sizes, rows now start with 3 ch to count as first tr and end with 1 dc worked into top of 3 ch at beg of previous row.)

Divide for front opening

Next row (RS) Patt 24 [28: 32: 36: 40: 44] sts and turn. Work on this set of sts only for first side of neck.

Keeping patt correct, cont straight until front matches back to shoulder fasten-off.

Shape shoulders

Fasten off, placing marker 12 [15: 18: 21: 24: 27] sts in from armhole edge to denote neck point.

With RS facing, rejoin yarn to last complete row worked before dividing for front opening, rejoin yarn to next st and patt to end. 24 [28: 32: 36: 40: 44] sts.

Complete second side to match first.

SLEEVES (make 2)

With 4.00mm (G6) hook, make 37 [39: 43: 45: 49: 51] ch.

Work foundation row as for back. 36 [38: 42: 44: 48: 50] sts.

Cont in patt as for back as follows:

Work 2 [2: 2: 2: 0: 0] rows.

Next row (RS) 3 ch (counts as first tr), 1 dc into tr at base of 3 ch (1 st increased), patt to last st, (1 tr and 1 dc) into last dc (1 st increased), turn. 38 [40: 44: 46: 50: 52] sts.

Next row 3 ch (counts as first tr), miss dc at base of 3 ch, *1 dc into next tr, 1 tr into next dc, rep from * to last st, 1 dc into top of 3 ch at beg of previous row, turn.

Rep last row 2 [2: 2: 2: 0: 0] times more.

Next row (RS) 1 ch (does NOT count as st), (1 dc and 1 tr) into dc at base of 3 ch (1 st increased), patt to last st, (1 dc and 1 tr) into top of 3 ch at beg of previous row (1 st increased), turn. 40 [42: 46: 48: 52: 54] sts.

Work 3 [3: 3: 3: 3: 1] rows.

Working all increases as now set, inc 1 st at each end of next and every foll 4th [4th: 4th:

4th: 4th: 4th] alt row until there are 50 [54: 58: 70: 82: 64] sts, taking inc sts into patt.

1st, 2nd, 3rd, 4th and 6th sizes only:

Inc 1 st at each end of every foll 6th [6th: 6th: 6th: 4th] row until there are 54 [60: 68: 74: 90] sts.

All sizes:

Cont straight until sleeve measures 30cm (11¾in) [38cm (15in): 46cm (18in): 47cm (18½in): 48cm (19in): 49cm (19¼in)], ending after a WS row.

Shape top

Keeping patt correct and working shaping in same way as for back armhole, dec 2 sts at each end of next 10 [10: 12: 12: 14: 14] rows. 14 [20: 20: 26: 26: 34] sts.

Fasten off.

MAKING UP

Join shoulder seams. Join side seams. Join sleeve seams. Insert sleeves into armholes.

Collar

With RS facing, rejoin yarn at top of right front opening edge, make the required turning ch, then patt 12 [13: 14: 15: 16: 17] sts of right front, patt across 24 [26: 28: 30: 32: 34] back neck sts keeping patt correct as set by right front sts, then patt across 12 [13: 14: 15: 16: 17] sts of left front, turn. 48 [52: 56: 60: 64: 68] sts.

Work in patt until collar measures 8cm (3in) [8cm (3in): 9cm (3½in): 9cm (3½in): 10cm (4in): 10cm (4in)] from pick-up row.

Fasten off.

Neck and collar edging

With WS facing, rejoin yarn at base of front opening, 1 ch (does NOT count as st), work in dc up front opening edge, around collar and down other front opening edge, working 3 dc into corner points and ending with ss to first dc.

Fasten off.

Pot pourri sachets

These dainty, picturesque pot pourri sachets are created using filet crochet. This technique features a background grid of mesh stitches that are 'filled in' to create a pattern or picture: here, we've used a heart and a flower shape. See pages 207–209 for more information on filet crochet.

PROJECT NOTES

MEASUREMENTS
Actual size: 18 x 18cm (7 x 7in)

YARN
1 x 50g (1¾oz) ball of 4ply 100% mercerized cotton in either white or red

HOOK
2.50mm (C2) hook

NOTIONS
40 x 20cm (15¾ x 8in) piece of fine white fabric
Pot pourri
160cm of 3mm-wide (63in of ⅛in-wide) ribbon

TENSION
27 sts and 10 rows to 10cm (4in) measured over pattern on 2.50mm (C2) hook, or the size required to achieve stated tension.

SPECIAL NOTE
All sachets are worked in filet mesh. At the sides of each square of chart there is a tr worked into a tr. For open spaces work (2 ch, miss 2 sts), and for solid blocks work either (2 tr into next ch sp) where solid block falls above an open space or (1 tr into each of next 2 tr) where solid block falls above another solid block.

THE PATTERN

SACHET WITH HEART MOTIF

With 2.50mm (C2) hook, make 50 ch.

Foundation row (RS) 1 tr into 8th ch from hook, (2 ch, miss 2 ch, 1 tr into next ch) 14 times, turn. 46 sts, 15 spaces.

Next row 5 ch (counts as 1 tr and 2 ch), miss tr at base of 5 ch and 2 ch, 1 tr into next tr, (2 tr into next ch sp, 1 tr into next tr) 13 times, 2 ch, miss 2 ch, 1 tr into next ch, turn.

Next row 5 ch (counts as 1 tr and 2 ch), miss tr at base of 5 ch and 2 ch, 1 tr into each of next 4 tr, (2 ch, miss 2 tr, 1 tr into next tr) 11 times, 1 tr into each of next 3 tr, 2 ch, miss 2 ch, 1 tr into next ch, turn.

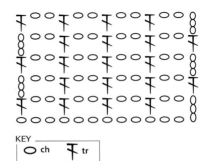

KEY
◯ ch   ⊤ tr

These 3 rows set position of filet mesh and chart.
Starting with row 4 of chart A, cont in filet mesh until chart row 17 has been completed.

Chart A

(Chart grid with row numbers 2–17 showing a heart motif made of solid blocks)

KEY
☐ open space (2ch, miss 2sts)   ☒ solid block (see note)

● Edging

Now work around entire filet panel as follows: 1 ch (does NOT count as st), work 51 dc down first row-end edge (this is 3 dc for each row-end edge), work 45 dc across foundation ch edge (this is 3 dc for each block), work 51 dc up other row-end edge, and work 45 dc across top of last row, ss to first dc. 192 sts.

Next round 1 ch (does NOT count as st), 1 dc into same place as ss at end of previous round, *3 ch, ss to top of dc just worked**, 1 dc into each of next 3 dc, rep from * to end, ending last rep at **, 1 dc into each of last 2 dc, ss to first dc.

Fasten off.

Chart B

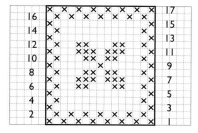

| □ | open space (2ch, miss 2sts) | ☒ | solid block (see note) |

SACHET WITH FLOWER MOTIF

With 2.50mm (C2) hook, make 48 ch.

Foundation row (RS) 1 tr into 4th ch from hook, 1 tr into each of next 2 ch, (2 ch, miss 2 ch, 1 tr into each of next 4 ch) 7 times, turn. 46 sts, 15 squares.

Next row 5 ch (counts as 1 tr and 2 ch), miss 3 tr, 1 tr into next tr, (2 tr into next ch sp, 1 tr into next tr, 2 ch, miss 2 tr, 1 tr into next tr) 7 times, working last tr into top of 3 ch at beg of previous row, turn.

Next row 3 ch (counts as 1 tr), miss tr at base of 3 ch, 1 tr into each of next 4 tr, 2 tr into first ch sp, 1 tr into next tr, (2 ch, miss 2 sts, 1 tr into next tr) 13 times, 2 tr into next ch sp, 1 tr into 3rd of 5 ch at beg of previous row, turn.

These 3 rows set position of filet mesh and chart.

Starting with row 4 of chart B, cont in filet mesh until chart row 17 has been completed.

● Edging

Work as given for sachet with heart motif.

MAKING UP

● Sachet

From fabric, cut out 2 pieces same size as crochet section, adding seam allowance along all edges. Sew fabric pieces together, leaving a small opening. Turn right-side out, insert pot pourri and close opening. Sew crochet section to front of completed sachet.

● Trimming

Cut four 40cm (15¾in) lengths of ribbon and tie each piece in a bow. Using photograph as a guide, attach bows to sachet.

Rose-red heart rug

This gorgeously plush, deep red heart-shaped rug uses a special loop stitch to create its unique texture.

PROJECT NOTES

MEASUREMENTS
Actual size: 106 x 72cm (41¾ x28in)

YARN
19 x 50g (1¾oz) balls of chunky 100% wool in red

HOOK
7.00mm (L11) hook

SPECIAL ABBREVIATIONS
dc2tog (insert hook as indicated, yoh and draw loop through) twice, yoh and draw through all 3 loops
loop 1 insert hook into next st, form loop of yarn around first finger of left hand and draw this loop out to approx 4cm (1¾in), now draw both strands of this looped yarn through st, yoh and draw through all 3 loops on hook
yoh yarn over hook.

TENSION
10 sts and 11½ rows to 10cm (4in) measured over pattern on 7.00mm (L11) hook, or the size required to achieve stated tension.

SPECIAL NOTE
The yarn quantity stated is the amount used for the rug in the photograph. If your loops are longer (or shorter), you may need more (or less) yarn.

THE PATTERN

RUG

With 7.00mm (L11) hook, make 3 ch.

Foundation row (WS) 1 dc into 2nd ch from hook, 1 dc into next ch, turn. 2 sts.

Cont in patt as follows:

Row 1 1 ch (does NOT count as st), 2 dc into first dc, 2 dc into last dc, turn. 4 sts.

Row 2 1 ch (does NOT count as st), (1 dc and loop 1) into first dc, loop 1 into each dc to last st, (loop 1 and 1 dc) into last dc, turn. 6 sts.

Row 3 2 ch, 1 dc into 2nd ch from hook, 2 dc

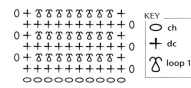

KEY	
O	ch
+	dc
ꝏ	loop 1

into first dc (2 sts increased), 1 dc into each st to last dc, 2 dc into last dc (1 st increased), turn. 9 sts.

Row 4 2 ch, 1 dc into 2nd ch from hook, (loop 1) twice into first dc (2 sts increased), loop 1 into each dc to last dc, (loop 1 and 1 dc) into last dc (1 st increased), turn. 12 sts.

Rows 5 to 20 As rows 3 and 4, 8 times. 60 sts.

Loop stitch: the loops are formed on the front only.

The back of the rug is sturdy double crochet.

Row 21 1 ch (does NOT count as st), 2 dc into first dc (1 st increased), 1 dc into each st to last dc, 2 dc into last dc (1 st increased), turn. 62 sts.

Row 22 1 ch (does NOT count as st), (1 dc and loop 1) into first dc (1 st increased), loop 1 into each dc to last dc, (loop 1 and 1 dc) into last dc (1 st increased), turn. 64 sts.

Rows 23 to 36 As rows 21 and 22, 7 times. 92 sts.

Row 37 1 ch (does NOT count as st), 2 dc into first dc (1 st increased), 1 dc into each st to last dc, 2 dc into last dc (1 st increased), turn. 94 sts.

Row 38 1 ch (does NOT count as st), 1 dc into first dc, loop 1 into each dc to last dc, 1 dc into last dc, turn.

Rows 39 to 48 As rows 37 and 38, 5 times. 104 sts.

Row 49 1 ch (does NOT count as st), 1 dc into first dc, 1 dc into each st to last dc, 1 dc into last dc, turn.

Row 50 1 ch (does NOT count as st), 1 dc into first dc, loop 1 into each dc to last dc, 1 dc into last dc, turn.

Rows 51 to 62 As rows 49 and 50, 6 times.

● *Divide for top*

Row 63 (RS) 1 ch (does NOT count as st), dc2tog over first 2 sts (1 st decreased), 1 dc into each of next 48 sts, dc2tog over next 2 sts and turn, leaving rem sts unworked.

Work on this set of 50 sts only for first side of top shaping.

Row 64 1 ch (does NOT count as st), 1 dc into first dc, loop 1 into each dc to last dc, 1 dc into last dc, turn.

Row 65 1 ch (does NOT count as st), dc2tog over first 2 sts (1 st decreased), 1 dc into each st to last 2 sts, dc2tog over last 2 sts (1 st decreased), turn. 48 sts.

Rows 66 and 67 As rows 64 and 65. 46 sts.

Row 68 As row 64.

Row 69 1 ch (does NOT count as st), dc2tog over first 2 sts (1 st decreased), 1 dc into each st to last 2 sts, dc2tog over last 2 sts (1 st decreased), turn. 44 sts.

Row 70 1 ch (does NOT count as st), dc2tog over first 2 dc (1 st decreased), loop 1 into each dc to last 2 dc, dc2tog over last 2 dc (1 st decreased), turn. 42 sts.

Rows 71 to 74 As rows 69 and 70, twice. 34 sts.

Row 75 1 ch (does NOT count as st), dc2tog over first 2 sts (1 st decreased), 1 dc into each st to last 3 sts, dc2tog over next 2 sts and turn, leaving last st unworked (2 sts decreased). 31 sts.

Row 76 1 ch (does NOT count as st), dc2tog over first 2 dc (1 st decreased), loop 1 into each dc to last 3 dc, dc2tog over next 2 sts and turn, leaving last st unworked. 28 sts.

Rows 77 to 80 As rows 75 and 76, twice. 16 sts.

Fasten off.

Return to last complete row worked before dividing for top, rejoin yarn to next dc and proceed as follows:

Row 63 (RS) 1 ch (does NOT count as st), dc2tog over first 2 sts (this is st where yarn was rejoined and next st) (1 st decreased), 1 dc into each st to last 2 sts, dc2tog over last 2 sts (1 st decreased), turn. 50 sts.

Complete second side of top as for first side by working rows 64 to 80.

Fasten off.

MAKING UP

Do NOT press.

● *Edging*

With RS facing, attach yarn to outer edge of rug, 1 ch (does NOT count as st), work 1 row of dc evenly around entire outer edge, working 3 dc into base corner point and ending with ss to first dc.

Fasten off.

Three-colour baby blanket

This cosy baby blanket is worked in three colours of a merino wool and cotton blend yarn, which combines warmth with resilience. This blanket uses a simple stitch pattern but the pretty combination of soft colours gives it visual interest.

PROJECT NOTES

MEASUREMENTS
Actual size: 68 x 95cm (26¾ x 37½in)

YARN
DK-weight 50% merino, 50% cotton mix yarn

A 5 x 50g(1¾oz) balls in cream
B 4 x 50g (1¾oz) balls in pale pink
C 4 x 50g (1¾oz) balls in pale blue

HOOK
3.00mm (D3) hook

TENSION
21 sts and 16½ rows to 10cm (4in) measured over pattern on 3.00mm (D3) hook, or the size required to achieve stated tension.

THE PATTERN

BLANKET

With 3.00mm (D3) hook and A, make 191 ch.

Foundation row (RS) 1 tr into 4th ch from hook, 1 tr into next ch, *3 ch, miss 3 ch, 1 tr into each of next 3 ch, rep from * to end, turn. 189 sts. Join in B.

Next row Using B, 3 ch, miss 3 tr at end of last row, *(1 tr into next missed foundation ch enclosing ch loop of previous row in st) 3 times**, 3 ch, miss 3 tr, rep from * to end, ending last rep at **, 2 ch, miss 2 tr, ss to top of 3 ch at beg of previous row, turn.

Join in C and cont in patt as follows:

Row 1 (RS) Using C, 3 ch (counts as first tr), miss st at base of 3 ch, (1 tr into next missed tr 2 rows below enclosing ch loop of previous row in st) twice, *3 ch, miss 3 ch, (1 tr into next missed tr 2 rows below enclosing ch loop of previous row in st) 3 times, rep from * to end, working last tr into top of 3 ch at beg of last-but-one row, turn.

Row 2 Using A, 3 ch, miss 3 tr at end of last row, *(1 tr into next missed tr 2 rows below enclosing ch loop of previous row in st) 3 times**, 3 ch, miss 3 tr, rep from * to end, ending last rep at **, 2 ch, miss 2 tr, ss to top of 3 ch at beg of previous row, turn.

Row 3 As row 1 but using B.
Row 4 As row 2 but using C.
Row 5 As row 1 but using A.
Row 6 As row 2 but using B.
These 6 rows form patt.

Cont in patt until work measures approx 63cm (25in), ending after 6th patt row and a WS row.

Break off B and C and cont using A only.

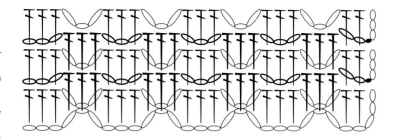

● *Work edging*

Round 1 (RS) 1 ch (does NOT count as st), 1 dc into st 2 rows below at base of 1 ch, (1 dc into next missed tr 2 rows below enclosing ch loop of previous row in st) twice, *1 dc into each of next 3 tr, (1 dc into next missed tr 2 rows below enclosing ch loop of previous row in st) 3 times, rep from * to end, working last dc into top of 3 ch at beg of last-but-one row, 2 dc into same place as last dc, now work down first row-end edge as follows: 1 dc into each row-end edge to foundation ch edge, now work across foundation ch edge as follows: 3 dc into first foundation ch, 1 dc into each foundation ch to last foundation ch, 3 dc into last foundation ch, now work up other row-end edge as follows: 1 dc into each row-end edge until dc has been worked into last row-end edge, 2 dc into same place as dc at beg of round, ss to first dc, turn.

Join in B.

Round 2 Using B, 1 ch (does NOT count as st), 1 dc into each dc to end, working 3 dc into each corner point and ending with ss to first dc, turn.

Break off B.

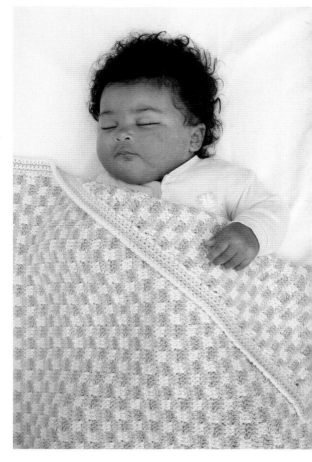

Three pastel shades create a pretty colour effect.

Using A, rep round 2 once more.

Join in C.

Using C, rep round 2 once more.

Break off C and cont using A only.

Rep round 2 once more but do NOT turn at end of round.

Now work 1 round of crab st (dc worked from left to right, instead of right to left) around entire outer edge, ending with ss to first dc.

Fasten off.

MAKING UP

Press carefully following instructions on the ball band.

Rainbow ribbon throw

The yarns used for this vibrantly colourful throw create a lush and velvety texture. These are chunky yarns that will work up satisfyingly quickly. The bold strips of colour are simply made from blocks of treble crochet.

PROJECT NOTES

MEASUREMENTS
Actual size: 150 x 150cm (59 x 59in)

YARNS
A 5 x 100g (3½oz) hanks of chunky-weight 90% merino, 10% nylon ribbon yarn in variegated turquoises

B 5 x 100g (3½oz) hanks of chunky-weight 90% merino, 10% nylon ribbon yarn in turquoise, pink and yellow

C 5 x 100g (3½oz) hanks of chunky-weight 50% wool, 50% cotton tweed yarn in variegated hot pinks

D 5 x 100g (3½oz) hanks of chunky-weight 50% cotton, 40% rayon, 10% nylon ribbon yarn in variegated greens and blues

HOOK
6.00mm (J10) hook

TENSION
11 sts and 7 rows to 10cm (4in) measured over pattern on 6.00mm (J10) hook, or the size required to achieve stated tension.

THE PATTERN

FIRST STRIP

With 6.00mm (J10) hook and yarn A, make 57 ch.

Foundation row (RS) 1 tr into 4th ch from hook, 1 tr into each ch to end, turn. 55 sts.

Cont in patt as follows:

Row 1 3 ch (counts as first tr), 1 tr between last 2 tr of previous row, *miss 1 tr, 1 tr between tr just missed and next tr, rep from * until tr has been worked between first tr and 3 ch at beg of previous row, turn.

This row forms patt.

Cont in patt until work measures 40cm (15¾in).

Break off yarn A and join in yarn B.

The colour changes create stunning effects.

Cont in patt until work measures 56cm (22in).

Break off B and join in C.

Cont in patt until work measures 64cm (25in).

Break off C and join in D.

Cont in patt until work measures 96cm (37¾in).

Break off D and join in A.

Cont in patt until work measures 102cm (40in).

Break off A and join in B.

Cont in patt until work measures 108cm (42½in).

Break off B and join in A.

Cont in patt until work measures 114cm (44¾in).

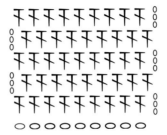

KEY

◯ ch

𝍉 tr

Break off A and join in B.

Cont in patt until work measures 150cm (59in).

Fasten off.

SECOND STRIP

With 6.00mm (J10) hook and B, make 57 ch.

Work foundation row as given for first strip. 55 sts.

Cont in patt as given for first strip as follows:

Cont in patt until work measures 10cm (4in).

Break off B and join in C.

Cont in patt until work measures 44cm (17¼in).

Break off C and join in D.

Cont in patt until work measures 60cm (23½in).

Break off D and join in A.

Cont in patt until work measures 80cm (31½in).

Break off A and join in B.

Cont in patt until work measures 90cm (35½in).

Break off B and join in C.

Cont in patt until work measures 130cm (51in).

Break off C and join in D.

Cont in patt until work measures 150cm (59in).

Fasten off.

THIRD STRIP

With 6.00mm (J10) hook and A, make 57 ch.

Work foundation row as given for first strip. 55 sts.

Cont in patt as given for first strip as follows:

Cont in patt until work measures 20cm (7¾in).

Break off A and join in B.

Cont in patt until work measures 24cm (9½in).

Break off B and join in D.

Cont in patt until work measures 28cm (11in).

Break off D and join in B.

Cont in patt until work measures 50cm (19½in).

Break off B and join in C.

Cont in patt until work measures 72cm (28¼in).

Break off C and join in D.

Cont in patt until work measures 110cm (43¼in).

Break off D and join in A.

Cont in patt until work measures 120cm (47¼in).

Break off A and join in B.

Cont in patt until work measures 140cm (55in).

Break off B and join in A.

Cont in patt until work measures 150cm (59in).

Fasten off.

MAKING UP

Press carefully, following instructions on the ball band.

Join strips together along row-end edges, placing second strip in centre and matching foundation ch edges.

Picture-perfect cushion covers

Crochet can be used to create shapes and motifs through combinations of stitches; here, the lush texture of double crochet fabric creates the perfect backdrop for motifs of bobbles and trellises, or panels of dainty flowers. The yarn is a sturdy cotton, so it will withstand household wear and will also be easy to launder.

PROJECT NOTES

MEASUREMENTS
Actual size: 45 x 45cm (17¾ x 17¾in)

YARN
All DK-weight 100% cotton
TRELLIS CUSHION COVER:
10 x 50g (1¾oz) balls in either gold or soft green
FLOWER PANEL CUSHION COVER:
10 x 50g (1¾oz) balls in either plum or taupe

HOOK
3.50mm (E4) hook

NOTIONS
5 buttons
46cm (18in) square cushion pad

SPECIAL ABBREVIATIONS
dc3tog (insert hook as indicated, yoh and draw loop through) 3 times, yoh and draw through all 4 loops on hook.
dtr3tog *(yoh) twice, insert hook as indicated, yoh and draw loop through, (yoh and draw through 2 loops) twice, rep from * twice more, yoh and draw through all 4 loops on hook.
rbtr relief back treble: work a tr in the usual way but working around stem of st, inserting hook from back to front and from right to left.
rftr relief front treble: work a tr in the usual way but working around stem of st, inserting hook from front to

back and from right to left; yoh = yarn over hook.
tr3tog (yoh and insert hook as indicated, yoh and draw loop through, yoh and draw through 2 loops) 3 times, yoh and draw through all 4 loops on hook.
ttr triple treble; dc2tog = (insert hook as indicated, yoh and draw loop through) twice, yoh and draw through all 3 loops on hook.

TENSION
17 sts and 20 rows to 10cm (4in) measured over double crochet fabric on 3.50mm (E4) hook, or the size required to achieve stated tension.

THE PATTERN

TRELLIS CUSHION COVER: FRONT

With 3.50mm (E4) hook, make 79 ch.
Foundation row (WS) 1 dc into 2nd ch from hook, 1 dc into each ch to end, turn. 78 sts.
Next row 1 ch (does NOT count as st), 1 dc into each dc to end, turn.
Next row 1 ch (does NOT count as st), 1 dc

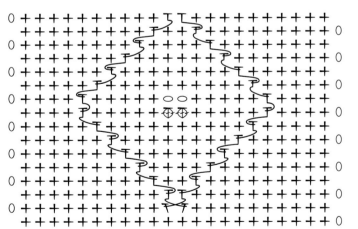

KEY
o	ch
+	dc
ꙅ	rbtr
T	htr
ꙅ	rftr
⊕	tr3tog

into each of first 10 dc, *1 htr into each of next 2 dc**, 1 dc into each of next 12 dc, rep from * to end, ending last rep at **, 1 dc into each of last 10 dc, turn.
Now work in patt as follows:
Row 1 (RS) Row 1 (RS) 1 ch (does NOT count as st), 1 dc into each of first 10 dc, *miss 1 st, 1 rbtr around stem of next st, 1 rftr around stem of missed st**, 1 dc into each of next

12 dc, rep from *to end, ending last rep at**, 1 dc into each of last 10 dc, turn.
Row 2 1 ch (does NOT count as st), 1 dc into each of first 9 dc, *miss 1 st, 1 rbtr around stem of next st, 1 dc into missed st, miss 1 st, 1 dc into next st, 1 rbtr around stem of missed st**, 1 dc into each of next 10 dc, rep from * to end, ending last rep at **, 1 dc into each of last 9 dc, turn.

Row 3 1 ch (does NOT count as st), 1 dc into each of first 8 dc, *miss 1 st, 1 rftr around stem of next st, 1 dc into missed st, 1 dc into each of next 2 dc, miss 1 st, 1 dc into next st, 1 rftr around stem of missed st**, 1 dc into each of next 8 dc, rep from * to end, ending last rep at **, 1 dc into each of last 8 dc, turn.

Row 4 1 ch (does NOT count as st), 1 dc into each of first 7 dc, *miss 1 st, 1 rbtr around stem of next st, 1 dc into missed st, 1 dc into each of next 4 dc, miss 1 st, 1 dc into next st, 1 rbtr around stem of missed st**, 1 dc into each of next 6 dc, rep from * to end, ending last rep at **, 1 dc into each of last 7 dc, turn.

Row 5 1 ch (does NOT count as st), 1 dc into each of first 6 dc, *miss 1 st, 1 rftr around stem of next st, 1 dc into missed st, 1 dc into each of next 6 dc, miss 1 st, 1 dc into next st, 1 rftr around stem of missed st**, 1 dc into each of next 4 dc, rep from * to end, ending last rep at **, 1 dc into each of last 6 dc, turn.

Row 6 1 ch (does NOT count as st), 1 dc into each of first 5 dc, *miss 1 st, 1 rbtr around stem of next st, 1 dc into missed st, 1 dc into each of next 8 dc, miss 1 st, 1 dc into next st, 1 rbtr around stem of missed st**, 1 dc into each of next 2 dc, rep from * to end, ending last rep at **, 1 dc into each of last 5 dc, turn.

Row 7 1 ch (does NOT count as st), 1 dc into each of first 4 dc, *miss 1 st, 1 rftr around stem of next st, 1 dc into missed st, 1 dc into each of next 4 dc, (tr3tog into next dc) twice, 1 dc into each of next 4 dc, miss 1 st, 1 dc into next st, 1 rftr around stem of missed st**, rep from * to end, ending last rep at **, 1 dc into each of last 4 dc, turn.

Row 8 1 ch (does NOT count as st), 1 dc into each of first 4 dc, 1 rbtr around stem of next st, *1 dc into each of next 5 dc, 2 ch, miss 2 sts, 1 dc into each of next 5 dc**, miss 1 st, 1 rbtr around stem of next st, 1 rbtr around stem of missed st, rep from * to end, ending last rep at **, 1 rbtr around stem of next st, 1 dc into each of last 4 dc, turn.

Row 9 1 ch (does NOT count as st), 1 dc into each of first 4 dc, *miss 1 st, 1 dc into next st, 1 rftr around stem of missed st, 1 dc into each of next 4 dc, 1 dc into each of next 2 tr3tog into next dc (leaving 2 ch of previous row unworked on WS of work), 1 dc into each of next 4 dc, miss 1 st, 1 rftr around stem of next st, 1 dc into missed st**, rep from * to end, ending last rep at **, 1 dc into each of last 4 dc, turn.

Row 10 1 ch (does NOT count as st), 1 dc into each of first 5 dc, *miss 1 st, 1 dc into next st, 1 rbtr around stem of missed st, 1 dc into each of next 8 dc, miss 1 st, 1 rbtr around stem of next st, 1 dc into missed st**, 1 dc into each of next 2 dc, rep from * to end, ending last rep at **, 1 dc into each of last 5 dc, turn.

Row 11 1 ch (does NOT count as st), 1 dc into each of first 6 dc, *miss 1 st, 1 dc into next st, 1 rftr around stem of missed st, 1 dc into each of next 6 dc, miss 1 st, 1 rftr around stem of next st, 1 dc into missed st**, 1 dc into each of next 4 dc, rep from * to end, ending last rep at **, 1 dc into each of last 6 dc, turn.

Row 12 1 ch (does NOT count as st), 1 dc into each of first 7 dc, *miss 1 st, 1 dc into next st, 1 rbtr around stem of missed st, 1 dc into each of next 4 dc, miss 1 st, 1 rbtr around stem of next st, 1 dc into missed st**, 1 dc into each of next 6 dc, rep from * to end, ending last rep at **, 1 dc into each of last 7 dc, turn.

Row 13 1 ch (does NOT count as st), 1 dc into each of first 8 dc, *miss 1 st, 1 rftr around stem of next st, 1 dc into missed st, 1 dc into each of next 2 dc, miss 1 st, 1 dc into next st, 1 rftr around stem of missed st**, 1 dc into each of next 8 dc, rep from * to end, ending last rep at **, 1 dc into each of last 8 dc, turn.

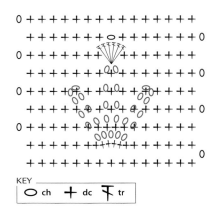

KEY

O ch + dc ⊤ tr

Row 14 1 ch (does NOT count as st), 1 dc into each of first 9 dc, *miss 1 st, 1 dc into next st, 1 rbtr around stem of missed st, miss 1 st, 1 rbtr around stem of next st, 1 dc into missed st**, 1 dc into each of next 10 dc, rep from * to end, ending last rep at **, 1 dc into each of last 9 dc, turn.

These 14 rows form patt.

Rep last 14 rows 5 times more, then 1st row again.

Next row 1 ch (does NOT count as st), 1 dc into each st to end, turn.

Rep last row twice more.

Fasten off.

LOWER BACK

With 3.50mm (E4) hook, make 79 ch.

Foundation row (RS) 1 dc into 2nd ch from hook, 1 dc into each ch to end, turn. 78 sts.

Next row 1 ch (does NOT count as st), 1 dc into each dc to end, turn.

This row forms dc fabric.

Cont in dc fabric until lower back measures 25cm (9¾in).

Fasten off.

UPPER BACK

Work as given for lower back until 5 rows fewer have been worked than on lower back to fasten-off point.

Next row 1 ch (does NOT count as st), 1 dc into each of first 10 dc, *2 ch, miss 2 dc (to make a buttonhole), 1 dc into each of next 12 dc, rep from * 3 times more, 2 ch, miss 2 dc (to make 5th buttonhole), 1 dc into each of last 10 dc, turn.

Next row 1 ch (does NOT count as st), 1 dc into each of first 10 dc, *2 dc into next ch sp, 1 dc into each of next 12 dc, rep from * 3 times more, 2 dc into next ch sp, 1 dc into each of last 10 dc, turn.

Work 3 rows.

Fasten off.

FLOWER PANEL CUSHION COVER: CENTRE FRONT PANEL

With 3.50mm (E4) hook, make 56 ch.

Foundation row (RS) 1 dc into 2nd ch from hook, (1 dc into next ch, 1 htr into next ch) 3 times, 1 dc into each of next 41 ch, (1 htr into next ch, 1 dc into next ch) 3 times, 1 dc into last ch, turn. 55 sts.

Now work in patt as follows:

Row 1 (WS) 1 ch (does not count as st), 1 dc into first st, (1 dc into next dc, 1 rbtr around stem of next st) 3 times, 1 dc into each of next 41 dc, (1 rbtr around stem of next st, 1 dc into next dc) 3 times, 1 dc into last dc, turn.

Row 2 1 ch (does not count as st), 1 dc into first st, (1 dc into next dc, 1 rftr around stem of next st) 3 times, 1 dc into each of next 41 dc, (1 rftr around stem of next st, 1 dc into next dc) 3 times, 1 dc into last dc, turn.

Rows 3 and 4 As rows 1 and 2.

Row 5 1 ch (does not count as st), 1 dc into first st, (1 dc into next dc, 1 rbtr around stem of next st) 3 times, 1 dc into each of next 20 dc, (1 dc, 10 ch, 1 dc, 10 ch, 1 dc, 10 ch and 1 dc) into next dc, 1 dc into each of next 20 dc, (1 rbtr around stem of next st, 1 dc into next dc) 3 times, 1 dc into last dc, turn.

Row 6 1 ch (does not count as st), 1 dc into first st, (1 dc into next dc, 1 rftr around stem of next st) 3 times, 1 dc into each of next 20 dc, miss (1 dc and 10 ch), keeping the three 10-ch loops at front (RS) of work dc2tog over next 2 dc missing the 10 ch between them, miss (next 10 ch and 1 dc), 1 dc into each of next 20 dc, (1 rftr around stem of next st, 1 dc into next dc) 3 times, 1 dc into last dc, turn.

Row 7 As row 1.

Row 8 1 ch (does not count as st), 1 dc into first st, (1 dc into next dc, 1 rftr around stem of next st) 3 times, 1 dc into each of next 17 dc, 1 dc into next dc picking up first 10-ch loop of 5th row and enclosing this loop in st, 1 dc into each of next 5 dc, 1 dc into next dc picking up third 10-ch loop of 5th row and enclosing this loop in st, 1 dc into each of next 17 dc, (1 rftr around stem of next st, 1 dc into next dc) 3 times, 1 dc into last dc, turn.

Row 9 As row 1.

Row 10 1 ch (does not count as st), 1 dc into first st, (1 dc into next dc, 1 rftr around stem of next st) 3 times, 1 dc into each of next 20 dc, 6 tr into next dc picking up centre 10-ch loop of 5th row and enclosing this loop in sts, 1 dc into each of next 20 dc, (1 rftr around stem of next st, 1 dc into next dc) 3 times, 1 dc into last dc, turn.

Row 11 1 ch (does not count as st), 1 dc into first st, (1 dc into next dc, 1 rbtr around stem of next st) 3 times, 1 dc into each of next 20 dc, 1 ch, miss 6 tr, 1 dc into each of next 20 dc, (1 rbtr around stem of next st, 1 dc into next dc) 3 times, 1 dc into last dc, turn.

Row 12 1 ch (does not count as st), 1 dc into first st, (1 dc into next dc, 1 rftr around stem of next st) 3 times, 1 dc into each of next 20 dc, 1 dc into next ch sp, 1 dc into each of next 20 dc, (1 rftr around stem of next st, 1 dc into next dc) 3 times, 1 dc into last dc, turn.

Rows 13 to 16 As rows 1 and 2 twice.

Row 17 1 ch (does not count as st), 1 dc into first st, (1 dc into next dc, 1 rbtr around stem of next st) 3 times, 1 dc into each of next 8 dc, (1 dc, 10 ch, 1 dc, 10 ch, 1 dc, 10 ch and 1 dc) into next dc, 1 dc into each of next 23 dc, (1 dc, 10 ch, 1 dc, 10 ch, 1 dc, 10 ch and 1 dc) into next dc, 1 dc into each of next 8 dc, (1 rbtr around stem of next st, 1 dc into next dc) 3 times, 1 dc into last dc, turn.

Row 18 1 ch (does not count as st), 1 dc into first st, (1 dc into next dc, 1 rftr around stem of next st) 3 times, 1 dc into each of next 8 dc, *miss (1 dc and 10 ch), keeping the three 10-ch loops at front (RS) of work dc2tog over next 2 dc missing the 10 ch between them, miss (next 10 ch and 1 dc)*, 1 dc into each of next 23 dc, rep from * to * once more, 1 dc into each of next 8 dc, (1 rftr around stem of next st, 1 dc into next dc) 3 times, 1 dc into last dc, turn.

Row 19 As row 1.

Row 20 1 ch (does not count as st), 1 dc into first st, (1 dc into next dc, 1 rftr around stem of next st) 3 times, 1 dc into each of next 5 dc, *1 dc into next dc picking up first 10-ch loop of 17th row and enclosing this loop in st, 1 dc into each of next 5 dc, 1 dc into next dc picking up third 10-ch loop of 17th row and enclosing this loop in st*, 1 dc into each of next 17 dc, rep from * to * once more, 1 dc into each of next 5 dc, (1 rftr around stem of next st, 1 dc into next dc) 3 times, 1 dc into last dc, turn.

Row 21 As row 1.

Row 22 1 ch (does not count as st), 1 dc into first st, (1 dc into next dc, 1 rftr around stem of next st) 3 times, 1 dc into each of next 8 dc, *6 tr into next dc picking up centre 10-ch loop of 17th row and enclosing this loop in sts*, 1 dc into each of next 23 dc, rep from * to * once more, 1 dc into each of next 8 dc, (1 rftr around stem of next st, 1 dc into next dc) 3 times, 1 dc into last dc, turn.

Row 23 1 ch (does not count as st), 1 dc into first st, (1 dc into next dc, 1 rbtr around stem of next st) 3 times, 1 dc into each of next 8 dc, 1 ch, miss 6 tr, 1 dc into each of next 23 dc, 1 ch, miss 6 tr, 1 dc into each of next 8 dc, (1 rbtr around stem of next st, 1 dc into next dc) 3 times, 1 dc into last dc, turn.

Row 24 1 ch (does not count as st), 1 dc into first st, (1 dc into next dc, 1 rftr around stem of next st) 3 times, 1 dc into each of next 8 dc, 1 dc into next ch sp, 1 dc into each of next 23 dc, 1 dc into next ch sp, 1 dc into each of next 8 dc, (1 rftr around stem of next st, 1 dc into next dc) 3 times, 1 dc into last dc, turn.

These 24 rows form patt.

Rep rows 1 to 24 twice more, then rows 1 to 16 again.

Next row As row 1.

Next row As row 2 but do NOT turn at end of row.

Do NOT fasten off.

SIDE FRONT PANELS (both alike)

With RS facing and 3.50mm (E4) hook, work down row-end edge of centre front panel as follows:

1 ch (does NOT count as st), 79 dc evenly down row-end edge to foundation ch edge (this is approx 13 dc for every 15 row-ends plus one extra), turn.

Row 1 (WS) 1 ch (does NOT count as st), 1 dc into each dc to end, turn. 79 sts.

Rows 2 to 7 As row 1.

Row 8 1 ch (does NOT count as st), 1 dc into each of first 7 dc, miss first 3 dc of 4th row, 1

Five buttons close the cushion at the back.

ttr into next dc of 4th row, *miss 3 dc of 4th row, dtr3tog into next dc of 4th row, miss 3 dc of 4th row, 1 ttr into next dc of 4th row, miss 1 dc of 7th row**, 1 dc into each of next 7 dc of 7th row, 1 ttr into dc of 4th row used for last ttr, rep from * to end, ending last rep at **, 1 dc into each of last 7 dc of 7th row, turn.

Row 9 1 ch (does NOT count as st), 1 dc into each of first 7 dc, *dc3tog over next 3 sts, 1 dc into each of next 7 dc, rep from * to end, turn.

Rows 10 to 14 As row 1.

Fasten off.

With RS facing and 3.5mm (E4) hook, attach yarn at rem free end of foundation ch edge of centre front panel and work up other row-end edge of centre front panel as follows:

1 ch (does NOT count as st), 79 dc evenly down row-end edge to foundation ch edge (this is approx 13 dc for every 15 row-ends plus one extra), turn.

Complete as for first side front panel.

LOWER AND UPPER BACK

Work as given for lower and upper back of Trellis cushion cover.

MAKING UP (both cushions)

Press carefully following instructions on ball band. Lay upper back over lower back so that fasten-off edges overlap by 5cm (2in) and sew together along side edges. Sew front to backs along all 4 edges. Sew on buttons.

Heirloom bedspread

This project is one that requires time and dedication. This bedspread is an heirloom piece that will take a long time to create with the fine cotton yarn, but will be treasured for a lifetime. You could work a smaller number of motifs to make, for example, a christening blanket for a precious baby. See pages 214–219 for more information on working motifs.

PROJECT NOTES

MEASUREMENTS
SINGLE BEDSPREAD:
193 x 261cm (76 x 102¾in)
DOUBLE BEDSPREAD:
261 x 261cm (102¾ x 102¾in)

YARN
77 x 50g (1¾oz) balls of 4ply 100% cotton in white for single bedspread;

106 x 50g balls (1¾oz) for double bedspread

HOOK
2.50mm (C2) hook

SPECIAL ABBREVIATIONS
tr3tog *yarn over hook and insert hook as indicated, yarn over hook and

draw loop through, yarn over hook and draw through 2 loops, rep from * twice more, yarn over hook and draw through all 4 loops on hook.

TENSION
Basic motif measures 17cm (6½in) square on 2.50mm (C2) hook, or the size required to achieve stated tension.

THE PATTERN

BASIC MOTIF

With 2.50mm (C2) hook, make 6 ch and join with a ss to form a ring.

Round 1 1 ch (does NOT count as st), 16 dc into ring, ss to first dc. 16 sts.

Round 2 5 ch (counts as 1 tr and 2 ch), miss first 2 dc, *1 tr into next dc, 2 ch, miss 1 dc, rep from * to end, ss to 3rd of 5 ch at beg of round. 8 ch sps.

Round 3 (1 ss, 1 ch, 5 tr, 1 ch and 1 ss) into each ch sp to end. 8 petals.

Round 4 1 ch (does NOT count as st), working behind petals of previous round: 1 dc around stem of first 'tr' of 2nd round, *5 ch, 1 dc around stem of next tr of 2nd round, rep from * 6 times more, 2 ch, 1 tr into first dc. 8 ch sps.

Round 5 5 ch (counts as 1 tr and 2 ch), 1 tr into ch sp partly formed by tr at end of previous round, *3 ch**, (1 tr, 2 ch and 1 tr) into next ch sp, rep from * to end, ending last rep at **, ss to 3rd of 5 ch at beg of round. 16 ch sps.

Round 6 Ss into first ch sp, 5 ch (counts as 1 tr and 2 ch), 1 tr into same ch sp, *2 ch, (3 tr into next ch sp, 1 tr into next tr) twice, 3 tr into next ch sp, 2 ch**, (1 tr, 2 ch and 1 tr) into next ch sp, rep from * to end, ending last rep at **, ss to 3rd of 5 ch at beg of round.

Round 7 Ss into first ch sp, 6 ch (counts as 1 tr and 3 ch), 1 tr into same ch sp*, 2 ch, 1 tr into next ch sp, 2 ch, 1 tr into each of next 11 tr, 2 ch, 1 tr into next ch sp, 2 ch**, (1 tr, 3 ch and 1 tr) into next ch sp, rep from * to end, ending last rep at **, ss to 3rd of 6 ch at beg of round.

Round 8 Ss into centre of first ch sp, 3 ch (counts as first tr), 2 tr into same ch sp, *(2 ch, 1 tr into next ch sp) twice, 2 ch, miss 1 tr, 1 tr into each of next 9 tr, (2 ch, 1 tr into next ch sp) twice, 2 ch**, (3 tr, 3 ch and 3 tr) into next ch sp, rep from * to end, ending last rep at **, 3 tr into same ch sp as used at

KEY
○ ch
+ dc
● ss
⊤ tr
⊼ tr3 tog

overlay panels

beg of round, 1 ch, 1 htr into top of 3 ch at beg of round.

Round 9 3 ch (counts as first tr), 1 tr into ch sp partly formed by htr at end of previous round, *1 tr into each of next 3 tr, 2 ch, miss 1 ch sp, (1 tr into next ch sp, 2 ch) twice, miss 1 tr, 1 tr into each of next 7 tr, (2 ch, 1 tr into next ch sp) twice, 2 ch, miss 1 ch sp, 1 tr into each of next 3 tr**, (2 tr, 3 ch and 2 tr) into next ch sp, rep from * to end, ending last rep at **, 2 tr into same ch sp as used at beg of round, 1 ch, 1 htr into top of 3 ch at beg of round.

Round 10 3 ch (counts as first tr), 1 tr into ch sp partly formed by htr at end of previous round, *1 tr into each of next 5 tr, 2 ch, miss 1 ch sp, (1 tr into next ch sp, 2 ch) twice, miss 1 tr, 1 tr into each of next 5 tr, (2 ch, 1 tr into next ch sp) twice, 2 ch, miss 1 ch sp, 1 tr into each of next 5 tr**, (2 tr, 3 ch and 2 tr) into next ch sp, rep from * to end, ending last rep at **, 2 tr into same ch sp as used at beg of round, 1 ch, 1 htr into top of 3 ch at beg of round.

Round 11 3 ch (counts as 1 tr), 2 tr into ch sp partly formed by htr at end of previous round, *3 ch, miss 3 tr, 1 tr into next tr, 3 ch, miss 2 tr, 1 tr into next tr, (3 ch, 1 tr into next tr) twice, 3 ch, miss 1 tr, tr3tog over next 3 tr, miss 1 tr, (3 ch, 1 tr into next tr) 3 times, 3 ch, miss 2 tr, 1 tr into next tr, 3 ch**, (3 tr, 3 ch and 3 tr) into next ch sp, rep from * to end, ending last rep at **, 3 tr into same ch sp as used at beg of round, 3 ch, ss to top of 3 ch at beg of round.
Fasten off.

Completed basic motif is a square.
In each corner there is a 3-ch sp between 2 blocks of 3 tr, and along each side there are a further ten 3-ch sps. Join motifs while working

The basic motif (shown in darker colour for clarity).

round 11 by replacing each (3 ch) with (1 ch, 1 dc into corresponding ch sp of adjacent motif, 1 ch).

MAKING UP

● *Single bedspread*
Make and join 165 basic motifs to form one large rectangle 11 motifs wide and 15 motifs long.

● *Double bedspread*
Make and join 225 basic motifs to form one large square 15 motifs wide and 15 motifs long.

●*Edging*
With RS facing and 2.50mm (C2) hook, rejoin yarn with a ss into a ch sp around outer edge and cont as follows:

Round 1 (RS) 6 ch (counts as 1 tr and 3 ch), *1 tr into next ch sp (or corner joining point of motifs), 3 ch, rep from * to end, working (3 tr, 3 ch and 3 tr) into each corner ch sp, and replacing (3 ch) at end of last rep with (1 ch, 1 htr into 3rd of 6 ch at beg of round.

Round 2 6 ch (counts as 1 tr and 3 ch), miss ch sp partly formed by htr at end of previous round, *1 tr into next ch sp, 3 ch, rep from * to end, working (3 tr, 3 ch and 3 tr) into

Edging detail (shown in darker colour for clarity).

each corner ch sp and ending with ss to 3rd of 6 ch at beg of round.

Round 3 3 ch (counts as 1 tr), miss st at base of 3 ch, 3 tr into first ch sp, *1 tr into next tr, 3 tr into next ch sp, rep from * to end, working across corner (3 tr, 3 ch and 3 tr) as (1 tr into each of next 3 tr, 3 tr, 1 ch and 3 tr into corner ch sp, 1 tr into each of next 3 tr) and ending with ss to top of 3 ch at beg of round.
Fasten off.

Press carefully following instructions on ball band and taking care not to crush flowers at centres of motifs.

Yarn details

The actual yarns and colours used in the projects on pages 130–157 and 256–311 are given below. If you have difficulty locating the yarns, see the suppliers list on page 314. Yarn manufacturers frequently discontinue certain shades of yarn within a yarn range, or discontinue a yarn range altogether. The information given here will allow you to source a suitable substitute yarn.

Page 131
Striped Scarf Jaeger Matchmaker Merino Aran (100% merino wool – 90yd/ 82m per ball)1 x 1^3/4oz/50g ball each in colours: **A** 775 Gloxinia; **B** 772 Clover; **C** 663 Light Natural; **D** 662 Cream
Plain Scarf Rowan Polar (60% wool/ 30% alpaca/10% acrylic – 109yd/100m per ball): 2 x 3^1/2oz/ 100g balls in colour 650 Smirk

Page 132
Flower Top Rowan Wool Cotton (123yd/ 113m per ball):
1 x 2oz (50g) each in colour: **A** 946 Elf; **B** 949 Aqua; **C** 952 Hiss

Page 133
Striped Bag Rowan Wool Cotton (125yd/ 115m per ball):
1 x 2oz (50g) each in colour: **A** 805 Wine; **B** 799 Glee; **C** 724 Bubbles; **D** 726 Bleached; **E** 800 Bud

Page 134
Cable Throw Rowan Rowanspun Chunky (100% pure new wool – 142yd/130m per ball); 3 x 3^1/2oz/ 100g hanks each in colours: **A** 981 Pebble; **B** 982 Green Water; **C** 983 Cardamom; 2 x 3^1/2oz/100g hanks in colour: **D** 984 Silver

Page 135
Place Mat and Coaster Debbie Bliss Cotton DK (100% cotton – 92yd/84m per ball) as follows:
3 x 1^3/4oz/50g balls in colour 13020 Bright Green

Page 136
Mittens Jaeger Matchmaker DK (100% wool – 131yd/120m per ball): 1 x 1^3/4oz/50g ball each in colours:
Tiger **MC** 898 Orange; **A** 681 Black; **B** 662 Cream; oddment of pink for nose
Bear **MC** 702 Dark Brown; **A** 874 Light Brown; oddment of black for face
Dog **MC** 874 Light Brown; **A** 663 Beige; oddment of black for face
Cat **MC** 787 Ginger **A** 662 Cream; oddments of pink for nose and black for face

Page 137
Rib Stitch Scarf Rowan Rowanspun Chunky (100% pure new wool – 142yd/130m per ball): 2 x 3^1/2oz/100g hanks in colour 992 Hearty

Page 138
Short Row Cushion 21st Century Yarns (100% silk): 2 x 1^3/4oz/50g skeins in colour Azure

Page 139
Striped Beret Jaeger Matchmaker DK (100% merino wool – 131yd/120m per ball):
1 x 1^3/4oz/ 50g balls each in colour: **A** 883 Petal; **B** 894 Geranium
Plain Beret Rowan Yorkshire Tweed (100% pure new wool – 123yd/113m per ball); 1[2:2] x 1^3/4oz/50g balls in colour 349 Frog

Page 140
Garden Plot Squares Throw Rowan Handknit DK Cotton (100% cotton – 93yd/ 85m per ball): 34 x 1^3/4oz/50g balls in colour 204 Chime

Page 141
Beaded Bag Rowan Lurex Shimmer (80% viscose/ 20% polyester – 104yd/95m); 2 x 1^3/4oz/50g balls in colour 332 Gold
1 pack of Jaeger beads colour J3001009 Bronze

Page 142
Sheep Toy Jaeger Matchmaker DK (100% pure new wool – 131yd/ 120m); 1 x 1^3/4oz/ 50g ball each in colours: **A** 661 White; **B** 681 Black

Page 143
Fair Isle Baby Blanket Rowan Wool Cotton DK (50% merino wool/50% cotton – 123yd/ 113m per ball):
1 x 1^3/4oz/50g ball each in colours: **MC** 900 Antique; **A** 933 Violet; **B** 953 August; **C** 909 French Navy; **D** 952 Hiss; **E** 954 Grand; **F** 910 Gypsy; **G** 951 Tender

Page 144
Scented Sachets and Cover Jamieson and Smith 2ply jumper weight Shetland Wool (100% shetland wool – 129yd/118m per ball); 1 x 1oz/25g ball each in colours: **A** 1A cream;

B 49 lilac; **C** 20 purple

Page 145
Lace Bags Jaeger Siena 4ply (100% mercerized cotton – 153yd/140m per ball)
Light pink bag 1 x 1^3/4oz/50g ball in colour **A** 404 Light Pink
Dark pink bag 1 x 1^3/4oz/50g ball in colour **B** 423 Dark Pink
Dark purple bag 1 x 1^3/4oz/50g ball in colour **C** 421 Dark Purple

Page 146
Adult's Funnel Neck Sweater Debbie Bliss Merino Aran (100% merino wool – 85yd/ 78m per ball): 15[16:17:18] x 1^3/4oz/50g balls in colour 325205 Blue Green

Page 147
Child's Funnel Neck Sweater Debbie Bliss Merino Aran (100% merino wool – 85yd/78m per ball): 12[12:13:13] x 1^3/4oz/50g balls in colour 325205 Blue Green

Page 148
Lace Cardigan Debbie Bliss Merino DK (100% merino wool – 109yd/100m per ball): 8[9:10] x 1^3/4oz/50g balls in colour 606 Lilac

Page 149
Baby Bootees Jaeger Baby Merino DK (100% merino wool – 131yd/120m); 1 x 1^3/4oz/50g ball in colour 224 Dawn

Page 150
Rose Brooch Jamieson and Smith 2ply jumper weight Shetland Wool (100% shetland wool – 129yd/118m per ball):
1 x 1oz/25g ball each in colours: **A** 43 Maroon; **B** 92 Green
Rose Button Fastening Jaeger Siena 4ply (100% mercerized cotton – 153yd/140m per ball):
1 x 1^3/4oz/50g ball in colour 421 Dark Purple. DMC Stranded Cotton embroidery thread:
1 hank in each of the colours: 718 Dark Rose; 605 Light Pink; 472 Green
Leaf Edged Sachet Jaeger Siena 4ply (100% mercerized cotton – 153yd/ 140m per ball):
1 x 1^3/4oz/ 50g ball in colour 404 Light Pink

Page 151

Gingham Check Bag Debbie Bliss Cotton DK (100% cotton – 92yd/82m per ball): 2 x 1³/4oz/50g balls in colour 13002 White.

Rose Brocade Bag Debbie Bliss Cotton DK (100% cotton – 92yd/82m per ball): 2 x 1³/4oz/50g balls in colour 13012 Mauve

Page 152

Patchwork Cushion Rowan Handknit Cotton DK (100% cotton – 93yd/85m per ball): 1 x 1³/4oz/50g ball in colour **A** 204 Chime
Rowan Wool Cotton DK (50% merino wool/50% cotton – 123yd/113m per ball): 1 x 1³/4oz/50g ball each in colours: **B** 933 Violet; **C** 952 Hiss; **D** 951 Tender
Debbie Bliss Cotton DK (100% cotton – 92yd/84m per ball) 2 x 1³/4oz/50g balls in colour: **E** 13020 Bright Green

Page 153

Valentine Card Jaeger Siena 4ply (100% mercerized cotton – 153yd/140m per ball): 1 x 1³/4oz/50g ball in colour 421 Dark Purple
1 skein of Caron Waterlilies 12ply silk embroidery thread in colour 084 African Sunset

Christmas Tree Card Jaeger Siena 4ply (100% mercerized cotton – 153yd/140m per ball): 1 x 1³/4oz/50g ball in colour 404 Light Pink
1 skein of Caron Waterlilies 12ply silk embroidery thread in colour 066 Jade

Page 154

Gift Bags see pages 14–15 for details

Page 155

House Sampler Rowan Yorkshire Tweed 4ply (100% wool – 120yd/110m per ball): 2 x 25g balls of colour 264.
DMC Tapestry Wool (100% wool – 8.7yd/8m per skein):
1 skein each of 7110 dark red; 7758 red; 7759 light red; 7306 dark blue; 7304 blue; 7505 gold; 7370 dark green; 7369 green
DMC Stranded Cotton 1 x 838 dark brown

Page 156

Intarsia Cushion Jaeger Matchmaker DK (100% pure wool – 131yd/120m): 3 x 1³/4oz/50g balls in colour **MC** 663 Light Natural: 1 x 1³/4oz/50g ball each in colours: **A** 857 Sage; **B** 886 Asparagus; **C** 876 Clarice; **D** 870 Rosy; **E** 894 Geranium; **F** 887 Fuchsia; **G** 896 Rock Rose

Page 258
Band of Bunnies

Miss Pink: 1 x 50g (1³/4oz) ball of Rowan RYC Soft Lux (64% extra fine merino, 10% angora, 24% nylon, 2% metallic fibre, 125m/137yd per ball) in Powder (002)
Mr Grey: 1 x 50g (1³/4oz) ball of Rowan Wool Cotton (50% merino wool, 50% cotton, 113m/123yd per ball) in Clear (941)
Sparkles: 1 x 50g (1³/4oz) ball of Twilleys Goldfingering (80% viscose, 20% metallized polyester, 200m/218yd per ball) in Pastel Rainbow (11)
Fluffy: 1 x 25g (7/8oz) ball of Rowan Kidsilk Haze (70% super kid mohair, 30% silk, 210m/229yd per ball) in Cream (634)

Page 261

Sunny Day Stripes Two shades of Rowan 4 ply Cotton (100% cotton, 170m/186yd per ball):
Sweater: A 2 [2: 2: 3] x 50g (1³/4oz) balls of Aegean (129); **B** 2 [2: 2: 3] x 50g (1³/4oz) balls of Honeydew (140)
Hat: A 1 x 50g (1³/4oz) ball of Aegean (129); **B** 1 x 50g (1³/4oz) ball of Honeydew (140)

Page 263

Precious Pastels baby Set Two shades of Jaeger Baby Merino DK (100% merino wool, 120m/131yd per ball):
M 2 x 50g (1³/4oz) balls of Petal (212)
C 1 x 50g (1³/4oz) ball of Mallow (221)

Page 266

Pretty In Pink Cardigan and Shawl Rowan 4 ply Soft (100% merino wool, 175m/191yd per ball) in Fairy (395): 3 [4: 4] x 50g (1³/4oz) balls for baby cardigan; 11 x 50g (1³/4oz) balls for shawl

Page 269

Autumn Colour Coat 14 [15: 16: 17] x 50g (1³/4oz) balls of Twilleys Freedom Spirit (100% wool, 120m/131yd per ball) in Fire (502)

Page 272

Corsage A 1 x 25g (7/8oz) ball of Rowan Kidsilk Haze (70% super kid mohair, 30% silk, 210m/229yd per ball) in Elegance (577)
B 1 x 25g (7/8oz) ball of Rowan Kidsilk Night (67% super kid mohair, 18% silk, 10% polyester, 5% nylon, 208m/227yd per ball) in Dazzle (609)

Page 273
Glorious Glamour Scarves

Classic Version: 4 x 50g (1³/4oz) balls of Rowan RYC Cashsoft DK (57% extra fine merino, 33% microfibre, 10% cashmere, 130m/142yd per ball) in Bella Donna (502)
Evening Version: 2 x 25g (7/8oz) balls of Rowan Kidsilk Night (67% super kid mohair, 18% silk, 10% polyester, 5% nylon, 208m/227yd per ball) in Fountain (612)
Silk Version: 4 x 50g (1³/4oz) balls of Jaeger Pure Silk DK (100% silk, 125m/137yd per ball) in Dawn (002)
Tweedy Version: 3 x 50g (1³/4oz) balls of Rowan Felted Tweed (50% merino wool, 25% alpaca, 25% viscose, 175m/191yd per ball) in Sigh (148)

Page 274

Peruvian-Style Bag Five shades of Jaeger Aqua (100% mercerized cotton, 106m/116yd per ball):
A 2 x 50g (1³/4oz) balls of Cocoa (336)
B 1 x 50g (1³/4oz) ball of Pumpkin (335)
C 1 x 50g (1³/4oz) ball of Olive (334)
D 1 x 50g (1³/4oz) ball of Rose (333)
E 2 x 50g (1³/4oz) balls of Salvia (329)

Page 277
Solomon's Knot Wrap

4 x 50g (1³/4oz) balls of Jaeger Pure Silk DK (100% silk, 125m/137yd per ball) in Cameo (008)

Page 278

Circles and Stripes Set Two shades of Rowan Felted Tweed (50% merino wool, 25% alpaca, 25% viscose/nylon, 175m/191yd per ball):
A 2 x 50g (1³/4oz) balls of Rage (150);
B 1 x 50g (1³/4oz) ball of Pickle (155)

Page 281
Seaside and Shells Set

Jaeger Siena (100% mercerized cotton, 140m/153yd per ball) in Ocean (430): 4 x 50g (1³/4oz) balls for belt, 2 x 50g (1³/4oz) balls for hat, 3 x 50g (1³/4oz) balls for bag

Page 284

Tartan-Style Set Three shades of Rowan RYC Cashsoft Aran (57% extra fine merino, 33% microfibre, 10% cashmere, 87m/95yd per ball):
MC 6 x 50g (1³/4oz) balls of Thunder (014);
A 2 x 50g (1³/4oz) balls of Poppy (010);
B 2 x 50g (1³/4oz) balls of Bud (006)

Page 286

Summer Sky Mesh Top 4 [5: 5: 6: 6: 7] x 50g (1³/4oz) balls of Jaeger Siena (100% mercerized cotton, 140m/153yd per ball) in Borage (424)

Page 288

Bead-Edged Beauty 6 [6: 6: 7: 8: 8] x 50g (1³/4oz) balls of Rowan 4 ply Cotton (100% cotton, 170m/186yd per ball) in Cream (153)

Page 291

Flower-Trimmed Cardigan
Cardigan: 18 [19: 19: 20: 21: 21] x 50g (1³/4oz) balls of Rowan Denim (100% cotton, 93m/102yd per ball) in Memphis (229)

Leaves and Flowers: five shades of Rowan Cotton Glace (100% cotton, 115m/126yd per ball):
A 1 x 50g (1¾oz) ball of Buttercup (825);
B 1 x 50g (1¾oz) ball of Damson (823);
C 1 x 50g (1¾oz) ball of Blood Orange (445);
D 1 x 50g (1¾oz) ball of Shoot (814);
E 1 x 50g (1¾oz) ball of Ivy (812)

Page 294
Multi-Coloured Motif Shrug Five shades of Rowan Pure Wool DK (100% superwash wool, 125m/137yd per ball):
A 3 x 50g (1¾oz) balls of Pomegranate (029);
B 2 x 50g (1¾oz) balls of Raspberry (028);
C 2 x 50g (1¾oz) balls of Cypress (007);
D 2 x 50g (1¾oz) balls of Gilt (032); **E** 2 x 50g (1¾oz) balls of Avocado (019)

Page 296
Lazy Stripe Wrap Jacket 18 [20: 22] x 50g (1¾oz) balls of Rowan Tapestry (70% wool, 30% soybean protein fibre, 120m/131yd per ball) in Moorland (175)

Page 298
Casual Comfort Sweaters 6 [8: 9: 11: 13: 14] x 50g (1¾oz) balls Rowan Calmer (75% cotton, 25% microfibre, 160m/175yd per ball) in either Khaki (474) or Coral (476)

Page 300
Pot Pourri Sachets 1 x 50g (1¾oz) ball of Jaeger Siena (100% mercerized cotton, 140m/153yd per ball) in either White (401) or Chilli (425)

Page 301
Rose-Red Heart Rug 19 x 50g (1¾oz) balls of Twilleys Freedom Wool (100% wool, 50m/54yd per ball) in Red (403)

Page 303
Three-Colour Baby Blanket Three shades of Rowan Wool Cotton (50% merino wool, 50% cotton, 113m/123 yd per ball):
A 5 x 50g (1¾oz) balls of Antique (900);
B 4 x 50g (1¾oz) balls of Tender (951);
C 4 x 50g (1¾oz) balls of Clear (941)

Page 304
Rainbow Ribbon Throw
A 5 x 100g (3½oz) hanks of Colinette Tagliatelle (90% merino wool, 10% nylon, 145m/158yd per hank) in Lagoon (138);
B 5 x 100g (3½oz) hanks of Colinette Tagliatelle (90% merino wool, 10% nylon, 145m/158yd per hank) in Jamboree (134);
C 5 x 100g (3½oz) hanks of Colinette Prism (50% wool, 50% cotton, 120m/131yd per hank) in Rio (140); **D** 5 x 100g (3½oz) hanks

of Colinette Giotto (50% cotton, 40% rayon, 10% nylon, 144m/157yd per hank) in Neptune (139)

Page 306
Picture-Perfect Cushion Covers Four shades of Twilleys Freedom Cotton DK (100% cotton, 85m/92yd per ball):
Trellis Cushion Cover: 10 x 50g (1¾oz) balls of either Faded Gold (7) or Soft Green (11)
Flower Panel Cushion Cover: 10 x 50g (1¾oz) balls of either Light Plum (12) or Taupe (6)

Page 310
Heirloom Bedspread 77 x 50g (1¾oz) balls of Rowan Cotton Glace (100% cotton, 115m/126yd per ball) in Bleached (726) for single bedspread; 106 x 50g balls (1¾oz) for double bedspread

Yarn suppliers

Contact the manufacturers for your local stockist or find stockists and mail order information on their website.

US

The Caron Collection
Thistle Needleworks, Inc, (The Shops at Somerset Square), 140 Glastonbury Blvd, Glastonbury, CT 060633
www.caron-net.com

The DMC Corporation,
10 Port Kearney, South Kearney, NJ 070732
tel: 973-589 0606
www.dmc-usa.com

The Handworks Gallery
2911 Kavanagh Blvd, Little Rock, AR 72205
www.handworksgallery.com

Jaeger
Westminster Fibres Inc., 4 Townsend West, Suite 8, Nashua, NH 03063

Tel: (603) 886 5041
www.westminsterfibers.com

Knitting Fever Inc
35 Debevoise Avenue, Roosevelt, New York 11575
www.knittingfever.com

Rowan and RYC
Rowan USA, 4 Townsend West, Suite 8, Nashua, NH 03063
Tel: (603) 886 5041
www.westminsterfibers.com

Royal Yarns
404 Barnside Place, Rockville, MD 20850
online ordering: www.royalyarns.com

UK

Colinette Yarns
Units 2–5, Banwy Industrial Estate, Llanfair Caereinion, Powys, SY21 0SG
Tel: 01938 552141
www.colinette.com

Debbie Bliss
www. debbiebliss.freeserve.co.uk

Designer Yarns Ltd
Units 8–10 Newbridge Industrial Estate, Pitt Street, Keighley, West Yorkshire, BD21 4PQ
tel: 01535 664222
www.designeryarns.uk.com

DMC Creative World Ltd
Pullman Road, Wigston, Leicester, LE18 2DY
tel: 0116 2811040
www.dmc.com

Green Lane Mill
Holmfirth, West Yorkshire, HD9 2DX
tel: 01484 681881
www. knitrowan.com

Jaeger Handknits
Green Lane Mill, Holmfirth, West Yorks, HD9 2DX
Tel: 01484 680050

Kangaroo
PO Box 43, Lewes, BN8 5Y
tel: 01273 814900
Worldwide online ordering: www. kangaroo.uk.com

Macleod Craft
West Yonderton, Warlock Road, Bridge of Weir, Renfrewshire, PA11 3SR
tel: 01505 612618

Rowan and RYC
Green Lane Mill, Holmfirth, West Yorks, HD9 2DX
Tel: 01484 681881
www.knitrowan.com
www.ryclassic.com

Shetland Wool Brokers Ltd,
90 North Road, Lerwick, Shetland Islands, ZE1 0PQ
tel: 01595 693579
Worldwide mail order:
www. shetland-wool-brokers.zetnet.co.uk

Shoreham Knitting
19 East Street, Shoreham by Sea, West Sussex, BN43 5ZE
tel: 01273 461029
UK online ordering:
www.englishyarns.co.uk

Twenty-first Century Yarns
Unit 18, Langston Priory, Kingham, Oxfordshire, OX7 6UP
tel: 07850 616537
Worldwide online ordering:
www. 21stcenturyyarns.com

Twilleys of Stamford
Roman Mill, Little Casterton Road, Stamford, Lincs, PE9 1BG
Tel: 01780 752661
www.twilleys.co.uk

AUS

Jo Sharp Pty Ltd,
ACN 056 596 439, PO Box 1018, Freemantle, WA 6959
tel: 08 9430 9699
www.josharp.com.au

Ireland Needlecraft,
4/2–4 Keppel Ave, Hallam, Vic 3803
tel: 03 702 3222

Sunspun,
185 Canterbury Road, Canterbury, Vic 3126
tel: 03 0830 1609
online ordering: www.sunspun.com.au

The Wool Shack
PO Box 228, Innaloo City, Perth, WA 6918
tel: 08 9446 6344
online ordering: www.woolshack.com

Needles and equipment
Available from your local yarn shop and at the online retailers above.

Acknowledgments

Claire Crompton:
I would like to thank Designer Yarns for their generosity in supplying all Debbie Bliss yarns. I would also like to thank DMC Creative World for supplying tapestry wools and embroidery threads.

Sue Whiting:
Many thanks to Christine Roberts, Mrs Palmer, Ann Casey and Caroline Ashman for their many hours spent crocheting. Thanks also to Ann Hinchliffe and Kate Buller at Rowan, to Jenny Thorpe at Twilleys, and Colinette Sansbury at Colinette Yarns.

The publishers would like to thank the models, Sharryn McGall and Emma Dyas, and thanks also to our young models – Joel, Kiera and Bryony.

Make-up by Sharryn McGall at www.sharryn.co.uk

Thanks also to Joyce Mason at Spin A Yarn for help with yarns and equipment on pp161–65. Visit her website at www.spinayarndevon.co.uk

Index